...AND HEAVEN SHED NO TEARS

To Daniel and Susan
Tenenbaum
our closest and dearest
"Family" and friends

Henry Herzog

N.Y. DECEMBER 14. 1995.

...AND HEAVEN SHED NO TEARS

Henry Armin Herzog

SHENGOLD PUBLISHERS, INC.
New York

ISBN: 0-88400-184-9
Library of Congress Catalog Card Number: 95–071057
Copyright © 1995 by Henry Armin Herzog

Published by Shengold Publishers, Inc.
18 West 45th Street, New York, NY 10036

Printed in the United States of America

THIS BOOK IS HUMBLY DEDICATED TO

My parents, Antonia and Emil,
who were taken away from their children
to gas chambers in Belzec.

My brothers, Nathan and Szymon,
who were captured, tortured
and executed in Płaszow.

Their memory will be in my heart forever.

In deep gratitude I feel like standing-up
and utter a prayer in Remembrance
to the noble hearts and deeds of our
dedicated Christian Polish friends,
Tytus and Luiza Zwoliński, who sheltered
my sister, and together with
Wladysław Łopatowski, helped us both
escape from Poland to Hungary.

Foreword

Since the first of September 1939, my determination, or better, obsession was to keep our family together. My parents, younger sister and two younger brothers moved throughout the miseries of war and oppression together. I was twenty-two years old, strong, and able to absorb all calamities of Nazi persecution, as long as my mother was protected from famine and squalor. We gathered every evening, after the inhumane labor conditions, around my mother. Death tested me the first time on the day my dear parents were sent to Belzec death camp in September 1942. My brothers and I wished to join them, but they commanded us to stay alive and take revenge. I saved our sister by putting her under the care of a noble Christian family. But the long arm of destruction claimed the lives of my dear brothers, during an escape attempt in November 1943. I made survival and revenge my aim. The tortuous ways of survival brought me to the point where I finally could take my revenge.

In July, 1944, I joined the Russian partisans and, alongside them, fought the Nazis until March, 1945. After that time, little was left to me except trying to adjust to life, and the determination to bear testimony.

For a very long time I found the task of writing quite difficult. Writing, I thought, should be left to writers but the inner compulsion to bear witness was overwhelming. I felt a deep need to recount the cruelties committed by Germans, civilians and army alike and the merciless behavior of the German allies. Further, I had to tell everything. For example, the tragic and naive cooperation of our *Judenrat* and Jewish police with our mortal enemies; the danger of our enemies from within; and the Jewish informers. Above all, I needed to reveal the devastation we felt at the silence of the western world's leaders as well as the ineffective action of Jews geographically removed from Nazi danger.

—H. A. H.

November, 1995

Introduction
by Jan Karski

I met Henry Herzog a few years ago on his initiative. He told me that I should lecture more often to both Jewish and Gentile communities. He would help me in organizing my appearances. He did.

Asked about his own past, he answered that it was not much different from my own. Absorbed in my work, I did not press him for more information.

Then a few months ago, he sent me a typescript of his book together with original documents, testimonies, photographs and other memorabilia which prove beyond any doubt that his story—incredible as it seems—is authentic. Written in unpretentious style—sort of a court testimony—it describes six years of his war life in Poland, Hungary and Slovakia—a life of despair, humiliation and pain. Also of stamina, dedication and bravery. The book will make a reader, any reader, understand the *uniqueness* of the Holocaust as a historical phenomenon. Let no nation, no government, no church adopt this sacred, this cursed term. Holocaust means destruction of six million Jews in Nazi-dominated Europe.

The Jews were totally helpless, abandoned by governments, by Church hierarchies, by societal structures.

Having lived in the Gentiles' world for centuries, they had no country of their own. No representation in the Allied war councils. They were doomed just because they were Jews. Even those who took part in the underground resistance—and there were thousands of them in every Nazi dominated country—had to conceal their Jewish identity to their co-conspirators—unless they would have exposed themselves to a double jeopardy. The only anti-Nazi groups where the Jews did not

Jan Karski, Professor Emeritus of Political Science, Georgetown University. In 1942, he was sent by the Polish underground courier for the Polish government in exile to transmit a report on the situation in occupied Poland, and in particular on the situation of the Jewish population. Karski visited twice the Warsaw ghetto where the Jewish leaders asked him to inform the western world of the desperate situation of Polish Jewry. In 1982, he was awarded the title of "RIGHTEOUS AMONG THE NATIONS" by Yad Vashem.

run a risk of being rejected or threatened—let it be said—were the Russian partizans.

Herzog joined them in the mountains of Slovakia. Not because of his political orientation but because of his indomitable determination to fight the enemy without hiding his Jewish identity.

Herzog's or now Adam's saga shows that not all humanity was insensitive to the Jewish Gehenna. There were thousands of *individuals*—educated ones and simpletons—who true to the Lord's Commandment *Love thy neighbour*—tried to help the Jews. Herzog met several of them. He remembers them tenderly and lovingly. The author emerged from the war emotionally wounded. He was understandably disappointed, vengeful. The title of the book reflects well his state of mind. No wonder. He suffered too much. In September 1942 his parents were taken to the Belzec death camp. In November 1943 his two younger brothers were murdered near Plaszow camp. Once he tried to take his own life. He saw too much. I understand him. Still, having read his typescript I feel compelled to include in this foreword my message.

Henry remember: we won the war against the evil. My own country, Poland, is free again. Out of the ashes of six million innocents, out of the armed struggle of the bravest among the brave Jews like yourself, the State of Israel came to life again. The Jews are no longer homeless and no longer helpless. We the surviving victors—Jews and Gentiles alike—have new tasks to perform. We must seek and find ways to join forces in combatting fanaticism, hatred, racism, bigotry, antisemitism wherever they raise their ugly heads. And although you didn't intend it—this is the crucial message your war reminiscences convey.

As the reader can readily ascertain, I am not a disinterested party. Indeed, the name of this book was taken from a title that I used for an excerpt from this book long before its publication, and the reader will find my name somewhere in these pages. This makes the writing of these lines even more difficult, as my tears mingle with the ink on the page before me. Heaven was silent and did not cry during the time covered in these memoirs, but the human emotion, the outcry of violated humanity, and the horror of the unimaginable are leaping from this text. At the same time it is a solemn hymn to the human spirit, to the level that one clings to life, and it is proof that determination can triumph over despair, deprivation and bestiality.

Let this be a reminder to all of us that there are people like the author of this book—yes, this is all true, not a figment of anybody's imagination. Let this be a memorial to those who died and testimonial of those that survived.

"Eretz, al t'hasi Damam"*—Earth, do not cover their innocent blood. JOB XVI, 18.

—DR. GIDEON FRIEDER
The George Washington University
Washington, D.C.

*Hebrew—Traditional cry and plea for heavenly justice for the innocent who were slaughtered.

Little Historical Poem

Banderowiec[1] punched him in his mouth,
Szaulis[2] kicked his behind,
German knocked all his teeth,
and later put a bullet in his head,
On his death bed
Someone curious asked him,
Who is your biggest enemy?
He, before he died coughed out—JEW!

Janusz Minkiewicz

This same poem in original Polish.

Banderowiec dał mu w gębę,
Szaulis mu siedzenie sprał,
Niemiec wybil wszystkie zęby,
Potem kulą, w łeb mu dał.
Nad śmiertelnym go barłogiem
Spytał ktoś ciekawski zbyt
Kto największm twoim wrogiem?
On nim skonał, charknął—ŻYD!

[1]Banderowiec: Ukrainian fascist.
[2]Szaulis: Lithuanian Fascist in the service of the German Police.

Contents

...AND
HEAVEN SHED
NO TEARS

1

Cracow, Poland
1939

I was born on April 27, 1917, in Spiska Stara Ves, a small town on the Slovak side of the Tatra Mountains, a few miles from the Polish border, where my mother, Antonia and her family had lived for many years. My father, Emil, was born in Jarosław in Galicia which had been part of the Austro-Hungarian empire. When World War I broke out in 1914 my father was conscripted into the Austrian army and sent to the Balkan front in Albania. On the way his unit made a stopover in Spiska Stara Ves. There my parents met and fell in love at first sight. They corresponded, and on his first furlough, Father returned and they were married. Stationed in Tirana, Albania, he was wounded, convalesced and returned to active duty. When the war ended in November 1918 he came back for Mother and me, took us with him to Cracow, in the newly independent Poland. He had many friends and connections in Cracow and felt at home there, and when Mother's five sisters and four brothers and her Mother decided to emigrate to the U.S.A. Father and Mother decided to stay in Cracow. Before long Mother felt they had made a mistake. She missed her family very much and could not adjust to Poland. Her mother tongues were Hungarian and German and she never became fluent in Polish.

I was the oldest and was followed by a sister, Fela, and two brothers, Szymon and Nathan. Life in Cracow was good; the Jewish community was large and proud, tracing its history to the tenth century when the first Jews settled there, fleeing persecution, pogroms, inquisition and forced conversion to Christianity. The Jews had been invited to Poland by King

1

Kazimierz the Great who pledged his personal protection. They contributed to the rapid growth of industry and commerce, but were never fully accepted by the population and had to live in ghettos, relying on the king's protection for their safety and pursuit of their way of life. The trade they brought to Poland was of great advantage to the country and made them prosper too. Soon they started building their own synagogues and centers of culture. In prewar Cracow there still were synagogues that had been built in the twelfth century.

The Cracow ghetto was called the Kazimierz quarter in honor of the royal protector of the Jews, but in time, was renamed as the city's eighth district. It bordered on Wavel castle where many kings of Poland had lived and reigned since Cracow had for centuries been the capital of Poland, until one of the kings moved to Warsaw. But even after the move all the kings were buried at Wavel castle, as were the heads of the Catholic Church and, in our time, the modern Polish hero Marshal Jósef Piłsudski. Wavel was one of the most revered historic sites of Poland.

Poland soon had the largest Jewish population in Europe and, though poor, contributed much to the rapid growth of Jewish culture, producing many writers, poets, musicians, scientists and spiritual and political leaders. The Catholic Church never resigned itself to the Jewish presence and preached hatred for all things Jewish. That permeated the nation and through the ages resulted in repeated outbreaks of persecution and pogroms, which culminated in the killing of nearly half the Jews by the cossacks under their bloodthirsty leader, Hetman Bohdan Chmielnicky in the seventeenth century.

Ever since I can remember, unconcealed anti-Semitism was a way of life for the three and a half million Jews who lived among the Polish population which totaled thirty-two million when World War II broke out. Three quarters of the Jews lived in large cities and towns. In Cracow we were about fifty-five thousand, split into two groups, the orthodox and the conservatives. Our family was conservative and were looked down on as heretics by the orthodox. In the twenties an assimilation movement started among the nonorthodox and a small minority opted for conversion.

When Hitler came to power in Germany in 1933 the traditional Polish anti-Semites took new heart and sparkle. The Jews followed Hitler's career with trepidation and a feeling of helplessness. Under foreign minister colonel Jósef Beck, Poland was the first country to extend a hand to Hitler, and the leader of the country, Marshal Piłsudski, signed a ten-year non-aggression pact with him on January 26, 1934. The pact was bitterly opposed in parliament (the *Sejm*) by the Peasant party under Wincenty Witos, by the PPS (the Socialist Party) and the few Jewish deputies. We watched in despair as just across the border Hitler named himself Fuehrer, appointed himself Commander in Chief of the armed forces, the SS and SA bullies and whipped the German nation into blind obedience under an oath of personal loyalty to him. When Hitler incorporated his native Austria into his Thousand Year Reich with the infamous *Anschluss* of March 1938, we were deeply troubled by the reports of the SS and Gestapo following close behind the jackboots of the German army (the *Wehrmacht*) to unleash a reign of terror, with the Jews as their prime target, while the enlightened western world stood silently by.

On October 28, 1938, all over Germany the Nazis rounded up ten thousand Jews of Polish origin who did not have German nationality and sent them to the Polish border. They ignored the protests of the Polish government, who refused to let the Jews into the country. Those unfortunates, who had been forced to leave all their possessions behind, were forced to stay in a no-man's-land for many days in very bad weather and shocking sanitary conditions until the Polish authorities "permitted" them to enter Poland. Some of them found their way to Cracow impoverished refugees, still confused by their sad experience, they lined up at our Kehila (Jewish Council building) for housing and food. Jews in Cracow received them with open arms.

On March 15, 1939, the Wehrmacht occupied Czechoslovakia. The SS and the Gestapo killers followed close behind the troops and started a round of arrests and killings of opposition leaders and Jews. In the ensuing panic many Jews fled for their lives, with only the clothes on their backs. Many came to Poland. Some of them arrived in Cracow and joined the ranks of the refugees. As Hitler moved ever closer, effectively surrounding Poland from three sides, we began to feel we were living a nightmare which, like bad dreams, we were impotent to influence. It did not take him long to move in, his propaganda preceding his *Drang Nach Osten*—Push to the East—to gain *Lebensraum* for his German master race. In August of 1939, with a diabolical master stroke, he made a pact with his arch enemy Stalin. Thus he secured his freedom of action and was ready to fall undisturbed upon Poland. He opened his unprovoked attack on our country before dawn of September 1, 1939.

I shall forever remember the day. It started in the early morning when loud explosions woke me from my sleep. I rushed to the window and saw thick smoke rising into the sky from the direction of the railroad station, eight blocks from our street. Sirens started wailing all over the town. Stunned, we switched on the radio and heard the announcer repeating over and over again, "*Uwaga-Uwaga!*" (Attention!) "This is not an air-raid drill; this is an attack. Our dear country, Poland, is under enemy attack since 4:45 this morning." Instructions were broadcast, urging the population not to panic, to follow instructions, and when the sirens sounded to immediately make their way to the nearest shelter and stay there until the all clear. As the sirens were already sounding we all dressed quickly and went downstairs to the air-raid cellars which soon filled up with bewildered neighbors. Only the older ones knew what war meant. When the all clear came we did not immediately go back into our third story apartment, in case it would not last very long. Already the rumors were flying. The railroad station had been hit and the military airport outside the city had also been bombed. Everybody had questions; few had answers. One of our neighbors who lived on the ground floor invited us to stay in his flat for the time being. His name was Władysław Lopatowski and his wife was Zofia. They had a son, Jan, who was a little younger than I. Mrs. Lopatowski made tea for us all and we sat around the radio to hear the news. First we listened to the Polish stations which reported that the assault started from the air, and at Danzig, the Baltic port, the German battleship *Schleswig-Holstein* was shelling from the sea. Simultaneously the Wehrmacht crashed across the border. There had been no warning, no ultimatum, no declaration of war. Our armed forces were obviously caught by surprise but the announcer, quoting the military command, bravely assured Poles that our army would soon push the Germans back from the soil of Poland. The German radio station we switched to told a different story. The jubilant Nazi announcer reported that the glorious Luftwaffe had bombed military targets, important rail junctions and bridges, and destroyed the Polish air force on the ground before the planes could take off while the German army was advancing on all fronts meeting little resistance.

Deeply disturbed we returned home but did not eat breakfast; we hungered only for news. Our radio station was admitting that our troops were suffering heavy losses and were falling back to new positions in many sectors, and it accused the Germans of deliberately bombing civilian targets causing thousands of innocent casualties. We stayed with the radio all day, switching between stations, and in the evening we went to bed with our clothes on, ready to run to the shelter at the first sound of the siren. The news was still sketchy. The Warsaw radio station admitted that our troops were suffering heavy losses and were being pushed back—retreating, the announcer put it—to new defensive positions. The German stations were jubilant with detailed reports of their successes on land, in the air and at sea. Their tanks were routing our cavalry and infantry; their bombers were wiping out Poland's most strategic sites, while their ships were imposing a blockade of the Polish Baltic coast. Meanwhile, western radio stations were reporting total surprise in their capitals, their governments stunned into lethargy.

Next morning the news had not improved. We realized that we were now in mortal danger. Mother was trying hard to control her tears. Like Father, she still remembered what tragedies the last war had caused just twenty years earlier. We avoided looking at each other. On top of the rape of Poland that Hitler had started without provocation, we as Jews had no illusions about our fate. Our Jewish press had, since 1933, kept us informed about what the Germans were doing to the Jews in their own country, in Austria and Czechoslovakia, and now here they were on the doorsteps of the three and a half million Jews of Poland.

It was now twenty-four hours since the assault began and we had been hoping for better news. But, in fact, it was worse. Our defenses had been broken. In Danzig, German "tourists" and the local German population came into the streets fully armed and attacked members of the Polish garrison and police. German "merchant ships" in the harbor were shelling Polish positions. The Germans there were hosting swastika flags and that same day Hitler simply annexed the city to the Reich.

Many places were reported as already being in German hands. We could not follow all the names, but it was clear that their forces were pushing relentlessly forward while our army was falling back. The western radio stations reported the situation as completely under German control. Their modern weapons were wiping out our pitifully outmoded, even ancient, arms. Their panzers were cutting down our mounted lancers, relics of battles of old. As our military leaders, operating by their dusty plans, concentrated their defense in the west, the Germans were attacking from the north, from East Prussia, and from Slovakia in the south, bypassing our forces and pushing behind them toward the Vistula River, Poland's natural second line of defense. The western announcers were calling the German campaign a *Blitzkrieg,* a war of lightning strikes they had developed, while the Poles were fighting a traditional defensive war, the kind they had studied in their old textbooks and manuals. Another new phenomenon of war, the infamous fifth column, here made up of Poles of ethnic German origin, was also reported to be helping the advancing Wehrmacht by acts of sabotage, stabbing our defenders in the back. There were two million of them and they had lived in Poland in dignity, accepted by the population as equals, while we Jews, Polish for a thousand years, had been discriminated against as a foreign entity, not only by the common people, but quite openly by the leaders of the country, and particularly the Catholic Church. Jews were kept out of senior ranks in government service and the army. The air force and navy would not accept Jews at all. But while many Jews were now fighting and dying for Poland, these German Poles were repaying their host country for its hospitality by cooperation with Poland's ancient enemy, Germany. The Polish radio was urging the population to remain calm and promised that our army would stop the German advance as soon as they would establish strong new defense lines. We were shocked, but a greater shock was in store, when it was reported that in the south two Slovak divisions had joined the German attack on our country.

We heard that Hitler had given a major speech in the Reichstag only a few hours after his troops had smashed across the border. He told his cheering henchmen that it was the Polish army which had attacked Germany, and Germany would defend itself. His nerve was incredible.

Late in the evening our President Moscicki also issued a proclamation to the Polish people, dramatically declaring before God and history that on this day Hitler had let his beasts out of their cages and they were running loose in Poland. The Germans were all killers, young and old. He asked the population to remain calm and cooperate with the authorities. This was a very sad proclamation. The radio called on all men of military age to go east to report for active service. I was of military age and Szymon a few months short. We had to decide what to do. Father and I went to the Jewish section of the town where we had many friends, to hear what the opinion was there. On our way we saw refugees who were streaming into our town in trucks, in cars and on foot, exhausted and sweating in the hot summer weather under the heavy loads of what possessions they could carry. As it was Saturday, the Sabbath day, the Jewish shops were closed and people stood around anxiously discussing the situation. As we approached the refugees, we noted their desperately sad looks. They had come from Silesia on the western border of Poland and had fled to keep out of the way of the SS who were following the soldiers.

We called on friends and learned from them that already many men had left Cracow to look for safer havens in the east for themselves and their families, intending to come back for them later. But many who owned large enterprises or properties did not want to abandon them. As we had no business to worry about we decided that Father, Szymon and I would leave next morning. Mother would stay with Fela and Nathan, who was under military age. We thought they would find it too difficult to make the trek in the hot weather, and the trains were not running. They strenuously opposed our plan and finally we agreed that we would all go together. Father and I went downstairs to tell the Lopatowskis of our plan and asked them to take care of our apartment while we were away. As we sat there listening to the radio the neighbors from the second floor came in and introduced themselves, a couple called Gelb. I noticed their German accent and that the wife indeed knew very little Polish. They told us the husband had been among the many Jews the Germans deported to Poland in October 1938. He had managed to get to Cracow and had found a job with a Polish scrap dealer. His wife was Aryan and had been allowed to stay in Germany but had decided to join him and arrived with their furniture and belongings a few months earlier. We became instant friends. Mr. Gelb told us that the attack on Poland had not been spontaneous as Hitler claimed, but had been carefully planned and prepared.

Cracow was in immediate danger, close to the Slovak border and the Silesian areas. We already knew that the Germans had broken through our natural defenses in the Tatra Mountains and the Jablunkowy Pass and were also advancing rapidly from Silesia. We went upstairs to pack our knapsacks. Mother was baking bread for our trip. We were all depressed, tense and nervous, and little was said. The radio reported the Polish army in full retreat on all fronts, suffering tremendous casualties with thousands of prisoners falling into German hands. German bombers were indiscriminately killing civilians in cities, towns and villages; "murderers from the sky" the announcer called them. First reports were coming in of atrocities committed by the invading Germans joined by the Polish-Germans in the western areas, burning, looting and raping. Frequent warnings were broadcast to look out for the German fifth columnists.

The German stations were jubilant, broadcasting gloating communiqués of victories issued by the OKW—*Oberkommando der Wehrmacht*—the Supreme Headquarters of the armed forces.

The western stations drew a clearer picture of the situation. Hitler had committed over half a million men to the attack. Two armies, "North" under General Bock, and "South" under General von Rundstedt, were under the overall command of Marshal von Brauchitsch. They comprised sixty German divisions, nine of them motorized, and two Slovak divisions. They were equipped with the most modern tanks and new weapons, many of which had never been seen before. They were backed by two thousand planes from two of Ger-

many's three air squadrons. Poland had seven hundred outmoded planes, one armored division, and ten cavalry
divisions. Horses against tanks; spears, lances and sabers of
our renowned cavalry, whose bravery was no match for the
steel of the German fighting machines. Most of their infantry
was motorized and moved fast while our men had to march.
But the biggest devastation was caused by their bombers
which, escorted by modern fighter planes, dominated the
skies, sowing destruction, confusion and panic in the ranks of
the army and civilian population.

Our leaders were publicly bitter about the inaction and
silence of France and England. They had pledged to stand by
us in a treaty signed not long before, but did nothing to help
as Poland was bleeding and its inferior army in retreat. We felt
we had made the right decision to move east.

We went to bed early to be ready for our journey into the
unknown. Early next morning we dressed, locked the doors
and gave the keys to Mrs. Lopatowski. She wished us all the
best and we stepped out into the dark and deserted streets,
blacked out since the start of the war. We knew there was no
use going to the railway station; the trains out of Cracow
had stopped running since many bridges and junctions were
destroyed by the German bombers. The buses were not running either, so we started walking toward Podgorze, the eastern part of the city, across the Vistula bridge. I knew the way
very well; it was the way to the chocolate factory where
Father and I worked. Soon the streets were filled with refugees
coming from all directions, burdened with suitcases and bundles, and not really knowing where to go. All the stores were
closed. We passed through Podgorze to the Plaszow suburb,
the industrial zone of Cracow. The roads were crowded with
cars, trucks and horse-drawn carts loaded and overloaded
with people and belongings, with a few soldiers on their way
to join their units. It was very hot and the traffic stirred up
clouds of dust, so we decided to walk in the fields, parallel to
the highway. There were many broken-down vehicles and
others that were stalled, having run out of gas, watched over
by the refugees anxious for their belongings. Some had found
horses to pull their cars while many refugees walked alongside
us. Every few hours we sat down in a field to rest. We were
very thirsty. Though we soon finished all the food we had

taken with us, it was the thirst that bothered us most. In the villages we passed through we tried to buy food but were turned away, so we picked up a few potatoes and turnips in the fields and baked them over a bonfire. Exhausted, we slept well in the open field. Father woke us early in the morning to allow us to make some headway before the sun came out. When it got hot we entered a forest and marched in the shade of the trees. Suddenly we heard the sound of low-flying planes, and, looking up were terrified by the sight of a swarm of planes coming straight toward us, like vultures closing in on their prey. We dropped to the ground under some trees keeping an eye on the planes. We saw bombs dropping out of their bellies and exploding loudly on the nearby highway, starting fires. People were jumping from burning vehicles but the German planes pursued them and cut them down with their machine guns like wheat being harvested. The Nazi pilots, unchallenged, took their time to do their lethal work. When they were satisfied, they soared high into the sky where God was presumably witnessing the slaughter of His children. We felt that since September 1, He had abandoned us to the German killers.

When the planes had disappeared we ran to the road which seemed to be going up in flames of total disaster. We heard the screams of the wounded, some lying on the ground, others running aimlessly around with blood streaming from their injured bodies, searching for aid. The road was strewn with corpses, torn bodies and personal belongings, all covered in blood. Wounded horses were groaning loudly, adding to the general feeling of horror until soldiers put them out of their misery with their rifles. People were raising the heads of the dead and wounded to identify their relatives and friends, crying over their dead or injured bodies. We helped carry the wounded into the forest where we had hidden from the attack. Soldiers began digging graves alongside the road. The uniformed dead were placed in individual graves which they marked with their names; civilians were placed in mass graves surrounded by mourning relatives. We helped the soldiers to push the burned and disabled vehicles off the road to clear the way for army convoys and then went back into the fields to carry on our march.

We were shattered by this first encounter with the horrors

of war: the dead who only a few moments earlier had been fellow refugees, their inconsolable relatives crying for them, the mangled horses and scorched steel. And all the time we continued marching. Many kept looking back as if once more to take leave of their dear ones. There were parents who had just buried their children, and children who had placed the bodies of their parents in the mass graves.

Now I realized that the radio reports of indiscriminate bombing of innocent civilians by the Luftwaffe had not been exaggerated. I had just witnessed those Nazi pilots doing their cold-blooded work. We moved slowly through the bumpy field with the sun beating down on our backs and heads. The sight of a village ahead cheered us, but the peasants would not even open their doors when we asked to buy food. They allowed us only to draw water from their wells, and that was a big relief. When darkness fell we stopped and tried to sleep, but sleep would not come. The scenes of the day haunted us and we talked compulsively about the tragedies we had witnessed. I was especially sorry for Mother and Fela. And this was only the beginning of the war. God only knew what might still be in store for us.

With the first light of dawn we moved on, staying on the road to walk faster and going back into the tree-shaped fields when the sun came up. Occasionally we came upon a stream or a river that was low because of the drought. We bathed our blistered feet in the water and drank deeply regardless of the consequences. Now it was the Germans, not the germs, that worried us. In the next village we met some peasants who told us they had no food to sell because the army had requisitioned all their reserves. As we left the village we were stopped by military police who were examining the papers of the hundreds of refugees on the road ahead and ordering some, whose papers were apparently not in order, to stand aside and wait. When our turn came I told them that Szymon and I were going east to try to join the army. I asked the officer where we might report. He didn't know, but told us to continue on east. The soldiers ordered refugees out of the vehicles they had arrived in and unceremoniously commandeered them, disregarding their protests. They also took over the stronger-looking horses, leaving the refugees stranded with their bundles of be-longings.

Depressed, we rested in a field and Father attempted to cheer us with the promise that we would soon reach Bochnia, a town where he had customers with whom he had been friendly for years. We decided that Mother, Fela and Nathan would stay there while the three of us would continue east to the Bug River. Marching on without further stops we reached Bochnia in the early evening. As we entered we noticed a big commotion and for the first time saw a Polish mob in action, looting. There were quite a few soldiers in the frenzied crowd, their rifles still slung over their shoulders, clutching stolen goods under their arms. Many were drunk with the vodka they had stolen. We sensed that drunken soldiers carrying arms were dangerous so Father quickly took us down a side street, keeping out of the way of the running crowd hurrying to take their loot home and go back for more. Father stopped near a small house and went round to the back where he knocked on the door and called the name of a customer he knew lived there. We realized that the homeowner must be frightened by the roaming mob but he opened a crack in the door, and when he recognized Father, he quickly let us in. He greeted us warmly and Father and he embraced. He suggested we change our dusty clothes and wash up, and was evidently amazed at the immense amount of water we were able to drink. By the time we had cleaned up, his wife had prepared a hot meal for us. Over the food they told us that the local police had left the city in the morning and the mob had taken over. The first victims were the Jews, their homes, stores and workshops. The mob was joined by Polish refugees who were passing through the town and welcomed the chance to put into practice the anti-Semitism they had grown up with. Some soldiers, who were supposedly on their way to their units, also joined in the plunder, throwing their training and discipline to the wind.

After the meal our host filled us in on the latest news. On September 3, England and France had at last declared war on Germany since Hitler had ignored the ultimatum they had issued. In Warsaw the news had been greeted with tremendous enthusiasm and exhilarated Poles danced in the streets outside the foreign embassies. But Hitler's armies were still pushing full steam ahead while our forces continued withdrawing to what were called "new" positions. The larger cities in the western part of Poland were already in German hands, including Katowice, Gniezno, Poznań, Bydgoszcz, Częstochowa and Torún. Our hostess prepared a room for us, and next morning Father asked our host to direct us to a Jewish family where Mother, Fela and Nathan might stay. He would not hear of it and insisted they stay with them. After breakfast we, the three men of the family, set out, going east again, reassured that our dear ones were in good hands.

A day or two later, as we were moving through the fields we heard the rumble of artillery fire behind us. Father said it was not far away. Occasionally low-flying German planes passed above us heading east. When we reached a river we washed and soaked our tired feet, which were swollen and covered with blisters. The sun beat down on us all day. Whenever we met an officer we asked for directions to report for service. None of them had any idea. Confusion reigned. In a few days we reached Sandomierz, a famous old town on the Vistula. As we entered it we again saw a Polish mob plundering Jewish stores, workshops and homes. There was broken glass all over the sidewalks, and empty boxes and broken vodka bottles everywhere. Again we saw armed soldiers enthusiastically joining the mob. We moved into the side streets to look for a Jewish family with whom to spend the night and came upon an old, bearded Jew standing in front of a small house next to a devastated store. Father approached him and asked him in Yiddish whether we might come in to wash and rest. The old man was so scared he could scarcely talk but finally agreed to let us come in if we would promise to protect him. We noticed that there was no one else around, but we refrained from asking where his family was. He just stood behind the curtain and watched the street. We washed and sat down to eat, and fell asleep sitting at the table. Early next morning Father woke us and the first thing we noticed was that the old man was still standing in the same spot at the curtained window as though he had been petrified. We realized there must be something wrong with him; perhaps he had lost his mind as the threatening mob had robbed his store. Even when we thanked him and wished him goodbye, he made no answer.

When we were back on the road Father said he had decided we should go back west to Cracow, given that till now we met only anarchy as the disorganized troops heading east lost control. We also worried about our loved ones. We marched through the fields but this time we stayed closer to the high-

way. We decided not to enter the villages but slept in the
fields, making our meals of whatever vegetables we could find,
baked if we could make a fire, raw when we could not, and
drank from the wells we came upon. We were not alone, there
were many refugees like us, some going east, others west, and
all the time German planes were overhead, flying east and
coming back again.

The artillery fire was drawing closer. One morning as we
were getting up, we spotted a big cloud of dust rising from the
highway, accompanied by the rumble of heavy vehicles coming toward us from the west. Drawing nearer the highway we
saw a big convoy of military vehicles heading east, and as
they passed us we were astonished to see they were Germans.
How different they looked from the retreating Polish army.
The convoy of trucks and armored vehicles was preceded by
motorcycles with side cars. Father explained to us that they
were the patrols. The soldiers looked fit and well armed and
were singing lustily. The heat and dust didn't seem to bother
them; the Polish army certainly did not. Ahead of them, the
few Polish soldiers still around were busily robbing the Jews
in the neighboring town. Father told us the German artillery
and equipment were very modern and of the finest quality. As
an old soldier he had an eye for military affairs. Our own
ancient army was no match for them; bravery alone could not
hold back panzers. We now continued our march on the main
road estimating that we no longer need fear the German
planes. After a few hours we were stopped at a military
checkpoint. We lined up to wait our turn. The younger men
were ordered to take off their caps or hats to provide the
soldiers an easy way of checking for deserters, since all
recruits had to shave their heads. We were checked out and
allowed to continue west. As we marched on we saw German
planes flying east, very low as though to guide the Wehrmacht
columns. The sky was theirs. There was no Polish air force,
and it seemed to us, no God either to stop them.

We slept just off the road and next morning woke to another
very hot day. In the villages we were again unable to obtain
food, but now the peasants opened their doors and told us
that the Germans had imposed order and were requisitioning
all they had. On our way we met more refugees still going

east, while we were heading back to Bochnia. They told us that Cracow had been taken by the Germans on the sixth, and Bochnia a day later. The German soldiers on the highways were mostly behaving correctly they told us, but warned us of the early curfews in many places.

The German patrols who passed us were very strict but fair. For the first time I saw German soldiers and officers at close range. They appeared well dressed and clean and very disciplined. Sometimes their field kitchens gave us food and Father, who spoke German well, got cigarettes from the older men. We marched on as fast as our blistered, tired feet would carry us, cheered by the thought that we would soon be reunited with our dear ones in Bochnia, and made it there before the curfew. Father guided us through the streets which were almost empty. The stores were open but there were no customers. A German foot patrol passed us but there were no hoodlums running wild. Now they were afraid of the Germans.

We located the house and our former hosts told us that our family had left to return to Cracow which the Germans had since taken. We were disappointed but could only hope they had reached home safely. Our hostess told us she had given them enough food to last until they reached Cracow so they need not ask the unfriendly peasants. We were invited in; washed and changed our clothes, and sat down to a fine meal. The host filled us in with the news we had missed on the road. German victories and Polish retreats. But for the first time we heard of atrocities carried out on Jews by the invading Germans. There were reports of plunder, beatings, torture, rape and killings. Jewish houses of worship were desecrated and burned. In Bochnia the Germans had restored order after their soldiers had looted what the Polish hooligans had left.

Polish radio announced that our political and military leaders were leaving Warsaw and foreign embassies were also evacuating from the capital. Only a few leaders of the opposition PPS Socialist party and the Witos Peasant party were staying on to resist. German forces were approaching Warsaw from the west, north and east from behind the Vistula. Our second line of defense was no more. It had dissolved into a few pockets of resistance.

We slept on the floor in the next room and in the morning found our hostess had prepared some food for the road, though they didn't have much themselves. We were touched by the kindness of these people and could not thank them enough. We wished them all the best for the approaching High Holidays and hoped that one day, when peace would return life to normal, we would get together again.

We marched on. We noticed a long convoy of trucks coming up behind us and soon saw they were Polish prisoners of war, crammed into the trucks, the healthy and the wounded with blood-stained bandages together, begging for water and food. The heavily armed German guards would allow no one near them. For these tragic figures the fighting was over, but who could tell what awaited them in the German camps, especially the Jews who might be among them. All the time long columns of Germans were going east with Luftwaffe planes flying ahead of time to clear the way. We preferred not to go into the unfriendly villages again and made do with the food we had, drinking water from the streams we passed. We had no trouble falling asleep; our exhaustion saw to that. When we discerned the tall smokestacks of Cracow in the distance we stepped up our speed to make sure we'd make it before curfew. In the late afternoon we reached Plaszow and then Podgorze. There were still no streetcars and we had to continue walking. The bridges over the Vistula had been blown up, presumably by our retreating army. We waited in a long line to cross on a military pontoon bridge and then we were back in Cracow. We were practically running now. There were many people in the streets and the stores were open. We saw German soldiers in trucks and on foot. At last we reached our building and looked expectantly up at the windows on our floor to see whether our dear ones were waiting for us. The windows were closed and shuttered. But when we knocked on the door, Nathan opened and shouted excitedly, "They're back! They're back!" Mother and Fela came running and we had a tearful reunion in each other's arms. The first thing Mother said was that we all looked so skinny and she made us take off our dirty clothes and wash. Before we had finished changing Mother was in the kitchen preparing food to fatten us again. She too was full of praise for the people who had taken care of us in Bochnia, and also for the Lopatowskis who had been very good to them when they returned, bringing food that was now hard to obtain. The food stores were empty since the peasants were not coming to the city to sell their produce as usual.

We were told that on the day the Germans had entered the city, they had shot eleven Jews who had been taken hostage along with some Poles, to make sure there would be no resistance. When the day had passed quietly the Poles were released, but the bodies of the Jews were found outside the walls of the old Jewish cemetery on Miodowa Street. The news of the executions spread like wildfire and caused a great panic, a frightening warning of what other Jews might expect.

The Germans wasted no time with their anti-Jewish measures. Already the first order requiring all Jewish business establishments, including those with 50 percent or more Jewish ownership, to paint a Star of David on their entrance to make it easier for the Germans to identify them. Almost immediately their soldiers, and the SS and Gestapo who had followed close on their heels, entered Jewish stores and took anything they fancied without bothering to pay. They also made raids into the Jewish section to round up Jews for all kinds of work. Trucks were taking hundreds of Jews to the barracks and buildings they had taken over to get them ready for their new masters. One truckload failed to return in the evening. Their families panicked but there was no way of finding what had happened to them. They never came back and rumor had it they had been taken away and shot.

After supper we went downstairs to greet the Lopatowskis who were happy to see us back. They admitted they had been worried for us because of the bombings and the killing of Jews by the Germans in many places, including the highways, of which we had known nothing. Mr. Lopatowski was very angry that our new allies, England and France, who had declared war on Germany, had done nothing to come to our aid. Their military pact turned out to be a scrap of paper, of no more help to us than they had been to Czechoslovakia. But he was ashamed of the Polish soldiers and civilians who had taken part in looting Jewish property.

Reports were coming in from western Poland of the atrocities committed by German soldiers, the special units of the SS and Gestapo, and the ethnic Germans, against the Polish population in general and the Jews in particular. The ethnic Germans now declared themselves members of so-called self-defense organizations, the Freischutz or Selbschutz. They were, in fact, a fifth column blindly serving Hitler. These traitors had apparently been well organized against the day of the invasion. Many held important positions in which they were able to supply the invading Germans with vital information.

President Roosevelt's declaration of U.S. neutrality was another shock for us. We had believed in America and its principles of democracy and human rights. Neutrality had, in fact, signified approval, or at least acquiescence in Hitler's attack and the indiscriminate killing of Poles. Polish casualties were high but the Germans had also suffered losses, if only a few. This was no "Flower War" of the kind that had greeted them in Austria and the Sudeten area of Czechoslovakia. The Poles fought back, heroically if pathetically, outnumbered and outgunned. In many places they were still defending encircled positions on the Baltic Sea, in the Hell peninsula at Westerplatte. Also near the Bzura River and in Kutno. Warsaw was under constant bombing raids and being encircled from all sides, with the Polish army falling back toward the capital to defend it. For the first time Mr. Lopatowski revealed to us that he was a leading member of the PPS underground but swore us to secrecy. He was very proud that his party had made the patriotic decision not to abandon Warsaw, whereas the anti-Semitic leaders of the country had run away with their families on September 5, like rats leaving a sinking ship.

Mr. Lopatowski told us that on Wednesday, September 6, the first motorized German patrols had entered Cracow at about six in the morning, coming from the west and south. The Polish troops had withdrawn the night before to save the historic city from destruction. The German patrols were followed by tanks and long columns of motorized infantry and behind them the heavy guns. The Germans took over most of the public buildings for their own use, and placed the main streets and important junctions under guard. Only a few people ventured out into the streets. Most preferred to observe the Germans from the safety of their homes.

In the afternoon large notices, in German and Polish, were prominently posted all over the city warning the populace not to attempt to conceal weapons, ammunition or explosives of any kind but immediately to surrender them to the nearest

German army post. Anyone found possessing arms would be shot. The notice also warned that any act of armed resistance or sabotage would be punished by death.

A curfew was imposed, from 6:30 p.m. to 5:30 a.m., and the blackout stayed in force. But everybody was ordered to report to their jobs next morning and all stores to open for business. Prices were frozen and looters shot on sight.

The Gestapo took over a government building on Siemiradzego Street and appointed Dr. Stanisław Klimecki, an unknown city official, as the new mayor.

We learned that Łódź, Poland's second largest city where two hundred thousand Jews lived, had been captured and the Germans changed its name to Litzmanstadt. They renamed many places, giving them new German names, an early indication of their plans for Poland. Hundreds of Jews were brutally beaten or killed, often pushed into synagogues and burned alive. Synagogues were profaned and some were put to use as stables or warehouses by the German army. Jewish women were raped. The local ethnic Germans seized the chance to grab Jewish property whose owners were banished. Allowed to take only small suitcases and a little money with them, they were turned into instant beggars. Many of them came to Cracow to look for shelter and our Jewish Council placed them with Jewish families.

Mr. Lopatowski told us that he and his son worked in the Zieleniewski metal plant, where he was a foreman. His wife was a school teacher. Mr. Gelb advised us not to go to the Jewish section during the mornings because that was when the Germans were hunting for Jewish workers. Our section was considered safe because it was gentile. Next evening Father, Szymon, and I went to the Jewish section to see friends. We noticed the Star of David signs on Jewish stores and restaurants, many of which were closed after having been looted, and their smashed windows were boarded up. Food in all stores was sold out and the peasants who were still bringing their produce to town no longer accepted money—they would take only goods in exchange. The tension was palpable. Every time a car or truck was heard, Jews ducked into doorways or stores and advised us to do likewise. They feared the German hunt for men to work outside of town, constructing their camps and doing humiliating jobs. But this morning the trucks were bringing not hunters but robbers. We watched as they stopped outside Jewish stores and forced Jews to help them load merchandise. We were told that German soldiers had been coming into Jewish stores accompanied by Poles, prostitutes, porters and odd-job men, who used to work for the Jewish merchants and knew where the best goods were, and who asked for anything they fancied. They laughed when the owners asked them for payment. The first German word their Polish companions learned was *Jude*.

There were many notices on the walls, orders signed by Kłimecki, all concerning the Jews. One of them forbade Jews to lock their apartments at any time, to make it easier for the Germans to enter as they wished. We met refugees from the Silesian areas and talked to some of them. They were bewildered by their sudden change of fortune, having been turned into paupers overnight. They had witnessed many atrocities and were happy that at least they had got away with their lives. Many of the occupied towns were already *Judenrein* (free of Jews). Hundreds of Jews had been killed, and those who remained alive had fled. Their old neighbors, the ethnic Germans, had guided the Gestapo and SS and had taken part in the massacres. Jewish refugees from Częstochowa, the Polish holy city, told us that when the Germans entered on September 3, they rounded up many Jews, ordering them to put on their prayer shawls, then herded them into a synagogue and burned them alive. At least two hundred Jews were massacred.

Mother was disappointed when we returned without any food. We told her about the peasants' "new currency," and she started preparing clothes for an exchange. We hoped for a miracle but the radio announced only German victories which the western stations confirmed. Their goal was now to encircle Warsaw and cut off the rest of the Polish army from behind the Bug and Vistula rivers, our intended second line of defense. Our president and his cabinet, as well as many political and military leaders, including Marshal Smigly-Rydz, had abandoned the capital and were fleeing east and south to the Hungarian and Romanian borders. Later in the evening the German radio announced that Hitler had appointed General von Rundstedt as military governor of occupied Poland, and Dr. Hans Frank, a Reich minister, as the head of the civilian administration. The Germans were evidently intending to rule us for good.

We got up early the next morning and left home as soon as the curfew was lifted. The streets were almost empty, but on the outskirts of town we met peasants whose wagons were surrounded by eager customers exchanging goods for food. We got bread, butter and enough potatoes to last us for ten days. We carried them home and then Szymon and I went to the chocolate factory where Father and I worked. Everything was in disorder with empty crates and cartons and broken glass lying all over. There was only one man in the office, Otto, who had been one of the employees and who was now the boss. None of us ever knew that Otto was an ethnic German. Now he was put in charge of the factory by his invading countrymen, replacing the Jewish owners who had built it up. He greeted me but would not shake hands and told me that immediately after the Polish troops had withdrawn, a mob from the neighborhood broke into the factory and looted everything they could carry away, including pieces of equipment and raw materials. There was no way to resume production for the time being. I asked him whether Father and I could return to work and he said that under his management there was no room for Jews.

The next morning we went to the Jewish section where Father had had many customers and hoped to find a job, but nobody needed workers. We were told that the evening before a German officer who was staying in the Hotel Royal, just a block from Wavel castle on the edge of the Jewish section, claimed that shots had been fired at him. He pointed at a nearby building and the Gestapo started a search, pistols drawn, terrorizing the Jewish inhabitants. They arrested twenty-six Jewish men and the next morning their families were ordered to come to the nearby St. Michael jail to pick up their bodies. A tipsy German officer had made an allegation and twenty-six Jews were dead! We realized that this was the New Order. No trials and no defense. The Gestapo were omnipotent—prosecutor, judge and executioner all in one. The news spread like wildfire and paralyzed the Jews. Everybody in the close-knit Cracow community had known the dead men.

Szymon returned home and told us that he could get his job

back, in a large wholesale textile company in the Polish section. In the evening I visited Mr. Lopatowski who told me that the Gestapo were arresting Polish patriots and intellectuals and sending them off to the Mauthausen concentration camp near Linz in Austria. Warsaw was now almost completely encircled and the Germans were driving toward Lwów in the south and Brest Litovsk in the north, their tanks advancing at incredible speed. He confided in great secrecy that his party, the PPS socialists, had nominated him as a leader in the underground movement they were forming against the German occupiers. We were proud to have such a friend from a party that we had always considered friendly to Jews.

In the Jewish section people were jumpy, disturbed by every approaching car, but the Poles appeared to feel quite safe and unconcerned. For the first time we saw the SS in action. They were driving around in long-bodied military cars, their number plates bearing the dreaded double lightning flash insignia. They wore dark green uniforms with silver skulls on their collars and peaked caps. To us they looked like death itself. When they came upon religious Jews in caftans, beards and sidelocks, they jumped out and made the frightened men jump and dance while they photographed and filmed them. Then they cut off their beards and sidelocks very slowly, to have their amusement recorded on film. When they finished taking pictures they kicked the Jews with their heavy black boots and the poor souls ran off, happy to be alive.

Father and I could find no jobs. Many Jewish workers were being dismissed without notice and replaced by Poles, and there was no demand for new Jewish workers. We were advised to try the Jewish Council, as the German companies and army units who needed workers ordered them from the Council. We went to the Council building on Krakowska Street. There were long lines of refugees outside waiting for food and lodgings. At the Community Kitchen in Dajwor Street there were more lines, supervised by Jewish men with vizored caps and OD arm bands. They were the new *Ordnungs Dienst* (Jewish Public Order Police), in charge of keeping order in the Jewish section. They were also used as couriers between the Council and the Gestapo which had set up its headquarters at number 2, Pomorska Street. There, Siebert who was appointed chief of the Jewish section, became our new master. We were deeply touched by the long lines of refugees who only a few days ago had been prosperous citizens and were now destitute, begging for food, a roof over their heads and jobs. They had fled from their homes to escape the Germans only to be caught by them in Cracow. There was nowhere left to run.

When we returned the next morning to look for work the section was very nervous and we were told to hide, the German *Chappers* (Catchers) were coming. The three of us hurried into the nearest building and a woman on the first floor let us in. From the window we could see the young SS men catching any Jew they could lay their hands on and kicked and pushed them into their trucks. As soon as their truck was full they drove off. A few minutes later the street was normal again and we were able to go down. On a side street we met some peasants with their wagons, but they had already sold all the food they had brought. We told them we would make them a good offer of goods in exchange for food and they promised to return in four days and come straight to our section. Szymon returned with good news too. His boss had allowed him to buy goods from his store at wholesale prices so that we were now able to join the popular new "black market," buying goods cheap and exchanging them for food. We could see nothing wrong with this; after all we had to eat.

Later, as we walked through the main business street of the Jewish section, Bozego Ciala, we heard shouts of *"Das sind Juden"* (Those are Jews) behind us. We looked back and saw some Poles pointing us out to uniformed Germans. The Germans motioned to us and called, *"Komm komm"* (Come along). We had no choice but to go to them, and they took us to a truck parked in a side street, kept out of sight to make it easier for them to catch unsuspecting Jewish slaves. They made us climb in the truck which was nearly filled with Jews. Polish bystanders were evidently enjoying the sight. The truck took us to the outskirts of Cracow to a large camp at the military airfield which had been taken over by the Luftwaffe. We were split up into groups of thirty men and ordered to unload supply trucks and carry the materials into the warehouses. They rushed us all the time, not allowing us to rest. The older men, who could not keep up, were beaten but had to go on working despite the blood streaming from their faces and bodies. When the trucks were unloaded we were taken into the barracks and made to clean them, always on the double. Our group was assigned to the latrines. They gave us a few buckets of water and disinfectants and we washed the floors and the latrines with our bare hands. The chemicals burned our hands and skin and the stench was terrible. All the time the Germans were screaming at us, *"Los, los"* (Hurry up). They gave us neither food nor drink. Late in the evening they told us *"Verschwinde"* (Get lost). As it was already past curfew time we decided to march in a long column, hoping this would spare us trouble. We reached home without further mishap and had a difficult time washing off the dirt and smell.

Early the next morning we went to the so-called Tandetta, a large open flea market where peasants were again bringing their produce. They took almost anything in exchange—old clothes, shoes, underwear, household utensils and bedding. We made some deals and were home before eight, which was the time the Germans came out.

On Saturday, I accompanied Father to the Jewish section to meet a refugee from Jarosław for news of his sister and her family there. The man said he knew they were all right. On our way back we were again denounced by some young Poles who pointed us out to an elderly SS man who was already known as the best "Jew catcher" of them all. Nevertheless it took him a long time to fill up his truck as there were few Jews on the street on the Sabbath. Then he drove us to a large government building and made us unload furniture they had confiscated. The heavy work did not bother us, but we were sorry for Father and the other elderly Jews. The Germans had taken the furniture from wealthy Jewish homes, mostly expensive pieces, many of them obviously valuable antiques. They were guided by the Polish janitors who often first took bribes from the Jews not to tell the Germans and then betrayed them. The janitors and porters were actually becoming the most dangerous people for us, guiding the Germans to hidden stores. We were repeatedly warned not to break or scratch any furniture on pain of being shot for sabotage. The upstairs rooms were being prepared for German officers and their families and we had to take the best pieces there. In order to protect the valuable furniture, the Germans did not rush us which at least was a piece of luck. When we finished in the evening they sent us off. Mother cried when we returned home, completely exhausted. For the first time she told us she regretted that we had not gone to America with her family before the war. Now it was too late.

The radio reported that everywhere the Polish army was being routed and only in the Westerplatte fortress in the Baltic were they putting up any real resistance, heroic but hopeless. We heard that two Polish submarines and three destroyers had gotten through the German blockade and reached ports in England. Symbolic victories. We told Mr. Lopatowski about the hoodlums who were cooperating with the Germans and terrorizing the Jews. He told us that the underground knew about them and were listing their names for retribution when the time came. We hoped we would live to see them punished.

A neighbor told us that one of the bakers in our section had received a supply of flour and would be selling fresh bread the next morning. He told us he intended defying the curfew to stand in line all night. Szymon, Nathan and I decided to join him and we lined up together. We were not alone. The queue was growing fast but the German patrols did not bother us. Early in the morning the baker opened his store but there was such a rush that he called the German police to restore order. By the time our turn came, some Poles were pointing us out as Jews and the Germans ordered us away. After having stood in line for eleven hours we had to return home without a single loaf to show for our troubles. We had known that the Poles were anti-Semites and always had been, but we had expected they would change their attitude in the face of our common enemy.

In the Jewish section we met some people who had just returned from their attempted march to the east. They told terrible stories of German military police separating Jews from Poles at the checkpoints. They allowed the Poles to go on but had marched the Jews to the nearest town where they had imprisoned them in synagogues and empty school buildings, together with local Jews. Many young women were raped in full sight of everybody. They were all kept locked up without food or water for a week and then let go, but had to leave their possessions behind. They were comparatively lucky. In some towns and villages they passed, Jews had been forced to dig their own graves. We too had walked along these same roads and now thought how lucky we had been to return safely.

How our lives had changed in such short a time. It was beginning to sink in that the world had abandoned Poland. In Cracow the Germans nominated a *Judenrat* to replace the Jewish Council, with Professor Marek Bieberstein as its president, and Dr. W. Goldblat as his deputy. We knew neither of them, but it did not matter. They were only tools to carry out Gestapo orders.

The next morning we reported to the *Judenrat* for work and were placed with an army unit. The soldiers took us to their base by truck and for the first time we worked for decent Germans. Many of them were older men and that might have been the explanation. They did not rush us, allowed us rest periods, gave us food from their field kitchen, and even some cigarettes for Father. Our job was to unload equipment at the railroad station and move it into their barracks.

When Szymon returned from his job he told us that in the morning a German civilian had walked into the store and presented some papers to the owner certifying that he had been appointed *Treuhand* (Trustee), actually the new owner of the business, by the German administration. He was the new boss and told the displaced owner he would allow him to stay as his manager, and promised he would keep all the workers too. All large enterprises which were owned by Jews, or had 50 percent Jewish ownership, were being taken over by the *Treuhands*. Most of them threw out the Jewish owners and their Polish partners and dismissed all Jewish employees. On the bright side the German troops and their Polish hoodlums could no longer help themselves in those Jewish stores. They had to pay the full price for goods.

In the evening the latest news was that the Germans were completing their occupation of Poland. In the southeast they were almost at the gates of Lwów and in the north General Guderian's tanks were fast approaching the fortress of Brest Litovsk. Our leaders were on their way out. Ukrainian nationalists were cooperating with the Germans in the southeast, sabotaging railways, roads and small bridges, providing information about the Polish forces, and even shooting at Polish troops.

Now the Germans had a sixth column in addition to the fifth

column of ethnic Germans—the Ukrainian nationalists who had made trouble for Poland ever since independence in 1918. But, unlike the Jews of Poland, they had not been harassed by discriminatory laws, economic boycotts and riots. We alone were a minority who were hated and officially discriminated against. We hoped that now at last decent Poles would realize who the loyal citizens were, and who were the traitors and collaborators. There were also reports of Ukrainians murdering Jews and looting their property immediately after the Germans arrived, and that the Germans tolerated their actions. To cap it all our western allies were doing nothing to help Poland, which was collapsing under the weight of the Nazi onslaught.

On Sunday morning, September 17, we watched the Poles going to church as usual showing no sign of fear or apprehension. We switched on the radio for the news and were immediately stunned. Russian forces had crossed the eastern border of Poland on a thousand-mile-wide front, meeting no resistance from the sparse border patrols, who, in fact, believed the Russians were coming to save Poland. The population enthusiastically welcomed the Soviet soldiers with flowers, but when the Russians met the first regular Polish columns they disarmed them and arrested their officers. Russian planes dropped millions of leaflets announcing they were coming to liberate the Polish workers and their families from their capitalist oppressors. They took Poland by complete surprise. We went downstairs to the Lopatowskis and found them in a state of shock. The Polish radio commentators were beginning to condemn the Russian invasion, while the western allies, who had stayed aloof during the German attack, were now criticizing the Russians for falling on Poland when it was on its knees and stabbing it in the back.

All hope for a miracle that might still save Poland evaporated. We realized that facing two fronts was the end. The German stations kept suspiciously quiet about the Russian move, but the Polish radio hopefully reported bloody skirmishes between Russian advanced units and the Germans. This illusion was soon dispersed by the Russian and German stations. In despair we realized that this was the calculated result of the deal of August 23 between Hitler and Stalin. They had carved up Poland between them and Stalin was now coming to claim his share. Poland had been independent for only twenty-one years and already her traditional enemies were busy dividing it up between them. This was the final blow, there was no way the outmoded Polish army could prevail against two heavily armed enemies on two fronts. It was also a tragedy from the political point of view. England and France which had, at least formally, declared war on Germany when it had attacked Poland, were not at war with Russia and not likely to risk one.

It was not long before we heard that the advancing Russians were carrying out mass arrests of landowners and industrialists, among them many Jews whom they accused of being capitalists. We stayed by the radio all night. How could we sleep while our country was being raped by two great bullies. The next morning, in the Jewish section, most people appeared happy that at least the Jews who would be under Russian occupation would be saved from the German murderers, and hoped that perhaps, with the Russians so close, things might take a turn for the better. Later in the morning the radio announced that advanced German columns were withdrawing westward to a previously agreed demarcation line behind the Bug River. They were relinquishing Lwów, Brest Litovsk, Białystok and Przemyśl to the Russians, evidently carrying out the terms of their August pact. General Guderian was personally handing over the fortress of Brest Litovsk to a Russian general. Our two biggest enemies were shaking hands there, over our prostrate body politic. The Russian radio stations were working overtime promising freedom and well-being for workers and peasants in the territories they were occupying. They urged the working classes to denounce their bosses and landowners to the Soviet officers and even called on the Polish soldiers to kill their own officers.

Siebert, the chief of the Jewish affairs department of the Gestapo in Cracow, accompanied by members of his staff, that morning drove into the Kazimierz section under heavy guard, and stopped outside the Jewish Council building. He was furious when there was no one outside to greet him, and as he stormed in, slapped and kicked the first executive he came across, in front of the office workers. He made it clear that the new development would make no difference to their Jewish policy and warned that from now on all Jews were under the jurisdiction of the SS and SD (Gestapo), and forbidden to question any German order, all of which had to be obeyed fully and immediately. The Council was to issue orders to close all Jewish places of worship and declare any assembly of more than two Jews a severely punishable crime. This meant that Jews could get together for prayer services only at great risk. Moreover, the religious Jews were required to shave off their beards and sidelocks, and Jewish ritual slaughter was no longer permitted.

We met some friends returning from the new demarcation lines who told us that the Germans had ordered Jews living on the German side to cross over the new border immediately. They were forced to cross the Bug or San rivers and many drowned trying to swim, or clinging to pieces of timber. In many places the Russians would not allow them in and forced them to go back only to be fired on by the Germans. Father started worrying about his sister and her family who lived in Jarosław which was on the demarcation line. The rumors coming from there were hair-raising. Near Rzeszów the Germans had thrown hundreds of Jews into deep wells, burying them alive. At Przemyśl, eight hundred Jews were murdered by the Wehrmacht. On the roads many Jews were shot on their way home. The Ukrainians were as bad as the Germans who were looking after them, taking them along with them as they withdrew to let the Russians in. Under the Russians things were little better for Jews; many were arrested as capitalist exploiters and shipped deep into Russia. But most harrowing of all were the reports that the N.K.V.D. secret police were arresting socialists and communists, among them were many Jews.

Meanwhile in Cracow, the Germans arrested the new mayor they themselves had recently appointed. Nobody knew why. Notices were posted announcing that a number of hostages had been shot in retaliation for an attack on German soldiers in the city, and we were again warned against any "hostile" activities. New hostages were taken to enforce the warning.

The Jewish High Holidays were approaching and on the day before Rosh Hashana, the New Year, the Germans issued an order that all Jewish stores must remain open on that holy day. The Jewish Council ordered all Jewish men to report outside the Council building early in the morning. The four of us joined a long line of Jewish men. We were issued shovels and marched through the streets to remove antitank obstacles and fill in outdoor air-raid shelters in the city parks. It was very hot and we worked hard until late in the afternoon.

New Year used to be a happy festival, but this day was a sad one. Jews were crying, supplicating the Almighty for succor in their distress. These were cries of anguish and despair washed by tears of blood. The religious Jews were fervently praying for the Messiah and believed that never before had the time been so ripe for His coming. In my heart I prayed for revenge against those who were humiliating, torturing and killing us. I cursed them and the mothers who brought them into this world.

There were few traditional festive dinners and many poor Jews hardly had bread on their tables. The next day, the second day of New Year, we too went to a synagogue. Lookouts were posted outside to warn us of approaching Germans. The rabbis shortened the service, which usually lasted until well after noon, to reduce the risk. Yet many in the congregation were dressed in their finest holiday garb, and a few still retained their beards and sidelocks which they tried to conceal as best they could behind high collars. God had abandoned us, but they still were faithful to Him. We heard that in Kalisz and Łódź, in the western part of Poland, the Jews were compelled to wear yellow patches on the front and back of their clothing. Refugees who had come from Mielec, a small town not far from Cracow, told us that on the eve of the New Year, when religious Jews were in the ritual bath to purify themselves for the holy days, Germans broke in, picked out about forty of them and marched them off naked, to the Jewish abattoir. There they hanged them one by one on meat hooks and then set the building on fire. I despaired over our prayers. God was not there in Mielec, or indeed anywhere at all in Poland.

Now it was the eve of Yom Kippur, the holiest day in the Jewish calendar. In muted tones, to avoid the attention of the Germans, the Kol Nidre prayer, the prayer that even the most irreligious Jew is familiar with, was recited. Never before did our synagogue hear such desperate cries so rigorously suppressed.

Soon many more German civilians with swastika armbands

on their coats were seen on our streets. At first we thought they might be tourists, come to see their newly occupied "Eastern Territories". But they were not tourists. They had come to run our city. The Jewish Council had to provide the best accommodation and furniture for them. Those who had come without their families were placed with well-to-do Jewish families outside the Jewish section who had to give them their best rooms. They made the Jewish matrons their cooks and servants. But the Jews, as always, found a bright side, they prominently displayed the names and ranks of their German lodgers on their front doors, and the nameplates did indeed act as a sort of talisman against unwanted visits by Germans, Polish hoodlums and burglars. The German officials who brought their families with them requisitioned the best Jewish and Polish houses and the Jewish Council then had to find accommodation for the Jews they displaced. The German radio reported only jubilant victories, including the sinking by their U-boats of a British aircraft carrier in its home port. The surviving Polish radio station announced the formation of a Polish government in exile, made up, we mused bitterly, of leaders who had abandoned their people to the German butchers. On September 27, just under four weeks after the war started, General Kutrzeba, the heroic defender of Warsaw, surrendered to the overwhelming German forces with his one hundred fifty thousand troops. The next day Russia and Germany signed a new friendship pact in Moscow, putting the final seal on the fate of Poland. Five days later, on October 2, the most heroic Polish troops of the war, the three thousand men under Admiral Unrug who had defended the Baltic fortress of Westerplatte, surrendered to the Germans.

Poland had lost the war and the world just watched. The Allies did not make good their commitment to stand by us. On October 3 the German radio, which was now "our" radio, reported that by order of the Fuehrer Adolf Hitler the territories Germany had been forced to cede to Poland in 1918, the Warthenau and parts of Silesia, were returned to the Third Reich. The next day Hitler visited Warsaw and took the salute at a victory parade of his jackbooted hordes. The Germans officially announced that their military operations in Poland had been completed. But not their operations against the Jews.

Every other day new regulations and restrictions were published on the walls. Their most popular word was *Verboten* (Forbidden). It was forbidden, under threat of death, to listen to foreign broadcasts, and *Juden Verboten* (Jews not allowed) signs appeared in the windows of many large stores, hotels, restaurants and even moviehouses. When we went to the Jewish Council offices to look for work, we found the offices staffed mainly by Jewish refugees from Austria, Czechoslovakia and Germany who knew German well. They looked down on us, considering themselves superior by virtue of their western culture. We called them "Yekes."

Since many Wehrmacht units had left the city, there were fewer roundups of men in the Jewish section and the Jewish Council was itself able to supply all the workers the Germans demanded. The pay we received from the Jewish Council was paltry, but after work hot meals in the community kitchen went with it. Only the old German masterhunter from the SS was still in action. He never missed a day, and became a feared figure to be given as wide a berth as possible. We prayed that he might be sent back to Germany, but like all our prayers this one too went unanswered.

The son of one of our neighbors, Mr. Hacker, returned from Warsaw where he had been stranded by the outbreak of the war. He had hair-raising stories to tell. At first the Stuka dive bombers, which we saw for the first time while running from Cracow in September, already the most dreaded planes in the German arsenal, had bombed and strafed the civilian population and later their artillery took over the job of reducing Warsaw to rubble. Thousands of soldiers and civilians were killed, many buried alive under collapsing buildings. The Germans destroyed the central water and electricity supply on the very first day, and diseases and epidemics were rampant. Thousands of Jews who were taking part in the defense of the capital became victims not only of the bombs and hunger, but of anti-Semitic Polish hoodlums who chased them away from the long lines for food and medical attention and, after the Germans entered, from the military soup kitchens with screams of *"Juden, Juden."* The Gestapo appointed an unknown Jewish engineer, Adam Czerniakow, as president of the Warsaw *Judenrat,* and he set up a committee of twenty-four members to tackle the difficult task of governing the three hundred thousand Jews of Warsaw, many of them in various stages of starvation.

One morning, while we were out, there was a knock on our door. Fela opened it and was confronted by two tall German *Shupos* (policemen), in light green uniforms and their peculiar helmets. They unceremoniously walked past her, and without saying a word went through all the rooms to look over the furniture. Finally they broke their silence but only to say that they were confiscating our big radio set and some of the best pieces of furniture. They called down to some Jewish workers they had brought with them to come up and take away their new property, which was loaded on waiting trucks. The two policemen knocked on all the doors in the building, but where the tenants were Poles, apologized politely and left them alone. They were interested only in Jewish apartments.

Many of our Polish fellow citizens also exploited the opportunity to rob Jews. The worst were the tax collectors who presented outrageous bills, and if a Jew were unable to pay, took away anything portable. On the other hand, Jews were no longer able to collect debts from Poles who put them off with threats of denunciation to the Gestapo on some trumped-up charge. Pensioners were particularly hard hit. The Germans simply stopped all pension payments to Jews. They also froze Jewish savings and commercial accounts, allowing the withdrawal of no more than 2,000 zlotys a month. This made it impossible for Jewish merchants to carry on regular trade and their reserves were being wiped out by inflation caused by the black market, which they were forced to join to survive. The Germans introduced new *Ersatz* (artificial) products. Saccharine replaced sugar, margarine for butter, chicory for coffee, and fabrics made of artificial yarns.

On the streets we had to run the gauntlet of plain-clothes Polish policemen called *Tajniaks,* who hunted for Jews carrying parcels and demanded bribes to save them from confiscation, and of course keep an eye open for the German police, and beware of informers. The one order that did not bother us was the forbidding of the sale of alcoholic beverages. Jews did not drink. There were only two bars in the whole of the Jewish section.

One morning a new order was published obliging all men and women over the age of fourteen to register at City Hall for identity cards. Jews got cards marked with distinctive yellow stripes and inscribed *Jude* in large letters.

In the evenings we spent more time with the Lopatowski and Gelb families, discussing the news and prospects, both of which were bleak. For the first time Mr. Lopatowski showed us an underground newssheet, published by the PPS Socialist party. It carried detailed reports of German crimes against the population, and particularly the Jews, and how they were systematically making many localities *Judenrein,* killing those Jewish residents they did not expel. It also warned informers and collaborators that they would pay for their crimes in due time. This was the only encouraging item in the paper which we studied as thoroughly as Holy Writ.

On October 26, the German military governor, General von Rundstedt, left Poland and the military government was replaced by a German civilian General Government to rule all of German-occupied Poland. Dr. Hans Frank was appointed governor general, and SS Gruppenfuehrer, Dr. Seyss-Inquart, who as chancellor of Austria had engineered the *Anschluss,* was appointed his deputy. The General Government made Cracow its new capital and Frank took over the Wavel castle for his headquarters. This was a symbolic slap in the face for Poland. The old royal castle was the country's most revered historic site. A few days later the Gestapo ordered the tenants and storeowners in six buildings around the castle, all of them Jewish, to vacate them within twenty-four hours. Soon after, wrecking crews demolished the vacated buildings to allow Dr. Frank a better view. Before we had recovered from this blow, reports came in about a massacre in Łódź. The SS machine-gunned hundreds of Jews in the streets and that day, October 6, immediately became known as Black Thursday. How many more black days were in store for us?

In Cracow many more prosperous Jewish families were driven out of their homes to make room for Germans who were arriving to staff the new General Government. Father got a job in a wholesale store where he met many out-of-town customers bringing in food and in turn buying goods to take home. From them he obtained food for us, and from them we heard that in the townships and villages Jews were no longer allowed on the sidewalks, but had to walk in the gutters.

To mark his installation, Governor General Frank issued a

proclamation denouncing the leaders of Poland and the western warmongers who had provoked Germany. He promised justice for all, except for the Jewish bloodsuckers, political agitators, and economic hyenas, for whom there would be no room in the territories under his rule. Himmler himself and other dignitaries of the Reich had reportedly come to Cracow for the great day. They divided Poland into four districts with Cracow, Lublin, Radom and Warsaw as their respective capitals, each headed by a district governor.

Almost immediately Frank issued an order for the registration of all Polish males between the ages of eighteen and sixty for compulsory work as needed. Jews had to register from the age of twelve. On November 2, the historic Wavel castle was renamed Krakauer Burg, Cracow Castle. Frank moved in with a procession of SS men on motorcycles and in open cars, their guns at the ready. Jews were ordered off the streets while the procession passed. The city's most popular newspaper, *Illustrowany Kurier Codzienny* was closed by the Germans, replaced by *Goniec Krakowski* which, though it appeared in Polish, was run by the Germans. It did not take long to start printing inflammatory anti-Semitic articles. All over Poland large posters were displayed with ugly caricatures of caftan-clad, bearded Jews sucking Polish blood. The Jews were blamed for Poland's misfortunes, including the war itself, as well as for the food shortages. Sadly, many Poles chose to believe these lies.

Our neighbor, Mr. Gelb, was hired by a large German company which opened a branch in Cracow, and was put in charge of collecting scrap and waste materials for reuse by the German war industry. He was given documents exempting him from compulsory labor and assuring him safe passage on the streets.

The Jewish Council ordered a new registration because the Germans wanted to know exactly how many Jews were now living in Cracow, following the arrival of so many refugees. A total of sixty-eight thousand five hundred were counted, about 25 percent more than there had been before the war. The refugees included two of Mother's uncles, Jozi, who had been deported from Czechoslovakia after he lost his whole family, and Einhorn, who had been expelled from Nuremberg in Germany. He had lost his wife, but his two sons had escaped to France. We promised to help them with money and the food we were still able to obtain, because Fela, with her Aryan looks, was able to buy in stores that were forbidden for Jews.

One day as I was walking through the Polish section, the Germans started rounding up Polish men to be shipped for forced labor in Germany, in addition to the many who had already volunteered to go. I was stopped, too, but when they saw my Jewish identity card they let me go. This time they were looking only for Poles.

On November 6, SS Obersturmbannfuehrer Bruno Mueller sent out personal invitations to the professors at the Jagielonski University for a discussion on the relations between the Third Reich and the Polish universities. Over one hundred eighty professors came, but when they sat down, the building was surrounded by SS and policemen, and Mueller, who was to address them, told them instead that they were all under arrest. They were taken to the jail the Germans had opened in the Montelupich building, a disused old Austrian armory, and most of them were deported to the Mauthausen concentration camp together with the deposed mayor, Kłimecki.

More refugees arrived form the western areas. They told us that the Germans were systematically clearing out the Jews, deporting them, with only hand luggage and small sums of money, to the new ghettos they were establishing in different cities. Only in Łódź, where the important textile industry was run mainly by Jews, were they allowed to stay because the Germans needed those products. The reports were very upsetting because they made us realize that we were beginning to live on borrowed time. Nor could we expect help from our Polish fellow citizens. Whenever I came across my former schoolmates in the street they turned their heads as though they had not seen me. At first it hurt, but soon I got used to it, as we had to get used to increasingly frequent humiliations at the hands of the Poles as well as the Germans.

Shortly before Poland's Independence Day on November 11, the Germans arrested one hundred twenty Poles as hostages to forestall disturbances or even the hoisting of Polish flags. November 11 was a Sunday, and the Germans ordered the churches to stay closed so that the streets were deserted. The Germans broke into the city's synagogues and took away the religious treasures, including our holy Tora scrolls and their silver decorations, rare books and carpets.

The Jewish Council had to supply hundreds of Jewish laborers to the Germans and they were paid 2.5 zlotys for a long day's work, which was not enough to buy a loaf of bread on the black market. Their families were saved from starvation by the meager meals the community kitchen provided. Many Jews who had assimilated, but for years had not maintained any contacts with the community, now converted to the Catholic faith in a desperate attempt to save themselves. The Church received them with open arms. It had always been its goal to gather in Jewish souls. We mused that Judaism wasn't losing much, nor the Church making great gains. In fact, their conversion eventually did not gain them even a postponement of the fate of the Jews, because very soon everybody who had a single Jewish parent, or even one Jewish grandparent, had to register as Jewish, which was a great shock for those who had long since opted out of the faith and considered themselves good Catholics to the point of their having become anti-Semites.

My brothers and I were often called in for compulsory work by the Jewish Council, together with the refugees and the poor, because we could not afford to buy our way out or bribe a doctor to exempt us for health reasons. These exemptions became a good source of income for many scoundrels. We usually worked in the city, cleaning offices for the new General Government, or in the barracks outside the city. Meanwhile the Jewish section was daily becoming more crowded as Jews were thrown out of their homes to make room for the newly arriving German officials and their families. Dr. Frank, who was a lawyer by profession though a butcher by inclination, bombarded Poland with new orders almost daily, many of them directed against the Jews. Jews were no longer allowed to sell or transfer properties or possessions; all tax exemptions were cancelled for Jewish nonprofit associations such as sports, charitable, medical, scientific, cultural and religious organizations; and Jews had to surrender all motor vehicles they owned, from trucks to motorcycles. He ordered the confiscation of all Polish government properties, and the property of Jews and Poles who had not returned from their

flight to the east, which they then handed over to collaborators.

Mother regularly wrote letters to her family in the U.S.A.
The post office accepted the letters, but she never received
any answer, and never knew whether the letters reached their
destination. She was now permanently sad and we did all we
could to save her from hearing about the worst excesses. The
week after Independence Day another blow fell. All Jews from
the age of ten, were ordered to wear identification band on
their right arms—a ten-centimeter white band with a blue Star
of David. We were to be easily spotted targets for the Germans
and the anti-Semites. Those, who like Fela, had been able to
get by on their Aryan appearance, would now also be marked
as Jews. Jews who would be caught not wearing those bands
faced imprisonment.

Next the Germans installed loudspeakers in the center of
the city for twice-daily broadcasts of their news bulletins and
propaganda in Polish. Poles were forbidden to wear uniforms,
from those of the veterans to the traditional school uniforms,
and only the Polish police were permitted to wear their dark
blue uniforms, but could carry no weapons.

Frank next ordered the establishment of *Judenrats* to replace the Jewish Councils in every town and city of Poland.
In the larger cities, the *Judenrat* was to comprise a president
and a deputy, and twenty-four members, and in towns with
less than ten thousand Jews the *Judenrat* was to be made up
of twelve members and a president.

Mr. Lopatowski showed us the latest underground newsletter which carried a list of names of Jews who were cooperating
with the Germans or acting as informers. The list included
several Cracow Jews and a few refugees from Germany whom
we had received with open arms when they arrived in 1938.
We were very angry that they had chosen this way to repay
our kindness.

During the night of December 4, German police, SS, Gestapo and some Polish constables sealed off the Jewish section, Kazimierz, in which almost 90 percent of Cracow's Jews
lived. No one was allowed in or out, and we had no way of
finding out what was happening in Kazimierz, but there were
plenty of rumors. More than fifty hours after the siege began
it was lifted and we went to hear what happened. The residents

had been awakened by the sound of trucks, shouted orders, and the tramp of boots. The Germans shot at anybody leaving their house and even at those looking out of windows. Then they began systematic searches of every building, room and attic, firing warning shots at the ceilings to intimidate the frightened Jews. They demanded that all valuables and cash in excess of 2,000 zlotys be handed over on pain of being shot on the spot. Wherever they discovered concealed valuables they beat or shot the owners. Jews were forced to dig up their own cellars to allow the Germans to check for hidden treasure and many, including women, were subjected to intimate body searches. Many women had their wedding bands and earrings ripped off. The Polish janitors guided the Germans to the wealthier apartments. More than sixty Jews were killed in the action, hundreds wounded or badly beaten, and the Jewish hospital was quickly filled with victims.

Some Gestapo men came to the *Judenrat* building where they found the duty manager, Max Reidlich, took him to the nearby Isaak synagogue, and ordered him to take the Tora scrolls out of the Holy Ark and burn them. When he refused they shot him.

The mayor ordered all Jewish schools closed. Jewish students were expelled from the Polish schools and all Jewish teachers were fired. The *Judenrat* was given power over the Jewish population by the Gestapo, in effect to carry out Gestapo orders, and through the Jewish police, who were subject to its authority, to make sure they were carried out promptly. In return the *Judenrat* and police officials were granted some privileges. They were allowed to keep their apartments, given special passes exempting them from the curfew, and allowed extra food rations. Worst off were the refugees from the west who had been thrown out of their homes by the advancing Germans, and had fled to Cracow for refuge. They had come in September, when it was still hot, with only their summer clothing and were now freezing. We collected winter clothes and shoes for them and when we delivered them were shocked by the "housing" they had been allotted by the *Judenrat*—abandoned buildings, most without electricity, gas, toilet facilities, or running water. Their children were starving and freezing in the terrible cold but the *Judenrat* leaders were well dressed and fed.

One day we were surprised to meet some Jewish men who were wearing Polish army uniforms on the street despite the ban. They were Jewish POW's who had just been released from the German camps. They were soon back in civilian clothes and one of them who had been my friend before the war, told me incredible horror stories—not about how the army had lost the battles, or how the cavalry was routed by German tanks, or even the breakdown of communications between the fighting units and the general staff—but how their Polish comrades-in-arms had turned on them the moment they were captured. Their own officers and comrades had denounced them to the Germans as *Juden* (Jews), and demanded to be separated from the them on the way to the POW camps. The Germans were pleased to agree. In those prison camps the Poles made their lives miserable, raided their barracks and stole their rations, their warm clothing, boots and blankets. Many fell ill and died of starvation or freezing. Their tragedies did not end even when they were released. Many whose homes were on the Russian side of the new demarcation line were shot by the German border guards.

When the heavy winter snowfalls started, the *Judenrat* ordered all Jewish males over fourteen to clear the streets and roads. We toiled in the freezing wind, continually shoveling the snow which heaped up again as soon as we cleared it. Outside the *Judenrat* building refugees from the Warthenau area were lined up in the freezing weather. They, as well as the Polish population from that western part of Poland the Germans had incorporated into the Reich, had simply been thrown out to make room for Germans. Because of the heavy snow the peasants who brought supplies to town failed to arrive, and there were serious shortages of food and firewood, so that we had to sleep in our heaviest winter clothes to avoid freezing during the cold nights. There were no Christmas or New Year celebrations in Cracow that first winter of occupation, except for the Germans. For Poles the holiday season was very sad, but for us Jews it was tragic.

2

Cracow, Poland
1940–1941

As we toiled to keep the streets clear of snow that winter, the passing Poles threw insults at us and laughed at our distress, telling us it was about time that Jewish parasites should do some work. Even our Polish foremen were embarrassed. Some of them were very decent men and worked hard alongside us. Inside the city we simply dumped the snow we shoveled into the sewers but on the highways, disposal was more complicated and meant even more work. The next blow was an order forbidding Jews to travel by train without special permits. Father, who had been trading goods for food with former customers who had come into town by train, was cut off from most of his sources by this order. Then the Germans established a new central bank, the Emisyjny Bank, and ordered the exchange of the old Polish bank notes. This was a great blow to those Jews who had cash assets in hand and were now forced to quickly find a Pole who could legally exchange the old zlotys for the new money. The Poles took advantage of their need and many charged exorbitant fees, making them suffer heavy losses.

We learned from Mr. Lopatowski that for the first time many monks and priests were arrested all over Poland and sent to concentration camps. Some were executed on charges of anti-German activities. The renowned Peasant party leader, Wincenty Witos, who had been arrested in Rzeszów several months previously, was brought to Cracow jail in very poor health. The Poles did not escape the Nazi cruelties either, and all over the country men were hanged in public squares for all kinds of crimes, real or trumped-up, and the populace was forced to watch the executions, to intimidate them against any notion of resistance.

On March 1, a new anti-Jewish order was published, not signed by the *Judenrat* as usual, but by City President Schmidt himself. It forbade Jews to travel in the front part of the streetcars, only in the rear coach. When the tram had only a single car, Jews were allowed only in the rear seats, after all non-Jews were seated. This made travel very difficult as the conductors often abused their powers to keep us out so as not to "contaminate" the Poles. But we got a revenge of sorts when the Germans started promulgating anti-Polish orders. Now Poles too were *verboten* to enter many restaurants, coffeeshops, grocery stores and moviehouses. Polish students were no longer allowed into the famed library at Jagielonski University. Mr. Lopatowski told us the Germans were staging mass arrests among the Polish intelligentsia all over the country, to eliminate potential leadership and resistance. Whenever the Gestapo did not find the man they came searching for, they simply took away a relative who disappeared into their concentration camps.

In the evening of April 9, Mr. Lopatowski came to our apartment very excited. He had just heard on the radio that the Germans had invaded Denmark and Norway without any warning. Denmark was overrun, but the Norwegians were putting up stiff resistance and the British navy had dispatched warships and troops, including the Polish units that had escaped to England. We were very proud and happy that at last the English were fighting, and we prayed they would soon defeat the Germans for, we knew by now, that was our only chance to survive. Hope was our last resort but the religious Jews were relying on the miracle of the coming of the Messiah.

On April 29 an order was published forbidding Jews to enter the city's main square and the famous old Sukienice market, where many Jews owned stalls, small stores and workshops. They had to leave their businesses, which had been passed down from generation to generation. Those establishments were allotted to ethnic Germans and Ukrainian and Polish collaborators. Despite all the restrictions, the very religious Jews somehow obtained matzos for Passover and secretly observed this ancient "Festival of Freedom" under the very noses of the Germans.

Then on May 10, the Germans launched their *Blitzkrieg* across the borders of Belgium, Luxemburg, Holland and France. The news created a sensation in Cracow. Strangers shook hands in the street and smiles returned to faces that had been sad seemingly for ages. Neville Chamberlain, the great appeaser, resigned and was replaced by a new leader, Winston Churchill.

But our hopes and elation did not last long. The British began withdrawing their forces from Norway, and in the west the Nazis quickly gained amazing victories, destroying everything that stood in their way. There was a spin-off in Poland too, where thousands of patriots were arrested, many of whom had been betrayed by former comrades. There were also many Jewish informers and as we did not know their identity, everybody became suspicious and very careful, which made our difficult lives even more uncomfortable.

Another big blow fell on May 18, 1940. The Cracow district governor, Wachter, issued an order calling on the Jews to voluntarily leave the city by August 15! Those leaving would be permitted to find themselves their own new places of residence and take all their belongings, and would also receive special permits to go by train. Only fifteen thousand Jews needed by the Germans would be allowed to remain in Cracow. A Resettling Commission was established on Lubicz Street where Jews in essential services were to be issued residence permits. Jewish war veterans from the German and Austro-Hungarian armies were included. But those who were not needed or who overstayed the deadline, would be deported with only a suitcase and 2,000 zlotys in cash. The commission was headed by an ethnic German, Reichert, assisted by the president of the *Judenrat,* Bieberstein, and his deputy Goldblat.

Our situation was very bad. Only Father, as a war veteran, Szymon and Fela, who had gotten a job with the parks department, were working. We appealed to Father's old friend, Mr. Hochwald who had a son who ran the biggest plumbing company in the district and was now working mainly for the Germans under a *Treuhand* trustee. A job there, we ventured, would be recognized as essential. There was panic among the Jews. Only those working for the *Judenrat* or the Jewish police could be sure of staying, and nobody knew which other jobs would be considered essential. Hochwald talked to his son on our behalf and encouraged us to go and see him. He received us very warmly and agreed not only to take us on, but made out a certificate to show we had been engaged four months earlier. Fela also received a working certificate from her park employer and the next day we went very early to Lubicz Street to file our applications, but the line was already so long that we had to wait six hours until our turn came. Then we could only hope.

Next morning the three of us, Nathan, Szymon and I, reported to Hochwald's office for work. He gave us tools and sent us out with a group of plumbers to a German office building. The work was hard and dirty, but we did our best and our fellow workers were pleased with our efforts. We were not rushed and were given rest breaks and were paid.

Panic was becoming the normal condition among the Jews. Everybody was scurrying to obtain an essential job, while at the same time looking for relatives outside Cracow they might join in case they would not get the permit, and setting aside the money they would need to move their belongings. Mother's relatives decided to move to Tarnów where her aunt had lived. Every other day Mother went to the post office to send letters to America. The place was full of Jews doing the same. But there was never an answer, and we felt the whole world had abandoned us, just as God had.

A typhoid fever epidemic broke out in the Jewish section among the poorer people, brought on by the harsh winter and the miserable living conditions. On Sundays we saw many Jews moving out, their goods piled high on trucks and horse-drawn wagons. Many younger people were going to the Russian border hoping to be allowed in. A new profession, *Macher* (wheeler-dealer), sprang up overnight. These *Machers* knew where to go and whom to see for favors, but charged high prices for their services. They were able, at least for a time, to obtain jobs from influential Germans who simply fired their own Jewish workers to make room for the high-paying new staff.

As the deadline drew nearer people became secretive, afraid of informers and would not even reveal where they intended moving, much less what jobs they had managed to get. More tragedies were taking place daily. Many Jews who had entrusted their valuables and money to Polish friends for safe-keeping found that now, when they needed them to finance their move out of Cracow, the old "friends" flatly refused to return anything, and when the owners insisted, threatened to denounce them to the Gestapo. There was nothing the victims could do but hope for revenge after the war, if they could survive it.

Our own plumbing jobs were good, our fellow workers taught us the trade and our German "clients" were satisfied. But, like everybody else, we could not be sure that we would be allowed to stay, so we sent a letter to Father's brother in Rzeszów to prepare him for our possible arrival, and also sent him many packages of things we would need. We did not know if any of them ever reached him.

The Gestapo was not satisfied with the slow rate of the Jewish exodus and ordered the *Judenrat* to close the shelters for the poor and the refugees as well as the community kitchen. A group of well-to-do Jews organized relief committees which distributed food, clothing and money to those of the homeless who were willing to move out. The *Judenrat* assured them there would be jobs waiting for them in the East in the Lublin area. We often saw them walking to the railroad station with their bundles, the children carrying the going-away gifts they had received. Every Jew who moved out made it safer for the *Judenrat* officials. Desperate, rich Jews were paying any price for essential jobs and appeared not to care if these came at the expense of poorer people they replaced. The Polish janitors were particularly vicious, waiting until the Jews had already packed their belongings and then presenting them with fictitious repair bills, forcing them to pay heavy cash bribes, or their best pieces of furniture, in order to be allowed to go. Then they made more money allowing Poles to move into the vacated apartments. Other Poles hung around the buildings and when the Jews were unable to load all their furniture on the trucks, offered to buy the surplus stuff, at a fraction of their value. These were the vultures waiting to pounce on the stricken, helpless victims. The Germans were quite happy with the chaotic conditions because this kept the Jews too anxious and nervous to think of resisting, while the

Poles were happy to see the Jews go and to get their hands on their possessions.

Occasionally we had to go into the Jewish section for materials for our plumbing work. It resembled a frantic anthill in the shadow of a descending boot. Jews were scuttling around trying to make deals with the Poles and peasants who were waiting on the sidewalks to buy Jewish property cheaply. In the evening we heard that the chairman of the Resettling Commission, Reichert, and his Jewish assistants, Bieberstein and Goldblat, as well as *Judenrat* members, Leinkram, Goldfluss and Mayer, had been arrested in the commission offices. The Gestapo charged the Jews with having bribed Reichert and having themselves accepted bribes as well. We were astounded. We had of course known about the corruption of the *Machers,* but had not realized that it had reached so far up. It was rumored that the commission had prepared thirty thousand residence permits, double the number the Germans had allowed, in order to make as much money as they could by selling them to trusting Jews, who innocently believed they were assuring their survival with the permits. The whole committee was replaced and the new one did not include a single Jew. The new committee worked round the clock to review the permits their predecessors had issued. Now, those Jews who had bribed the committee through their *Machers,* panicked and paid any price to move out.

The news of the lightning German victories in western Europe did not make our already desperate situation any easier. Europe was in Hitler's hands, all the Jews in it at his mercy, and we already knew, only too well, that he had no mercy.

As if to rub in the fact that they were here to stay, the Germans in Cracow started to demolish all the statues of Polish heroes, starting with that of the beloved national poet, Adam Mickiewicz, in the main square opposite St. Marie church. They also ripped out the commemorative plaque on the spot in the main square where Tadeusz Kósciuszko, the Polish-American hero, swore allegiance to Poland on March 24, 1794. To cap these calculated insults to Polish feelings, they renamed the main square "Adolf Hitler Platz."

All Jewish doctors and dentists were ordered to mark their shingles with the Jewish star. The German director of the

Board of Health, Dr. Waldbaum, issued a letter to make the seizure of their apartment-clinics legal, putting the official stamp on what had already been done. Jewish lawyers were forbidden to appear in the courts. Rumors had it that the new chairman of the Resettling Committee, Pavlu, was talking of only ten thousand residence permits and not the fifteen thousand that had been announced in the official order. This meant that our chances for staying declined by a third and caused another panic. The richer Jews were moving out while the rest of us were doing our best to sell our belongings in the Tandetta, where the peasants were giving better prices than the scavengers who were hanging around Jewish buildings hoping to make cheap purchases.

For the first time a Jewish newspaper, the *Gazeta Zydowska* (Jewish Gazette), made its appearance. It was a tragicomedy for us. Nearly half the Jews of Cracow were gone and now they were putting out a Jewish newspaper. Actually, it was merely a vehicle for the publication of official orders and communications from the *Judenrat*. A very fine German-Jew named Seifert was its editor.

The Germans again warned the Polish population that listening to foreign broadcasts was strictly prohibited and punishable by death. Non-Germans were also forbidden to display Nazi emblems or flags. Frank's deputy, Seyss-Inquart, was promoted by Hitler to commissioner of occupied Holland. At the same time Hitler erased the name of Poland even from the General Government of Occupied Poland, which he himself had given to it, and shortened it simply to General Government. As far as the Germans were concerned Poland had ceased to exist.

In the mountain resort areas south of Cracow, all Jews were ordered to leave immediately to make room for German vacationers from the General Government employees and for families from Germany which was now being bombed by the British.

Meanwhile some of the Jewish poor who had been sent away to nearby communities were drifting back to Cracow complaining bitterly that the local *Judenrats* had done nothing to take care of them, had failed to provide any sort of housing or food, and they had not found any jobs. Most tragic were those coming back from the Lublin area. They arrived in rags and were barefoot, starving and exhausted. They had to come back on foot unless they could find some honest peasants to take them a distance on their wagons. Only the young and strong had been able to make the trip at all. They told us the real facts about the Lublin "Agricultural and Industrial Center" by which they had been lured to leave Cracow. It simply did not exist at all. When they had arrived in Lublin by train they found themselves alone with nobody willing to help them or able to give them information. They were advised to go to the nearest towns where Jews were still living. There they found out that thousands of refugees from Warthenau, Łódź and Kalisz were already living in shacks and tents, without water or electricity on the outskirts of the towns. Hunger and death were rampant and corpses littered the streets while the sick waited in vain for treatment. In Lublin itself there were many displaced Jews living on the streets without even a community kitchen. There were hordes of beggars, mostly small children and old people, imploring the Jews who had nothing left to give. The arrivals from Cracow received no attention at all from the *Judenrat,* not because its officials were heartless but because there were so many Jews needing help that the small community was unable to give any more.

This then was the Germans' so-called Lublin "Reservation," the promised land for the Jews of Cracow. The young returnees had witnessed many deaths, including their own relatives but told us that despite everything there were still many pious Jews faithfully observing every tenet of the Jewish religion and serving God with all their heart.

The final irony was that most of those who were causing their misery, the Nazi killers, sported the motto *Gott mit uns* (God is with us) on their belt buckles as they were killing the Jews who died with His name on their lips.

We provided clothing, shoes and food to the poor souls who had returned but advised them to leave again at once and try Wieliczka, Bochnia and Tarnów where the situation was reportedly better. If they stayed in Cracow informers would soon tell the Gestapo. They all left within a few days and their stories spread throughout the Jewish community. There were no more volunteers for the Lublin Reservation. The ground under our feet began to burn and those who had made plans to leave and had prepared their destinations, were now in a

hurry to get out to places where they might yet fare comparatively well. Many could no longer afford to hire trucks and
opted for the cheapest available transport, the boats on the
Vistula River. They brought their belongings to the mooring
near the Debnicki bridge, but the boatmen, sensing a chance
to make money from the Jews, raised their prices to the sky.

Mother's aunt and two uncles came to say goodbye. They
were leaving next day by train for Tarnów where Aunt's
children lived. Mother was very sad and could not control her
emotions. She cried until our hearts were bursting. We had
never seen her crying like this before. She tried to hold her
relative back, sobbing over and over that she would never see
them again, that this was the end for all of us. Finally they
sadly tore themselves away and we accompanied them to the
corner of the block. Mother sobbed and cried all night calling
to God and begging Him for help.

We received a card from our relative in Rzeszów informing
us that none of the packages we had mailed to them were ever
delivered. They were probably pilfered by the post office
workers who felt quite safe stealing parcels sent by people
with Jewish-sounding names.

Every day our parents went to bid farewell to more friends
who were leaving and returned from these visits broken in
spirit. They aged terribly in those hard days. Mother continued to write letters to the U.S.A. but no reply ever arrived.

We heard reports that the Germans were planning a ghetto in
Warsaw, whose Jewish population had doubled to six hundred
thousand in the past year, and that Jews had already been put
to work erecting fences around the most dilapidated sections
of the city for this purpose.

At this time the Cracow Resettling Commission's decisions
were being delivered by mail to individual Jews. Those who
got the permit were happy but the rest of us were nervous. We
made our plans in case we would be refused. Mr. Lopatowski,
who had nothing to gain from his aid to Jews, had become like
a guardian angel for us—a most noble human being. Every
evening, on our return from work, we could see by our
parents' faces that no answer had yet come for us. Some of
our next-door neighbors received rejection slips together with
orders to report to the resettling center on Mogilska Street

within twenty-four hours, with no more than twenty-five kilograms of belongings and 2,000 zlotys per person.

A new and urgent panic swept through the community. German and Polish policemen were bringing the rejection slips into the Jewish section. They ordered the families to get ready at once, and stood over them telling them to hurry as they allowed them to pack only a single suitcase each. They would not even permit them to say goodbye to their neighbors or to their relatives who were at work, but took them away to the Mogilska Armory. Other desperate Jews, anxious not to have to go to the death trap in Lublin, were running around to find any kind of vehicle to take them out of the city. Some left with their loads on their backs or in baby carriages, on the way to the boats. Before we left for work we urged our parents to go to the Lopatowskis because we feared that the police might come and take them away to the Mogilska Armory from which it was almost impossible to escape.

Those were the hardest days we had yet experienced. But one evening, on our usual gloomy return home, we were welcomed with broad smiles. Mother and Father rushed to embrace us and kept repeating, "We can all stay." We felt that our jobs with Mr. Hochwald's company helped us. Immediately we went downstairs to tell the Lopatowskis the good news. They told us that during the day Mrs. Gelb had also received a permit for her husband, whose job was apparently essential. We told Mother to keep the permit in a very secure place together with Father's Austrian army papers.

Meanwhile, in the Jewish section, bedlam reigned. As people tried to get out, the janitors locked the main doors on them and demanded bribes. The peasants arrived to help the Jews move their goods on their carts, but at a price which they themselves fixed. Carts were desperately sought by those Jews who had received negative answers and were anxious to leave at once, because tomorrow might be too late. They parted with their best possessions, in return for being driven out of the city, no matter where as long as they might get to the other side of the Vistula. Hundreds of trucks and wagons were moving Jews and their belongings. The Poles were fighting each other for the best stores, apartments and furniture which the hurrying refugees were abandoning. Next morning another blow descended on us—a new order forbidding Jews to leave the city by train—closing the net of helplessness around us even tighter. Many older religious Jews who had not applied for residence permits were now illegals; illegal in the town they and their forefathers had been born in. The roundups for these illegals, and for those who were given negative replies continued rapidly. Polish and German police made house-to-house searches in the Jewish section. The Poles were eager to help the Germans round up Jews, but what dismayed us was the fact that our Jewish police, once they had obtained their own residence permits, were also taking part in the hunt for their brethren. Those they caught were taken to Mogilska, the next stop being Lublin, the black hole of Polish Jewry.

The conditions in the Mogilska Armory were terrible. The building had long ago been abandoned. It had no wooden floors, gas, electricity, water or toilet facilities. Those who were brought there under armed guard, were completely cut off, since nobody was allowed near the building. Only the *Judenrat* community kitchen brought them watery soup, hardly lukewarm, and a little bread. But, for the right price Jewish policemen were taking messages from those trapped inside to their families. It was rumored that for really big money it was sometimes possible to get out, but this was a possibility only for the richest. The poor Jews were on their own, abandoned by God and man.

In the evening, Mr. Lopatowski brought home the latest underground newsletter which reported that in Warsaw and Lublin the ghettos were being closed off. In Warsaw, the ghetto which was located in the dirtiest part of the capital, was sealed on November 15, 1940, with ten-foot-high walls topped by broken glass. It was guarded on the outside by German and Polish policemen, and by Jewish police inside the walls. A few Jews who had obtained special permits were allowed out into the city for a few hours. Every morning thousands of workers were taken under heavy guard, for work outside and they were marched back in the evening. Hunger and disease were rampant among the Jews who had been squeezed into a very small area. Every room was occupied by a whole family, often with two families in the kitchen. All school buildings, synagogues, closed-down factories and warehouses were used as shelters for thousands who were dependent on the miserable food the community kitchen was able to provide. Anyone caught trying to climb over the wall was shot. Nevertheless, thousands of small children, who, because they were under twelve years of age were not obliged to wear the Jewish identification armbands, daily crawled under the walls into the Polish section to beg for bread and scraps of food for themselves and their families. Hundreds were dying of hunger, exposure and disease. Their corpses were put out into the street to be picked up by the burying parties. They were stripped by the living poor who needed the clothes and shoes to survive a few more days. The families of the dead would not admit their relationship in order not to have to pay for their burial.

The destruction of the Jews of Poland was in full swing and the Germans did not even have to waste their bullets on us. They simply forced the Jews into overcrowded ghettos and left them to die, under the supervision of the Jewish police of the *Judenrat,* who still entertained the illusion that they might survive because the Germans were still allowing them to keep their apartments and even to heat them.

One day the German police came to our next-door neighbors, the Hackers, while their son was at work, informed them that their residence application had been denied and gave them a few minutes to pack essentials. Then they marched them away. Mother was a witness to their tragedy and she described to us how they had gone off, stunned and anxious, forced to leave behind all they owned. When the son returned home Mother told him what had happened. He ran out to try somehow to do something, but soon came back because relatives warned him that there was no way to get his parents out of the Mogilska Armory and that he might well be taken in himself. Next day he did not go to work but started selling their possessions in a last desperate bid to bribe his parents free. Unfortunately he did not succeed.

For the first time Jewish informers were coming out into the open, aiding the police in ferreting out hidden Jews. A few days later the Germans carried out their biggest raid yet in the Kazimierz section, deploying more than four hundred policemen. They stopped all passers-by and checked their identity papers. Many Poles were arrested and taken away for forced labor. All Jews who did not have residence permits were put on trucks and taken to the Mogilska Armory. Many of the Jewish informers were well-known to the Jews of Cracow, some even from religious families, selling their souls to the German devils. We knew many of them and when we met them in the street, looked past them as though they did not exist. They were despised, as were the Jewish police and the *Judenrat*. Polish truckdrivers were still offering to take Jews and their belongings to neighboring villages. The poor souls gave away everything they had to hire a truck, just to avoid the Mogilska, while others tried to get away on the cheaper river boats.

One Sunday a next-door neighbor burst in, out of breath and almost too agitated to talk. He told us that the last two leading rabbis of Cracow, rabbis Kornitzer and Rappaport, had been arrested by the Gestapo a few hours earlier. Their crime was daring to appeal to some influential Poles to intervene with Governor Frank on behalf of the town's Jews. They went to see Sapiecha, the Archbishop of Cracow, and Count Roniker, a nobleman who was chairman of the Citizens Relief Committee, and begged them to help save the remnant of Cracow Jews. The Gestapo's response was swift and harsh. The two rabbis were arrested and sent off to the Oswiecim camp, Auschwitz, as it was now known. A few days later their families received a card from the camp commandant informing them that their relative had died of pneumonia, and ordered them to send 25 zlotys each for their ashes. The ashes arrived and though no burial was permitted, all of us deeply mourned the two courageous spiritual leaders who had paid with their own lives for their efforts to save the lives of their flock. They had lived one block away from our house when we lived in the Kazimierz section, and I had often seen them on Saturdays and Jewish holidays, walking to the synagogue at the head of their followers.

The search for illegals went on without letup. We were often stopped, going to or returning from work, to have our papers examined. About fifteen thousand Jews were left in the city. Mother had no more relatives to visit so we saw the Lopatowskis more often. One day some SS trucks pulled up outside the Mogilska Armory and the SS men selected about four hundred young men and took them away to their Pustkow camp near Debica, east of Cracow. We had not heard of this camp before and did not know what was going on there.

As the snowstorms started and the early frosts caused many pipes to burst we were kept very busy, working seven days, eighteen hours a day. From the underground newssheets we heard about the bombing of both German and British cities. They also reported that the underground was informing their people in London about the happenings in the General Government, the arrest and execution of Polish patriots, the "resettling" of Jews in ghettos, and their sufferings. We were sure that the representatives in London must have informed the British and American governments and the Vatican too, but they did nothing to help us. The Pope, Pius XII, who had previously been the Vatican's Nuncio in Germany, never condemned Hitler for the murders his henchmen were committing in Poland.

Heating became a problem. Jews were not allocated any coal, and the peasants who brought in firewood demanded high prices for it. The Germans started to set up a section of their own in the city and ordered many Polish families to vacate the buildings they earmarked for themselves. But unlike the Jews, the Poles were allowed to take their possessions with them.

A new order gave the illegals until December 2 to report to the Mogilska Armory. The heavy snow now made it impossible for them to leave the city, except on the sleds of the few peasants who still brought their produce to town, but they demanded high prices. They were willing to take the risk of transporting Jews because the harsh weather was keeping the police indoors. As the snow heaped up into veritable mountains the mayor declared a snow emergency, and ordered all Jews to be put to work clearing it. Our boss had to release us from work and we had to report to the Jewish section of the labor department. There we were given big shovels and Polish foremen marched us to the outskirts. Conditions were terrible—icy winds and almost zero visibility. But since we had done this job the year before, we were prepared and wore our thickest winter clothing. Our foremen turned out to be decent men who allowed us to enter houses now and then to warm up. Many of the Polish householders, who were ordinary working people, were very kind and sometimes served us hot tea, which was a great help. In the evening we returned home with hurting backs. As before we were not paid for the work.

The weather forced the Germans to suspend their searches for illegals, but when the snow stopped they resumed the roundups with the same determination. The biggest roundup yet took place in the Podgorze section. Hundreds of German and Polish police cordoned off the main streets and checked every adult. They were hunting mainly for Poles for forced labor in Germany. The Poles realized that since there were so few Jews left in Cracow, the Germans had more time to devote to dealing with the Poles. The Gestapo appointed a new president of the *Judenrat,* a Dr. Rosenzweig.

We returned to our plumbing job temporarily. When the snowstorms started again we were once more ordered out for snow clearing. Mayor Schmidt worked out a new idea to get more Jews out for the harsh work. Every Jew between the ages of sixteen and sixty had to report for twelve days of snow removal, from early morning to nightfall. On completing the day's work our permits would be stamped by the Jewish police. After we completed the mandatory twelve days we would have the full complement of required stamps on the back of our permits. Only those with all twelve stamps would be allowed to apply for renewal of their residence permit. It did not escape us that though we had only just received our permits, the Germans were already talking of the need to have them renewed. Schmidt's scheme worked, and many who had not reported for snow duty before, now eagerly turned up, which made it easier for us to cope with the mountains of snow. However, it was evident that bribery was rife. We never saw many of the richer Jews in the snow lines. The job was in the hands of the Jewish police and they got their bribes safe in the knowledge that the labor department officials would never know, because they did not venture out of their heated offices. In the evenings, after we had our permits stamped, we lined up for hot soup at the community kitchen, the only recompense for our hard work.

We got through our twelve days and next morning reported back to Mr. Hochwald. He was happy to have us back, because there was a lot of plumbing work to be done and he was quite nervous lest he would not satisfy our German masters, who had no intention of being kept waiting by Poles or Jews.

The snow kept falling and the mayor issued another order for twelve more days of snow duty, with a warning that all lacking twenty-four stamps on their permits would be deported forthwith. Everyone came for no one wanted to have to leave Cracow. As bad as it was here, it could be even worse elsewhere. We had received no news from those who had left, voluntarily or as deportees. Some rare and vague messages did reach us, brought in by the peasants, from those who had gone to nearby villages. We heard nothing from our relatives in Tarnow and Mother was very worried.

It was February of 1941 and rumors were circulated about the imminent formation of a ghetto in Cracow, accompanied by much speculation about which section would be chosen. This kept our shrinking community occupied until it was time for filing the applications for new residence permits. We had our twenty-four stamps and Father was quite confident when he went to the commission to fill out the applications. Meanwhile we were working, and as the weather improved, the pressure of work eased, and since the peasants had also returned to town with food and firewood, it seemed that things were looking up for us. But it did not take long before another blow fell. An order from district governor, Dr. Wachter, was posted on the walls early one morning, announcing mandatory new applications, annulling the twenty-four stamp privilege. Only those who could prove that their jobs were vital for the Germans were permitted to apply at all. He announced that *Judenrat* and Jewish police officials now also had to apply for permits. Exemptions for war veterans were no longer mentioned. Applications had to be filed before March 10. All the promises to those who would work for their twenty-four stamps had merely been a device to get us out into the snow. It was not the first promise the Germans had broken. Our own problem was that only we, the three brothers had vital jobs, or at least jobs we believed were vital. Fela was not working because the weather had closed the parks. Our parents were unemployed, and Father's war veteran papers were now worthless. When we came home from work we discussed our situation. There was clearly no hope that all of us would be allowed to stay. We three brothers could apply, but did not want to be parted from our parents and Fela. We decided to leave Cracow and go to Rzeszów. The next morning Father would try to meet his Polish truckdriver friend who had a regular Cracow to Rzeszów route. He knew where the driver lived, but was unable to find him. We didn't go to work next day but went instead to look for the driver and began to prepare our move. We went through our belongings and sorted out everything we did not urgently need, to sell at the best price we could raise. The four of us took the stuff to the Tandetta and sold it to peasants who were still giving better prices than the local speculators. In the evening we went to see the Gelbs and told them of our decision. Mr. Gelb, who had a secure job, sympathized with our plight. Then we went to see the Lopatowskis and asked them to accept the furniture we had left. They declined, but we eventually convinced them with the argument that after the war they would be able to return it to us.

On March 3, another new poster signed by Dr. Wachter announced the establishment of Jewish living quarters in Podgorze in the eastern part of Cracow. He gave the Jews seventeen days to move in. It no longer concerned us. We were ready to leave.

Next morning Father and I found our truckdriver as he was making deliveries to a warehouse, and asked him to take us to Rzeszów. We agreed to the fee he asked, which was high, but the risk of transporting Jews, now forbidden, was even higher. He asked us not to bring a lot of things and to wait for him in a quiet side street in the evening. We gave him the address where Father's close friend lived. We packed our things while Mother prepared some bread for the journey, and when we finished we took our leave from the Gelbs and Lopatowskis. It was very sad and emotional moments for all of us. Late in the evening we left. We went two at a time, each carrying a bundle of belongings, to the meeting place we had arranged with our truckdriver. I went out with Mother who was crying, and some Polish neighbors whose curiosity was aroused, followed us. We had to be very careful. We were now refugees in full flight. As I left the building I wondered whether we would ever see our city and apartment again. In our friend's home the wife had prepared a light meal for us, but we could hardly swallow the food. We were anxious only for the darkness that would bring our driver. We started listening for the sound of a motor or a footstep on the stairs. At last we heard both, and with a hurried goodbye to our friends, the last people we saw in Cracow, went out to meet the driver. He had parked his truck in a dark spot and urged us to hurry. When we were aboard he drove to the warehouse and finished loading his cargo which he arranged around us completely concealing us. We sat on the floor, in the cold and dark, but it did not matter, as long as we would get out of Cracow unnoticed in the curfew. Outside the city there was still snow on the roads which were very bumpy. We knew that the trip should normally take about five hours, but in the winter conditions the driver had to be especially careful. He planned to reach Rzeszów early in the morning and get us off before he could be spotted unloading Jews from his truck. We had not had a chance to inform our relatives of our coming and hoped they were all right. We sat in silence, all of us steeped in our own thoughts. Whenever our driver slowed down our hearts missed a beat, fearing we might be stopped and discovered at a military checkpoint. It would be dangerous not only for us but for the driver too, who was risking his truck and his freedom by transporting Jews. He was doing it because he had become a good friend of the family while doing business with Father and had visited us quite often when he was in Cracow. At last the truck came to a complete stop and the driver came to the back and told us we had reached the outskirts of Rzeszów. He asked Father to take off his white armband and come and sit next to him in the driver's cabin to guide him to our uncle's home. Another twenty minutes of anxiety and we arrived. We got off and were careful not to arouse attention, though the street was still deserted. We reached the house safely and the driver helped us carry up our bundles without waking the neighbors. We thanked him and said a whispered goodbye to a very fine man.

3

Rzeszów, Poland
1941

Father knocked quietly on the door and soon our cousin Franka came out, still half asleep. She was taken aback and said nothing to us. Father explained that we had had to run away, and she then asked us to come in and took us into the kitchen. Uncle and Aunt came in and they too were astonished to see us, so much so that they omitted embracing our parents. They appeared to be wondering what we were doing, coming to their house so early. Father apologetically told them we had had no time to notify them of our arrival. They asked no questions and seemed surprisingly disinterested. Finally the aunt asked us whether we'd like some hot tea and we accepted. For us children, it was the first time we had met our aunt and cousin Franka. Uncle we knew from his business trips to Cracow in the past, when he used to stay in our home as a welcome guest. He was older than Father and, as I recalled, they had always been very close which made it hard to understand their distant, hostile behavior now. Father told them about our life in Cracow and how it had become imperative to get out when our efforts to obtain residence permits failed, but as his story was obviously making no impression, he gave it up. He asked only where we might put our bundles. Aunt showed us to a room and told us this would be our temporary accommodation. I wondered what she meant by "temporary" but let it go, so long as we were far away from Cracow, and had a roof over our heads. The room had only a single bed so we sat on the floor to rest from our exhausting journey. At least the room was warm. We sensed that Father, the kindest of men, had been hurt by his kin's indifference, but he said nothing. Mother and Fela busied themselves with the unpacking, and we three looked out of the window at the people going about their business in the street below. After some time Uncle came in and invited us to the kitchen for breakfast. We hoped the ice was now broken since Uncle started telling us about his own two sons. They had been caught on the Russian side of the new line and decided to stay there. For the first time Father learned from him news about their sister and her family who, Uncle told us, had at very short notice been thrown out of their home-town, Jarosław, with little more than the clothes on their backs. He was in touch with them through letters conveyed by smugglers from Przemyśl on the Russian side.

Our relatives were, however, still considering us as six uninvited, and unwanted, intruders. Indeed, we seemed to make them uncomfortable, so we thanked them for the food and returned to our room. There Father confessed he had been deeply hurt by our cold reception. He blamed it on the aunt whom he had known to have a distant personality. But this was wartime and we were close relatives, refugees in trouble, seeking shelter. When they left for work we asked Father to show us the city, which he knew well from his business trips. It seemed that our relatives' home was in a nice building in a good Polish section. In the streets we saw many Jews, prominent by their white armbands. Father went into several stores and was warmly greeted by the owners with whom he had done business for many years before the war. They were happier to see him than his family had been. They told him our relatives were now in business, in a store that had belonged to Aunt's brother. The large six-room apartment had also been his. He had left everything behind when he ran away to the Russian occupied zone. Aunt had found a friendly *Treuhander* for the store, an ethnic German she had known before the war, and all three of them worked there. For Uncle it was a great improvement. Before the war he had been a traveling salesman making only a meager living. Father's friends assured him he had nothing to worry about. Aunt's business was big enough to employ all of us, and they would surely give us jobs.

In the Jewish section we noticed that things appeared much

more normal than in Cracow. There was none of the nervousness at the sound of approaching trucks, and there were few Germans, though the Jews made sure to greet each one of them, and step aside to let them pass. There were not very many Polish policemen either, or many beggars or badly dressed Jews. Comparing Rzeszów with Cracow of the past few months was like contrasting day and night. We felt secure, and on returning home told Mother that we would be able to manage without our relatives' help. They had been home for lunch and had gone through the motions of inviting Mother and Fela to join them, but they had declined. Fela had been particularly upset by Cousin Franka's silent treatment and her failure, since she was a little older than Fela, to ask her any personal questions or enquire if she needed anything.

When they returned home Franka invited us for supper and insisted when we demurred. But, confounding our expectations, they remained quite cold to us and made their indifference plain by not reacting at all to our impressions of the city. Not wishing to appear rude, we sat at supper but retired to our room as soon as it seemed proper. Father and Mother slept in the bed and we bedded down on the floor in our winter clothing since Aunt had refrained, pointedly it seemed to us, from offering us blankets, or pillows. Perhaps she didn't want them to get dirty on the floor.

The next morning we all went to the *Judenrat,* to register and get identity papers, and then to the Jewish labor department. After we had waited for some time, the clerks asked us more questions in a few minutes than our relatives had done all day. How we had arrived and why, whether we had any furniture, and similar questions. Finally they issued us documents granting us legal status and sent us on to register for compulsory work. We were told that there were temporary daily jobs available with German army units for which we must line up before seven in the morning. Father went to see one of his old wholesale customers who offered him a good-paying job in his store, which at least would save him the daily line-up. It was our first break in Rzeszów. When our relatives returned home they forestalled possible requests for jobs in their store, telling us they were themselves only humble employees of the *Treuhander,* with no say in the management.

The next morning the four of us lined up for work. Fela got

an assignment before we did, and went off in a truck with some other women. Soon a large military truck arrived and we were ordered to get in. The back was uncovered and there were no seats, so we had to stand and hold on to one another. After a short trip we arrived at a large farm compound, Staromiescie, on the outskirts of the city. The other Jews told us that before the war it had been the headquarters of the Polish general, Kazimierz Fabrycy, commander of the Karpaty army of the southeast, and was now used by the German army. We were put to work in a large warehouse unloading military equipment and when we finished were taken to the Staroniwa freight railroad station. I was amazed at its size, out of proportion for so small a city. We knew that Rzeszów had, since 1936, been the center of Poland's so-called Industrial Triangle, established as a great military and civilian industrial-commercial complex. The project went into full operation in 1937 and, with the thousands of engineers and skilled workers it employed, had brought prosperity not only to Rzeszów but to the whole region. The influx of skilled workers from the western regions had also brought many anti-Semites, and even before the war, many Rzeszów streets were closed to Jews.

There was a lot of activity at the station, with many military trains being loaded and unloaded. It was obviously an important center for the Germans. When we finished loading our trucks we were taken back to the camp and were told to line up for a meal. I could not believe my eyes. No cursing, no one to push or kick us, only straightforward working orders. The meal was good, indeed, to us it was excellent. Afterward I noticed some of our workmates making deals with the soldiers, mainly buying cigarettes. When we finished unloading we were told to clean the barracks. I screwed up the courage to ask a German sergeant to sell me some cigarettes. He told me to wait and soon came back with a few packs. I didn't know the price but he told me what the other Jews were paying, which seemed fair. I was happy because Father was a heavy smoker and was miserable without cigarettes. The sergeant also sold me some canned food. I could not believe that there were still Germans behaving as he did. Apparently the complex staff were older men of the regular army. After work we were driven back to the labor department. How different from having to run home to beat the curfew in Cracow. We were paid 5 zlotys each for our day's work. Father was delighted with the cigarettes and Fela told us she had got a job that might be steady, in a huge uniform warehouse where they had to sort out uniforms for the different military and Waffen SS formations. Treatment had been fair there also, and she was happy. We hurried to have our supper so that we could decline our relatives' expected half-hearted invitation, and went to bed early.

As we lined up again the next morning, our fellow workers, who were mostly refugees from Kalisz, told us they had come to Rzeszów in December 1939. When the Germans marched into Kalisz they had immediately started throwing the thirty thousand Jews out, deporting them in open coal wagons in which many died of cold and hunger. The Rzeszów *Judenrat* had allotted them abandoned buildings and synagogues to live in, and fed them in the community kitchen. But in time they had found their own accommodations with local Jews, and many had found jobs, even good ones for those with skills. We asked them how to deal with the German soldiers and what prices to pay in order not to spoil the market for them.

That morning we loaded some very heavy equipment, and after our field kitchen meal, bought a lot of things from the soldiers, including army bread and cosmetics some of them had brought from their previous station in France. We spent all our money but got good things, and in the evening didn't even bother to wait for our pay because we earned more selling our treasures. However, our elation turned sour on returning home. Mother was crying and told us that in the morning two Jewish policemen had delivered relocation orders from the *Judenrat* for us. Our relatives wanted us out and had evidently enlisted the help of the *Judenrat*. We were upset, but comforted Mother that we would now have a place of our own, and even if it would be inferior, the only thing that mattered now was to survive the war. We stayed in our room all evening to avoid having to face relatives who did not want us, and even at a time like this were unwilling to share their big apartment with us. Next morning we reported to the *Judenrat* and a Jewish policemen took us into the Jewish section to a first floor apartment in a dilapidated old building, where a young woman was ordered to give us one of her four rooms. Next to her was a boy about eleven years old. She was very nice and asked us to move in in the evening, when her husband would be back from work. We went to the store where Father worked, told him about our new home, and asked him to borrow a pushcart to move our things before our relatives returned. Mother was shocked by the look of the building, but I assured her that it was nice inside and that the landlady was very pleasant. We waited for Fela at the labor department and took her straight to our new home. She told us the German warehouse supervisor had informed her she could stay on the job, which was a lucky break. When we reached our new apartment the landlord was home and came out to welcome us. While we were unpacking he came to invite us for tea. He told us he was a custom tailor working for a large Jewish tailoring shop in the town center of the Polish sector, which was now managed by a German *Truehander*. Their customers were Polish professionals and businessmen, and he was making a living, which was not easy with the black market prices. He provided a large bed for our parents, promised to obtain camp beds for us, and his wife brought us blankets.

Over tea he told us the Germans had entered Rzeszów on September 8, just two days after they captured Cracow. They immediately started persecuting the Jews, aided by Poles who guided them to Jewish homes with young girls, and they raped many of them. The Poles also took them to the homes of the richer Jews to help themselves to some of the best belongings.

He told us that during the High Holidays many religious Jews were killed. German soldiers, accompanied by SS and Gestapo men, had come to the synagogues during the prayer services and ordered everyone out. Firing in the air, they made the Jews, still clad in their prayer shawls, some wearing the solemn white shroud under them, get out of the synagogue and forced them to run to the Wisłoka River. They took pictures all the way, kicking and pushing the elderly who could not keep up, and on reaching the river forced the frightened Jews to jump into the water, firing their guns to hurry them. Many, especially the elderly, drowned. The Germans then made off, still laughing. This went on until a new military commander arrived and put a stop to the anarchy, as well as the random roundups of Jews for work.

Everything must go through the *Judenrat,* he decreed. He personally had lost many relatives in the nearby small town of Dynow. On the day the Germans entered it they ordered all male Jews to assemble in front of the synagogue and cut off the beards of the older men, while their comrades photographed their handiwork. Then they made the Jews leapfrog over each other and in general amused themselves tormenting them. Finally they ordered them into the synagogue, locked the wooden building, poured gasoline around it, and set it on fire. The screams of the poor souls being burned alive rose to high heaven, the most shocking holiday prayer ever heard. When younger men tried to escape from the inferno through the windows they were picked off by the Germans. Then they looked for more Jews, chased them through the city and forced some of them to jump into wells and the others to bury them alive in them. These killers had been men of the regular army, not the feared SS special extermination units.

The chief of the Rzeszów Gestapo's Jewish section, Adolf Schuster, appointed a *Judenrat* with a Mr. Kleinmann as president, Beno Kahana his deputy and three most unpopular members, Hirschhorn, Spiro and Landau. Schuster's henchmen, Johann Gawron and Heinman, frequently presented the *Judenrat* with demands for levies and gifts. An Austrian, Pablu, was appointed mayor and quickly showed himself to be a sadist, eager to prove his loyalty to the Reich. Only the military commandant was fair to the Jews. The Gestapo also terrorized the Polish intelligentsia with wanton arrests just to keep them scared.

The next morning again we lined up for jobs at the labor department. The truck from our previous job did not arrive so we were taken to a communications unit to dig holes for telephone poles. The frozen, mud-covered ground made the work strenuous and exposed us to the cold wind and freezing rain and our shoes were soon caked with heavy clay. We were given no food or rest periods and worked continuously until it was dark, when they took us back to the *Judenrat* where we got some hot soup from the community kitchen. Father heard that the Jewish labor department was under pressure to supply large numbers of Jews to work for the army and SS. The officials worked through the night to prepare lists, but the demand for slave labor grew as tremendous numbers of soldiers and their equipment were expected to make camp in the region. Fortunately for us, our old army sergeant came to pick up workers next day and we asked him to take us and if possible, give us steady worker status. He agreed and arranged it with a labor department official. Fela told us that in her depot they were also kept very busy handling a huge turnover of uniforms.

Rzeszów was an important German military junction. Our landlord told us that all available Jewish carpenters, mechanics and electricians had been mobilized to put up new barracks outside the town, and to renovate the many buildings the Germans had commandeered to house troops. The *Judenrat* had to supply the furnishings.

I got on very well with the sergeant who sold me everything he could buy in their canteen. One day I asked him why so many Germans were cruel to the Jews. He answered that when the Germans crossed the Polish border the "why" had died, and advised me never again to ask why. It was good advice.

We did not have to work on Sundays and enjoyed the day walking around the town with our parents and Fela. We envied the Poles who looked so unconcerned as they went to church, well dressed and fed. Coffeeshops and some restaurants were full and there were few beggars on the streets. Mother told us that in the public markets, where she shopped during the week, Jews were allowed only between eleven in the morning and three in the afternoon, because the Polish population had complained that peasants preferred to sell their produce to the Jews for higher prices. Now they could come only after the Poles had bought the best produce and make do with the leftovers.

When we came to work one morning our sergeant told us their unit was being moved out of Rzeszów. It was a blow for us because the job was good and yielded many side benefits, but we had no problem getting other work. Many trucks were waiting for Jewish workers and on our first assignment we were taken a long way out of town toward the Jasło district, where we were put to work covering a long tunnel-shaped bunker with earth. We saw many electric generators outside, and inside hundreds of soldiers and men of the Todt organization were busy. Jews were not allowed inside the tunnel. We learned that some months earlier the whole area had been cleared of peasants, and Stepina village, which had stood on the site, had been completely razed to make room for a military airfield and the bunker.

Our landlord told us he had heard that the Germans had invaded Yugoslavia and Greece and were advancing rapidly to occupy both countries, while in the western desert, General Rommel, with his so-called Afrika Korps, was advancing to Egypt and the Suez Canal, putting the British to flight. We became fast friends with the landlord and his family and they were of great help to Mother when she was home alone during the day.

One morning we and a large group of other workers were put on SS trucks which took us a long way south in the direction of the Dębica area. Finally our truck left the main road and drove into a forest in which we spotted a very big camp surrounded by high barbed-wire fences with tall watchtowers armed with machine guns. There was feverish activity in the compound. We saw young SS men, probably recruits, being trained while tanks were negotiating obstacles and water barriers, and low-flying airplanes were dropping bombs on ground targets. We were taken to a large open-air storage area where thousands of crates were standing outside some barracks. We were ordered to carry them inside and were warned they contained explosives. The crates were heavy but we were not rushed, and as almost all of us were young, we coped. The many Jewish workers who were already old hands there told us they had come from Dębica and Tarnów. Some were even from Cracow, where they had been selected from the Mogilska Armory for the work last year. They told us this was the Pustkow Waffen SS camp for special training and weapons tests. When we left in the evening the guard towers had already turned on their searchlights and foot patrols with guard dogs were making their rounds. The next morning we were sent, together with some women, to the residence of the district governor, Ehaus. We noticed that those in the know tried to evade this assignment. The residence was a beautiful old palace that had belonged to some Polish nobleman. I was put to work with a bucket of water and a bunch of old newspapers to clean the windows. I started on the top floor of the three-story building and worked my way down. It was dangerous work. I had to hold on with one hand as I leaned out and cleaned windows with the other but I was left alone, being warned only to finish the job before dark. The German civilians were screaming and cursing all the time, kicking every Jew they thought was not working fast enough. By now it was clear to me why the oldtimers tried to shirk this assignment. They told me that when Ehaus was there, he often personally directed the ill-treatment of Jews, especially young women whom he beat with a rubber truncheon. When we finished working we had to pass a fire station manned by Poles who had orders to play their hoses on us. It was uncomfortable, but we were told we were lucky. It could be worse in winter when the water was near freezing. We passed another building in the palace park and were told it was the county jail, the most feared place in Rzeszów, where many Polish patriots and Jews were imprisoned and tortured, and only a few ever came out alive. We were glad our job there was done.

When we came home Father examined our shoes and found they had rotted from exposure to the cold and wet. We had to buy *drewniaki* (wooden-soled shoes), something like the well-known Dutch clogs, though not as good. Father was now receiving commissions on his sales in the store and with our combined wages we could manage, modestly but adequately. He also had the chance to buy bread and other foods from his Polish customers. Every day we saw more German soldiers and airmen in town. Our Polish truckdriver told Father, when they met, about the changes that had taken place in Cracow since he had taken us away. The Jews were now all confined to the Podgorze ghetto and many had been killed by the Gestapo. Nevertheless, there were sixteen thousand Jews in the ghetto, far more than the eleven thousand Wachter had planned. Many had gotten in illegally and the Germans apparently didn't bother about them. The old Jewish section of Kazimierz was now inhabited by Poles.

The next morning an SS truck took us east to a beautiful palace where we were ordered to bring out furniture and objets d'art, and load them on specially padded trailer trucks. They were the most beautiful pieces I had ever seen, all antiques, and included some very large, wonderfully polished mirrors that took four men to carry. All the time the SS men were screaming and warning us to take care of the goods and threatened to shoot us for sabotage if any piece would be damaged. When the trailers were full we were driven to the railroad station, and from its name, Lancut, we realized that we had been picking bare the estate of the legendary Count Potocki, to be shipped to Germany.

That evening, May 10, 1941, our landlord excitedly told us that Hitler's deputy, Rudolf Hess, had flown a plane to England, bailed out by parachute and been captured. We were not sure what to make of this extraordinary news. It could mean many things, but we chose to hope that perhaps something was happening in Germany which might lead to peace and our salvation. Everybody was very excited, but our life was unchanged, working all day to come home for exhausted sleep.

We were sent to a new assignment with the *Ostbahn* (the Eastern Railways), where Germans in black uniforms and armbands inscribed *Deutsche Reichsbahn* (German Railways), were in charge. I was sent to work in a locomotive maintenance pit while Szymon and Nathan had to handle heavy rails. The foremen were old Polish railroad workers, good men, who showed us what to do. My job in the pit was to clean the pipes of the engines that came in for coaling and watering. The cleaning was done from below, and my Polish workmates warned me to watch out for the hot steam and dripping oil. The job was hard and had to be done fast as each engine had an allotted time. We did well because our German foreman told us he wanted us as steady workers and gave us requisition orders to take back to the labor department which endorsed them. We were happy not to have to line up outside the department every morning to be trucked to constantly changing jobs. Now we could walk to the *Ostbahn* on our own. Very soon we were on a first-name basis with the Polish workers who shared their food and taught us the tricks of the trade. When we came back home in the evening we learned that the Gestapo had imposed another levy of 500,000 zlotys on the Jews, to be collected by the *Judenrat* within twenty-four hours. When the Germans came to count the money they found the sum was 500 zlotys short. Without further ado they shot the two Jews who had been in charge of the levy and the four Jewish policemen who were on duty at the time. Six Jews dead for 500 zlotys!

One of the Polish foremen at the railroad asked us whether we were related to a certain Lonek Herzog from Rzeszów, and when we told him he was a cousin who, with his brother, had fled to the Russian zone, he introduced himself as Mr. Zwolinski and told us that Lonek, had been the leader of the PPS movement's youth section in Rzeszów before the war, and that they had worked together in the PPS. He told us in great secrecy that he himself was now one of the leaders of the local PPS which was part of the underground, and if we needed anything we should not hesitate to come to him. We became very friendly with Mr. Zwolinski, who was a twenty-five-year railroad veteran.

The station was becoming a hive of feverish activity with unending traffic of troop trains on their way east and freight trains heading west with Russian products. We were kept very busy and I had to do a lot of overtime, working more than twelve hours every day of the week cleaning the engines, and our breaks were shortened. I returned home late every night, soaked in oil, and all of my clothes were quickly ruined. It was lucky I had the wooden shoes.

Our landlord told us that the highways also were packed with long columns of troops going east, horse-drawn artillery as well as motorized units and tanks. Since we were only eighty kilometers from the Russian border we speculated that the Germans were fortifying their front against the Russians, who had attacked Finland and occupied the Baltic states of Estonia, Latvia and Lithuania, as well as the northern part of Romania. We learned from Mr. Zwolinski that the last British troops had evacuated Crete, leaving the island to the German paratroops, so all of western Europe was now in German hands. Reinhard Heydrich, Hitler's favorite SS officer, the butcher, cynically misnamed the "Protector" of Bohemia and Moravia, had been killed by Czech patriots. In retaliation the Germans had razed the village of Lidice, killing all the men and sent the women and children to concentration camps.

At four, one Sunday morning in June, we were awakened by the sound of trucks driving into the Jewish section, and within minutes Jewish policemen were knocking on doors and ordering all men under sixty to come out. Father, my brothers and I, were ordered in the trucks and taken to the railroad station, where many Jews were already at work, loading military equipment which was arriving by truck and freight train. The soldiers were wild, pushing and yelling, *"Los, los, schnell, schnell"* (Get a move on), and when anybody dropped something, mainly older Jews, they were beaten but had to continue working. Not a moment's rest as more trucks and empty trains were arriving all the time. When the sun came out the heat added to our discomfort and it was long after dark before we were finally allowed to go home, totally exhausted. We had worked like slaves and as I fell asleep I recalled the biblical story of the Jews in Egypt, enslaved by Pharaoh, to build storage cities for him.

When we returned to work next day, our Polish mates excitedly told us that yesterday, June 22, 1941, the Germans had attacked Russia, without a declaration of war or any warning. Powerful German armies, with thousands of tanks, and supported by the mighty Luftwaffe, had crossed the border on a thousand-mile front at 3:15 in the morning. We saw and heard the planes flying east. Now we knew where all the trains had gone these last few weeks. All of us were happy, including the Poles, despite their traditional hostility for Russia. Already there was one benefit, many of the Poles who had been openly anti-Semitic now started being nice to the Jews, in case the Russians should soon be here. We felt that the Russian giant, once they could recover from the surprise, would cut the Germans down to size. We dared to dream that the Russians might soon be in Rzeszów to rescue us from the German yoke. In the town Poles were shaking hands with Jews. The Russians were only a few hours of tank-driving time away. Meanwhile a blackout was ordered and we covered our windows with blankets, but since we had no definite news we fed on rumors.

As day after day passed without a Russian in sight, our joyous expectations turned to confusion. What had happened to the Russian giant and all those tanks and planes they had deployed to occupy the eastern part of Poland? We did not have much time to speculate because we were kept very busy at the rail station. Troop trains were arriving from the west without a letup, continuing east after we had serviced them. We had to work late into the night and the blackout made the work dangerous. The news was getting worse each day—only German advances. One after the other they were occupying former Polish cities, Wilno, Brest Litovsk and many smaller and less well-known ones, which they had so generously ceded to the Russians when they carved up Poland twenty months ago.

Mr. Zwolinski supplied us with the correct news, and it was bleak. Many local populations in Latvia, Lithuania, Estonia and Byelorussia were aiding the advancing Germans, after welcoming them with flowers. Worse still were the reports of the massacres of Jews by the SS special killer units—the Sonderkommandos and Einsatzgruppen—who followed hard on the heels of the advancing Wehrmacht, producing a bloodbath without precedent. No longer random killings and cutting off beards for amusement, but stark genocide.

The Polish engineers told us that because the Russian railways had a wider gauge, the Germans had to quickly adjust their trains since their panzers were pushing east at incredible speed. The Russians were suffering tremendous casualties, and thousands were taken prisoner every day. Mr. Zwolinski said the English felt safer now. They were no longer standing up to the Germans alone. The threat of invasion had receded and they signed an alliance with the Soviet Union which they had long despised.

At our station we saw the first Red Cross trains coming back from the front bringing the seriously wounded to the military hospitals the Germans had built in Rzeszów. Many of them were dead on arrival. This time there was no lusty singing by the Germans and none were taking pictures of humiliated Jews. Many of these wounded or killed might have been killers of Jews in Poland and Russia. It was a start of the vengeance we had dreamed of—blood for blood. If only all of them would suffer as they had made us suffer. However, they were still advancing victoriously, and more and more names of places we knew so well were in the news. Lwów, the largest city in eastern Poland was captured, and so were Równe, Stanisławów, Kolomyja and Białystok. What worried us most were the hundreds of thousands of Jews who lived in these cities. Many Rzeszów Jews had close relatives there and feared for their safety, compounding our anxiety that the German terror would close in on us too, and make life even worse than it was already. Our fears were reinforced almost immediately by the appearance of large posters with carica- tures of ugly Jews sipping blood, burning churches, and smashing crucifixes. The captions, in Polish and German stated that these were the Jewish Bolsheviks at work. The German-controlled radio stations and newspapers pulled out all the stops to describe the attack on Russia as an all-out war against the Bolsheviks who were out to destroy Christianity, and they singled out the "Jewish commissars" as the spear- head of the anti-Christs. The Germans did not have to incite the populace very much. As soon as they entered a town or village the local anti-Semites turned on the Jews, killing many before the Nazis could get their hands on them. The Nazis were massacring the Jews according to carefully prepared plans. In Lwów, where one hundred fifty thousand Jews lived, the bloodbath continued without stop from the day the Germans entered the city on June 29 until July 3. Gangs of Ukrainians slaughtered Jewish men, women and children whom they dragged from their homes. Their excesses were applauded by the Germans who laughed as they photographed the killings. In Vilnius, thirty-five thousand Jews were re- ported to have been killed by Lithuanians. In Białystok a thousand Jews were burned alive in synagogues and another thousand buried alive in mass graves. But even as we mourned for our brethren our will to survive was strengthened by these atrocities. We must live to exact revenge. Governor Frank announced the enlargement of the General Government by three more districts in the newly conquered areas of southeast Poland, where six hundred thousand Jews lived, Lwów, Stanisławów and Tarnopol.

At the railroad station the first trains came through carrying Russian POW's, tightly packed in cattle cars. They were closely guarded and no one was allowed near them, but we could hear their cries for food and water. The tracks were littered with dead Russians thrown out of the trains. These were the soldiers on whom we had pinned our hopes for liber- ation.

Sometimes we managed to bring home some food we had bought from our workmates and, when the weather started turning cold, we managed to steal pieces of coal at the station and smuggle them home in our clothing. We shared everything with our landlord. When by a miracle the first Jewish refugees from the newly conquered areas arrived, their stories were hair-raising. The Germans had placed the Jews at the mercy of the Ukrainians who, together with the SS and Gestapo instituted a reign of terror. *Judenrats* were appointed and before long many of their officials were shot on some charge or other, and hostages were taken from the Jewish population. At the front, whenever Russian prisoners were taken, the Germans first searched for Jews and commissars and always found men who were ready to betray their comrades. We asked the refugees why the Jews had not gone east with the Russians and they explained that in many places the Germans came so fast that there was no time to run. Many did not want to leave their families and possessions. None of them really believed the stories of the German massacres in our part of Poland from September 1939.

Coming to work one morning we found our Polish workmates highly excited. They had heard that the Japanese had launched a surprise raid on the American fleet in Pearl Harbor. The day was December 7, 1941. They inflicted tremendous damage and many casualties. The U.S.A. was now at war with Japan and Germany. This was a new glimmer of hope for us. The Americans would once more come to rescue Europe from the Germans, as they had done in 1917. And the Russian winter which had already started would, we hoped, rout the Germans as it had done Napoleon's army in 1812, even if the retreating Russians would themselves prove unequal to the task. Our landlord told us that at his place of work he had a chance to glance at German newspapers, and had seen hundreds of obituary notices for Germans killed in action on the Russian front. That was good. Not enough, but a start. All the blood in Germany could never wash their hands clean of the Jewish blood they were spilling.

There were persistent rumors that a ghetto was to be established in Rzeszów and some even claimed they knew exactly where it was to be set up. The same rumors had preceded the establishment of the ghetto in Cracow I recalled, and while I wondered how the rumors started, I could not ignore the fact that all of them that had foretold some new disaster for the Jews had been proved right by subsequent events. Perhaps the Germans were themselves spreading these rumors, as a way to keep the Jews too frightened to think of escape or resistance.

It was not long, as we came out to go to work one morning, we saw a crowd around a new wall poster, a *Judenrat* announcement of the formation of a Jewish living section—the rumored ghetto. Officially it was established for "health reasons." The streets and squares to be included in the ghetto area were specified, and it would be closed on December 31, 1941, giving us, and the converted Jews who had not been exempted, ten days to move in. Only those possessing valid passes issued by the German authorities would be allowed to go out of the ghetto to work. Anybody else found outside the ghetto after it was closed would be shot. Poles would not be allowed in without special permits, on pain of imprisonment and heavy fines. We found that the building we lived in was located within the ghetto limits so we would not need to move, while that of our relatives was not. We could not feel very sorry for them. But the store Father was working in would be in the Polish section and he would lose his job. Many Jews had to move out of their homes, find accommodations in the ghetto and move their belongings. Jewish businessmen had to find new stores and workshops, all in ten days, and without the help of Polish truck drivers who were forbidden to move Jewish property.

We had been through such panic situations twice in Cracow, first in the summer of 1940 when fifty thousand Jews had to leave the city within three months, and again in March 1941, when the formation of the ghetto in the Podgorze section was announced. We advised those of our acquaintances who would have to leave their homes to first try to secure accommodations in the ghetto, and then to enlist whatever help they could to move in as much of their property as they possibly could.

Our German supervisor told us that we could get passes to allow us to keep on working for the *Ostbahn,* and we would have to be brought to work in as groups, under guard. On our way home that evening the town was buzzing with activity like a nervous beehive. Jews and Poles were busy making deals, selling belongings and making exchanges of apartments and stores, which had to be legally approved by the *Judenrat* and City Hall. Outside both of those buildings the lines stretched for blocks in the miserably cold and wet weather.

Everybody wanted to be first, to get the best locations, and
Jews were rushing to make deals with Poles who had apartments and stores located inside the new ghetto limits. The
Poles had the upper hand as there were many Jews willing
to pay any price. The muddy streets filled with pushcarts,
wheelbarrows, and even baby carriages, transporting property
into the ghetto. Here too the *Machers* appeared, as though
from nowhere, extracting big fees to fix things with the authorities for those who could pay and thus avoid standing in the
long, cold lines. Many *Judenrat* officials and policemen also
took the opportunity to make money. Here and there peasants
were offering their carts to desperate Jews. God only knew
how they found out so quickly that here was another chance
to make money. Janitors also came into their own. Fully
aware that the ground was burning under Jewish feet, they
could extort large sums without much trouble. Many Polish
owners of property inside the ghetto made fantastic deals,
exchanging hovels for fine apartments and choice stores in the
Polish section. Some of them were not satisfied even with
such one-sided exchanges and stripped their premises bare of
everything but the walls before handing them over. They also
had the advantage of available transport to cart things away.
It seemed like Cracow all over again, down to the trusted
Poles who had accepted Jewish valuables for safekeeping and
then, when the Jews needed them most, flatly refused to
give them back. It was plain that the Poles welcomed this
opportunity. At a single stroke they were rid of their Jewish
friends and kept their property. On the streets the common
hoodlums lurked to grab things from passing Jewish carts
and prams. Poles and Germans enjoyed watching the Jews
struggling through the muddy streets, but the unkindest blow
of all were the Jewish scum who waited until their unfortunate
brethren had unloaded their goods on the sidewalks, then
pounced and made off with the best items they could snatch.
If the new homes were too small to accommodate all the
belongings, Poles appeared as though through a trapdoor to
offer negligible sums for the surplus. Occasionally some crafty
peasants outbid them with offers of firewood and food which
were more important than money for the Jews.

As the Poles moved out, and the Jews moved in to the
designated area, Jewish artisans were put to work fencing in

the ghetto. The *Judenrat* was working round the clock finalizing accommodation arrangements and preparing passes. In the evenings some of the officials, as well as Jewish policemen, were quite openly helping those who could pay to get the best available apartments. The converts, some of whom had no connections with the Jewish community at all, were particularly hard hit. Despised by the Jews who considered them turncoats, and themselves looking down on their former co-religionists, they were now forced to come and live with us as Jews.

Our landlord was forced to take in another family, the Horns, very religious Jews who had come from nearby Tyczyn not long before. Now we had a family in each room, all sharing the single kitchen and toilet. There were loud and bitter arguments in almost every building, and the *Judenrat* and their police had to intervene in many cases to restore order. Jews were still passionately concerned about the size of their rooms and their furniture. On the whole, it was perhaps better that such matters of minor importance were still occupying us, keeping our minds off what was in store for us.

Even before everybody had settled in, a new order was posted on December 24, 1941, Christmas Eve, obliging Jews to surrender all furs and fur-lined clothing, as well as any skiing equipment they might own, to the Germans. We were given twenty-four hours to bring them to the *Judenrat*. Many Jews preferred to give them away to Poles, or sell them for small sums to the speculators, rather than let the Germans have them to protect their soldiers in Russia from the cold. We prayed they might all freeze to death before they could wrap themselves in their ill-gotten Jewish furs. We ourselves had no furs or ski equipment. The next day the Gestapo drove up to the workshop of a Jewish furrier to confiscate his stock. When he told them he had already turned in all his furs and showed them the receipt, they shot him in front of his family.

Our new religious neighbors assured us that the times were now so tragic as to make it virtually certain that the Messiah would shortly appear to save us. They consoled themselves that in the ghetto they were at least rid of Germans and Poles, and free to pray and grow their beards and sidelocks again. We, on the other hand, were unable to convince ourselves to be as sanguine because we realized that it would take a miracle to put roses in our future, and we doubted the miracle would happen. The ghetto fences, with three gates built in, were completed, and a large *Arbeit Macht Frei* inscription was painted on top of a death-head emblem warning that entry was strictly forbidden "for health reasons." There were some heart-breaking farewells between Jews and Poles and then the gates closed. We were now at the mercy of the Germans, conveniently crowded together for them to do with us as they wished, and they had not made a secret of what they wished for us. Finally they gave the ghetto a German name, *Ghetto Reishof,* not an auspicious omen.

4

The Ghetto, Rzeszów
December 1941–March 1942

Many Jews whose windows faced the Polish section watched as the German and Polish police took up their sentry duty outside the three gates, in Mickiewicza and Lwowska streets, and at Plac Wolnosci, while Jewish police were stationed on the inside of the gates. The SS also maintained a station inside the ghetto, in a building on Garncarska Street.

All outside groups were escorted to work by their German guards. Fela's Mr. Zwolinski brought along some extra food for us to take home and our workmates told us they would exchange food for certain goods we could purchase in the ghetto. Outside the ghetto on the streets some Poles gave us messages for Jewish friends inside. Since the guards made no attempt to search us at the gate, we understood that smuggling would present no problem, so we might be able to make some extra money to augment our meager income, which was now made even smaller by Father having lost his job. The *Judenrat* was the de facto authority inside the ghetto, issuing food coupons and passes for going outside the ghetto, distributing the rations, assigning rooms and stores for professional offices and workshops, administering the hospital, finding shelter for refugees, and running the community kitchens and orphanages. It moved its offices into a large building which belonged to the Schiff family. Its officials and the policemen took the best and most spacious apartments for themselves. There were audible arguments everywhere, mostly over living space and toilet facilities. The newcomers had not yet gotten used

to their new situation, but we knew from our own experience
that they soon would, like it or not. But we were appalled by
the callous behavior of some of our officials who heartlessly
deprived the poor and elderly, evicting them from their homes
and moving them into cellars, many damp and dark and
lacking the most fundamental facilities, including electricity
and water, in favor of those who could pay. There were a few
who would not properly heat their rooms, though they were
able to do so, because they did not want the others in the
same apartment to enjoy their warmth. It was disgusting how
quickly selfishness had infected us, nor were we cheered
when, on our way to work, we saw Poles blithely opening the
stores that only last week had belonged to Jews. For them
Governor Frank had kept his pledge of October 26, 1939, that
he would rid them of the "Jewish bloodsuckers." In the ghetto
we saw the poor souls who had been confined to airless cellars
coming out in the morning as we marched to work, gasping
for air and jumping around to warm themselves after the night
in their frigid quarters, victims of greed that should never have
been allowed to raise its head in our sad new circumstances.
On the other hand, the Jewish policemen were wearing leather
coats and high boots to make themselves look like our German
masters. They kept their wives and girlfriends well dressed
too. Their power had completely turned their heads. It was
left to more decent Jews to help the poor wretches with gifts
of food, clothing and fuel, sharing their own meager supplies
with them. Prices in the ghetto were far higher than on the
outside and bread was particularly expensive, up to ten times
more costly, so that bakers who managed to get flour were
soon on a level with the elite of the *Judenrat* and police, who
had free access to bribes. On the other hand, beggars, young
and old, started making their appearance in the ghetto streets.

Smuggling became the biggest industry, and we had no
choice but to join the trade as the only way to keep alive.
Coming and going every day as we were, and in close contact
with Poles, we were in a good position to do so. Others
engaged in the illicit trade across the fences, connecting roofs
and cellars of the buildings adjoining the Polish areas. But the
biggest smugglers were the Jewish police themselves. At night
they had Polish speculators who brought them whole truck-
loads of essentials and bribed the German and Polish police

on the other side of the gates to turn a blind eye on their nighttime activities.

Only the religious seemed not to mind the ghetto. They were again able to organize religious instruction classes for their children, spent long hours in prayer and study, and persuaded themselves that their earthly suffering was of no significance because it had a higher purpose, to bring the coming of the Messiah nearer. They were expecting the miracle of redemption to occur at any moment. Some even looked happy. The converted Jews, on the other hand, were unable to adjust to the hostile environment. Some risked their lives to flee to other towns where they might not be recognized. The boys were not circumcised and they knew all the Catholic prayers, so they might have a chance to make it.

One day all the Jewish sick who had been in hospitals outside were dumped into the ghetto, and Dr. Heller, who was running the small ghetto hospital, somehow took care of them. His efforts earned him the gratitude and admiration of all. The worsening winter weather compounded our troubles. The peasants could not bring their produce to town and the deep snow made smuggling across the fences nearly impossible. There were many cases of the poor breaking into the apartments of the better-off to steal food and fuel—desperate acts of honest people who now had no other way to keep alive. Our Polish workmates did what they could to bring us some bread to work. They themselves had little other foodstuffs at this time. In my cramped workpit I at least kept warm, though wet, but my brothers and the others who were working outside suffered, many got frostbite and had to stay away from work, which deprived them of the bits of food and coal they might have taken home to their families.

Our only satisfaction was to see the many sick and wounded German soldiers the trains were bringing back from the front. We watched surreptitiously as they were carried from the trains into ambulances that took them to the military hospitals. Many had frozen limbs and faces, some were without noses or ears, but the smell of rotting flesh was like fine perfume to us. Many had died on the way and were covered before they were taken out of the trains. Nature and the Russians were repaying them for our torments!

Mr. Zwolinski informed us that the Russians were launching

many successful counterattacks. But from the Warsaw ghetto
the reports were tragic. Hundreds of Jews were dying every
day of cold, hunger and disease. From Cracow came news
that six thousand Jews had been brought back from the
neighboring villages to which they had been banished by the
Germans in 1940 and 1941, and the ghetto was extremely
overcrowded. How brutal a game the Germans played with
them. First they made them leave and now, when winter of
1942 was at its worst, they were bringing them back and
packing them into the already overcrowded ghetto.

Some Poles were still allowed into our ghetto, mainly the
utility inspectors, and they were visitors we could have done
without. They did not hesitate to disconnect whole buildings
if one poor family in it could not pay the charges. The most
vicious were the tax collectors, demanding payment of taxes
long paid, and waving aside the receipts with threats of denunciation to the Germans. The only concession they made was
to take paintings, objets d'art, rugs, or fine furniture in lieu of
money—heartless scavengers feeding on our misfortune.

Although the snow was high some people risked their lives
to smuggle goods across slippery frozen roofs, while others
desperately dug tunnels to the adjoining Polish buildings.
Anything to survive a little longer. The poorest were fading
away, shadows of their former selves, reduced by hunger and
cold. We did what we could to aid those living near us, once
dignified human beings turned into beggars. When the weather
improved the Polish contacts again brought the goods the
black marketers ordered and tossed them over the fences. In
the crowded streets people were openly buying and selling
every conceivable merchandise. The Germans who occasionally drove through did not interfere. They only photographed
the caged Jews, and our beggars earned cigarettes by posing
for them. Only the religious were scared and had to hide their
beards until the Germans left again.

Dr. Heller and his heroic aides were worried by the rising
mountains of rubbish. Outside the shelters, in which the
poorest were living without toilet facilities, the garbage was
combined with excrement. Rats and mice roamed freely
through the shelters and people were dying every night, their
corpses removed next morning by the ghetto undertaker,
Oszerowicz, and his crew. If no preventive measures were to

be taken, diseases would rage out of control in the hot summer. But the *Judenrat* officials were too busy with immediate problems, and looking after their own welfare, so that the appeals from doctors were ignored. The old and sick died before their plight was considered and dealt with. On the other hand, enough trouble was taken to mobilize carpenters to build wooden overpasses above the Polish streets that divided some parts of the ghetto. Previously these streets had been guarded by the police, now we had to walk above them.

One evening we found our landlord in a happy mood. He had found a job in a cooperative newly formed by a Mr. Eintracht who persuaded the Germans to approve the opening of a series of workshops, which he called cooperatives, to make and repair uniforms and boots for the Wehrmacht, the SS, the Luftwaffe and other German concerns. The scheme created hundreds of jobs for tailors, shoemakers, and many other artisans, men and women who had been idle, hanging around selling their dwindling belongings to keep body and soul together. Now they received wages, special ration coupons as well as meals at work. After he had worked there for a few days, our landlord told us that Eintracht was making an income on the side selling fictitious jobs in his cooperative to rich Jews, and even obtained exit passes for them as "buyers." Others, who had no idea how to hold a tool, he engaged as management assistants and clerks. The *Judenrat* now started evicting people from the better ground-floor apartments to make room for doctors and dentists to open their offices. Many of those evicted were dumped into the hellish shelters. As the snows continued the Germans ordered the *Judenrat* to provide men for snow removal work, and Father had to put in many days on hard work that was backbreaking for a fifty-seven-year-old man. He was not the only one. Every man up to the age of sixty was obliged to take his turn. Only the rich and influential were able to buy, or arrange, their way out. We passed these forced labor parties on our way to and from work and it was agony to see the very poor toiling in their inadequate rags which were quickly soaked, hanging on their emaciated bodies like heavy loads. The food situation grew progressively worse and people became more selfish, forgetting the more desperate poor. Hunger and cold were now busy doing the Germans' work of exterminating Jews.

They only had to sit back, issue orders, and let the *Judenrat* and the Jewish police enforce them.

Our Polish workmates told us that the Russians had launched a counteroffensive under the umbrella of the terrible winter and were wreaking havoc on the German soldiers. All the Jewish furs they had stolen did not protect them. Deep inside Russia, where their triumphant advances had taken them, their panzers and other equipment were frozen fast, and so were the men. Mother nature was avenging us on these inhuman killers. And in the west the Allies were now bombing German cities, and even the Russians had started to bomb Berlin, paying the Germans back in their own kind. In Moscow, General Sikorski, Prime Minister of the Polish Government in exile, signed a friendship pact with Stalin overcoming, for the sake of the common goal of defeating the Nazis, the traditional enmity between Russia and Poland, and overlooking Stalin's connivance with the Germans for the dismemberment of Poland in 1939. Stalin agreed to let two hundred thousand Poles leave Russia to join General Anders' army in Britain.

In our station we handled many troop trains going east. Lately we noticed that the soldiers were either very young or old. Hitler was running out of his human reserves. The cream of his armies was being inexorably ground down by the Red army and its great ally, General Winter. We were happy to see it but our happiness was short-lived, lasting only until our workmates told us of the mass murder of Jews in many towns not far from Rzeszów. They mentioned Bochnia, Mielec, Radom and Tarnów—towns we knew to have large Jewish populations. We got the eerie feeling that doomsday was moving in on us, and we were helpless to protect ourselves against its coming. One evening we were told that the district governor, Dr. Ehaus, accompanied by his colleague, Major Weiss of the German police in Rzeszów, had come to the ghetto gates and ordered the German and Polish police to immediately begin thorough searches of the returning Jewish workers. Substantial quantities of food and other items were discovered and confiscated, and many Jews were mercilessly beaten, some of them given up to seventy-five lashes. For us it meant that we now had to be more careful, and we agreed with our Polish contacts that it would be safer for them to bring the goods to the fences in the evening and throw them across to us at the agreed spots. We would settle the accounts the next day.

Our guards at the *Ostbahn,* whom we called the Black Police, because of their black uniforms, were fair and tolerant, closing their eyes to our many transactions with our Polish workmates. Compared to other outside jobs ours was excellent. "Our" Germans demanded only that we do our work properly and fast. Pressure was growing and we speculated that the Germans were planning another spring offensive. Mother, protected from roundups by the identity papers of a parent of essential workers in steady jobs, kept our clothes, which wore out at an amazing speed, in shape, while Father was still working on snow clearing outside the ghetto. Every day open peasant carts were bringing in more Jews who had been ordered out of the neighboring villages by the Germans, allowed to take only twenty-five kilograms of belongings, which they held onto as they sat freezing in the carts. The peasants took them to the *Judenrat* to line up for a roof over their heads. The lucky ones found relatives who squeezed them into their own apartments. They made a terrible sight, dirty and unshaven completely bewildered by their suddenly changed circumstances. Many of them knew no Polish, and had never before left their villages in which they had lived in poverty for generations, sustained only by their religious faith. The Horns also found some relatives among the new refugees and brought them into their home. Next morning, on our way to work, we saw many of the poor souls lined up outside the *Judenrat* and we were furious that the officials had not come to work earlier to make it a little easier for these desperate men, women and children, many of whom were suffering from illnesses because the Polish doctors had not been allowed to treat Jews.

The one bright spot in our life was the continued arrival of hospital trains carrying German wounded. There were now so many that some of them arrived in cattle trains, like the Jews had been transported in 1939. But disease was now threatening us too, and Dr. Heller and his assistants were fighting an unending battle against epidemics, lice, and disease-carrying vermin. There were no public bathhouses and very little disinfectants in the ghetto. Younger men and women were organized to help the doctor, many buildings were designated as quarantined, and the shelters were closely guarded by the Jewish police. Our fear that the sadistic Ehaus would find out and kill us all was as chilling as the danger of disease itself. To conceal the situation hundreds of dead were buried under the cover of night without any ceremonies. Even the *Judenrat* bureaucrats were concerned, now that the danger was coming closer home.

One day in March of 1942 a large group of German Jews was dumped in front of the *Judenrat* by the Gestapo. Their appearance amazed us. They looked as though they had come for a visit or vacation, dressed in their holiday best, complete with hats and gloves and carrying smart luggage. On Sunday we had a chance to talk to some of them. The Germans had tricked them into believing they were sending them to the east, in passenger trains, to essential jobs their inferior eastern cousins were incapable of doing properly, but when they arrived in Rzeszów, the Germans confiscated their valuables and most of their luggage. Nevertheless they were still making plans to return home once they would finish their work here. Almost none of them spoke Polish or Yiddish, a big handicap for them. The *Judenrat* found rooms for all of them with the richer Jews.

The weather was still wintry rough, and the military trains continued going east unabated. One day our Polish workmates brought us the most devastating news yet. Thousands of Jews in Łódź, and the whole Warthenau area, were being deported to a place called Chelmno near Kolo, allegedly for special work. But as soon as they arrived they were herded into specially constructed, hermetically sealed trucks. As soon as a truck was loaded to capacity it drove off, and its deadly exhaust gases were piped into the sealed compartment, killing everybody inside by a slow and painful process of poisoning and asphyxiation. By the time the trucks reached the camp all inside were dead and their bodies were removed by Jewish prisoners who had been formed into corpse-processing units. They had to strip the bodies and search clothing for concealed valuables which they saved for the Germans. Then they had to throw the naked corpses into open pits and cover them with quicklime. We refused to believe the stories, but the Polish underground had carefully confirmed them. This was planned mass murder, no longer random executions by roaming SS death squads. Thinking it over we reached the conclusion that when the Germans smashed across the Russian border on June 22, the year before, that was the day they started to put their long-range plans for the Jews into operation, and now the mass murders were gathering momentum. We decided not to tell our parents or Fela what we had heard. In fact, we found Mother quite happy because for the first time since the war started she had received a sign of life, albeit indirectly, from relatives in the U.S.A. Some small food packages from Portugal, mailed by a Lisbon forwarding company, containing chocolate, cocoa and sardines, undreamed-of delicacies for us. They must have been ordered by our relatives because only they had our address, from Mother's letters.

Now a new trouble hit us. The *Judenrat* had at last responded to the fact that the mountains of frozen filth they had allowed to accumulate during the winter must be removed before the summer sun would melt them, and turn them into virulent disease spreaders. Our Jewish police were given quotas of workers they had to mobilize for the job, and as they would not touch the rich who had paid them off, they came for us. They forced us to get up and come with them refusing even to look at our *Ostbahn* passes. We worked with the poor souls from the shelters all night, and in the morning went to work at the station. Our German supervisor quickly noticed that we were not working like our former selves and ordered the three of us to report to the *Ostbahn* chief. We were terrified he would dismiss us for our poor performance, so we told him the truth. He was very angry, and in the evening sent a deputy with us to the ghetto. Mother and Fela were terrified at the sight of the black-uniformed German, but we explained. He waited out of sight. When our police came up and refused to listen to our pleas that we needed to rest for our *Ostbahn* jobs, he showed himself. The two policemen were paralyzed with fear and lamely tried to explain they had made a mistake. He ordered them to accompany him to the Jewish labor department where he talked to Pfeifer, the German chief. Pfeifer was furious. He called in a Jewish official and ordered him to take away the policemen's papers, caps and badges of office, and send them to the rubbish-clearing sites, to do the work they had forced us to do. We returned to the station and were not bothered by the ghetto police again.

As it was getting warmer many started selling their winter clothes. They needed the money now and desperately hoped that by next winter the war would be over and they could get new clothes. Others, with nothing left to sell were reduced to begging, and their ranks were swelled by unemployed free professionals, while musicians, some well-known artists, took to playing in the streets for morsels of food or pennies. The food the *Judenrat* and community kitchens were distributing was quite insufficient. Officially, Jews were supposed to receive half the rations allocated to the Polish population, and those were only half of what the Germans were getting. However, even the pittance allowed us did not always reach us, part of it got lost en route. Only the bakers, food merchants, and skilled workers with steady jobs got enough. Everybody else survived somehow from day to day but the warmer weather made it a little easier.

At the station our work became harder each day as the train traffic accelerated and I realized that with the food we were getting, we would not be able to hold out much longer. I came up with an idea I thought might save us. We knew from our previous work that there were great amounts of scrap and waste material lying around the many military compounds, and also that Mr. Gelb, our former neighbor in Cracow, was working for a large German company collecting scrap for the war industries. Why not set up a Rzeszów branch? I discussed the idea with the family and we decided it was worth giving a try. I wrote a postcard to Mrs. Gelb which a Polish workmate posted for me. A few weeks later, when we returned home from the nightshift, we found an elderly German talking to Father. Later we learned his name was Hermann Mueller. We guessed that Mr. Gelb had informed him of my plan, and he had apparently considered the idea important enough to come to see us himself. He asked us to tell him everything we knew about the waste materials we had spotted and then took us to see Pfeifer, who gave us passes and excused us from our *Ostbahn* jobs to show Mueller the scrapheaps.

Outside the ghetto a chauffeured car was waiting for Mueller and we directed him to several military installations. From the respectful reaction of the guards to the papers he presented, we understood that he was an important man. We took him behind the barracks and warehouses and he made notes of what he saw, but never said a word. Later we traveled to the Pustkow SS camp, which was the largest of them all, and there for the first time he made a remark, namely that he could not believe that so much material was allowed to rot. From there we drove to the Szebnia SS base where we saw a Russian POW camp. The prisoners there were obviously being ill treated, reduced to little more than skeletons, and lying on the ground or dragging themselves around. If this was how they treated POW's all those stories about the Jews we had refused to believe must be true. Where was the International Red Cross?

We returned to the ghetto at a late hour and Mueller told us he would submit his observations to his main office in Berlin. Next morning we returned to work hoping that something would come of our meeting, our one hope to survive. One day a strict security regime was imposed, a trainload of SS men arrived to guard the station and its vicinity, and we reckoned that a very important personality must be expected. Our workmates even speculated that Hitler himself may be coming in his personal armored train. Mr. Zwolinski told us that Hitler had indeed had a bunker built for him not far from Rzeszów in 1941, and I recalled how we had worked for a week on a huge bunker in the spring of that year.

On returning home one evening we were met by unusually happy faces and guessed something good had happened at last. Father told us that Pfeifer's office had ordered Father and the three of us to report next morning. This could only mean one thing, our scrap collection scheme was maturing. Next morning Pfeifer told us he had assigned us to work for the Ravo Abfall und Rohmaterial concern, the German company specializing in scrap and raw materials. We were to leave our *Ostbahn* jobs and he provided us with individual passes which could be signed only by him, the Gestapo, and the district governor's office. Mueller, who attended our meeting, told us his project had been approved by Berlin and Cracow, and he would personally open a branch in Rzeszów. He wanted Father for manager and asked us to take him immediately to the Eintracht cooperative to order materials and pushcarts for us. When we showed our new passes to the

German police at the ghetto gate they studied them for a long time before they let us through. They had evidently never seen passes like that before. Mueller took us in his car to a large warehouse near the freight railroad station which had already been assigned for us by the Ravo company. It was a large, dilapidated building and needed a lot of cleaning and renovation. Mueller had a group of artisans brought from the ghetto, and with the materials from Eintracht cooperatives they were soon at work.

Our passes allowed us to leave the ghetto unescorted and gave us the freedom to move about in the whole Rzeszów district, including entry to military compounds and we also received green bands inscribed with the Ravo name to wear with our white armbands. Father changed completely, a new man, happy and proud to be working again and with his own three sons. We picked up our pushcarts from Eintracht, and after another lengthy examination of our passes at the gate, walked out of the ghetto and got down to work. We started at a large military compound in the suburbs where we had worked the year before. A soldier took us to the barracks where scrap had been dumped. We picked out the best pieces and estimated there was enough material there to keep us busy for a week.

As we pushed our carts through the streets the Poles stared at us. They were not used to seeing Jews walking through their section unguarded. They appeared to be pursuing normal lives and looked quite well dressed and fed. There were no beggars in rags here, and nobody selling his last shirt, or playing and singing for a piece of bread. The store where father had worked now had a Polish name, the vultures savoring their prey. The buildings looked clean and there were children playing on the sidewalks. And only a few hundred yards away stood our ghetto, in another world of misery and sadness, as though the fence around it was intended not only to keep the Jews in, but hope and happiness out.

We dumped our scrap at the warehouse and Mueller, whom we called Chief, checked it but said nothing. We told him we were going back to the compound and he left it up to us to find the best scrap. Before it got dark and after making sure there were no customers inside, we went into a Polish food store and asked to buy some bread. We watched fascinated as the owner put a loaf in a brown bag as though it were the most natural thing in the world, paid him and went out. All we had done was buy bread but we felt as though we had worked a miracle.

Before we left the warehouse to make our rounds next day, Mueller asked Father to make him a list of what we would need for our job. Father asked for some men to help us and more pushcarts, and Mueller wrote out a requisition order for the Eintracht cooperative and promised to get Pfeifer's office to assign us collectors and warehouse workers. The new men assigned to us included four from Cracow, Mr. Wiesenfeld and his son Artek, and his brother-in-law Mr. Kranz and his son Kuba. We had heard of them in Cracow, religious Jews who had a wholesale leather business on Dietla Street. With more collectors at work our scrapyard quickly began to fill up and Mueller seemed satisfied. We continued buying foodstuffs in Polish stores, under the pretext of picking up their empty bottles, and they asked us to bring items we could buy in the ghetto. By taking the pushcarts into the ghetto with us in the evenings, to conceal our purchases under the scrap, we were able to get a nice little black market business going. The German policemen were used to us and only gave us a perfunctory look. But we had to be careful of the Jewish police and informers. As Mueller seemed very happy with the way our work was coming along, Father proposed he permit us to collect scrap inside the ghetto too. He approved and this gave Father an opportunity to give jobs to some of the older men, including his old boss from the store.

When the time came to start sending the mountain of scrap we had collected to Germany, we got the opportunity to visit the station again, to deliver our goods. We had a happy reunion with Mr. Zwolinski and our old workmates there. Mueller ordered the peasants to put a certain number of their horsecarts at the disposal of the Ravo company with which to move our scrap to the station. We got a good trade going with the peasants, exchanging clothes and other articles for foodstuffs. Father, who was well liked by all the Jewish workers despite being Mueller's right-hand man, warned them not to be greedy so as to enjoy our good fortune as long as it should last, thus harmony reigned in our yard and we were not plagued by jealousies or arguments.

Mueller agreed to employ some of the peasants with their carts to make the collection more efficient which was a break for us, because they brought us bread and food at lower than store prices. In addition we didn't have to push the handcarts any more. In the ghetto many of the people who had at first looked down on us as *shmatte* (rag-and-bone men), now appealed to Father to employ them and even offered bribes, but Father knew that there was a limit to a good thing and did not attempt to stretch our luck. During our visits to the station we got the latest news from Mr. Zwolinski, and it was very bad. Jews were being deported to extermination camps by the thousands, and many of the local inhabitants in the Ukraine, Bialorussia and the Baltic countries were aiding the SS, as auxiliary police, to round up Jews to be killed.

One night in April of 1942 we were awakened by the arrival of a convoy of cars. We ran to the window and saw a lot of Germans, some of them in uniform, and guided by the Jewish police to whom they gave what looked like lists, went into certain buildings. A few minutes later shots were heard and they then returned to their cars and drove off. We knew they had shot some people, but not who or why. We could not sleep, but it was not until the next morning that we found out that Oszerowicz and his undertakers had removed forty-two bodies. All of those killed were former communists or members of the Bund, a left-wing Jewish party. They had been shot in front of their families and in a few cases, when the Gestapo, who had obviously been guided by informers, could not find the man they were looking for, they simply shot somebody else from his family. When we told Mr. Zwolinski the next time we came to the station, he informed us that similar actions had been carried out all over Poland and that several thousand Jews had been shot that night. At the same time Polish patriots were also being hunted and killed and many Poles were transported to Germany for forced labor. A few weeks later another Gestapo raid took place in the dead of night. This time they walked straight to the room of the Lew family and shot them all. No one knew why, but the whole ghetto mourned for the family because they had been very charitable and helpful to us. Before the ghetto had time to recover, another night raid took place, this time for the Kanarek family, one of the wealthiest in the ghetto. The

Gestapo first ordered them to surrender all their cash and valuables and then broke up the furniture, took up the floor looking for hidden treasure, and finally ordered them to dig up their cellar, before shooting them all. Now panic gripped the ghetto every time the black cars with the POL license plates drove in. Obviously that was just what the Germans wanted, to keep Jews in a state of constant fear, suspicious of informers in our own ranks and thus to break our spirit and make us docile victims.

We usually had Sundays off from work and on one of them, while strolling in the ghetto, we noticed the first encouraging sign of cooperation and common effort. Everywhere young men and women were planting vegetables in every inch of soil they could put together on balconies, flat roofs and in courtyards. It was a heartwarming sight holding out the hope that by fall there would be extra food.

As the spring weather warmed up, epidemics of typhoid fever, dysentery, scurvy and tuberculosis, swept through the ghetto killing dozens of people every day, undoubtedly caused by the filth that brought rats, birds and many bugs. Our doctors were desperate, and every able-bodied man and woman joined in to clear the remaining accumulated garbage and burn it. We were particularly frightened of what the Germans would do if they found out. I came down with a fever and Mother, who was frightened out of her wits, alerted Dr. Heller, who diagnosed diphtheria and insisted I go to the hospital at once. But Mother begged him to let me stay and personally looked after me night and day, while the rest of our family stayed with men from our workplace to reduce the danger of infection. Dr. Heller came to see me from time to time, despite his tremendous workload. I recovered slowly while all over the ghetto people were dying, their bodies removed at night by Oszerowicz and his burial party. The families were not allowed to attend the interments in order not to alert the Germans. Thanks to the superhuman efforts of Dr. Heller and his assistant, Dr. Hauptman, helped by many noble and devoted unknown Jews, the epidemic was contained, but the other dangers stayed with us.

When I returned to my job I did paperwork until I was strong enough to do physical labor again. At the station Mr. Zwolinski told us that the German spring offensive had begun and they were making advances along most of the front. Only Moscow, Leningrad and Sevastopol were holding out. Mueller urged us to intensify our efforts as the German war machine needed more scrap. We visited many large German enterprises, and even went to the Gestapo building on Jagielonska Street, as well as to the office of the district commandant and the jail. We knew that many of the Poles and Jews who entered these buildings did not come out alive and after a few days Oszerowicz was called to take their tortured bodies for burial in the ghetto. He sometimes buried Polish patriots alongside the Jews. They had died together because they had not been Germans, and therefore inferior.

When working in these buildings we saw the cold faces and dark uniforms with the shining death heads all day, and were almost paralyzed just having to look at them.

One morning on our way out, we found another large poster on the wall, an order, signed by the *Judenrat,* for the registration, within three days, of all Jews over twelve years of age. We wondered what new troubles the Germans had in store for us. Some elderly men dyed their hair to make themselves look younger, others bribed officials to change their own and their children's birthdates on their identity papers. Everybody wanted to be fit for work categories. When we went to register early next morning there were already long lines outside the *Judenrat.* We were directed to the desk dealing with those who were working for the Germans outside the ghetto. Mother was accepted into this category too since there were five of us working.

One day we met our truckdriver from Cracow on the street outside the ghetto. He told us that the ghetto in Cracow had been besieged by the Germans for ten days, from May 31 to June 10, 1942. Shooting was heard all the time and every day large groups of Jews were marched out of the ghetto to the Prokocim railroad station where they were squeezed into cattle trains and sent off, going east—nobody knew where. We mourned for the Jews of our city but realized that the deathtrap was closing on us too. Soon there were reports that similar actions had been carried out in Bochnia and Tarnów, with many killed or sent off to a fate we were afraid to guess at. Tarnów was only sixty kilometers from Rzeszów. Some Jews in our ghetto started preparing bunkers to hide in, and those who had a lot of money contacted Polish friends to plead for hiding places in their homes. The *Judenrat* tried to calm the ghetto by saying the rumors were exaggerated, that Jews of these cities had been resettled in labor camps.

But the truth could no longer be suppressed, even the BBC, which some daring Poles listened to, was reporting the facts and giving the names of the cities where Jews had been murdered or sent to extermination camps. While the reports made us shudder they were also a macabre encouragement, giving us hope that now the west knew what the Germans were doing. They had actually warned them that they would be held responsible for their actions when the war was over. However, the only change that occurred was that the German police at the ghetto gates checked everybody coming and going more carefully. It was done under the supervision of Gestapo men, and we were experienced enough to realize that it could bode no good. Every change the Germans introduced was always for the worse. Soon more men were rounded up in the ghetto for a special assignment to level an old abandoned Jewish cemetery on Mikoszka Street. They were ordered to have the job finished in three days. We also noticed that in the *Judenrat* and labor department buildings the lights were burning all night even though the registration had long since been completed. When Pfeifer himself came to check out the cemetery work, we took it as another bad omen, because he did not usually concern himself with work inside the ghetto.

But however ominous our fears, we had to go on working. If anything, we worked harder, hoping to collect enough scrap to make a shipment necessary. That would take us to the station and give us a chance to talk to Mr. Zwolinski. We were actually picking up so much wastepaper that Mueller got a machine to press it into easily handled bundles that were more convenient to ship. The arrival of the new machine raised our spirits. We reckoned that things must surely be quite normal if the Germans were taking the trouble to supply an expensive press for our work. It was a reasonable hope, a straw to clutch, and it cheered us up. But our elation was not to last for very long. Indeed, no longer than a few days.

5

Rzeszów, Deportations
July–September 1942

O n our return to the ghetto on the evening of July 6,
1942, there was a crowd standing in front of a new
poster: a "Resettlement" order. We knew now just what
resettlement meant when carried out by the Germans. The
order divided us into two classes. One for those with proof of
employment outside the ghetto for the German forces or
enterprises, and officials of the *Judenrat,* the Jewish police,
the labor department and the Eintracht cooperative. These
persons were required to report in front of the labor department with their families. The second group comprised all
those who were unemployed along with their families, and
they must assemble on the grounds of the old Jewish cemetery
along the Mikoszka River, bringing no more than twenty-five
kilograms each of personal belongings and enough food for
two days. The date of assembly was July 7, the very next day,
at six in the morning. Noncompliance would be punished by
death. We chose to assume, and certainly to hope, that we
belonged to the first group.

Though stunned, people did not waste time but started
hurrying home to prepare. The streets became a beehive and
the people in our building were in a panic, running about with
little purpose trying to get advice from each other. Mother
and Fela already knew the essence of the order, for the bad
news had spread through the ghetto. Seeing that even the high
and mighty officials of the *Judenrat* and police were scared
only added to the general confusion. Since we could not be
absolutely sure that we would be included in group one,

Mother packed rucksacks with our personal things and prepared food and thermos flasks of hot tea. Before she finished, the young son of our landlord burst in to tell us that the Jewish police and officials of the *Judenrat* and labor department were making the rounds of the ghetto with lists in their hands. The tension mounted as we waited to hear the final word on who would be sent away and who might stay. A Jewish policeman soon ended our uncertainty. List in hand he told everybody where to go tomorrow. All six of us were to come to the labor department along with our landlord, the Horns, and the new couple who were living in the kitchen. We were saved, but who could tell for how long? When other neighbors were informed that they were to be deported we could not muster the courage to look them in the face. At this terrible hour of reckoning everybody was thinking only of themselves, and those who had been reprieved thought only of their lucky escape. Ideas of fleeing were quickly nipped in the bud for large numbers of German, Ukrainian and Polish police arrived and surrounded the ghetto, the headlights of their trucks illuminating the fence that had overnight become a wailing wall. The whole ghetto trembled as this last lifeline was blocked. Children who saw their parents sobbing started crying and screaming, and that night nobody slept as we helplessly listened to the clocks ticking away the minutes to the fatal hour of six.

It was not quite light yet when policemen began screaming in Polish and Yiddish to get out and hurry to our designated places of assembly. The dim dawn lent an eerie air of doom to the streets full of despairing people unwillingly to meet their inevitable fate. Most tragic were the young mothers pushing their infants in baby carriages to face the merciless Germans, and the old and sick being helped on their last journey by paramedical volunteers. Then the children from the orphanage marched past, their appearance so neat that they must have dressed under the motherly care of the teachers who were accompanying them. We saw some religious Jews wrapped in their prayer shawls or wearing their morning prayer phylacteries, praying to God as they walked. Oblivious of the grim reality, they looked as though they were already entering the next world, the world that according to Jewish tradition is "wholly good." But it was not the Messiah who was awaiting

them at the gate this dire day. Again and again policemen
shouted warnings that no one was to be in their homes after
six on pain of being shot on the spot. They screamed to be
heard above the shouts of people calling goodbyes to friends
and relatives. Even this bedlam made room for one last rumor,
that the Gestapo were already inside the ghetto. It chilled
everybody to the marrow.

We reached our assembly place and squatted on the ground
on top of our bundles. It was heartbreaking to see the others,
those of the second group, passing by us downcast, seemingly
resigned to what they could not alter. Last of all came the
poor wretches from the cellar shelters, their rags inadequately
covering their emaciated bodies. The few small bundles they
carried were all they possessed. Some had tied them around
their necks for safety. Most had nothing at all to take with
them. The Germans laughed as they hurried them along with
their rifle butts and whips. For generations our rabbis and
elders had taught us to accept God's will without demur. If all
was well, it was because God was pleased with us, but if
things went wrong it was to allow us to continue atoning for
our sins, an atonement that had continued since the destruction of the Second Temple nearly two thousand years ago. We
had been trained to accept our fate as divine judgment and to
expect a better life only in the next world.

At six o'clock sharp the trucks, filled with fully armed
police and SS men, drove through the three gates. The killers
fanned out, took their rifles off their shoulders and faced
helpless men, women and children, who were already more
dead than alive. We were ordered to form a line and come one
at a time to a long table the Germans had set up. They checked
each identity document against their lists. I recognized Pfeifer,
Ehaus, Pablu and the feared Gestapo chief, Schuster, oversee-
ing the tragedy. When our turn came to present our papers, it
took the Germans what appeared to us an eternity to check
them, before they grudgingly acknowledged with a cold nod
that we were allowed to stay. Not all in our group were
so lucky, for we saw the Germans gleefully tearing up the
documents that were confidently presented by people from
the Eintracht cooperative. Their world was destroyed in that
fleeting moment of tearing paper. They tried to plea, but the

SS men with their rifle butts, pushed them to the resettlement assembly point from which there was no return.

Many families were divided. Some appeared to freeze as the selection was carried out and were separated without apparent feelings, like robots. Others burst into tears or began to scream, but were quickly dealt with by the SS guards. Still others refused to be separated and though they were allowed to stay, joined their dear ones at the other place, preferring death rather than be torn apart. Now and then shots could be heard from the buildings where the Germans had found some Jews attempting to hide, or others who had not left their homes in time.

When our confusion at last gave way to realization, we noticed that there were many Ukrainians among the SS. We used to call them *Junaki*. Besides their rifles they also carried *batogis,* whips made of long, thick leather thongs, tipped with sharpened pieces of metal. They did not spare their *batogis* from the people who were passing by them, laughed at the discomfort and injuries they wreaked.

When the selection was completed some of the deportees were ordered to climb in the trucks which quickly drove them away. We saw mothers separated from their small children when a truck was filled, but their cries of anguish got them only a blow or kick. The children were screaming *"Mamusiu! Tatusiu!* Ratuj!'' (''Mummy! Daddy! Help!''), but their parents were prevented from jumping into the trucks. Invalids and the very old were also pushed into those trucks. When all of them were gone, the remaining Jews were ordered to line up four abreast, and the long columns were marched out of the main gate, closely guarded by the SS men. Some brave ones still found the strength to wave to us, or maybe they wanted only to hide their tears behind their hands. My own hand was heavy, as though made of lead, as I tried to wave back. Finally the gate closed. It was all over.

We who remained were then ordered to return to our homes and stay inside to await further orders. There were still many SS men in the streets, their rifles at the ready. As we entered our building we saw some bloody bodies sprawled on the floor, those of the unfortunates who had not left fast enough, and the few who had hoped, to their last breath, to escape their fate. Perhaps they were better off dead. They no longer had to travel the long, tormented path to death.

As dusk of this endless day fell at last, we ventured out. There were bloody, beaten bodies lying everywhere. Now we realized what the early morning shooting had been about. The old and sick from the hospital and old age homes, and the mentally ill who had been confined to attics, had been gunned down, some pushed out of windows, to save the Germans the cost of transporting them to some other death. The SS men who had carried out the day's dark deeds were members of the so-called *Vernichtung* and *Ausrottung Kommandos,* the special destruction and extermination units. Soon Oszerowicz and his gravediggers appeared, to gather up the corpses that we had seen plus many more from all over.

So many of God's children were dead but there was no God in the ghetto, nor indeed in Rzeszów or in the whole of Poland. All the piousness and prayers had been in vain, at least in this world. Perhaps they were now resting in another, more benevolent one. We could only wish it.

Mother and Father sat on their bed and said nothing. Father had lost many friends this day, and all of us had seen so much fear, pain, anguish and cruelty. We could not even think of eating and went to bed hungry but alive forlornly hoping that maybe tomorrow might be a better day.

The next day dawned and we left for work, tired and depressed. The Polish speculators who used to swarm around us like flies, now left us alone. They knew what had taken place in the ghetto and were decent enough to leave us alone with our pain. We forced ourselves to work, and when we came to the station, Mr. Zwolinski was waiting for us. He could not hold back his tears as he fervently shook our hands. He had not been sure he would ever see us again. But he had terrible news for us. All the old, the invalids, and the children, who had been taken away in trucks, all those who had been unable to march to the railroad, were in fact driven to the Glogow forest on the way to Dynow, not far from Rzeszów, ordered to get off and undress, and were then shot one by one. Polish workers had thrown their bodies into long pits they had dug the day before. When the pits were full, the SS men threw in some handgrenades to kill anybody who might still have a spark of life left. Even so, when the Polish workers covered them with earth it moved for many long moments before it lay still.

Those who had been marched away were taken to the railroad station in the Staroniwa suburb, and under heavy guard forced into cattle cars, one hundred twenty squeezed into each car that usually carried forty soldiers or eight horses. There was no water or sanitary facilities in them.

No Pole was allowed at the station while the Jews were loaded, but they could see what was going on from a distance. Only the Polish engineer was on board his locomotive, guarded by SS men. The floors of the cars were covered with dry straw and lime, and barbed wire was stretched across the small air openings to prevent escape. When no more Jews were left, the cars were sealed by the SS. The train stood in the scorching heat until the evening when it moved off to the east. Hundreds of bundles, lost or abandoned, were picked up at the station and along the route the deportees had marched. Ukrainian guards picked them up and threw them on their trucks.

Our emotions notwithstanding, we had to force ourselves to continue working. Mueller ordered us to report to him in his office before we left for home in the evening. He, and all other German bosses employing Jews, had received orders, Father told us, to collect the identity papers of his Jewish workers for inspection and stamping by the Gestapo. We sensed that this unusual procedure indicated a new misfortune hanging over our heads, a sinister shadow. We got through the day, working like automatons, and when we surrendered our ID cards to Mueller in the evening he promised to take care of all of us. He was a gentle chink in my solid hatred for all Germans.

When we returned to the ghetto a heartbreaking emptiness met us. There were a few people about and they told us their ID cards had also been taken away, as was Fela's. A new fear gripped us. This could only mean that the Gestapo was already planning a new disaster for us. Everybody knew what had happened in the Rudno forests, and many had had close relatives among the victims. Only yesterday we had chosen to believe that the SS were being kind to those unable to walk by taking them on their trucks. Now that we knew the truth we were furious that there were still those in the *Judenrat* and the

Jewish police who cooperated with the Germans in the vain hope of mollifying them. But the future was now more urgent than the past. The ID cards belonging to the children of those working in essential jobs had not been taken, and there were still a few Jews in the ghetto who did not have any real jobs. They now rushed to get some kind of secure employment.

On our way to work next morning the Polish speculators again approached us but we preferred dealing with the peasants. Mueller told us he had been summoned to the Gestapo office to pick up our ID cards. We wondered about those mysterious stamps.

Our rounds took us into the ghetto and we were able to smuggle in some food on two peasant carts used for our pickups. Our collectors in the ghetto told us that a few hours earlier some SS trucks had brought a load of bundles and suitcases to the Eintracht cooperative to have their contents cleaned and sorted for shipment to Germany. When the workers opened them they got a severe shock. They were the personal belongings of the people who had been deported yesterday. Some even recognized items belonging to their relatives and friends. A commotion of anguish erupted and Eintracht, who feared an inspection, begged his staff to start working again, lest the Germans should kill them all.

Late in the afternoon Mueller returned to our warehouse and from his smile we knew he was bringing good news. In fact, he had gotten stamps for all but two men who were both over sixty years of age. Mueller told them there was nothing he could do since he could not appeal a Gestapo decision. The rest of us held our ID cards tightly and checked and rechecked the life-saving red stamps all the way home. Meanwhile at home tragedy had struck our landlord. He and his wife received the red stamps but their young son was refused along with the couple who had been living in the kitchen.

We soon learned that many *Judenrat* officials and Eintracht workers had also been refused stamps. The *Machers* who, for large fees, had been able to do so much, were now themselves staggering around like poisoned cockroaches, desperately seeking help.

Our landlord and his wife sat and discussed what to do— abandon their son to the Germans or go with him? If so, should both or only one accompany him, and if only one which one of them? How distressing it was for us to see these two kind people, who had treated us so decently, trying to reason out a life-and-death decision for themselves and their only son. There was nothing we could do for them, not even offer advice.

It was hard to fall asleep, and we had barely done so when Mother woke us. She had heard suspicious noises from the street. We looked out of the window and saw people running. The ghetto was surrounded by the Germans and we were trapped again. Pandemonium broke out everywhere in the ghetto. The people with the life-saving red stamps were the minority, and the others realized that this time the selection would be one they could not survive. They were already marked. All they could do was tremble and hope against hope.

Very early in the morning, police and *Judenrat* officials made the rounds shouting orders for everybody to assemble on the Mikoszka Square, with twenty-five kilograms of personal belongings, some food and all their valuables. No one was to lock their rooms and apartments. The Germans intended making searches. It was still dark outside and we could not make out individual faces, only a blurred, stumbling procession of the helpless. While we were still making our way to Mikoszka Square, the trucks came in, this time through all three gates. The men, some Ukrainian *Junaks,* others with fierce dogs on leashes, jumped off and started screaming at us, calling us the most humiliating names while hitting out with their whips and clubs. When they came upon a Jew who had his prayer shawl wrapped around him (a last desperate try to keep out this evil world), they ripped it off and beat him about the head. The snarling dogs terrified the mothers of trembling children.

In Mikoszka Square the SS guards ordered everybody to lie on the ground, facedown, not to talk or raise our heads. Now and then we heard shots being fired and soon there was a terrible stench of excrement. We heard faint prayers, God's abandoned children still expressing their faith in Him. The sun came out and beat relentlessly on our backs adding to our discomfort, but all appeals for water, mainly by the young mothers, were ignored by the SS men who amused themselves by tormenting the elderly, making them do exercises their bodies were incapable of performing.

At last we were ordered to get up, form a line, and pass by a long table that had been set up at which German officials had taken their seats. Everybody tried to wipe off the dust to make themselves more presentable to the German judges of life and death. The SS guards ordered the few who were still wearing their prayer shawls and phylacteries to take them off, but their officers told them to leave them alone. For what purpose? I noticed that this time the selection was much faster, the line was advancing at unusual speed. At the table those whose ID cards had the red stamp were ordered to the right where they were surrounded by armed SS men. Those without the stamp had their cards taken away and torn up. I recognized many *Judenrat* officials among them and they made a last desperate attempt to talk to the officers they knew and had blindly served so well. The officers ignored their pleas and sent them off for deportation. Many of those SS decisions were tragedies. Husbands were separated from their wives, children torn away from their parents, and it was now up to them to decide whether to grasp the straw or voluntarily join their dear ones and face the ultimate fate together. The religious were the most dignified and did not beg for mercy, but on being selected moved slowly to the deportation group reciting silent prayers.

The SS men shouted for us to move faster, take off our hats when facing officers, and cursed at us all the time.

I recognized Pfeifer, Mayor Pablu, and Shupo commandant Weiss, sitting in judgment. They asked no questions and offered not a word, just checked the ID cards and occasionally glanced at their lists before motioning which way to turn, to live or die. One shake of their finger decided the fate of a human being. It was soon apparent that those with the life-saving stamps were few, whereas the group of the condemned kept growing. SS men were moving among them making random selections, especially of the better dressed, for personal searches. They did not hesitate to make body searches of women too, in full sight of everybody.

Total silence descended on the square, broken only by the shouted orders from the SS guards, and occasional shots exploding from the direction of the buildings. When we heard the furious barking of the dogs we knew they had discovered another desperate Jew. The barking was followed by a quick shot and then silence again. Our turn came. Mother and Father went first and walked the length of the table until the last officer motioned them to the right. I saw Pfeifer looking at me and felt he remembered us. One way or another, we all came together again, saved! We embraced with silent tears. Others in our group who had been separated from their families called out to them, but the SS guards quickly shut them up. Some suddenly ran across to rejoin their kin among the condemned. They had made their decision and the SS men did not stop them. Now the president of the *Judenrat*, Kleinmann, the mightiest Jew in Rzeszów, and his family were standing before the crucial table. There he was reduced to being only a Jew. He with all his family were motioned off for deportation—all he had done for the Germans had not saved him!

The scene unfolded before me as though I were watching a horror movie I did not want to see, as if I had gone into the theater by mistake. Suddenly our uncle, aunt and Franka appeared at the table. The parents were sent off, but Franka, who had a job in Pfeifer's office, joined our group. At that moment all our grudges against them evaporated and we wept for them. Father weakly waved to his brother whose name he kept repeating under his breath. Many policemen and their families were sent off and yet their colleagues were busy serving the German judges cool lemonade, and loading the baskets of confiscated valuables on the trucks. How incredibly sad it all was. Some SS officers started a secondary selection, picking out the fittest young men from the deportation group and ordering them to the trucks. They needed them to work for them. By noon it was all over. Everybody's fate was decided. The German officials got up and left, talking unconcernedly as they got into their waiting cars. Only the SS guards remained.

Our group was ordered to return home and stay there to await further orders. The streets were forbidden to us. From the windows we watched the columns, four abreast, marching to the main gate in the direction of the Staroniwa railroad station. Those left behind called to relatives being marched away and their cries dissolved into uncontrolled sobbing. Father quietly repeated the name of his older brother over and over, until the column disappeared on the other side of the gate. Jewish policemen warned us to stay inside until the SS left the ghetto. We saw some with their vicious dogs, and their no less vicious Ukrainian assistants. Any hidden Jew that was discovered was shot on the spot. Once they found a bunker in which some Jews were hiding and offered to leave them alone if they would surrender their valuables. The desperate souls began passing out jewelery to them whereupon they broke in and shot them one by one.

The heat was terrible. We washed off the dust and drank lots of water, and then sat in exhausted, helpless misery, the silence ruptured first by the dogs and guns and then by the crying from the Horns' room. Only two sons were left. Leon and Hersch. Their parents and all other members of their family had been deported this day. Our landlord and his wife did not return. They must at the last moment have decided not to abandon their son, and went with him, knowing full well where they were going. The couple who had lived in our kitchen were also gone. Our building was more than half empty. We looked cautiously out of our window and saw that the street had been taken over by SS men and their Ukrainians, with Jewish policemen doing their bidding. Many seemed to be drunk. No doubt they had found some vodka in the abandoned homes. There were many pieces of luggage lying in the street and here and there empty baby carriages and wheelchairs. Their owners would not need them any more. At last the tragically tumultuous day turned to dusk and we saw the SS marching off to the number 3 gate, where their trucks were waiting. When the last one left the Jewish police gave us permission to come out. People began running from building to building to see who of their friends and relations may still be left.

Some Jewish policemen came in, for the first time friendly. At last they had learned their lesson. Serving the Germans had not in the final analysis paid off, not for the police or for the *Judenrat* officials. To the Germans they were, after all, just Jews, regardless of their position or duties. They told us how the SS had searched for bunkers, and flooded or threw poison-gas canisters into those they found. The ghetto was still under siege, closely guarded, and only Oszerowicz and his gravediggers were allowed out in order to remove the many corpses.

We did not sleep well that night and before it was over another astounding occurrence confounded us; a long column of peasant carts arrived, all loaded to capacity with Jews from other localities, who were dumped outside the shelters which had been emptied of their previous inhabitants only a few days ago. Next morning when we left for work the peasants who had brought the Jews told us they had come from the small towns around Rzeszów, including Lancut, Kolbuszowa, Tyczyn, and Blazowa. They were the last Jews in these places. The Poles quickly took over their property.

Somebody warned us that the Gestapo was hunting for Jews who had reportedly escaped from the ghetto so we asked Mueller to let us work inside the warehouse for the day and he agreed. He was not interested in losing his workers. During the day we learned that as the Jews were marching to the Staroniwa station the day before, an SS man ran up to a woman who was unable to keep up with the column and pushed her forward. When her husband tried to protect her, the SS man shot him on the spot. The shooting alarmed other guards who did not know what had happened, and they started firing wildly into the column and killed two hundred forty Jews in a few moments. Their bodies were left lying in the street for Oszerowicz. In the panic many Jews dropped their sorry bundles which were picked up by the Ukrainians. All this took place in front of the city postoffice in full sight of the Polish population. It was the first time they had actually seen Jews being wantonly killed.

But the German death machine did not rest. When the burial party interred the many bodies in a large common grave in the Jewish cemetery, one of the men wrote in Hebrew on a nearby wall "Here lie anonymous Jewish martyrs." A Gestapo man who arrived to inspect the grave noticed the inscription and asked what it meant. The translation infuriated him and he demanded that the man responsible come forward. The man, who was a religious Jew who had wanted to perpetuate the memory of the dead, stepped up and immediately the SS man shot him. The others had to wipe off the inscription, so that not even a memory remained.

There had apparently not been enough trains to take all the Jews away the day before because some were returned to the ghetto and thrown into the abandoned old Austrian army barracks, dilapidated relics from the First World War, unfit for man or beast. The heat inside must have been unbearable, but no one was allowed to approach them and we could do nothing about their desperate cries for water.

When we returned from work in the evening, Mother told us that some people had managed to bribe the Ukrainians, who wanted money for vodka, to get relatives out of the barracks. One rescued family moved into our building and they told us of their ordeal. On their march to the station many Poles laughed at their distress, and when families were separated as they were pushed into the cattle cars they begged the SS to allow them to reunite, but were curtly told that at the last stop they would be together again for good, in the *Himmelkommando* (Heaven Unit), and were roughly pushed into another car.

Next morning another action was started and the Jewish police ordered us to stay inside. Everyone was quiet. There were no children left to cry and the grownups had no tears left. The SS drove in once again to take away the poor souls in the barracks and the Jews from outside Rzeszów who had been brought in the day before. We were not allowed to go to work. From our windows we watched forlornly as the now-familiar action was carried out in all its brutality, until the last of the deportees had marched or stumbled through the gates.

One day carpenters started taking down the ghetto fence and moved it closer. The Germans were putting some of the buildings nearest the Polish sectors outside of the ghetto limits because the space requirement had shrunk. The *Judenrat,* now headed by a new Gestapo appointee, Benno Kahane, who was known for his blind obedience to the Germans, had to move those still left in the excluded buildings to the inside. Our building, which was well inside the ghetto, got more tenants and we helped them to move in. The labor department formed special units that they called *Raumungskollone* for clearing and cleaning the evacuated buildings to ready them for Poles who were impatiently waiting to move in. The belongings and furniture left behind were taken to the Eintracht cooperative for sorting and repair. Now only three thousand Jews were left in the ghetto.

Our warehouse had filled up again and we began another shipment which gave us a chance to meet with Mr. Zwolinski at the freight station. He told us that Jews had fared ill all over Poland. From Lwów, thousands were deported to Belzec and thousands more shot in the nearby Lesiencice forest and in the sanddunes of the Janowska camp. Near Kiev, one hundred thousand Jews were machine-gunned in a place called Babi Yar, and there were no Jews left there. The Polish underground gave more details about the Belzec camp. It was in the eastern part, and almost all Jews were gassed after they were brought in.

That evening in our building we met two young men who had miraculously managed to escape from the deportation train cattle cars by tearing holes in the wooden floors and jumping out when the train slowed down. Their parents had urged them to make this last desperate bid to survive, to tell the world and to avenge them. Many others were killed as they jumped but even those who landed safely had to face the risk of stealing back to Rzeszów through the hostile Polish environment. Now they had only one purpose left in life, to survive and to take revenge. A few days later more Jews were brought in from Jasło, Krosno, Rymanow, Sanok and from as far away as Nowy Sacz, all of them south of Rzeszów. They were happy when the Germans made them get off the train at Rzeszów, for they had feared that they were on the way to Belzec where they knew gas chambers were waiting for victims. Now they hoped for another miracle to see them through the war.

At the station Mr. Zwolinski told us that since July 22, 1942, at least six thousand Jews were being sent daily from the Warsaw ghetto to nearby Treblinka, where an extermination camp had been set up. The next day, on July 23, the Warsaw *Judenrat* President Czerniakow committed suicide when he was ordered to provide ten thousand Jews a day, and the Germans took to trickery to fill their quotas of victims. Through the Jewish police they made all kinds of promises for a better future for those who would report for work in the country, and some starving, desperate Jews voluntarily reported for deportation merely to benefit from the promise of bread and marmalade. What was most amazing was the fact that the Jewish police was completely in charge of the deportations. They delivered those selected to the SS killers waiting at the train station. The water and electricity supply to the ghetto was cut off. Many committed suicide to escape the fate that was awaiting them in this extermination camp.

Mr. Zwolinski also told us that for the first time armed Polish partisans had started operating against the Germans in the forests and mountains, mostly made up of former members of the anti-Semitic Endek Party. They called themselves *Armia Krajowa,* the Home Army. Mr. Zwolinski, who was a socialist himself, had opposed the Endeks since before the war. He was ashamed to tell us that some Jews who had escaped and wanted to join them in the common cause against the Nazis were killed by them. They still hated Jews as much as the Germans, unable to overcome their innate prejudice even in Poland's present desperate situation. We were dismayed for it meant that we could not hope for salvation from the partisans. Another lifeline was blocked.

In the ghetto I was sad to see the vegetable patches the optimistic young people had planted a few months ago. Their vegetables were ripening now, but they were gone and would not enjoy the fruit of their labor. They had planned months ahead but for us a few days, or even a few hours, was now too far for planning; fate was moving in on us at a dizzy rate. God had long since abandoned us, now even time was against us.

The Gestapo frequently called on Kahane in the *Judenrat* with demands for more money, valuables and luxuries, always to be delivered within twenty-four hours. They kept him and Eintracht busy ordering and cajoling those of the rich who were left to supply the required goods and cash.

Somehow the demands were met, a high price for another day of being left alive in the ghetto. Meanwhile at work, a new rumor started making the rounds concerning an upcoming action against young women. According to one version, the Germans wanted them to work on farms in Germany, but another held they wanted girls for their field brothels. We had learned early on that the worst rumors were more likely to be realized, so we feared the second version, and thought immediately of the danger to our sister Fela. All four of us agreed that her only chance was to hide out with the Zwolinskis for a few days. We felt sure that this wonderful human being would do it for us. That evening, on our way back to the ghetto, we lingered until Fela's group arrived from their work.

While Szymon and Nathan looked out for the Germans, I walked alongside her. I explained the situation to her and stressed that it was imperative she leave at once. I gave her Mr. Zwolinski's address, and after hesitating only a moment, she agreed. I advised her to take off her white armband, fall behind, and hide in the nearest corner until the column would be gone. Szymon and Nathan nodded that the coast was clear and we left her. We were deeply worried but felt that with her Aryan looks she had a fighting chance. When we reached home we immediately told Mother. She was stunned, but when she got over her shock agreed that we had acted for the best. To evade informers we decided to keep Fela's flight a close secret. We spent another sleepless night, and next morning took our pushcarts to the railroad station to look for Mr. Zwolinski. I spotted him and sidled up to him, making sure not to attract attention. When he finally looked up and noticed me I could see from his face that Fela had made it. He assured me that they would look after her, and treat her as though she were their own daughter, whatever it would take. On our return to the warehouse we quickly told Father and his care-worn face lit up.

Mueller obtained passes for us from the district Gestapo chief, Hans Mack, to collect scrap in some large local factories in the Rzeszów district and also in the nearby military camps. At our first stop, the Huta Stalowa Wola iron works which, before the war had been part of the Central Industrial Region and was now called the Hermann Goering Werke, we saw many Jews at work. They were dragging themselves around, in very poor physical shape, more like skeletons than men. Our hearts bled for them. Mueller was very satisfied with our harvest and told us to go next to the former Polskie Zaklady Lotnicze aircraft factories, renamed now the Daimler Benz and Heinkel works, in the outskirts of Rzeszów. After a few days we had filled our scrapyard up again and started deliveries to the railroad. There Mr. Zwolinski told us that Fela was already looking better. His wife had given her some dresses and nightgowns, and she was a great help to Mrs. Zwolinska. We promised to smuggle some of her clothes to him.

When we returned to the ghetto that evening, August 7, 1942, we were met by the terrible news we had feared. During the day the SS had come again and this time ordered the

Jewish police to round up all the younger women and children for a special registration. When they had all lined up outside the labor department they were surrounded by the SS. Then the trucks drove in and they were ordered to get in. Panic broke out and young mothers threw caution to the wind and started fighting for their children, setting on the SS men with their bare hands, while the children, frightened out of their wits, started screaming. Of course it was all to no avail. A few shots where fired and soon all had been pushed into the trucks which drove off at once. The whole thing had happened so fast that the men in the nearby Eintracht cooperative had not been aware that their wives and children were being taken away. But soon someone told them and they all stopped working. They might be accused of sabotage and shot, but they no longer cared. Desperately they rushed out to their homes and when the empty rooms confirmed the rumors they went berserk, and heartbreaking wailing arose. When we reached our room we were profoundly relieved to find Mother safe at home and Father held her in a close embrace for many, many minutes. Later, as more men returned from work and found their women and children missing, and were told that the Jewish police had taken part in the roundup, a last desperate protest was staged. They gathered outside the *Judenrat* and demanded that the policemen be delivered to them. But very soon SS trucks arrived, apparently called in by the *Judenrat,* and the men were dispersed helterskelter, to face the anguish of their empty homes and the memories their wives and children had left behind.

We all felt totally betrayed. While we were away working for the Germans, other Germans had come to take our women and children, more than a thousand of them, aided by our own Jewish police. The taciturn heavens had collapsed on us. Next morning, as we marched off to work, the men were still not resigned to their wives and children being gone. They kept looking back at the windows to see whether, against all odds, their dear ones might yet appear to wave to them, as they used to do every morning. But the windows remained empty, as empty as our hearts and our lives. For many among us life had indeed ceased yesterday. We promised the bereaved men that we would get to the railroad station somehow to find out where the women and children had been taken. But we drew a blank, no women had been brought there, and no trains had come to take them away. Their fate was a mystery. It was days later before Mr. Zwolinski established from his underground sources that the SS trucks had taken them directly to the Pelkinia SS camp near Jarosław, where they had been shot on arrival. We had known that Pelkinia was a Russian POW camp where almost all the Russians had died of hunger, cold and disease. It was now an auxiliary extermination camp. It was terrible for us that evening to report what we had found out, extinguishing the bereaved men's last hope. Some collapsed on hearing the news.

And still more Jews were being brought to our ghetto, the remnants of the Jews from the neighboring localities. In some places the SS had not bothered to deport them, but made them dig their own graves in nearby fields and strip naked to be shot. The Jewish burial parties were themselves shot after finishing their work. The Poles who lived nearby were allowed to keep the victims' clothing, after it was checked for valuables.

We had by now picked our scrap sources dry. Mueller was restless and we feared losing our jobs which were our life insurance. Soon Mueller got orders from Cracow to ship off all the scrap we had collected and start liquidating the Rzeszów branch. The constant loading work did open another avenue for us. We now had to make frequent trips to the station. This gave us an opportunity to try to get our jobs with the *Ostbahn* back again. I went to see the German supervisor and asked him to take the three of us on, and if possible Father too. He told us there was a freeze on Jewish workers, but since he remembered how well we had worked, he would talk to his chief all the same. The next day he told us he could hire the three of us, but not Father. Once again even the best news was spoiled by a new blow. We could not hold back our tears for Father would be in a tight spot. We knew that older Jews could no longer get outside jobs. Even in the ghetto many younger men, most of whom had been brought in since the great deportation, were unemployed as well. Only a few of the able-bodied were taken on to clean out the abandoned buildings.

Mr. Zwolinski tried to cheer us with good news from Fela. She had settled into their home and was doing well. We proposed he write to Mr. Lopatowski in Cracow, who also had good underground connections, to obtain forged papers to make her "legal." A few days later, after we had loaded our last scrap, the Ravo company in Rzeszów was closed and we had to turn in our passes to Pfeifer's office. However, the request from the *Ostbahn* for our services was approved and we went to work again the very next day. I got back my old job in the pit and Nathan and Szymon were put to work loading coal on the tenders of the trains.

Mother and Father were downcast. Another rumor about a new wave of deportations throughout the General Government, did nothing to dispel our gloom. In addition, the German armies were still victorious. They had almost reached the Ural mountains deep inside Russia, and were pushing the British back into Egypt. Mr. Zwolinski told us they were closing in on Stalingrad, and their Luftwaffe was systematically destroying that strategically vital industrial city.

Some time later, on a Monday morning, Mr. Zwolinski beamed at us when we came to work, telling us that Mr. Lopatowski had personally visited them the day before, bringing a birth certificate and other necessary papers for Fela. She was now Felicia Zwolinska, their niece, born in a village that had been destroyed by the advancing Germans in September 1939, and no records were left there that could be checked. When we told our parents that evening, we saw their faces light up for the first time in many long days. But this encouraging interlude, like those before it, did not last long, as though to emphasize that good luck was not for Jews anymore. The Gestapo came to the ghetto, picked up Kahane and the chief of the Jewish police, Garelik, and took both of them away. They returned late in the afternoon but neither of them would say what the reason for their absence had been, either because they had been warned not to, or were afraid. But we knew it could bode no good. The rich Jews started building bunkers and some of the young women who were left, risked their lives to go over the fence to the Polish side. The next day the Gestapo returned and imposed a levy of a million zlotys on the ghetto. They gave Kahane twenty-four hours to collect them, their price they told him, for leaving us in peace in the future. It was a huge sum now that most of the richer Jews were no longer with us. But the promise was so immense that everybody scraped their resources and somehow the sum was raised. What a relief when we saw the Gestapo leave with bulging briefcases. The tension gradually relaxed until, during the night between the 14th and 15th of September, 1942, we were awakened by Jewish policemen who told us that the Germans were encircling the ghetto once again.

We sensed that the moment we had feared had arrived. Our parents no longer enjoyed the protection of having three sons working in preferred jobs. Ironically it was they who tried to calm us: We were working for the *Ostbahn,* important jobs, and as a final resort we could surely trust God to show His hand at last. But Mother was also practical, and once again started packing rucksacks with food for each of us, putting in a few pieces of winter clothing. Everybody resigned themselves for the worst and next morning, before the day had dawned, the Jewish police came to order everybody out, with twenty-five kilograms of belongings and all our valuables. Anybody found hiding inside would be shot. We left our apartment together and walked to the assembly square. There was dead silence. Even the few children who were left suppressed their crying; their mothers had promised them candy if they would keep quiet. The square was surrounded by SS men and their Ukrainians had rifles at the ready. When everybody had arrived we were ordered to lie down on the ground, which was covered with dust that had turned into sticky mud by the damp of the night. We were all instantly dirty. It was the least of our troubles. The SS men were shouting and kicking with their heavy boots at anybody who raised their heads, until they ordered everyone to get up and produce our documents and valuables. The three of us stood in a line in front of Mother and Father, a futile shield. Again the long selection table we knew and feared, again everybody trying to wipe off the dirt to make themselves more presentable, and again the bated breath as the selection began.

The lines began moving and our hearts sank when we saw that the Germans were not even looking at the documents of the older people. This meant that our parents had no chance. Our turn came. I presented my papers first and after a short examination the German judges of life and death motioned me to join the group who were allowed to stay. They never uttered a word. Soon Szymon and Nathan joined me, and we watched fearfully as Father approached the table. The official simply tore up his papers, and then Mother's. Our world stood still as we saw them moving resignedly to the other side. As though we had planned it, the three of us rushed forward regardless of the risk to embrace our parents, and swore that come what may we would stay by their side. But they would not hear of it. They had lived their lives, they told us calmly, and all that still mattered to them was the thought that the four of us were safe. An SS man ran over to us and we had to make an instant decision. It was not really a decision, for our parents' looks made it an imperative. We moved back to the survivors, but not before the SS man managed to get in a few blows with his rifle butt.

We were totally devastated. What good now was our healthy physique, three tall, strong young men in our prime, paralyzed by fear and unable to lift a finger to save our parents. Soon awareness returned and we heard the familiar screams, the firing in the air, and the tramp of shoes as the condemned marched off four abreast, to certain death. As they marched past they waved a brave goodbye and both Mother and Father lifted their hands to signal the traditional blessing of parents on their children. We blew them kisses and called their names. It was the last time we saw them.

We were ordered to go back to our homes, and again we saw bodies lying about. We had not heard the shooting by killers searching out those who had dared to hide from the Germans. We had been so totally immersed in the anguish of our parents' departure. There was nobody left to greet us in our room and we fell on our beds facedown in order not to have to look at each other, and our bodies shook with sobs we made no attempt to hide. Yes, we were men, but there were some things even men could not accept dry-eyed. Some neighbors came to console us, many of whom had themselves been through similar experiences during the past few months, but we waved them away, not wanting to talk, or even to see anybody. Eventually we fell into fitful sleep only to relive the nightmare. Next morning, tired and dejected, we went back to work; absence would not be excused. It struck me that now I was the head of the family and dutybound to be the younger brothers' guide. I wondered what I should have Mr. Zwolinski say to Fela. I did not have to wonder, my face told the story, and he cried with me. I told him how we had tried to go with our parents and he assured me that we had made the right decision. We were young and strong and might yet survive and get revenge. He offered us some bread and hot food but we could not eat. Over and over I relived yesterday's events in my mind, examining every detail to see whether we had done wrong. How could we have let our parents go away alone? Was it numbness, exhaustion brought about by the continuous blows we had suffered these past two years, or was it our Jewish training of submitting to authority? Somehow we got through work without doing anything wrong and returned home for another disturbing night of fitful, dream-haunted sleep. The next morning before work started, Mr. Zwolinski whispered to us that Fela was fine, but he could say no more with the other men standing around. During our break he told us that when he had broken the news to her about our parents she nearly fainted and then cried long and hard. He also gave her our letters. When she recovered sufficient to talk, she maintained we should not have abandoned our parents. Mr. Zwolinski explained to her that no one could have saved them. Finally she wrote a letter which he had brought for us. When I opened it I saw the ink was blotted by tears, but Fela assured us that she had accepted and approved of what we had done, and regretted only that she had not been there to kiss Mother and Father for one last time. Later I showed the letter to Szymon and Nathan and then destroyed it. When I had a chance to think it over coolly I came to the conclusion that it was better that Fela had not been with us. At least she had been spared the agony of seeing them standing together, holding hands, helpless against the hostile world, and then waving bravely to us as they walked away. Now we had to try even harder to survive and to avenge their deaths. A few days later Polish train engineers informed Mr. Zwolinski that the September 15 deportation train had arrived in Belzec the morning after. We knew that they were dead.

In our building the Horns and the Guttman brothers were still there, but of the Wiesenfelds and Kranzes who had worked with us for Ravo, only Kuba was left. Our work kept us busy and we put in long hours since the traffic was heavy with many trains going east filled with men and equipment.

We hoped that the Russians were waiting for them and if they could not wipe them out, that the winter soon would.

More Jews were brought into our ghetto, many of them from the areas near the Slovakian border. I asked them why they had not fled to Slovakia but they told us that those who succeeded to cross over the border were deported in 1942 back to Poland together with thousands of Slovakian Jews. We became very friendly with Chaim Moshe Halberstam and were able to bring him some food and old German newspapers which the Polish workers had picked up while cleaning the trains. The Halberstams, who came from Rzeszów where Chaim was born, belonged to one of the oldest rabbinical families in eastern Europe. Chaim had emigrated to the U.S.A. many years earlier and had served as a rabbi in Brooklyn, New York. He had returned to Poland in April 1939 to visit his parents and family and was caught by the war. The Gestapo did not honor his American passport, nor that of other Jews, and most of them were sent to Belzec.

There were some tailors and shoemakers among the new arrivals and they were put to work in the Eintracht cooperative. They smuggled out clothing and bedding to us, that we in turn smuggled out of the ghetto in exchange for food that we shared with them. It was a good arrangement for everyone. Sometimes we even had cake that Fela baked brought to the station by Mr. Zwolinski. He always refused the gifts we offered him, because he thought that was how a human being should act. He was a noble being in a world of brutes. One day he told me about the Russian general, Vlasow, who had surrendered in 1941 to the Germans along with hundreds of thousands of men. The Germans needed all the help they could get and accepted them into their forces. He kept his rank of general. He raised an army of Russian traitors for the Germans and even had planes drop leaflets behind the Russian lines with a call to the soldiers to desert their Bolshevik masters and join him on the German side. He also urged the civilian population to aid their German "liberators."

For as long as he could, Mr. Zwolinski told me only the good news—Hitler's fortunes were gradually reversing, and German advances in Russia had been almost completely halted. German cities were being intensively bombed. Rommel and his Afrika Korps had lost the initiative and were being chased back by the British, while tens of thousands of his Italian soldiers were surrendering. But finally Mr. Zwolinski came out with the bad news from Poland itself—tens of thousands of Jews from the big city ghettos had been deported, or murdered on the spot in massacres perpetrated in Warsaw, Cracow, Bochnia, Tarnów, and Wieliczka. The lethal net was closing around us. Our future was being wiped out in the streets of the ghettos, in the mass graves in the forests, and in the most devilish of all German inventions, the extermination camps.

With fall came the cold and rain and our clothes were worn out. When we begged the Eintracht cooperative foremen for winter clothing they turned us away. "Without money, no honey," they told us. They were handling mountains of clothing that had been left by the thousands who had been deported, and they could have given us some without risk to themselves. But they wanted money and our wages were a mere 5 zlotys a day, if we were paid at all. I personally had another problem. Being unusually tall for a Jew, it was hard for me to find shoes to fit me. I could manage with smaller-sized clothing, but the shoes had to fit. It hurt to see that so soon after they had witnessed the misery of deportation, and had themselves been saved only by luck, their hearts had turned to stone against their own brethren.

We befriended some of the young men from the Eintracht concern who had been moved into our building, but they were not able to smuggle out anything but some small pieces of clothing that they hid under their clothes. In the long evenings they sometimes recounted their experiences. A few of them had miraculously escaped from the Pustkow SS camp near Dębica where they had been taken, together with other young men from the Mogilska Armory in Cracow in the fall of 1940. They had been forced to work from dawn until late in the evening, seven days a week, in all kinds of weather. Their food consisted of an undefined liquid that was called coffee and some bread that tasted like sawdust in the morning; and in the evening a so-called soup made of potato peels and turnips, with another piece of "sawdust" bread.

Any "offense" was immediately punished by the foremen, who were Jewish or Polish, with cruel beatings. The camp guards were Ukrainians, whose major qualification for the job was their bestiality. They shot anyone too weak or sick to work, as well as anyone found in the barracks during working hours. They slept on damp straw mattresses in wooden bunks that were overrun by bugs and lice that fed on their emaciated bodies and spread disease. The barracks had no windows and the roofs leaked so that they were exposed to permanent damp, nor did their thin blankets keep out the winter cold. New men brought into the camp were searched and warned to surrender all valuables on pain of death for themselves and their relatives. Many were indeed shot, and the younger men had to bury them in a nearby forest. What they had gone through defied human imagination. Now we had to face the possibility that we might end up in camps like that ourselves.

Meanwhile our ghetto was again bursting at the seams as more refugees were brought in from the localities that had been made *Judenrein,* free of Jews. Many had lice and the fear of epidemics again became a reality. In November another order was posted on the walls ordering all unemployed and those working inside the ghetto to register the next morning. The outside workers were to register on the two following days. As always, the poster produced wild rumors. When it was our turn to register we saw that separate lines had been arranged for workers from the different workplaces, and for different professions and skills. We did not know the purpose for the segregation and it worried us.

The registration ended but the constant uncertainty made people selfish and secretive, looking out only for their own interests, unwilling to share the bunkers they were digging, or plans for escape to the Polish side. Some parents even abandoned their own children at the selections, a decision no human should be forced to make. I refused to judge, much less condemn them.

We were preparing to go to work in the morning, when the Jewish police swarmed into the buildings and ordered everybody out immediately with twenty-five kilograms of belongings and enough food for two days. They took us by surprise. The ghetto had already been surrounded by the SS guards and there was no time to flee. The weather was miserably wet and cold. Mothers brought their children to the assembly square, wrapped in blankets and quilts. The SS and

Ukrainians were already at work with their trigger-happy guns and snarling dogs. They were well dressed against the cold rain, as were Pfeifer and the other officials who had come for the selection. There was the usual examination of documents and the check against prepared lists, culminating in each of us being motioned to go one way or the other. I noticed that those selected to stay were ordered to the so-called *Appellplatz* (assembly ground). But I also saw that many people from the outside working groups were being ordered to the dreaded collecting place, the *Sammelplatz*. Their strength and skills had been used up and now they were being thrown away like squeezed-out lemons. When the turn of the *Ostbahn* workers came, we were all sent to the *Appellplatz*. We watched many *Judenrat* and police officials who had been marked for deportation pleading with Pfeifer and his henchmen, but to no avail. Their word was law and brooked no appeal. These Jewish officials, who had begun to feel they would be not touched, were particularly hard hit by a blow they had not expected. Their incredulous faces turned white as chalk. And the whole accursed action was played out against the background of riflefire and barking dogs as those who tried to hide were discovered. The nightmare of the condemned, including Eintracht workers who had in the past refused us warm clothing in order to better serve the Germans, marched off to their doom and the gate closed behind them leaving the usual baskets of valuables on a truck. I forgave them—foolish people who had tried to save themselves—they had not understood that the Germans made no distinction between Jews. All were eventually to be wiped out. I realized that some of our SS guards were speaking neither German nor Ukrainian. They were Estonian, Latvian and Lithuanian volunteers who were now a new breed of murderers in the Germans' extermination squads.

When the gate closed we were immediately sent back to our homes, but the hunt continued for those who attempted to hide. For the first time I personally witnessed how the SS murderers lined up men, women and children against a wall and gunned them down. The most horrifying sight was the way they took infants by their feet and smashed their heads against a wall in front of their parents, who were then themselves shot dead. Finally the killers ripped watches and jewelery from the still warm corpses and pocketed them.

The falling rain washed away the blood, while Oszerowicz and his men removed the corpses. All that night the scenes I had witnessed kept repeating themselves in my mind's eye, and I wondered how long it would be before we too would have to tread the same path. The next morning, the few of us who were left went out of the ghetto to our jobs. Mr. Zwolinski was there, but I kept away from him, not wanting to compromise him further. He had taken a big risk taking in Fela. Only much later, when we had a chance to be alone, did I give him our letters with the details of the previous day's events. He had known in general terms about the new deportation but not about the cruelties which he pledged he would report in full to the underground, against the day when they might be able to make their reckoning with the Germans. The underground would also tell the world, Mr. Zwolinski promised. We got many inquiries from Poles who asked about their Jewish friends. I was touched by their concern until I was told that they were only anxious about the valuables they held in safe-keeping for their Jewish friends which they need not return if their owners were dead. I told them I did not know and had no way to find out. The least I could do was not encourage the vultures.

The cold gave us a good excuse to wear several layers of clothing without raising suspicion, and we were able to trade some of the clothes for food, soap and medicine, all of which were in short supply or nonexistent in the ghetto.

Mr. Zwolinski's mood seemed to turn more optimistic and he told me that reports of German defeats were coming in from all over. The snow and bitter cold had helped the Russians to stop the German advances and they were counterattacking, inflicting tremendous losses. Stalingrad was developing into a graveyard for the Nazis and in Cyrenaica, Rommel was on the run since the Americans had landed in North Africa. But there was no good news for Jews. Massacres were being committed throughout Poland. The SS and police chief in the General Government, General Krueger, announced that only five ghettos would be left in the Cracow district: Cracow, Bochnia, Przemyśl, Rzeszów and Tarnów. All others would be eliminated to make their locations Judenrein. For the first time the name "ghetto" was used in an official announcement. Until now they had still tried to disguise them as euphemistic *Juedische Wohnbezirke,* (Jewish residential sections). Evidently they no longer found it necessary to try to mislead the world. The world already knew about the ghettos, the deportations, the mass shootings and the extermination camps built all over Poland, but did nothing. We were abandoned by God and the world. We could only selfishly console ourselves that Krueger was letting our ghetto stand.

One evening on returning home, Mr. Horn told us that a German commandant had been appointed for our ghetto. During the day and had gone to see Pfeifer, and Beno Kahane, the *Judenrat* president. Of what new tragedy was *he* the harbinger, we wondered. Immediately our Jewish philosophers, and that meant all of us, started speculating what new plans the SS would have for us. The next morning, when we assembled on the *Appellplatz,* we found a new, tall SS officer already there. I noticed that he held a senior rank of Hauptscharfuehrer. He was gray haired, tall and slim, about fifty-five years of age. His eyes were blue steel, cold and cruel, as though such eyes were standard SS issue for its killers. He just stood there, not saying a word, only observing. We stood in the bitter cold and shivered, but not only from the biting frost, but the thoughts we entertained about what this new persecutor had in mind for us. We also feared there would be exacting body searches this morning, and that would land many of us in trouble since we were carrying concealed goods to trade for food. Luckily nothing untoward happened and we were marched off to our workplaces as usual. At the *Ostbahn* we handed the goods to our Polish contacts but told them that for the time being we would suspend our smuggling until we could read the Hauptscharfuehrer's mind. Instead we made appointments to meet them later in the evening, at specific places along the ghetto fence, for over-the-fence deals. It would be safer, provided we were careful.

6

Rzeszów, 1942–1943
The Division of the Ghetto

When we returned home the commandant was not in evidence but something new had occurred. Ten-foot-high barbed-wire fences had been put in the middle of the ghetto on Baldachowska Street, and there were more bales of barbed wire lying nearby. The ghetto was being divided into two separate parts, A and B, the eastern and western sections respectively. This was the first order the commandant had issued. He had in fact been in such a hurry that he had given it orally, even before he had taken the time to put it in writing.

All unemployed men, and the wives and children of working men, would be concentrated in B section. All working women had to move into an isolated building in A section which was fenced off and put under guard to prevent visits. The *Judenrat* had to make arrangements for moving people between the two sections, and though we would remain where we were, all beds were to be removed to be replaced by bunks the Eintracht carpenters were ordered to build.

The commandant decided to set up headquarters for himself in the ghetto, and chose a small but modern building, in the center of A section, which belonged to the Zucker family. The tenants were unceremoniously thrown out to make room for him, and their furniture was confiscated.

Though we were prepared to face almost any new adversity, this latest order caused great confusion and dismay. Our philosophers, who always had a lot to say, were quiet this evening, as bewildered as everybody else. From the windows we could see people moving their belongings to their new homes, on carts or on their backs.

This was our second division, first we had been separated from the Aryan world in December 1941, and now our own little world was itself partitioned. The dividing line was clear. Those who were still of use to the SS and those who were not. We carried our beds down to the pavement where they were picked up by the removal squad who provided straw sacks until the bunks would be ready. We consoled ourselves that at least we had saved Fela from the troubles the new commandant brought with him.

The next morning he was on the assembly ground, accompanied by Pfeifer, Kahane, Garelik and some other officials. He introduced himself as Hauptscharfuehrer Bacher, and announced that the ghetto was now *Zwangsarbeitslager Reishof*—Forced Labor Camp Reishof. This was the first morning rollcall and there would be rollcalls every day from now on, mornings and evenings. He warned that he would permit no excuse for shirking, demanded maximum work performance, and total unquestioning obedience to his orders. Those who were working would get food rations but the "Jewish parasites" in B section would not. He would tolerate neither laziness at work nor dirt in our homes, and would enforce both by personal inspections.

He then motioned to a Jewish police officer to take over. The officer unfolded a long list from which he called the names of the groups and the individual workers in each of them, checking them off as each of us confirmed our presence. We stood there for quite a while in the bitter cold, when at last we were given the order to march off to work with our guards. When we returned in the evening the rest of the barbed-wire fences had been put up and a new gate installed, with a guard booth on either side of it, manned by Jewish policemen. Movement between the two sections was allowed only by special pass, only close relatives would be allowed to apply for them, and only on the days they were off from work. The passes would be issued by the *Judenrat,* the Jewish police and the labor department. I mused bitterly that this would provide them a new opportunity to extort bribes.

The bunks were put into our room, three high, to squeeze more Jews into less space. The Guttmans and Leon Horn were still with us. Leon's brother, Herschel, was assigned to the PZL works on the outskirts of the city, where a large group of skilled mechanics were working, accommodated in barracks adjoining the factory that were guarded by Ukrainians.

We took the morning rollcall in our stride, because everybody reported at the same time. It was soon over and thus tolerable. But in the evenings, when we returned home exhausted from a long day of hard work, we sometimes had to wait in the bone-chilling wet and cold until the last group returned. Fortunately the men from the house-clearing unit who were billeted in our room were able to bring us some warm clothing and high-top shoes, and in exchange we brought them all the food and coal we could smuggle in. I struck up a friendship with one of the cooks in the community kitchen, Mrs. Kleinmuntz, a fine lady whose son Benek was working with us. She always ladled our soup from the bottom of the cauldron where it was thickest, and saved some remnants that we could pass to the poor children waiting at the fence.

Bacher proved himself a zealous taskmaster. We were told that during the day he made innumerable inspections in both sections, turning up suddenly, and almost paralyzing the people with his cold stare and death-head insignia, which looked remarkably alike. His presence was especially hard on the rich who had bought their way out of their duties by bribing the *Judenrat* and police officials. Now they had to work like everybody else. But our officials were licking Bacher's boots, hoping for his favors. In fact he took over all authority and reduced Kahane to the function of a clerk. Bacher was constantly accompanied by a very young Jewish policeman by the name of Icek who was not a local man. Nobody knew where he had come from. At rollcalls he stood next to Bacher and instituted body searches. While Bacher looked on, he often discovered some pathetic pieces of contraband, whereupon he would order the culprit to drop his pants, and he flogged the poor man with the riding whip he always carried, twenty-five to seventy-five lashes on the bare behind. Bacher appeared to draw sadistic satisfaction from the sight of one Jew beating another. He was very rough, and besides his curt orders the only words we heard from him were curses. If anyone had entertained hopes of bribing him to alleviate our distress, his behavior quickly put a stop to them. We cursed him back silently and in private.

Food was issued from a community kitchen and when our Polish contacts could not, for some reason, throw any food over the fence for us, we took the hot meals. They had improved now that the cooks no longer dared skim off produce for sale. Bacher was likely at any time to spring an inspection, appearing suddenly like a jack-in-the-box. Nevertheless, some policemen still sold part of our rations to the starving Jews in the western part of the ghetto if they could pay the astronomical sums they charged for them. We could see starving children begging for food, and when they came near enough to the fence, we would throw them whatever we had, while the men of the house-clearing unit brought them warm clothes and blankets whenever they were able to.

The German Jews disappointed us. Because Bacher could converse with them with ease, he appointed some of them as foremen and they did their job with German thoroughness, threatening to report any shirkers to him. This was no empty threat. It could easily cost one's life. But those we hated most were the Jewish policemen, living well on their bribes while so many of us were starving. Everybody despised Icek. Short and skinny, he followed the tall Bacher about and we called him dog, both for his behavior, and because he was always fussing about Bacher like a lapdog.

Heavy snowstorms created a snow emergency in Rzeszów and Bacher mobilized men from the B section for snow clearing. Though the work was hard, and the men were inadequately dressed for it, it did at least give them a chance to buy some food from the Poles.

Once in a while new transports arrived and Bacher immediately ordered the newcomers into the western section, which was soon so crowded that two families had to share a single room. Bacher ordered a registration in that section, creating an instant panic, but it was intended only to find skilled workers for Pfeifer. The few who were found were transferred into our section, overjoyed at their new lease on life. There was a man in the B section called Serog, who rose to the situation like a true humanitarian. He convinced Kahane that we were all dutybound to look after the less fortunate in the B section who were facing starvation. Kahane organized a small kitchen from which meals were surreptitiously put across the fence in the evening after Bacher had retired to his well-heated house.

The winter of 1942–1943 was severe and we all suffered from the cold, but the news that the frost was killing off Germans by the thousands in Russia warmed our hearts. The Russians were attacking them on all fronts, Mr. Zwolinski told me, and Stalingrad was becoming a symbol of the Nazis' vincibility. Alas, it was too far away and too late for us. Only the German cattle cars with red crosses on them comforted us. We gloried as the dead, the wounded, and the frozen were taken off, and I was happy to clean the engines quickly so that they might go back for more. I enjoyed the sight but realized that we ourselves were living on borrowed time and it was running out. I entreated Mr. Zwolinski to help us get away and join the *Armia Ludowa* (People's Army), partisans we had heard about, who were not anti-Semitic. He promised to do his best and would write to Mr. Lopatowski in Cracow to enlist his help. We prayed for a miracle and though there were no rumors of new actions, knew they might erupt at any moment. When an epidemic was reported from the western section a general panic broke out. Dr. Heller and his assistants did everything they could and even enlisted our help to obtain some vaccines and disinfectants from our Polish contacts. We trembled that Bacher would hear of the epidemic, or be told by informers. That would be the end for all of us. We kept our room squeaky clean and on Sundays took out the bunks and scrubbed them with hot water.

Whenever Bacher, on his frequent inspections, came across Hebrew prayerbooks, Bibles, volumes of the Talmud, or other religious requisites, he ordered them destroyed. Though we were secular, we did not want our holy books profaned by our enemies. So, together with Chaim Moshe Halberstam and Leon, we collected prayer shawls, phylacteries and holy books from the surviving religious Jews, and buried them late one evening. We knew the religious always buried worn-out holy books because it was considered wrong to destroy them, and felt we were committing no sin by stretching a point and burying the items while they were still usable. It was better than to have them fall into the hands of the Germans. There could be no worse profanation. But even without their holy books the religious went on praying. They knew the prayers by heart, and also observed the holy days as best they could, hoping and trusting for a divine miracle. I could not blame them. Though they seemed to me to be betting against the odds, their faith did keep them going and prevented them from putting an end to their desperate lives, a mortal sin for Jews.

One evening when we returned from work and were lining up for the rollcall, we noticed that the ice-cold Bacher appeared uncharacteristically edgy. He kept slapping his boots with his riding crop and screaming at Garelik and his deputy, Markuzy. Obviously something was wrong, but we could not find out what it was. Finally, when the last of the workers returned and the rollcall confirmed that all were present, Bacher gave us a speech. He told us that six members of the Jewish police had disobeyed his orders. They had been lenient with workers who had broken his rules, and as an example he had decided to dismiss them and send them to the B section as unemployed.

He called their names, and when they hangdoggedly lined up in front of him, he took away their badges, armbands, and caps, and had them taken straight to the B section. Then he strode through the ranks of the assembled workers and inspected each of us closely for replacements. One, two, three, four, five, and then to my horror, he stopped in front of me and motioned me to step forward. I knew better than to deny him, or even let him see my objection. As much as I hated the policemen, I understood that their position between the hammer and the anvil, was hardly an enviable one. And now I was to become one of them, perish the thought! Garelik ordered the six of us to report to him for duty at eight the next morning. Meanwhile he handed to us the caps Bacher had taken from the dismissed men. When I reached home I was so upset that I could not eat, or even talk. After agonizing about my ill luck for a while I made up my mind. I went to Garelik's office and appealed to him to pick somebody else in my place. Polite as always, Garelik quietly told me that as Bacher himself had picked me there was not a thing he could do. All night I tossed and turned in my tight bunk unable to reconcile myself to the disgrace I would bring on myself and my brothers. At last I got an idea. I got up early and went straight to the gate to wait for our German guard who came every morning to pick us up for the *Ostbahn* group. He knew us very well, and when he arrived I took him aside, told him of the disaster that had befallen me, and begged him to ask Bacher to release me on the grounds that my specialized work in the engine pit was essential for the *Ostbahn*. He promised to try. As soon as Bacher turned up he walked over to him and saluted. I watched, tense and nervous, as they talked. Then I heard my name called and saw our guard motioning to me. I ran up and stood stiffly at attention in front of Bacher. He asked me whether I preferred to continue my work with the *Ostbahn*. I confirmed that I did as nonchalantly as I could, in order not to spoil this last chance, because I knew he would refuse if he thought I was eager. He curtly told me to return to the *Ostbahn* group. I could hardly believe my luck, because there had never been any indication of consideration for Jews by the icy Bacher. So before he could change his mind I took off my police cap, threw it to the group of policemen and, on the double, rejoined my workmates for the rollcall. When we marched off I thanked our guard. All my mates congratulated me. Nobody liked the Jewish police and everyone despised their caps, their badges, their armbands and their nightsticks. I had a good day. By the time we returned in the evening the news of my audacious appeal to the unapproachable Bacher had spread and a stream of well-wishers came to express their admiration. They told me that the policemen had been stunned by my action, but now they knew unmistakably just what we thought of their job.

A few mornings later, when we were marching off after the rollcall, we were ordered to halt. Little Icek came running up, called our roommate Sender out of the ranks and ordered him to drop his pants. He was wearing two pairs and Icek had noticed. Brandishing his whip with obvious relish he slowly gave the poor boy seventy-five vicious lashes while Bacher watched with a smile on his icy face. In fact almost all of us were wearing extra clothes to barter for food. It was the safest way to smuggle. All were sorry for Sender who had been found out by the despised Icek. It could have been any one of us.

Whenever Bacher was away, or holed up in his heated headquarters, many people came out to meet Polish contacts at the fence. Others went to visit the women, or just to meet with each other. But the moment there was the slightest sign of Bacher everyone melted away, disappearing as though dissolved by a magic wand. Sometimes on Sundays Bacher received visits from his friends, most of them SS men and their families. When the weather was good he took them around his two ghettos, but they spent most of the time in the western section where the amusement was greater. Unfortunate Jewish children, women, old and poor, made lovely pictures for their cameras. As a special treat Bacher would take them to his terrace and give them rifles to take potshots at the unsuspecting souls on the other side of the fence. He even let the young boys, all uniformed members of the Hitler *Jugend* (the Nazi youth movement), practice shooting at living targets. Killers, all of them, even the boys. I informed Mr. Zwolinski through our letters to Fela. He then undertook to report it to the underground.

One evening we were told of a new peak in Bacher's cruelty. Two men had been cleaning a sewer near his headquarters, one of them inside the manhole, and the other standing on top to receive the buckets of dirt he passed up. Unfortunately for him, Bacher happened to look out of his window when he was standing still, waiting for the next bucket to come up. Bacher came out, revolver in hand, and ran up to the unsuspecting young man who was paralyzed when he saw the tall black figure with his pointing gun. Bacher shot him on the spot, not allowing him as much as a single second to explain why he had apparently been idling. Then, replacing his smoking gun in its holster, he went back without a word. From then on, whenever anybody had to work in the ghetto his comrades would look out for Bacher's approach.

The weather turned even harsher. We were all freezing and hungry because the driving snow was preventing the peasants from coming to town, and we could not barter food with them. Our hearts bled for the poor souls across the fence who were far worse off then we were, but we could do nothing for them. Our only consolation was that in Russia it was much colder and the Germans there must be freezing just as we were.

Early on the morning of December 15, 1942, as we were walking to the assembly ground for the rollcall, we were stopped by the Jewish police and ordered back home. It was still dark but we had no difficulty making out the chilling sight of a small convoy of SS trucks driving into our section. The police ordered us to return to our rooms, pack and come back immediately. Once more we had been taken by surprise, though by this time nothing should have surprised us. We packed hurriedly, as well as we could, and went down. As we emerged we saw some of the trucks, filled with SS men, driving through the Baldachowska gate into the western section, while their comrades had fanned out in ours. We were all ordered to the collection place which was already surrounded by the SS and their volunteer henchmen from the Ukraine and the Baltic states. With a chill we saw that there was a machine gun, manned by an SS man, on each truck. This was an ominous departure from their usual procedure. We had heard of so many liquidations of ghettos that we were scared almost stiff, but there was nothing we could do but stand in the cold and wait, God alone knew what for. Soon a column of cars drove in bringing high German officials, in their warm winter uniforms, to observe the action that was evidently to be carried out. But the usual selection table was not set up.

Bacher gave some orders to Garelik who commanded everyone to line up in the different working groups, and to drop all our valuables into the baskets his policemen were putting into place. Bacher and Pfeifer gave Garelik some lists which he consulted and then ordered various selected groups to move over to the assembly ground where they were surrounded by SS men. Our group's turn came, and we were ordered to join them. Other groups were left standing on the assembly place, together with some *Judenrat* officials. Bacher and Pfeifer went up to them and made a personal selection, motioning to some of them to go over and join us. Some of the *Judenrat* officials who were left standing there tried to plead, but to no avail. The two killers simply went on to the next group, the labor department clerks. Some of them also tried to talk to Pfeifer, but for him they obviously did not exist anymore. They had served him as long as he needed them, and now that he had no more use for them he discarded them like so many soiled workshirts. We noticed our cousin Franka among those ordered to stay and were sorry for her. Last were the Jewish police and their families. Bacher himself made the selection. He picked out those who had served him most assiduously and allowed them to join us. They included Icek and Markuzy.

I recognized several men among the German officials who had watched the selection: the district governor, Dr. Ehaus; Mayor Pablu; the chief of the Rzeszów Gestapo, Mack, and the heads of his Jewish department, Schuster, Gawron, Gold and Pottenbaum. There were also some senior Nazi party officials I had never seen before, wearing their brown uniforms with swastika armbands, observing and commenting to each other. When it was all over they joined Bacher and Pfeifer and all went to the B section whose inhabitants were already lined up to await their fate. The selection there was very short. An officer picked out a few young men, and Bacher and Schuster picked out a few people who had been unofficial leaders in the section. The selected were brought over to our group. Soon the Nazi bigshots dispersed and the show was over.

We stood and watched in silence as the condemned people in the B section were marched through our section to the exit gate. Many of them were in pitiful rags and hardly able to drag themselves along. They were ordered to surrender all valuables they might possess, a bitter joke for most of the poor wretches. As though to rub the joke in, some body searches were made. As soon as they had gone, those people in our section who had been selected for deportation were commanded to form a column and began to march out. We watched with horrid fascination as they dropped cash, gold coins, watches and pieces of jewelery into the baskets, their final tribute to the German oppressors. Bacher, who stood by the baskets, ordered frequent body searches because the baskets were not filling up fast enough. The men had to take off their coats and jackets and some were ordered to drop their pants for rectal searches. Some of the women were also subjected to personal searches.

One of the SS officers stopped a young woman and ordered her to undress. When she had stripped he poked his whip into her vagina. She spat in his face. He was taken aback and cringed for a moment but then straightened, slowly wiping his cheek, and shot her down. I recognized her. She was the daughter of Mr. Wiesenfeld who had worked in the Ravo company with us. He had been deported, together with the rest of his family, with our own parents. The daughter had been spared at that time because she had been working for the Wehrmacht. Without further ado the SS killers ordered the column to march on, past her lifeless body. We saw Franka and some of our friends who had worked in the home-clearing units, as well as some of the skilled workers from the Eintracht cooperative, marching with the condemned. After they had gone we could still hear some of their anguished cries of *"Shema Yisrael"* ("Hear O Israel," the ultimate prayer). The western section was now Judenrein. Later we have learned that the SS officer who shot Miss Wiesenfeld was Amon Goeth, the commandant of the Plaszow camp.

When Bacher returned he ordered the Jewish police to join his SS men and their dogs to once again search for hidden Jews in the western section, in every nook and cranny, cellar, attic, roof and even in chimneys. He ordered us to stay where we were, freezing in the cold, until the operation would be completed. We stood there witnessing the SS killers shooting everyone they caught, leaving their bodies on the snow. Soon the search parties brought out a small group, apparently several families who had hidden together, lined them up against a wall and shot them one by one. When the first victim fell the others covered their faces and loudly recited their last prayer. Then the SS and their helpers searched their pockets and ordered the Jewish policemen to strip off their clothes for inspection. It was almost dark, and we were frozen stiff before Bacher allowed us to return to our rooms. Now at last we survivors were able to give vent to our emotions after a long day of watching, numbed in body by the cold, and in soul by what we had been forced to watch. Our anguished crying was a strangely fitting ending to a terrifying day. Of the *Judenrat* only a few remained, among them Kahane. Unable to eat anything we had some hot tea and soaked our frozen feet in warm water. The brutal deportation had been aggravated by the despicable behavior of some of the Jewish policemen, who were still seeking to benefit from our common tragedy, taking over vacated apartments and searching for valuables the departed might have left behind.

The ghetto, depleted of so many of its inhabitants, was unnervingly quiet, until we were awakened again by loud noises from the street. From our window we saw columns of Jews being marched to the western ghetto. We were no longer able to make sense of the German actions, shifting people around like chessmen on a board for no apparent reason except for the clear final objective, to sweep all of us away.

In the morning we found out that the newcomers were refugees, about one thousand of them from the ghettos in Krosno, Sanok and Jasto. Next day, Bacher and Pfeifer, accompanied by a few Jewish officials, made a selection for skilled workers. They sought mainly shoemakers and tailors. Only hours ago they had deported many skilled workers to their deaths and now they were looking for new ones. Those selected were brought into our A section and two of them, Altman and Goldberg, who had practiced law in Krosno before the war, were assigned to our room. They had registered as skilled mechanics to evade immediate deportation. Their families had been murdered, but at least they could recite the Kaddish mourning prayer for them. Hundreds of thousands of other Jews had been murdered, with no kin left to say Kaddish.

The western section, the B ghetto, was what we called a "*Schmalz* (animal fat) Ghetto", a melting pot of the condemned, and people would go to any lengths to try to get out of it. The winter may have frozen the German war machine in Russia to a standstill, but it did not halt their murder machine in Poland. The gas chambers and crematoria, the forests and mass graves, were all working at full speed, swallowing up masses of Jews.

We learned that two men from Cracow had been moved into our building, Maciek Fiedler and Mr. Brand. Brand was in his late fifties. I remembered him. He had had a fur shop on Grodzka Street. He had been selected to work in the Eintracht concern, making fur coats for the front. He had lost all his remaining family members in the closing of the Krosno ghetto. Fiedler was a little older than I, and had a twin brother Ludwik. He came from a highly respected Cracow family. His father had been a well-known educator and principal of a high school in the heart of the Jewish section on Miodowa Street. Maciek himself had been a high school teacher. He had escaped from Cracow to Tarnów and then to Krosno, where the Germans caught up with him. He knew Eintracht and was put to work in the Eintracht concern as an upholsterer. Mr. Brand was depressed and said very little, but Maciek, after overcoming his initial distrust, opened up. He told us that his young wife had been deported from Tarnów in July 1942. His twin brother, who also had the looks of a typical Pole, was living as an Aryan with the rightist Polish underground.

Our *Ostbahn* working group had become a very tightly knit band and we had complete trust in each other. We were able to bring back bread we exchanged for bedspread covers and pillow cases, which were easy to smuggle out under our winter clothes. We got them from the workers in an Eintracht warehouse which handled the eiderdown quilts and pillows collected from the homes of the deported. They had to sort and clean the eiderdown and pack it for shipment to Germany, but were able to give us the covers. Some of the Eintracht workers ran their own smuggling trade from their workplace near the outside fence. The Breitowicz brothers were prominent among them. Their profits enabled them to eat well. They spent their evenings gambling for high stakes. One evening they were surprised by a police patrol headed by Markuzy. He tried to confiscate the money on their table but Jankiel Breitowicz pulled a knife on him and warned him not to touch the money. Markuzy ignored the threat and Jankiel slashed his arm. Markuzy ran out, screaming with pain, and Jankiel was arrested. His brothers tried to buy him out but Markuzy was adamant and informed on them to Bacher who ordered Jankiel to be brought before him. But when he confronted the big man something extraordinary happened. They suddenly recognized each other. They had both been butchers in the Polish city of Katowice in Silesia, where many Germans had lived. Bacher ordered Markuzy to release Jankiel. The story created a sensation in the ghetto. Bacher was human after all! But Markuzy swore he would have his revenge on Jankiel.

The SS came regularly to pick workers from the B section. We noticed that sometimes an elderly civilian, dressed in the green "loden" coat and feathered hat of the Tyrol, came with them. We found out his name was Schmidt, chief of the Biesiadka camp, where he had a reputation for outstanding cruelty, even by SS standards. He was looking for free labor and Bacher could supply it. Many women lost their husbands or sons to him, and since Bacher approved his selections, there was no appeal. Through him Markuzy eventually got his revenge. One day when Schmidt came for more workers,

Markuzy promptly selected Jankiel Breitowicz and delivered him to Schmidt and his SS men, to be taken to Biesiadka.

Our rumor mill, reliable as always, informed us that Bacher was in trouble with the Gestapo over an authority dispute. It was not long before he was indeed removed. We were jubilant, but our enthusiasm was dampened by the older men who told us that Jewish tradition enjoined us to pray for the reigning king because his follower might be worse.

Soon Bacher was driven away in a Gestapo car. His successor, Schupke, who held the same rank of Hauptscharfuehrer, arrived with his deputy Oester, a younger man with the rank of Oberscharfuehrer. Some of our friends from Sanok knew Schupke from his post of a commander in the Zaslaw SS camp, which was near Sanok. It had the reputation of being an extermination camp, one of those auxiliary ones, like Pelkinia near Jarosław, Rozwadow and Trawniki, near Lublin. Zaslaw had originally been built for five thousand prisoners but the SS squeezed in eleven thousand Jews, many of them forced to stay in the open. They worked and lived in inhuman conditions, were given garbage for food with dirty water as coffee or soup. People died from exposure, hunger and every kind of disease and sickness, and were buried in large mass graves. Only the very highly skilled workers were given slightly better conditions, though their families also died like flies. The younger and stronger men were picked for the gruesome task of burying the thousands of dead, often including their own relatives. Finally, the survivors, with the exception of the few hundred skilled workers, were transported to Belzec death camp for quick extermination:

Schupke deprived Icek of the favorite position he had enjoyed under Bacher. He became just another nobody, avoided by his former comrades and heartily despised by all of us. Markuzy also lost his authority.

The people who worked in Schupke's office told us that he was an older man, gray haired, and surprisingly kind and fair to them, smiling and even talking to them occasionally. He chose for himself a personal barber, Hilda, a Jewish woman from the Sudetten region. For a butler, Berkowicz, who was a shoemaker by trade, and also his son on his personal staff.

The conditions in the ghetto became a little more relaxed

and it was easier to obtain visiting permits to the B section. The Jewish police, taking their lead from the new circumstances, became more humane and stopped terrorizing us. However, Oester, who concerned himself mainly with the western section, enforced a very strict regime there. He frequently came into the streets to inspect homes and the barbed-wire fences which no one was allowed to approach. But usually on Sundays both he and Schupke were out, and for the first time since the ghetto was divided, Szymon, Nathan and I went over to see the western section. The police at the gate tolerated free passage. It was like entering a world of misery, even for us who were no strangers to misery. There was more activity there than in our section, created by the many children, older men and women and families. Everywhere people were making exchanges, poverty evident in their sad eyes and drawn faces, their shabby clothes and rags. There were many beggars, young and old. We met some people we knew and spent a while talking with them of old times.

Soon after there was another night when we were awakened by the sound of cars driving in. From our window we saw Gestapo men getting out of the cars joined by Jewish policemen. They split into small parties and fanned out, soon returning with some half-dressed men and women, prodding them with their weapons. They lined them up against a large wall and shot them at close range. Then one of the Gestapo men went over to the corpses and kicked each one to make sure there was nobody left alive before they took off. Our police waited until Oszerowicz arrived with his men to remove the bodies. The Gestapo had carried out these killings while Schupke was away. Supreme killers, they could deal death over the heads of all established authority. They had arrived with prepared lists of their intended victims and knew exactly where to find them. After so many deportations and changes of rooms it could only have been the work of informers. Most of those killed were young people who had been members in the Haschomer Hatzair movement, a left-wing Jewish youth organization whose objective was immigration to Palestine to live in a Kibbutz. Rumors had it that they had organized a secret society which had planned resistance to the Nazis.

Once a month the SS trucks from Biesiadka came to the

western ghetto to return the young men they had taken from the ghetto in the past, and "exchange" them for fresh, healthier young men to work at the Biesiadka camp and the Huta Komorowska works. Schmidt always came with them to personally oversee the exchange. The young men they brought back were like the living dead, animated skeletons with prominent eyes staring out of two huge sockets. Schmidt exploited their young bodies to the last drop of their strength and then dumped them. He brought back so many "bodies" to Schupke and Schupke had to replace them with an equal number of fit young men. The books were balanced. Those who came back this evening were so weak that the Jewish policemen had to carry them off the trucks straight to the clinic. Only a few of them could walk the short distance unassisted.

Schmidt stood by, watching silently while his trucks were filled with fresh young men. When they drove off, they left behind a lamenting ghetto and weeping relatives who knew what awaited their dear ones. The half-dead bodies they were replacing told the story. From the Breitowicz brothers we learned that Jankiel had been among those brought back that evening. He was in very bad shape and they took him out of the clinic to the home of close friends who promised to try to keep him alive.

When we returned home the next evening Mr. Brand told us that a terrible massacre had been carried out in the western section during the day. The Gestapo had arrived in the morning, parked their cars near the clinic, and ordered all the men who had been returned yesterday to be brought out. As they came out the Gestapo shot them one by one, got back into their cars and drove off. Try as we might we could not fathom the depth of German depravity. First the SS took away healthy young men for slave work in their camps. Then they brought back the worn-out shells of their bodies to be replaced by fresh slaves, and finally they came to kill those who had survived the ordeal. Killed them with gloved hands in order not to come into contact with their wasting bodies.

Then another disaster we had long feared overtook us. A typhoid epidemic broke out in the western section probably brought in by the poor slave laborers. Dr. Heller and his assistant, Dr. Hauptman, who had taken over the health care in the western section, worked like Titans with their devoted nurses to stem the fever and prevent its spreading into the eastern section. But the situation became calamitous when Dr. Hauptman himself succumbed to the fever. Dr. Heller carried on alone and performed unbelievable deeds to contain the disease. Schupke and Oester had to be kept ignorant, for they would not hesitate to kill us all to stop the typhoid. Hundreds died and were secretly buried at night, but in a few days Dr. Heller had achieved a miracle and the epidemic subsided.

One day, as we passed the dividing barbed-wire fence, we heard our names called, and coming closer found Jankiel standing there. We would not have recognized him. He was a mere shadow of his former self, his sad eyes large and prominent. We could hardly understand what he was saying but he was obviously very hungry. We asked him to wait there and I ran to the community kitchen where Mrs. Kleinmuntz gave me some hot soup, while Szymon and Nathan brought all the bread we had from home. We knew that those who had somehow survived typhoid were ravenously hungry and there was little food in the western section. We watched Jankiel eat hungrily and entreated him, for his own good, to eat slowly. He nodded and kept on eating the bread, and drinking the soup. We promised we would meet him at the fence every evening on our return from work to bring him more food. We kept our promise and were happy to see him recover until he was allowed back into our section, and got his old job back in the home-clearing unit. Markuzy pretended not to see him. Under Schupke he was a very little man, bereft of authority.

Jankiel was very grateful to us for saving his life. One day he told us of his experiences in the Biesiadka and Huta Komorowska camps. They were put to work, in all kinds of weather cutting down trees with handsaws in the adjoining forest, and then carrying the logs on their backs to the works. The complex was under the management of the German Fischer Company which specialized in lumber and concrete work. Johann Robert Schmidt was a veteran manager with the company and had been sent to Poland to run the branch. Jews from all over Europe were brought there as slave laborers, guarded by cruel Ukrainians under SS officers who had graduated from the Pustkow school of killers.

The slaves had to work eighteen-hour days, seven days a

week. They were given meager meals mornings and evenings, consisting of indeterminate hot water, allegedly coffee in the morning and soup in the evening. The slightest mistake at work was punished by immediate death. Hundreds died from hunger and overwork and were buried in mass graves. They did not shoot many more only because Schmidt needed live bodies to exchange for fresh slaves from our ghetto.

It was March 1943, and our *Ostbahn* workmates told us that the news from the Russian front was improving. They had even overheard some Germans saying that the defeat at Stalingrad was an ill omen and Hitler was losing the war. Mr. Zwolinski informed us that another Polish army had been established in Russia. The Kosciuszko army, commanded by a Colonel Szyling.

Since no searches were now being made at the ghetto gates, some people started dealing in gold and foreign currencies. We called them *Waluciarzes* (the currency men). Leon Horn was one of them. Garelik, who was a fair man, had a good influence on Schupke and we started getting a little more food. The western section, however, continued to suffer because the stern Oester was always about to assure his orders were carried out.

One day Garelik asked us to come to his office. When he saw that his invitation scared us, he reassured us that he only wanted to form soccer and volleyball teams in both sections, and had obtained the permission of the two commanders for the project. He had heard that we used to be members of the Cracow Maccabi sports team and wanted us to play. The next evening he held a meeting of young men and made arrangements for practice. Schupke supplied the balls, and the Eintracht cooperative gave us good shirts, shorts, shoes and socks. The scheme caused a sensation in the ghetto, and combined with the improved weather, and news of German defeats in Russia, raised our spirits and even called forth some cautious optimism. Schupke was "all right," but Oester had to be watched.

One evening we saw Oester walking about with a big Dalmatian on a leash. She was a vicious-looking dog almost as tall as a young calf, and he called her Lottie. A Jewish policeman suggested to him that he should have the dog trained and recommended a man named Zahn, who had been a professional dogtrainer before the war. Oester engaged him and we were soon joking about Zahn and Lottie, two dogs who had found each other. But it did not take long before the joke was on us, in fact, no longer than until her training was completed. If anyone in the western sector went near the forbidden barbed-wire fence, Oester would set Lottie on him and she would maul the poor soul and hold on until Oester called her off. He took pleasure taking his time and watching the unfortunate one screaming with pain and fear. Lottie quickly became the terror of the western ghetto and all of us avoided Zahn, who became a virtual outcast, though hardly through any fault of his own. Some ghetto leaders talked to Schupke but he would not intervene. It seemed that nobody could stop an SS officer from tormenting Jews. Oester, in fact, made a sport of letting Lottie hunt Jews.

One evening a *Judenrat* official brought us a postcard addressed to "Herzog." It was from our cousin Awrumek from Father's hometown Jarosław, sent from the notorious Janowski camp near Lwów, and apparently meant for our uncle. It seemed to be written in blood and was a desperate cry for help. But there was nothing at all we could do.

In the troop trains going to the front through the station, there were now many foreigners—Belgians, French, Hungarians, Italians and Spaniards. Hitler evidently needed help from anywhere he could get it. Halberstam, who read between the lines in the pieces of German newspapers the Poles found in the trains, believed the Nazis knew they were in trouble. They were now bragging only about their U-boats sinking Allied ships, while they carried many obituaries for their fallen.

We took advantage of the improving weather to practice our soccer, and one sunny Sunday we played our first match, on the western side of the ghetto, against a team of young men also from the western side. Somewhat to our surprise a very large crowd turned out to watch. We knew we were not very good and starving Jews were not particularly great soccer fans, but evidently our Jews needed something to take their minds off their plight. The match was hard-fought but fair and we won, providing a couple of hours of entertainment for our fellow inmates. The next Sunday we played a team of Jewish police, and Schupke and Oester came to watch. We won again. What we liked best was how the crowd booed the police players. The matches made the three of us famous in the ghetto and we were soon known as the "three playing brothers from Cracow."

We told Mr. Zwolinski about the matches and he was happy for us, but we never forgot that time was running out, and begged him to make every possible effort to get us out. Rumors reached us that the ghettos in Częstochowa, Kielce. Kolomyja, Lublin and nearby Nowy Sacz had been liquidated. While bloody operations had been carried out against the Jews in Bochnia, Cracow and Tarnów. The end was coming closer.

Mr. Zwolinski had news that on April 19, 1943, an uprising had been started in the Warsaw ghetto. It made us proud that our brethren were fighting back, though they had no chance of prevailing against the might of the Wehrmacht with a few pathetic weapons and homemade Molotov cocktails which were bottles of gasoline that broke into flame on impact. Many Jewish fighters were falling in Warsaw, but not in vain, for they were killing Germans. Our Polish workmates came over to shake our hands and congratulate us. Their admiration was sincere. But, as always, there was bad news too. Thousands had been killed in the Janowska camp and the old mass graves there were being reopened and the bodies burned to wipe out all traces of the crime. Did this mean that the Germans already feared that they would lose? The Soviet armies were on the move and were pushing toward the Polish border, but too late for the Jews who were dying in Janowska, Cracow and War-saw, and everywhere else in Poland.

Then another blow fell, the head supervisor told us and a few others not to report for work again. We were terrified. We had done nothing wrong, and our job was our only life insur-ance. Our Polish workmates were genuinely sorry and it was hard to take our farewell from Mr. Zwolinski who was our link to Fela and the outside world. He promised he would do everything in his power to get us safely away. The next morning we again lined up at Pfeifer's labor department in the ghetto and were lucky to be assigned to the home-clearing unit, cleaning the buildings vacated by the last deportations. We were saved, for the time being at least, from being sent to the western section as unemployed, the last stop before death. We had long since got used to living for the day, in the spirit of the Psalms: "Bless the Lord day by day." The work itself was terrible, but that did not matter. Some of the buildings had already been boarded up and were overrun by rats and mice feasting on food left behind by those who had been deported, rushed to their doom by the Jewish police and SS. The smell was overwhelming and millions of insects, of all sizes and colors, were crawling and flying over us. We opened all the doors and windows and quickly chased off the mice, but the rats stood up to us. Bitterly we reflected that even rats were not afraid of Jews any more. We stripped almost naked to cope and were soon covered with insect bites, but when we managed to get some Lysol things were better. We had to move out all the furniture and household articles to be taken away to the Eintracht complex for sorting and repair. We kept the best clothes for ourselves and broke up the silver articles. The silver was easier to conceal and would make barter treasures. We kept religious requisites separate and in the evening buried them, with the help of Leon Horn and Halberstam, to save them from the bloody hands of the Germans. Our foremen were mainly German Jews who could not stay inside with us for very long. They were still too delicate to face so much filth, so we were more or less left alone. We were told that the Gestapo was pressuring Schupke to complete the cleaning quickly because there were Polish families, whose homes were earmarked for the families of German officials, waiting to move in. We heard that many German families were coming to Poland to escape the bombing of their cities by the Allied bombers.

Some of the best pieces of furniture were kept aside for shipment to Germany and this gave us another opportunity to go to the station to see Mr. Zwolinski. He told us that after our dismissal new Jewish workers had been brought to the station warehouses but nobody could fathom the logic of these bizarre exchanges. He also told us the Warsaw uprising was over and that the Jewish fighters had put up a heroic resistance against the Germans who had been commanded by a General Stroop. Mr. Zwolinski said he would try to keep us in touch with Fela by letter, getting one of his trusted friends to carry it. He gave us an exact description of the man and we told him where we could meet him at the fence. We waited for him every evening.

In one of the buildings that faced the Polish section, we

found a large hole in the wall through which the tenants had obviously been carrying out a barter trade with the Poles. We waited until a Pole passed by and called to him. He was eager to barter with us and told us that he used to trade with the people who had lived in this building until they were deported. We told him what we could offer him and asked for foodstuffs in return and he soon returned with the goods. This was the safest way we had found yet, but to be quite safe we posted one of our group as a lookout. It did not last long. When we completed cleaning the building we could not reenter it anymore. Schupke ordered us to cart all the second-class furniture and household utensils to the collection square. The next morning the gate of our section was thrown open, and the Polish populace was permitted in and allowed to take whatever they fancied. Hundreds of them arrived with all kinds of carts. There were also some peasants with horsecarts. We stood by frustratedly watching as they picked the place clean. These goods had been in the possession of Jewish families and how they must have cherished them. Now they were prey for these vultures. Everything was cleared out, down to the last safety pin, in an unbelievably short time. Our artisans were then ordered to immediately move the fence closer in, making the ghetto smaller still.

The arranged time for Mr. Zwolinski's courier was due and we watched the Polish street. Soon the man, who walked with a distinct limp, passed by and we called his name, Jozef Magrys. After we made sure that there was nobody around to see us on either side of the fence, he approached, gave us Fela's letter, took ours for her, and promised to come again at the same time in exactly one week. It was good to hear from Fela, who wrote that she was worried about us and that they were doing all they could to get us out. After we had read it several times over, we destroyed it.

The next Sunday, Garelik arranged another soccer match and as the weather was warmer and more pleasant, the crowd was even bigger than before. It was a heaven-sent opportunity to forget our troubles in the excitement of the game, at least for a couple of hours.

Because the ghetto was smaller now, it became harder for us to smuggle goods for food and we had to find new places at the fence. In the western section things were easier because

Oester was appointed inspector of the P.Z.L. camp at Lysia Gora. Hundreds of highly qualified Jewish mechanics were being held there, guarded by the cruel Ukrainians, to work in the aircraft factory. Oester had to be there every day but returned each evening to terrorize the ghetto as he walked around with his dog, Lottie.

We had more furniture to take to the station and met Mr. Zwolinski to discuss our planned escape. He asked us to have some small photos of ourselves to give to Mr. Magrys. Getting away from the ghetto would be the easiest part, but we would then be exposed to a hostile population only too eager to give Jews away to the Germans. In the forests the anti-Semitic partisan group, the Armja Krajowa, would be as eager to kill Jews as Germans. Mr. Zwolinski told us there were many Poles hunting Jews who dared to enter their Aryan world. First they blackmailed them, and after squeezing them dry, handed them over to the Gestapo. In a final twist of duplicity they collected the reward for delivering a Jew. The underground was aware of these so-called *Schmalzowniks* and a few had even been shot as a warning, but they did not desist.

While I was at work in one of the vacated buildings, a fellow worker came running to warn me that Nathan was in trouble. He had found a good pair of overalls among the clothing in the building he was cleaning and put them on. A German Jewish foreman noticed him and, with typical German instinct for order, told him to take the overalls off. Nathan explained that he was harming no one, but the foreman insisted and finally tried to force him to put the overalls back. Nathan, who was very strong, pushed him away and the man fell to the ground, got up in a fury, and said he was going to report him right away to the Schupo guards. That would be extremely dangerous for Nathan. When I ran up, I saw the foreman already on his way. I tried to reason with him, but he was very angry, insisting that Nathan must be punished for disobeying orders and using force against his foreman. I apologized for him, but he would not be appeased. I promised I would make Nathan himself apologize to him in front of the whole cleaning unit. He finally agreed and when we returned to the building I called Nathan, slapped his face, and ordered him to apologize. He did, took off the overalls and returned them to the pile of clothing. It was the first time I had raised my hand to my brothers and I felt terrible about it, so much so that I would gladly have cut off my hand. It was a very sad moment for me, but I had no choice. The German Jews were dangerous because they were so naive. Though there were mountains of clothing which our unfortunate brethren had left behind, their job was to keep the clothing for the Germans who had appointed them. They obeyed orders automatically, virtually by reflex, without a thought for the consequences. That was their character. We called them *Yeke Nar* (stupid German Jews).

Again the gates were opened and again the Poles streamed in to help themselves to abandoned Jewish possessions. The peasants had the good sense to bring us food so that we would help them find the best stuff. That way we got some food that would keep us going a little longer. I felt sure that our dead brethren would not have begrudged it.

As we were helping the peasants to load their new treasures, a young woman came over and quietly told us she was Jewish, living in Rzeszów as an Aryan. She was running out of money and in desperate need of help. We instinctively suspected a Gestapo trick, but at our request she said a few words in Yiddish and told us her Hebrew forename. We had no cash on us and asked her to wait while we would go to ask our mates for an emergency collection. They were happy to contribute and we collected a few thousand zlotys. We handed her the money in a package, as though she had picked up something from the Jewish property. She was moved to tears and thanked us brokenly. We watched her until she had gone through the gates back into her hostile world. We hoped we had helped her to hold on a while longer.

Meanwhile, since the ghetto area had again been reduced in size, it was more difficult for us to meet Mr. Magrys across the fence, and told him we would have to look for some other way to meet him. Leon Horn was still working on the outside and we confided in him, the first person we told about Fela living as an Aryan in the town. We were actually putting her life and ours, as well as that of the Zwolinski family who were sheltering her, in his hands. But we trusted him implicitly and he was glad to serve as our courier, risking his own life too.

Schupke appeared to be undergoing a change, and for the worse. He was more active, made frequent inspections of our workplaces and sometimes came into our homes at the crack of dawn. If he should catch religious Jews at prayer, wrapped in their prayer shawls with their phylacteries on their forehead and left arm, he would become very angry, tear the prayer-books out of their hands, throw them to the ground and stamp on them with his black boots. He would order them to take off their prayer requisites and forbid them ever to pray again, telling them that their prayers were in vain because God so obviously paid them no regard.

One early morning as I was shaving, I felt that somebody was staring at my back. I turned around and found myself looking at Schupke. I overcame my instinctive shock and greeted him, "Good morning, Herr Hauptscharfuehrer." He nodded and asked how I could make so much noise shaving. I explained that razor blades were hard to come by in the ghetto and I had to use an old one over and over again, sharpening it as best I could by rubbing it on the inside of a wet glass. He watched me doing that and then told me to come and see him in his office after work for some new blades. I could not believe my ears but, I speculated, he might have recognized me from the soccer match, and liked my playing. After work I washed and went to his headquarters where I met Hilda, his secretary-barber, who knew me well. She told Schupke I was there and he came out. After I identified myself he went back into his office and brought me a few packages of new razor blades. It was hard to believe, but this elderly SS man could still be a human being, one among the many thousands of those black beasts.

In the evenings, Icek Goldberg from Krosno, who now lived in our room played violin and was accompanied by my brother Szymon who played on the mouth harmonica and sung. Szymon had very fine voice. Their performances became soon the ghetto entertainment. The audience filling our room and the corridor. One evening Schupke and Garelik came in while they were playing. We all jumped up and stood at attention, but Schupke told us to relax and carry on. He sat down on one of the bunks to listen and nodded his approval. He stayed for a long while and when he left he said, *"Danke schoen"* (thank you). The two small words, addressed to us by an SS officer, were a sensation for us.

Once when we were busy cleaning one of the buildings, we heard some Gestapo cars driving in. From the window we saw

SS men going into Schupke's office. They came out with him and Garelik, and entered a neighboring building. A few moments later they were pushing out a large group of Jews, older men, some women and a few children. The Gestapo lined them up against the wall of their building, drew their pistols and shot them one by one at close range. The whole nightmare lasted no longer than fifteen minutes. Then they saluted Schupke and drove off. In the evening we found out what had happened. The Jews had been hiding in the building and some unknown informer must have given them away because the Gestapo killers had gone straight to a certain room, pushed aside one of the bunks and underneath the carpeting found a trapdoor which led into a bunker where those Jews had been living for some time. They were the relatives of working Jews who lived in the rooms above the bunker, which they had probably built to hide their families. The workers involved were later taken from their workplaces by the Gestapo and never seen again.

The three of us then met in secret with a group of other young men to discuss ways of discovering the informers before they would do away with all of us. There were too many things we could be shot for if we were found out: smuggling, dealing with Poles over the fences, everything we did to keep alive. In fact, only our breathing was still legal. We decided to keep our eyes wide open and especially to watch out for anybody seen going to the German guards. Since nobody in the ghetto had a phone, betrayals could be carried out only by word of mouth. Within a few days one of our lookouts noticed a young boy walking over to the main gate and handing something small to the German Schupo on guard there. It might have been money, but it might have been a written message. We knew the boy. We called him the cake boy. He used to hang around the ghetto peddling small cakes and rolls that had been baked secretly on the west side and smuggled into our section at night. There were many boys like him in the western section, orphans of deported parents, so small and skinny they could hide anywhere and slip through the smallest gap. Some of them used to beg for food at the fence and we would help them to the best of our ability. Somehow they kept themselves alive. This cake boy was the only one in our section and did good business because everybody loved something sweet.

That same night the Gestapo drove in again, entered two buildings and came out with nearly fifty half-dressed men, women and children. They ordered them to lean against a wall and shot them. We put two and two together and guessed that the paper the cake boy had passed to the guard must have been a message for the Gestapo. He entered all the buildings while making his rounds with his cakes, and could easily find out what was going on, and where. We waited until the cake boy turned up in the building we were clearing to offer his wares, and sent him up to the third floor. There we grabbed him and questioned him. He started to cry and denied everything but we told him that he had been observed handing his message to the Schupo. Confronted with the evidence he begged for mercy. But we decided he was too dangerous and though we were really sorry for him, he had to be removed. One of the men smothered him with a pillow and disposed of his body in a cesspool. We pledged to keep the affair a secret. Even telling a close friend might be fatal. But our satisfaction at having got rid of the informer soon soured, for another one was at work. When the men from the outside work groups returned home one evening the Gestapo was waiting, and from a prepared list, called out thirty-five names, all from the *Ostbahn* group. They put the men against the fence and shot them. All of them had been members of influential families.

The Gestapo had arrested Brunner, the chief of the *Ostbahn,* in his office and accused him of selling jobs to rich Jews. One of the *Machers* who had access to Brunner had informed on him, supplying the full list of those he had taken bribes from. But only the Gestapo, and those who bought their jobs through this particular *Macher* knew his identity. The Gestapo was not saying, and the recipients were dead. For what it was worth, now we knew why we had been dismissed from the *Ostbahn* not long ago, to make room for them. Everybody was on their toes again, being extra careful, and we got a message to Fela to redouble the efforts to get us out. A few quiet days were followed by another night visit from the Gestapo. They fanned out with the Jewish policemen and brought out a lot of Jews whom they took away on trucks. Again they had prepared lists and again their victims had been members of prominent families. It soon got around that all of them had been in a plan to escape to Hungary with the help of a Polish smuggler. They had paid him in advance and he gave them away to the Gestapo.

More men, mainly skilled workers, from the western section were taken away for forced labor, this time to the Szebnia SS camp, depriving their families of their breadwinners. I had a chance to observe the SS trucks and recognized one of the drivers, a man from Cracow, called Lolek Kluger, who had been one of the stars of the Maccabi cycling team. He recognized me too, but as there was an SS man in the cab with him he could only nod and whisper he would talk to me next time. I was amazed to see a Jew driving an SS truck.

We were ordered to establish a warehouse for abandoned property and found that the building adjoined the Polish section, with a common wall with a Polish house. This raised the possibility of trading. We closely observed the tenants of the Polish house and when we saw one of them alone called to him and proposed trading goods for food. When he agreed we arranged to meet him at seven every morning, before he went to work. We knocked a hole in the connecting wall, in the cellar, and did a good trade, obtaining food for all of us. But one day, when our lookout was not in place, Schupke walked into the warehouse and caught us handing a few items down into the cellar. We were taken completely by surprise and froze, paralyzed. He warned us to stop our smuggling and went off. We could not believe our own good luck but when the lookout came back we almost killed him. He had lost us a good and safe trading post. But necessity is the mother of invention and we quickly found an alternative.

One morning a workmate came to tell me that an SS truckdriver was looking for me. Of course it was Lolek Kluger. He had brought some SS men to pick up materials from the Eintracht warehouses for their Szebnia camp. This gave us a chance to talk. He told me he had lost all his family in Cracow, and in the summer of 1942 he had been one of a large group selected for Szebnia. In Szebnia he was picked to drive a truck. They had been the first Jews in the camp, after most of the Russian POW's there had been killed and buried in a nearby forest. He was lucky to get a good job. He had a relatively easy life as a driver and a few other Jewish men also had good jobs, but the rest suffered all kinds of tortures, hardships and humiliations, starting from the moment they arrived when they were subjected to demeaning searches for valuables. Every week their barracks were searched and anyone caught still possessing valuables was a dead man. The dead were constantly replaced by skilled workers from surrounding ghettos which were being liquidated. They were worked to the bone until they were unable to do any further service for the Germans, when they were shot. In fact, death was a blessing in the camp, because the so-called living conditions were so deplorable, the food meager and bad, and the slightest offense was punished by torture, hanging, or, if the poor offender was lucky, shooting. There was no clinic in the camp. The sick were simply shot. The camp commandant was an ethnic German, Jozef Grzymek, who had been transferred from the Janowska camp. He was sarcastically nicknamed "Uncle" by the inmates, because he was nice when he talked to prisoners, but an unspeakable sadist underneath his veneer of courtesy. No children were permitted in the camp but many parents smuggled their children in and kept them hidden. Grzymek learned of this and through the Jewish *Kapos* (camp police), spread a rumor that a kindergarten was being opened, run by Jewish girls. The mothers were taken in by the rumor, and brought their children to the place. For a few days they were happy, but then, while the parents were at work, Grzymek and his SS men put all the children on trucks, took them to the nearby forest and killed them. They were buried in a big common grave by a Jewish burial unit. When the parents returned from work they were desolate, but there was nothing they could do. The Ukrainian guards saw to that. Lolek told me that Grzymek often held wild parties in the camp for visiting SS bigwigs, complete with young Jewish girls he supplied, who were shot when the party was over. Among those visiting Grzymek was Amon Goeth, his superior. My two brothers and I faced this cold blooded killer twice in Rzeszow when he was in charge of the deportations.

I told my brothers and we were all very upset because we knew that many young men from the B section of our ghetto had lately been sent to the Szebnia camp. Indeed the latest persistent rumor was that our ghetto was shortly to be liquidated too, so unless we could manage to get out, we might also end up in Szebnia. Even our Jewish policemen were depressed, expecting the worst. When Schupke ordered the closure of the Eintracht warehouses all the workers panicked. We had to take the equipment to the station to be loaded for dispatch to the Szebnia camp. This did, however, give us an opportunity to meet Mr. Zwolinski again. He attempted to reassure us with the good news from the front. Perhaps the advancing Russians would soon reach the old Polish border and save us all. He also told us that Mussolini had been deposed by his own people and the Allies had landed in Sicily. But all this was taking place far from our ghetto and we needed help immediately. We sensed it would soon be too late.

Soon after that I learned that Lolek Kluger had escaped to Slovakia. He simply drove his SS truck to the border and his SS number plate got him across. Grzymek was furious at his audacious flight and had fifty camp inmates tortured and hanged in retaliation. Their bodies were left hanging for many days to intimidate the surviving inmates.

Early on September 3, 1943, four years after the cursed war had started, Jewish policemen woke us with the news that the Germans were surrounding the ghetto. Though we had sensed this was coming for some time, we were nevertheless shaken now that it was actually happening. We dressed in a hurry and packed our backpacks, putting in winter clothes and the strongest shoes we had, as well as some bread and thermos flasks with hot tea. Nobody talked. We were resigned to the worst. The ghetto was swarming with armed SS men. We had never seen so many before, notwithstanding the fact that the ghetto was already very small. I mused whether they could still be fearing resistance from us, worn down as we were by four years of fear, pain and suffering. Soon the sound of intermittent shooting echoed from the western section where the Ukrainians and SS men were running wild, indiscriminately beating and shooting people. When we came to the collection square as ordered, the selection tables were already set up. Schupke and Pfeifer said something to Garelik and he ordered each working group to stay apart. Our home-clearing crew was the largest. When everybody had arrived and lined up as commanded, the high officials got out of their cars and took their places at the table: Ehaus, Pablu, Schuster of the Gestapo, and their aides. Pfeifer gave Garelik a list and he called out the names of the groups, starting with those who were to be deported en bloc. Leon Horn's group was the first, and it was followed by the *Ostbahn* group. When the turn of the Eintracht workers came, some Gestapo officials at the table got up for personal selections and picked a few shoemakers and tailors.

Then it was our turn. There were about five hundred men and women in our group. We were ordered to line up in double file and the selection was carried out by Pablu, who picked those who were to stay. We three brothers stood next to each other in the front row. When Pablu reached me he motioned for me to join the selected to stay, but he passed Szymon and Natan condeming them to be deported. I stood transfixed, waited for a few seconds, and then raised my hand for permission to address Pablu. I asked him to let my brothers come with me. Pablu did not say a word but simply raised his whip and hit me very hard on the head. I started bleeding profusely and stood as though nailed to the spot. Schupke came over and demanded why I was not moving to the assembly ground as ordered. I told him, and pointing to my brothers, added that we had never been separated before and had always done good work as a team. He looked at Pablu and then told the three of us to move to the parade ground. We did not hesitate but ran across before they could change their minds again. From our position we could observe the selection and watched the resigned, careworn faces of our brethren, already totally indifferent, resigned to whatever fate would be decreed for them. They included our roommates Leon Horn and the Gutmann brothers, Mr. Brand, and most of the boys who had played soccer with us. Mrs. Kleinmuntz of the community kitchen, who had been by-passed by Pablu but picked by Schupke stood next to me, and Hilda also had been saved. Many Jewish policemen were left standing for deportation and only a few were with us. Icek Goldberg joined us, but Jankiel and his brothers were condemned. So was the German Jewish foreman who had forbidden Nathan to take an abandoned pair of overalls. But I could not see Halberstam, his nephew and sister-in-law, nor Maciek Fiedler, and I hoped they had managed to hide themselves and would not be discovered. It was touch and go. Already the SS dog handlers and their bloodhounds were getting ready.

When the Jewish policemen brought up the baskets for

valuables, we knew that the selection was over and that soon the condemned would start on their last journey. There were only about a hundred men and ten women with us, everybody else was gone. On the western side there was no selection at all. They were simply forced to lie facedown on the muddy ground and wait. After all the condemned from our section had passed through the exit gate, they were allowed to get up and ordered to march out. Some men and women among them were picked at random and ordered to undress for personal searches. That was enough to quickly fill up the waiting baskets.

When the last of them had gone a deathly silence descended on the grounds, in effect the silence of death. When we were dismissed and returned to our rooms, the empty bunks brought home to us what we had just survived. Our building was almost empty, but the searches for hiding Jews continued, in both sections of the ghetto, until darkness enveloped our tragic abode. As we watched from our window we saw one of those selected for deportation approach an SS officer and talk to him. After a few moments we saw a few SS men accompanied by our Jewish policemen who carried some shovels, enter one of the buildings, accompanied by this man. After a long time to our horror we saw a large group of men, women and children coming out from this building followed by the SS men. They were placed against the building and shot one by one. The Jewish man who stood next to the SS officer was the last to be shot. This Jewish man was an architect, a German Jew. He had told the SS officer about a bunker that he had built. They promised him that he would be spared. According to those policemen who entered this bunker it was the best hiding place they have ever seen. He was a traitor to the Jews who trusted him and probably had paid him a fortune.

The next morning we found the western ghetto, the B section, gone. There was nobody left, except for some bodies Oszerowicz would soon cart off. When we assembled to go to work we saw four hundred women, who had been picked out the day before from the B section, still standing in the space between the fences, wet and cold, guarded by SS men who were not Germans. We learned that Icek and Markuzy had been among those deported and we shed no tears for them. Schupke ordered half of our group to the Eintracht buildings to load the SS trucks for the railroad. At the station we looked for Mr. Zwolinski, preferring for safety's sake not to ask for him. When we found him, he had already heard that only a few Jews had been left in the ghetto and was happy we were among them. He told us that yesterday's deportation train had not gone east as in the past, but had headed for Auschwitz. He told us the Allies had landed in Italy and that the Germans were retreating along the width of the Russian front, burning everything behind them. But we were scarcely interested. It was all too far away from us, and certainly too late for the unfortunates who had been taken away yesterday.

When we returned to the ghetto we were told that the four hundred women had been taken away to the Szebnia camp. We were ordered to stay indoors until the hunt for the hidden, which was resumed at dawn, would be completed. In our warehouse we found Maciek Fiedler. It was like a reunion with one returning from the dead. He told us that when the ghetto was being surrounded the day before he had decided to risk all and had hidden in the vegetable plot behind the Eintracht buildings.

In the western section the SS were still firing from time to time, and we could hear the screams of the people they caught and beat mercilessly before they shot them. Some of the SS men came into our warehouse to rest and drink and we heard them coolly recounting how they had cleared out the Jews in the Przemyśl ghetto a few days before. They talked about the murders they had committed as though they had been some routine jobs satisfactorily completed. We learned that yesterday the SS had brought small Polish boys with them to help in their searches. The skinny little kids could squeeze through small gaps to find hidden bunkers, which the SS men then dynamited. As a reward they allowed the boys to take home some of the valuables found in the debris. The SS had smashed every attic and chimney, torn up floors and broken down walls to make sure no Jew could get away. We believed that those who were shot were better off than the poor souls who had been taken away. At least for them it was all over, and the Germans could inflict no more tortures on them. Oester and his dog were transferred from the now-empty B section to the PZL works. Halberstam and his family emerged from the place where they were hidden, and we put them up in our building. Once the SS had left, Schupke no longer cared. He knew very well how we would all end up anyway.

The reports of the deportations from all over the district caused panic among the few Jews who were still living clandestinely in Rzeszów and other small towns. They appealed to their Polish friends, to whom they had entrusted their possessions, to shelter them. Many of these "friends" betrayed them, and they were picked up by the Germans and killed. The luckier ones were given shelter for a few days and then turned out. Miraculously they returned to the ghetto and were questioned by Garelik who passed on their stories to Schupke. Schupke went with them to their Polish hosts and forced them to return their valuables to the Jews. A few days later a woman from our ghetto, Lotka Goldberg, managed to escape from the Szebnia camp, the only person from Rzeszów to have accomplished this feat. But she was denied entry by the German guard and collapsed at the gate. Schupke, who was called to the gate, ordered the guard to let her in. We were amazed but delighted by this hint of humanity on the part of Schupke. It was more, much more, than we had come to expect from SS officers. One coworker who knew the woman well, brought her over to our room and she told us of the horrors of Szebnia. The Jews brought there were exploited to the last drop of their strength and then killed. Her own escape was no less than a miracle. She urged all of us to flee while we were still alive because in the camps certain death was awaiting us. Her terribly run-down physical condition no more than a broken shell of a human being, and her mental despair affected us profoundly, and put us into a very somber mood. Though she was a young woman she was unable to work, and we kept her alive with smuggled food.

The last deportation had again made the ghetto too big and it was once more reduced. We had to vacate our building to make room for Poles who were waiting for apartments. We were put to work clearing and cleaning the vacated buildings. This time we decided not to leave the furniture to the Poles whose children had helped the Germans find hidden Jews, perhaps the owners of this very furniture. We smashed it, piece by piece, and the Jewish policemen who came in while we were doing so, no longer cared. The September 3 deportation had at last awakened them to the fact that they were not immune, and all they did was sort through the wreckage for hidden treasure to provide new means for them to get drunk and gamble for high stakes. We took our time and Schupke did not hurry us. He named the three of us as foremen of the home-clearing unit to replace the German Jews who had been sent away. I made sure that Halberstam and his nephew were in my group and I did not allow them to lift anything heavy. Only the Jewish police bothered us. They wanted a cut of the most valuable items we found. One day Szymon found a beautiful shirt and put it on. One of the policemen saw him and coveted it for himself. He commanded Szymon to take it off and hand it over. When Szymon refused and the policeman started pushing him around, Szymon gave him a good beating. The man ran to Garelik and demanded he report Szymon to Schupke. I appealed to Hilda who talked to Schupke and he released Szymon. From then on we didn't allow any policeman into the buildings we were clearing.

One morning Maciek, who was in our group, did not turn up for work, and almost immediately we heard the sensational news that Eintracht had also fled. I guessed that the two who had been close friends, had gone over the fence together, and that either Maciek's brother, Ludwik, who was with the Polish underground engineered their escape, or that Eintracht, who was known to be very rich, had bought their way out. The Gestapo arrived to investigate Eintracht's escape. Nobody cared about Maciek. A few days later, Halberstam, along with his nephew and sister-in-law disappeared also, probably helped by some peasants they had been friendly to.

The ghetto was now so small that its very diminution brought home to us that getting away had become a life or death matter for us. The tens of thousands of Jews who had lived in the ghetto at one time or another were gone, never to return; the children who had played in the street, the mothers and fathers who made superhuman efforts to bring home bread, all gone. Even the sunshine that the proverb tells us follows the storm, failed us.

And beyond the shrinking fences the Poles were impatiently waiting for the vacated apartments, and for the "open-house," when they could come and pick over the abandoned Jewish possessions the Germans did not consider good enough to be shipped to Germany. At least we were able to make their pickings poor. We saw to it that they would get nothing but junk. We also killed two birds with a single stone when we broke up the heavy furniture and threw the pieces out of the windows, denying them to the vultures and, not having to carry it down, saving our backs.

A few of those who had managed to escape returned to the ghetto voluntarily, their experience outside being too harrowing. From them we heard how they had been exposed to blackmailers who, after squeezing all their money and jewelery from them, betrayed them to the Gestapo. Moreover the Gestapo's hunt for Jews went on around the clock, as though that was the Germans' only worry. Yet, notwithstanding their hair-raising stories of the outside, more escapes were attempted and every now and then somebody else was missing.

One morning several cars with the dreaded POL number plates drove in and went straight to Schupke's office. We knew that the Gestapo never came just to say hello. Something big was going on. There was a lot of coming and going in Schupke's office and finally we learned that Oszerowicz, the ghetto undertaker, was missing. The Gestapo had called for him to pick up corpses from their vile cellars but he was not to be found. He was the one Jew the Gestapo really needed and the only one allowed in and out of the ghetto day and night. They obviously intended to find him. He knew too much—how many victims he had buried, and what the corpses looked like when the Gestapo had finished with them. A large reward was offered for information leading to Oszerowicz's capture. Perhaps they would not find it easy to locate him. He had amassed a macabre fortune, stripping valuables from the dead and smuggling food in his death cart, the same cart he had used to smuggle out his two daughters a few weeks earlier. He had established the sort of connections with the Poles outside that only money could buy. Schupke was furious and probably frightened as well. As a result he changed, and became irritable and demanding. Only Garelik could still talk with him, for an uncanny chemistry existed between the two men from the time Schupke had taken over command of the ghetto.

7

Rzeszów, Our Escape
Early November 1943

It was the beginning of November, winter was coming again, and we feared we would not live through it unless we could escape. There were only about one hundred Jews left in the Rzeszów ghetto out of nearly thirty thousand who had passed through. It was obvious that the final liquidation was approaching. The Eintracht cooperative buildings were almost empty, and when we went to the station to ship off the last of its machinery, we met Mr. Zwolinski. He assured us that with Mr. Lopatowski's help he expected shortly to get us safely away. Only the final details still had to be worked out. He told us that with the Russians already on the Dnieper River, the Germans in Poland were becoming edgy, and turning on the Poles. Governor Frank had issued a proclamation holding all Poles collectively responsible for any action against the Germans and threatening the strictest punishment. Already hundreds of Polish hostages had been hanged in public, particularly in Warsaw. We arranged with Mr. Zwolinski that we would wait at a specified, relatively safe place in the ghetto every evening, so that if he had any message for us, Mr. Magrys could safely deliver it. We also hid a ladder in an isolated corner, ready to take off when the time came. We spent many evenings waiting for Magrys but he did not come. Finally one evening we spotted him, walking faster than usual and obviously excited. After we made sure we were not being observed, he approached us and told us that though he had no letter he had good news. We were to leave the ghetto that very evening, before the curfew in town, and come to the

Zwolinskis' home. He gave us forged ID papers, urged us to be very careful so as not to spoil everything at the last moment, and wished us good luck. His one hope was to meet us again after the war and see us in person and in daylight. Then he made off, faster even than before, his limp notwithstanding. We made our way quickly back to our room and examined our new papers. We all had different names, which we quickly memorized. But our birthdates and birthplaces were unaltered. We changed into the dirty work clothes we had prepared for our flight, and smeared dirt on our faces to make us look like workmen coming home from work. We then left our rooms, and to make sure that no one would accidentally come upon us, hid in the dark outside. Just after eight we went to the fence, to the spot we had prepared and looked around. It was cold and quiet and there was nobody about. We put our hidden ladder in place and climbed across the fence into the Aryan world. I went last and pulled the long ladder after me and the three of us carried it in the middle of the road trying to look like workers going home. It was a dark and very cold November evening and there were not many people about, and fortunately no police patrols. We walked briskly but not hurriedly in order not to draw attention to ourselves. We knew the city well from our scrap collecting days, and when we reached the block in which the Zwolinskis lived, we stopped for a moment and put our ladder down, both to look around to make sure we were not being watched and also to let our urgently beating hearts slow down.

The street was empty and we looked for the Zwolinskis' house number. When we found it we put the ladder down outside and Nathan knocked on the door. Mr. Zwolinski opened the door and quickly brought us in. We told him about the ladder and he went out and took it to his garden behind the house.

Then Fela jumped at us and all four of us embraced and kissed and cried, patting each other's back and crying some more. At last she freed herself and stepped back to examine us and study our faces. Finally she remarked that we had all gotten very skinny. We noticed that she was a light blond now and looked very well. When we got over our first excitement we noticed Mrs. Zwolinska, whom we had never seen before, and went over to kiss her hand. She was less formal, kissed and embraced us, and told us she knew all about us from her husband and Fela. All this time, Mr. Lopatowski, our old friend from Cracow, stood on one side, patiently awaiting his turn to be greeted. We ran over to him and embraced him. We were all crying, but Mr. Lopatowski brought us back down to earth with his plan of action. We were to leave in about an hour and follow him and Fela, who would go in front, to the railroad station. He would buy tickets for the five of us and warned us not to get into conversation with anybody at the station or on the train, only to politely answer any questions we might be asked. He also advised that we keep an eye on each other. Since it would have been suspicious for us to travel without any luggage, Fela had prepared a small bundle for each of us. We washed the dirt off our faces and were ready.

Now it was time to say goodbye to the Zwolinskis. How can you thank people who have risked their lives to save yours? The only way we knew was to clasp their hands, cry, and tell them that from now on we lived only for the day when we might meet again after the war. Fela cried like a baby and could not tear herself away from her two saviors, until Mr. Lopatowski practically pulled her away. With one last look back we walked out following Fela and Mr. Lopatowski. The streets were almost deserted. We did not meet any policemen and made it safely to the station. Because of the blackout the whole station was pretty dark. We waited until Mr. Lopatowski brought us our tickets and then rejoined Fela. There were a lot of people on the platform and most of them were carrying large packages. The wartime Polish merchants were taking their merchandise to outlying villages where food was available. When the train arrived we had to push to get into the same compartment with Fela and Mr. Lopatowski. The darkened train was nearly full. At each stop more people squeezed in, all carrying bundles. We pretended to be sleeping on our feet. Early in the morning the train reached our destination, the Cracow-Plaszow station, and with some apologizing and pushing we got off. Pretending to be tightening our bundles we allowed Fela and Mr. Lopatowski to precede us following a little distance behind. It was still dark, and with the exception of some workmen on their way to work, the streets were deserted. Finally Mr. Lopatowski stopped outside a house and knocked on the door and we all went in. Our hosts were an elderly man and his wife who had no children. They nodded to us with a smile and asked us to sit down and relax. We were safe now. Mr. Lopatowski talked to the couple for a few minutes and then told us his plan. We would soon disperse to different homes of Polish patriots to wait for instructions and would meet up again the next day for the next stage of our trip by train to the Slovak border. There underground contacts would guide us across the border and put us in the hands of a Jewish committee who would help us to travel on to Hungary where another Jewish committee would help us settle. We were not the first Jews they had sent along this route and all of them had made it. We were in good hands and need not worry too much. Mr. Lopatowski reassured us and then shook hands with our hosts. He kissed us goodbye, wished us all the best and turned to leave because he had to go to work. We thanked him as best we could in the short moments we had left and I told him I wished for nothing more than to be able to come back after the war and really thank him for all he had done for our family.

A few minutes later two young boys arrived to take us to our different safe houses. Fela went first and then they came back for Szymon and Nathan. I was to stay there. The boys soon returned and reported that they had safely delivered my sister and brothers.

The lady of the house made breakfast but I was too tired and excited to eat. What a twenty-four hours we had spent and how fast everything had moved. Yesterday at this time we were still in the ghetto musing about whether we would be able to flee before the Gestapo came for the final roundup and here we were back in Cracow, waiting to continue on our way to freedom. I fell asleep at the table and when I awoke it was already late in the afternoon. My host told us that next morning the four of us would meet in a certain house from which we would be taken to the station in the evening. Then they gave me a hot meal and I lay down to sleep on a couch.

At eight the next morning my host told me the time had come to move on. A young boy came and took me to the house where my two brothers were staying, a two-story building. After giving me the name and apartment number, he left, hardly giving me time to thank him. I entered the lobby. As I looked for the name I had been given I noticed a doctor's shingle on the ground floor. I found the right door, on the second floor, and knocked. The door opened and I walked in.

As I did so the world collapsed around me. Szymon, Nathan and another, unknown man, were lying on the floor in the middle of the room with their arms handcuffed behind their backs. Hearing the door closing they raised their heads and saw me. Their eyes expressed a desperation that struck me dumb. Then I noticed two men standing in the room besides the man who had let me in, and more people sitting in the next room. I guessed that the three men were plainclothes Gestapo men and indeed they ordered me into the other room. They searched me and asked for my papers. I seemed to satisfy them and then they asked me in German why I had come there. I hesitated for only a split second and then told them in Polish, that I had come to see the doctor and gave his name which I had noticed on the shingle. I still had some unhealed cuts from my work in the ghetto on my hands and held them up for them to see. All the time I felt the desperate eyes of my brothers directed at me as they lay there helplessly. Then it struck me that Fela was due at any moment. I was sure she would not have my strength and would go to pieces at the sight of our brothers lying shackled on the floor, and give all of us away. So I turned to go and the three men, apparently satisfied by my story and wounds, let me pass undisturbed. I summoned every reserve of strength and willpower to keep a straight face and only allowed my eyes to articulate a silent last goodbye to my dearest brothers.

Then I moved fast, flying down the stairs, to intercept Fela before she would walk into the trap. The moment I got into the street I saw her approaching, accompanied by one of the boys of yesterday. I ran up to them and told them to turn around, start walking away and not to stop till the end of that street. They were bewildered, but did as I told them. When I joined them again, I asked the boy to take us straight back to the place he had picked me up from. I forestalled Fela's questions by quietly, but firmly, telling her that something had gone wrong and that she must go on walking normally to avoid drawing attention to us. The boy knocked on the door and the Poles immediately enquired anxiously what had happened. I recounted the whole story, sparing no detail. Fela broke down and both of us wept uncontrollably. I did not even try to suppress my emotions. I wept for all those years we had somehow overcome until this blow, just when we were on the brink of salvation. I do not know how I had mustered the strength and presence of mind to keep myself in check when I had come upon Szymon and Nathan lying fettered on the floor. Perhaps the fear that Fela might come in and give the two of us away also gave me an inner strength I did not know I possessed.

Now I held Fela in my arms and tried to comfort her, but how could we be calm in the face of our great tragedy? Both of us repeated their names over and over again, and our hosts, who were deeply touched as well, tried to divert our attention from the misfortune. They introduced a practical note and told us that it was vital we get in touch with the man who had brought us from Rzeszów. It would be dangerous to stay in their apartment after dark. He did not know Mr. Lopatowski's name. It was an elementary precaution used in the underground movement operating under the noses of the Germans. In the afternoon he told us he was arranging for a horse and buggy and the driver would take us to the man. The buggy ride through the wet, dark, deserted streets seemed to last for an eternity. As the horse clip-clopped through the streets I knew so well, I felt my life passing before my mind's eye, even as I kept agonizing about what must be happening to Szymon and Nathan. I knew the Gestapo had probably taken them to their headquarters in Pomorska Street and were torturing them to extract information about their forged papers, and who had helped them. But I knew my brothers and I was sure they would not betray our benefactors, no matter how badly they would be tormented. When we reached the street in which the Lopatowskis lived, I paid the driver, and after checking up and down we went to their house and knocked on the door. The young Lopatowski opened it and after overcoming his surprise at seeing us, called his father. When Mr. Lopatowski saw our tear-swollen faces he knew that something terrible had happened and helped us into chairs. Mrs. Lopatowski kissed us and wanted to make tea, but we declined. The three of them listened carefully, not taking their eyes off us as I told them our tragic story. When I had carefully recounted everything, I assured them they need not worry. Our brothers would not betray them. Mrs. Lopatowski was relieved and her husband said firmly that he trusted them and did not fear. He would go at once to find out what had gone wrong, make sure there had been no betrayal, and also to work out new plans with his comrades for the two of us to go on to Slovakia as intended. We waited tearfully and impatiently for his return. Thinking of our brothers, I seemed to feel their ordeal for I knew what the Gestapo was.

When Mr. Lopatowski returned a few hours later, he immediately told us there had been no betrayal. We had been victims of a tragic coincidence. The people in whose house we were all to meet were Jewish, but had Argentinian passports and were registered as protected aliens with the Gestapo. By the worst of bad luck, some Gestapo men had come to make a routine passport check just as our brothers, and the third man, also a Jew on the run, had arrived to wait for us and our guide, a concatenation of circumstances that only a truly cruel fate could have designed. But it could not be helped, and now we had to look to the future. His party ordered him to personally accompany us to the border and hand us over to the guide who would take us across to the Slovak side. The young Lopatowski went out to get us a buggy, and his mother quickly made us some sandwiches and gave us sweaters for the mountain crossing. The ride to the Cracow-Podgorze station took about half an hour. I knew every inch of the way. It used to be my daily route to work before the war, and the station itself was only half a block from the chocolate factory. Mr. Lopatowski bought the tickets and when the train came and there was a rush for seats, we made no effort to secure seats for ourselves, preferring to stand in the dark passage. When the train had pulled out and gone a little way, a young man came over to me and quietly told me that he knew I was a Jew on my way to the border. If I would hand over all the cash and valuables I had, he would leave me alone, otherwise he would hand me over to the Germans at the next stop. The young Lopatowski sensed that something was going on and came over to us. I was on edge but told him. He quickly brought his father and together they pushed the stranger against the door. They told him that they were Poles who were protecting me, and warned him that if he made one false move they would throw him off the moving train. He swore he would not harm me and proposed to get off at a subsidiary station where there were unlikely to be police patrols, and with their assent he did so. There were *Schmalz-ownikies* even on the trains, looking for helpless Jews to blackmail, and then turn them over to the Gestapo all the same to earn the extra reward. Mr. Lopatowski told me the underground was aware of these scoundrels and had actually killed some of them as an example, and he had warned this stranger that he would have to reckon with the patriots.

8

Slovakia
November 1943

F ela was very upset when I told her what had happened, but I pointed out that it was over and we must think only of the future. We arrived at our destination, a small station that was not patrolled. Mr. Lopatowski recognized his contact man and we followed him to a small house on the outskirts of the little town, where we were introduced to the man who would take us across the border, which was close by. The two Lopatowskis did not delay, but quickly said goodbye with hardly enough time for us to thank them once more, and left. Our guide said that we must leave immediately to take advantage of the dark. We followed him through part of the town into a forest. There he asked us not to talk, to walk very slowly, watch our step, and keep an eye on him all the time and that we must do exactly as he did in case he should spot a patrol. It was a dark November night, but we did not care about the cold or even feel the wet. We walked silently for several hours over difficult terrain and then our guide stopped, letting us catch up, and told us we were already in Slovakia. He was leaving us for a short time to meet his Slovak contact. We felt more relaxed now that we had left Poland behind us. He soon returned with the new guide and introduced us to him. He then bade us farewell and disappeared into the dark. Our new guide told us there was no danger of Germans on this side of the border but we had to watch out for the infrequent Slovakian border patrols who might be about. He assured us that he knew his job well and asked us only to stick close to him in the dark forest, and promised that we did not have very far to go. Actually we walked and stumbled on for several hours more until we spotted some lights in the distance. He told us they were the lights of his village and he soon led us through its deserted streets, disturbed only by the barking of dogs, to his home. His wife greeted us, served us some tea and bread, and took our wet clothes and shoes to dry. We noticed their children were sound asleep. Our guide told us that he would be grateful if we would let him have our remaining zlotys since they would be of no further use to us, and any of our valuables we could spare to augment the small fee the Jewish committee paid him for his dangerous work. I gave him the few zlotys I still carried, and though he did not conceal his disappointment, he told me he had guessed we were not rich. He asked only that we not mention his request to the Jews we would soon be meeting. We assured him we would not, and regretted we had no more to give him, but expressed our profound thanks.

We sat down by the fireplace and both of us fell into a deep sleep, waking only when the children got up and started chattering loudly. Our clothes had dried and our hosts urged us to dress warmly, served us breakfast of tea and bread, and then the husband took us to the station. It was November 4, another dark winter morning. Nothing unexpected happened on the way to the station, but all the way the thought gnawed at my heart that but for our great bad luck our brothers would now be with us, and the persistent regret was like a spike in our happiness and relief to be free at last. While the guide was buying the tickets we noticed that the few peasants who were standing on the little platform were better dressed and better behaved than Polish peasants. There was no pushing when the train arrived and we had no trouble following our guide into a compartment. We traveled for about two hours through mountainous country and got off at a small station in a place called Poprad. In the street we met a few people evidently on their way to work and soon our guide stopped outside a building. He took us up to a first floor apartment where we were greeted in Yiddish by a middle-aged couple. The woman assured us we were quite safe, and told us to take off our coats and come have some tea and bread in the kitchen. Our guide wished us luck and left to return to his home.

After breakfast we both had a bath and went to sleep in

clean beds, wearing pajamas. When we awoke, well into the afternoon, our hosts told us that the next morning they would take us shopping. That evening some Jewish men came by and asked us many questions. One of them concentrated on me and asked for every detail I could remember of the camps and the German officials I had met during the four years of occupation. He particularly wanted exact names. He wrote down everything I told him and said that the report would be taken to Switzerland by courier so that the world could be informed. They sympathized with our emotions as we recalled our terrible experiences, but were at a loss to understand why we were still so obviously sad now that we were safe. Finally Fela broke down and told them about the misfortune that had befallen us in Plaszow a few days earlier. They cried along with us.

Then they gave us a short review of the situation in Slovakia, which was now ruled by a president who was a Catholic priest, Father Tiso, an unblushing puppet of Hitler. In Bratislava, the Slovak capital, the Nazis had a representative named Vislicenny, who was officially an "observer," but who actually gave the orders which the fascist Hlinka guard enforced. There had been about ninety thousand Jews left in the entire country when Hungary took over part of eastern Slovakia, where fifty thousand Jews had lived, but now there were only thirty-nine thousand left in Slovakia. The fascist Hlinka guards made their lives miserable, breaking into their homes and stores at will to rob and beat. Jews had to wear yellow stars, were dismissed from government service, and Jewish doctors and lawyers were not allowed to practice. Since March 25, 1942, there had been deportations to Poland, forty thousand able-bodied men and women. The authorities assured the Jewish leadership that they had only been sent there to work. For some time they had indeed sent home optimistic postcards about being well. But rumors that they were sent to the extermination camps Majdanek, Trawniki and Auschwitz seemed more probable. Many young Jews had run away to Hungary, choosing not to trust the Germans and their Hlinka puppets. Following intervention by the Catholic Church of Slovakia and the vatican envoy, a commission was established to ascertain the truth and they found that in fact, only three hundred of the Jews who had been deported to Poland were still alive. A few conscientious Catholic priests repeatedly protested to Father Tiso and the deportations were eventually stopped. He also granted many Jews "presidential exemptions" which allowed them to work and continue their businesses.

I could not but envy them their devoted leadership, the *Ustredna Zydowska* (Jewish Central Office), which comprised Rabbi Weismandel, Rabbi Armin Frieder and Gisi Fleischman, who dedicated herself to rescuing Jews, particularly Jewish children from Poland. In Poland the first thing the Germans had done when they marched in was to eliminate our devoted leaders. Those who had not fled were replaced by flexible personalities who would unquestionably carry out their will.

Now the plans for our escape were completed. Two Jewish men would take us to the Hungarian border where a Slovak guide would take us across, and bring us to the Jewish committee in Kosice for rail passage to Budapest. There, finally, the Polish-Jewish committees would take care of us. We spent the day looking around the city, amazed at how normal everything looked. In the Jewish stores the owners fitted us out with new clothes from head to foot. We were overwhelmed by their generosity and eagerness to help. We also acquired some luggage because we were told that in Hungary it was safer to travel well dressed and with suitcases.

In the evening our hosts asked us to get ready for the two young men who would guide us were coming. For the first time in four years I put on new clothes, not the old garments the deported and the dead had left behind. Somehow it was difficult to part from our old clothes so we put them into our suitcases.

Our guides took us to the station, bought the tickets, and got on the train with us. It was not as crowded as in Poland and the people were much more relaxed and polite. The passengers in our compartment were well dressed and friendly, but we evaded conversation by pretending to be asleep. We did not want them to hear us talking Polish, or Yiddish, though the Jews had told us it would be quite safe to do so. We were instinctively unable to take chances. We traveled for more than five hours until our guides signalled us that we would be getting off at the next stop, which was a small station. They led us through the darkness to a little

house, the home of our Slovak guide. They handed us over to
him and left. He told us he was taking us immediately to the
Hungarian border. We entered a small woods, and after we
had walked for a short time the guide told us we had just
crossed the border and were now on the Hungarian side. He
told us to wait there and soon returned with another man, our
Hungarian guide. He left us in his care, bade us goodbye
and left.

My family in Cracow, Poland, 1938.

My mother, father, my sister Fela and I in
Rzeszów ghetto.

Bescheinigung.

Poświdczenie.

Herzog Irene

wohnhaft in *Kraków* Strasse *Kottlaźga* Z. *11.*
zamieszkały   uka   l.

hat der Anordnung des Chefs der Zivilverwaltung vom 22 September 1939
zadość uczynił zarządzeniu Szefa Zarządu Cwilnego z 22 września i tutaj się zameldował.

entsprochen und sich hier gemeldet.

Krakau, den *23-X-* 1939.
Kraków, dnia

Siegel
pieczęć

Kurm Konszkiur

Leiter des Bezirksamtes der Stadtverwaltung.
Kerownik Miejskiego Urzędu Obwodowego.

German identification papers, Cracow, 1939.

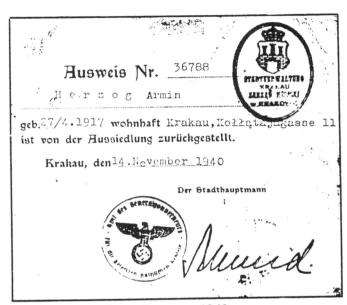

Permit to remain in Cracow, 1940.

Gestapo's stamp on my exemption from deportation, Rzeszów ghetto, 1942.

3) w mięsie z przodku. Kocham
pewno to jest ta drobn...gdy
nie to w drugi raz przyszły.
Do prania dajemy ...a...
b...ą do pralni... ...
za ... Do ... ...
...le na obiad podwójne
części porcja obiadu ...
na wieczór chleb też podwójny
(Nitek z kuchni i ... też
sobie ... coś ... ...
Masła też mamy nawet w
tym tygodniu bardzo dużo i też
nic Was nie kosztuje.
Proszę Cię więc abyś nam nic
...r za ... ...l ...
nie przysyłać bo nam nic
doprawdy nie brakuje.
Tylko Ty bądź nadal
ostrożna uważaj na siebie
stale. Gazet codziennie czytamy
i doprawdy dużo można z nich
... D napewno znacznie
... więcej wie... ale to wszystko jeszcze
nie jest to na co my czekamy.
Pora obięć domu i mieszkania
prawie, że nie wychodzimy z nikim
się nie ... tylko z ... kto
przyjmiemy i mieszkamy.
Pozostawiam miejsce dla N. i S.
by ci z myśl tego ...

Letter that my brother and I wrote to Fela,
which she received while hiding with
Zwoliński family.

In Csorgo Camp, Hungary, 1944.

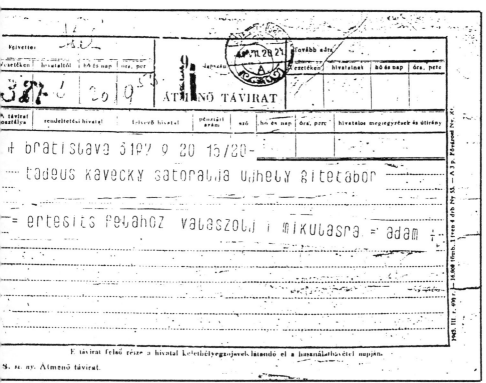

My telegram to my sister Fela, informing her that my escape
from Hungary was successful.

As a partisan in Slovakia
Mountains, 1944–1945.

Slovakia, 1945.

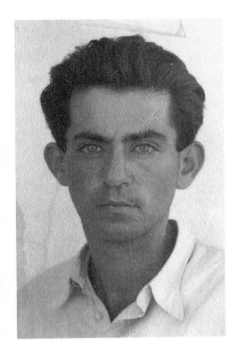

I met paratrooper,
Chaim Chermesh,
when he and other
members of British-
Jewish Brigade
parachuted in
Slovakia, 1944.

Gideon Frieder, 1995.

Czechoslovakian partisan identity papers.

SDRUŽENIE FAŠISTICKÝM REŽIMOM RASOVE PRENASLEDOVANÝCH SRP V BRATISLAVE

MINISTERSTVO NÁRODNEJ OBRANY

č. 10 He 91 .... Kleg. 5 oddel. 1947

Vlastnoručný podpis majiteľa

Číslo partizanskeho preukazu 7000

Meno a priezvisko Armin Herzog

narodený dňa 27.4.917 Sp. St.Ves

pol. okres Kežmarok , nar. polská

je podľa zák č. 34/1946 Sb

ČESKOSLOVENSKÝM PARTIZÁNOM

Bol príslušníkom partizánskej jednotky

Stalin Jegorov

od 15.11.1944 do 7.3.1945

a konal službu ako partizán

nosiľ partizánsky odznak čís XXX

Za ministra

Luiza and Tytus Zwoliński.

Wladysław
Łopatowski
and his family.

THE UNITED STATES HOLOCAUST
MEMORIAL MUSEUM

gratefully acknowledges a contribution
In Honor of the 75th Birthday of Henry A. Herzog, for
giving my life a second chance on October 27,1944.
from

Gideon and the Frieder Family

This gift will be used to create an American institution that will insure
that the Holocaust and its lessons are forever remembered.

9

Betrayal in Hungary
November 1943

The Hungarian guide told us, in Slovak, to follow very close behind him because there were border patrols active in the area. At one spot he told us to stop and wait very quietly as he was going ahead to check out the situation. We were still awaiting his return when we suddenly heard loud voices. Before we could figure them out, two armed Hungarian border police were upon us and our guide was with them. One of them, who spoke Slovak, ordered us to get up and walk ahead of them warning they would shoot us if we made any attempt to escape. I checked with a backward glance and saw that they were indeed pointing their rifles at us.

We were terribly upset, certain that our own guide had betrayed us. But why? We had hardly exchanged a word with him and he had not demanded any money. We walked in front of the rifles for only a short time when we spotted lights in the distance and arrived at a border post. Inside, an officer was sitting at a desk, and after he talked to our captors in Hungarian for a minute or two, we were ordered to surrender our papers and empty our pockets on the table. They also examined our luggage. The officer, who was writing what looked like a report, said nothing and did not look at us. When he completed his report he gave a short order and the Slovak-speaking guard told us to put on our coats, pick up our suitcases and come with them. They marched us through a small, dark village, to a little railroad station, where a few peasants were sitting on the benches, waiting for a train. We stood apart, in a corner, and when the train arrived waited

until everyone had got on and were then pointed into a
compartment by our guards. One of them left and we sat with
the other, who kept his rifle at the ready. The other passengers
stared at us curiously but nothing was said. After about an
hour the guard motioned us to get up and I noticed that the
station we stopped at was called Kassa. I knew that this meant
Kosice, which was the largest city in eastern Slovakia which
had been detached from Czechoslovakia and handed over to
the Hungarians by Hitler in 1938. The station was busy with
hundreds of people and many trains. For the first time we saw
Hungarian policemen, and some uniformed men wearing hats
with long feathers, whom I could not place. I spotted what I
believed were some Jewish people but could not catch their
eye. It was still quite early in the morning as we walked
through the bustling streets and I noticed many Jews among
the shopkeepers who were opening their stores, and many
Jewish-looking people in the crowd, and reckoned that we
must be in the Jewish quarter. But my attempts to address
some of them were ignored. I was desperately looking for
help. My biggest fear was that we would be sent back to
Poland where our lives would be worthless, but the Jews
avoided our looks. How different from their brethren in the
part of Slovakia from which we had just come, as though the
border the Nazis had drawn passed through their hearts too.
As we walked on I whispered to Fela and we agreed that since
we had different names on our papers, we would present
ourselves as an engaged couple, and not as brother and sister.

We soon left the Jewish quarter and reached a large modern
building guarded by police—the local jail. Our guard took us
into an office where an officer asked us something, first in
Hungarian, and when he realized we did not understand him,
switched to Slovak. But he only read out our names from our
papers which were on his desk, and when we acknowledged
them, he told the guard to take us out. He led us to the third
floor where we were separated. Fela kissed me and was led
away by a woman guard, while another warder put me into a
cell across the corridor, in which there were already several
other men, lying on some wide wooden benches. They addressed me in Hungarian but when they saw I did not understand, paid no further attention to me. I just sat there huddled
up for several hours until a guard brought us food, hot soup

and bread, in a tin dish. It was good but I was not concerned about eating. I tried to get some rest, spreading my coat on a bench and making a pillow of my jacket, but could not fall asleep. The events of the past forty-eight hours kept going through my head and I worried for Fela.

The next morning we were awakened with breakfast, weak black coffee, and some bread. Then I was called, for the first time by my new Aryan name, Adam Budkowski. I got up and gathered my belongings, but the warden motioned to leave everything in the cell, and took me to an office on the main floor, where a few men in plain clothes were sitting at a table. I was told to sit down facing them and they began questioning me, first asking whether I preferred Slovak or German. I told them I was a Pole and would speak Polish. As my answers then had to be translated, I had a little time to think. I maintained I was a Catholic whereupon one of them ordered me to drop my pants and pointed out that I was circumcised, but I stuck to my story. They were furious, and told me they did not believe a word I said, and considered my papers to be forged. Asked why I had come to Hungary, I told them I was looking for my family, that Fela was my fiancée and we hoped to make a new start in Hungary. While my answers were translated I could study their faces and realized that these were professional investigators who really did not believe me. I estimated that they must have guessed we had fled from Poland. It was reasonable to assume that we were not the first refugees betrayed by their guides.

When all my answers had been written down they called a policeman to take me back to the cell which was now empty. Again I huddled on a bench and when I heard loud voices from the yard below, looked out of the tiny window and saw young men drilling, no doubt new police recruits being broken in. A new man, who spoke German, was brought into the cell. He told me that the men who questioned me were officers of the Secret State Police, the highest authority in the Hungarian police force, and the most feared. I spent another almost sleepless night and the next morning was taken back to the same office for more questioning, but there was only one officer from yesterday at the table, and this time they all spoke Slovak. They shot questions at me but I remembered my story and stuck to it.

The next day, Sunday, there were no interrogations. The food was better and there was even a piece of meat in the soup. My German-speaking cellmate, who was an elderly, very intelligent man, told me he was a political prisoner, charged with being a communist, and that this was no regular prison but the headquarters of the Secret Police in Kosice in which prisoners were kept only for the duration of their interrogation. He refrained from asking any personal questions and I took my lead from him. For the next two days nothing happened, but on the third morning a guard took me downstairs into the office in which we had been received, where all my personal belongings, except my papers, were returned to me. A few minutes later Fela was brought in. We kissed but did not talk and when we were fully dressed two armed policemen escorted us out, and marched us through the deserted early morning streets. We had a chance for a short whispered conversation as we walked, and Fela told me she was fine, but fearful as to what they would do with us. We reached the station and one of the policemen boarded a train with us and took us into a compartment, from which he kept other passengers out. Fela and I were both very nervous, afraid that the train, which by its high speed seemed to be an express, was going to the Polish border. Certainly the length of the trip ruled out going to Poland, which was only a few hours from Kosice. After about five hours our guard got up and told us to get ready. We were overjoyed that the name on the large station we were entering was Budapest, and not some Polish station as we had feared. The guard took us to a streetcar, and made us stand on the open rear platform, away from the other passengers. It was a lovely city and seemed almost painfully normal, with open stores, well-dressed shoppers with packages, and bustling cafés and restaurants. The streetcar passed through what was obviously the Jewish section where we saw some religious bearded Jews, and some food and butcher stores with the Kosher sign. It seemed like a dream to me. We were only a few hundred kilometers from the accursed Poland and Jews were going about their business in peace, evidently considering their own shops and synagogues as quite normal.

After a long ride the guard told us to get off and took us to a very large building, a block long, with some guard booths

manned by policemen, at its front. Another jail. He took us in
and handed over our documents to an officer who, when he
realized we knew no Hungarian, motioned us to sit down.
Later he had us follow him into another room where we were
ordered to leave our luggage and personal belongings. On the
second floor Fela was again separated from me and handed
over to a female guard, and we cried as we parted. I was taken
up to another floor and put into a large room that was actually
a cell with tightly barred windows. There were a lot of men
sitting or standing about, but I could discover no Jewish-
looking faces among them. Another guard came in and, when
he had sorted out the language problem, motioned me to
follow him and took me to a storeroom where he gave me a
green blanket and wrote my name on it with white paint. He
also gave me a tin dish and spoon and returned me to the cell.
As there were no bunks or benches I sat down on my blanket
on the cold tiled floor. An hour later food was brought and
following my cellmates' example, lined up and got some hot
soup and bread. When I finished, I again did as they did, and
washed my dish and spoon at the faucet. A little later there
was a loud buzz, obviously the lights-out signal, and like all
the others, I spread my blanket on the floor and lay down,
covering myself with my coat and using my jacket for a pillow.
It was cold and noisy, with snoring, coughing and annoying
talk, but I was so exhausted, mentally and physically, that I
soon fell asleep. We were awakened the next morning by the
buzzer and lined up at the faucet to wash and shave. Then we
cleaned the cell which, despite being so crowded, was in fact
remarkably clean and orderly.

Soon a guard called my name and took me into a room
where some plainclothes officials were sitting at a table faced
by a single chair, into which they motioned me. The man
opposite me started questioning me in German and I asked
him to speak slowly and bear with me as I did not know the
language very well. First, reading from a paper in front of
him, he repeated the questions I had been asked in Kosice,
and then questions were shot at me by all of them, mainly
regarding my political background. I told them the only organization I had ever belonged to was a sports club in Cracow,
adding that I loved sports and played soccer and volleyball,
and also skated and liked mountainclimbing. Finally they

asked me about Fela and I stuck to our engagement story. They were curt but polite and made no threats, and when they got through had me taken back to my large cell. I walked around hoping to hear some Polish or Yiddish and finally did find two men conversing in Polish. I asked whether I might join them and they were quite glad to meet another Polish-speaking person. We introduced ourselves and for the first time I used my assumed name when talking to civilians. They were Mieczysław (Mietek) Kuczera from Przemyśl, and Henry Lubelski from Katowice. We did not mention religion, but I sensed they were both Jewish. Kuczera had been in this prison, which was called Tolonzhaz, for two weeks and Lubelski had been brought in a week later, and both of them were, like myself, waiting for the decision on their fate.

For lunch we got green-colored soup and some bread, and after we washed our dishes were taken down into the yard, which was enclosed by high, barbed-wire-topped walls. We walked up and down, four abreast, several hundred of us, some dressed in light clothes despite the cold, probably having been in the prison since summer. Henry told me there were many professional criminals in the jail, thieves and even murderers, but not in our cell, which held only politicals. It was good to stretch my legs and breathe the crisp cold air after the smells of the crowded cell, and I was happy to hear that we got to walk in the yard every day, one hour after lunch. I was interrogated several times more, and one afternoon was called out of the cell and taken down into the yard to meet Fela. We kissed and examined each other, and found that both of us looked fine. We were not the only couple in the yard, and Fela told me that she also had been interrogated several times but had no trouble with her answers. There were about forty women in her cell, which was very clean. She had been told that couples were permitted to meet twice a week. When I returned I told Henry and Mietek about my meeting with Fela who, I said, was my fiancée. At our next meeting Fela was radiant and told me that as a Polish citizen she was to be released in two days. But her happiness was marred by the thought that I would still be in Tolonzhaz. I wondered how she would manage in the strange big city without knowing the language, without friends, and with no money. But my new friends assured me that in Budapest there were many organizations aiding refugees from Poland.

The next morning I was again taken for interrogation, but this time it was a very short one, and the man who seemed to be in charge told me that I was to be sent to a camp. He named it, but I could not remember the complicated Hungarian name. I informed Kuczera and Lubelski and they told me that they were waiting to be sent there as well. Henry even knew the name, Csorgo Internalo Tabor. Both of them now confided that they were Jewish, and so did I. In fact the camp was for Jewish prisoners only. I tried hard, but without success, to get a message to Fela and was anxious because she would not know what had happened to me.

Once a week a man in a white coat, a doctor or paramedic, came into our floor with a lot of identical pills in a large white basin. If anyone had a complaint, no matter what, he gave him one of the pills, without as much as looking at the "patient." He never examined anybody. There was also a barber, who worked in the corridor, unceremoniously shaving off everybody's hair, and never said anything but *"Kevet keze"*, which meant "next." When he got through we all looked like common criminals, or as the more optimistic preferred to think, raw military recruits. To pass away the time Mietek told me his story. His family was sent from a small town to the Przemyśl ghetto and from there his parents were sent, in a cattle train, to the Belzec extermination camp in the summer of 1942. He and his two brothers were also put on a train to Belzec a year later, in September 1943. He was a mechanic by trade and brought along some tools and they managed to pry open the door of the car and jump out. Mietek made it, but his brothers and a few others who had dared to jump were not so lucky. They hit telegraph poles or rocks, and were killed. Now the only member of his family to survive, he wandered alone through the Polish countryside, avoiding cities but going into some villages to beg for food. Never staying in any one place for long to avoid betrayal, he managed to reach the Hungarian border and actually got across. But he was caught soon after he had walked several miles, and passed through a series of prisons until he ended up in Tolonzhaz. Henry told us he had fled from his hometown, Katowice, shortly after the Germans occupied it and reached Kolomyja near the Romanian border, which had been occupied by the Russians but subsequently taken by the Germans in June 1941. He escaped from Kolomyja a few weeks earlier and had managed to get across the Hungarian border on his own, but was captured and brought to Tolonzhaz.

It was almost Christmastime and a rumor swept the prison that some commission, probably from the International Red Cross, was coming to inspect our jail. We were put to work cleaning the place up, ostensibly for the holiday, and even began to discover bits of meat in our monotonous lunchtime green *Borszo levez* (lentil) soup. But the commission never came and the meat quickly faded out again. I was not very disappointed. From my experience in Poland I knew that the Red Cross was never very concerned about Jews. The cold became severe, and since many inmates only had summer clothing there were a lot of colds and fevers, and the coughing and sneezing made sleep a very fitful affair. As usual, all complaints were treated with the routine "wonder pill" dispensed from the basin by the man with the medical-style coat.

One morning a guard carrying a list, called Henry, Mietek and myself and took us downstairs to pick up our belongings. There we met other prisoners from other cells and all of us were taken out by armed policemen who put us on a nearby empty streetcar which took us to the railroad station. I noticed from the direction sign on the train they put us on that it was going west to Kassa, where I had come from in November. We had a compartment to ourselves, watched over by the guards who calmly ate their breakfast while we, who had not even been given the weak coffee and bread that morning, watched them hungrily. But worse than hunger was my concern for Fela and how she was managing all alone in the big city. The journey lasted for several hours until we were finally ordered to get off at a place called Satorja Ujhely which, our Hungarian fellow prisoners told us, was near the Slovak border. The guards took us through the snow-covered streets of the town to the country highway. The snow made walking difficult and the poor men in summer clothing had to jump about and flap their arms to keep warm, but there was nothing they could do about their light shoes which were almost immediately soaked through. We passed through a village and into the hills to an isolated building standing in the middle of nowhere.

10

Hungary, Csorgo Camp
January 1944

The building stood about three hundred meters from a railroad track, and when it came into sight we moved faster, anxious to get into a warmer place. It was a modern three-story building, enclosed by a high wooden fence topped with barbed wire, and secured by guard booths manned by armed sentinels. A policeman opened the gate for us and we entered the yard at the back of the building. There we were ordered to form a single line and wait, under the curious eyes of the prisoners who were looking out from their little barred cell windows above us.

A police captain and two sergeants came out, took the lists from our escorts, dismissed them, called and checked off our names and marched us in. All the talking, and except for the rollcall there had not been much of it, was done by the sergeants, the captain never said a word. Anyway, I did not understand anything. Inside, we were handed over to some men in civilian clothes, evidently trusties, who issued us blankets, pillows and tin dishes. One of the Hungarians in our group told them we had had nothing to eat all day so we were given some hot coffee with plenty of bread. When we had finished eating, we were taken upstairs and assigned cells and bunks. Henry and I were put into one cell and Mietek into the adjoining one. The first thing I noticed was that the bars on the window were ominously massive. We were obviously in a closely guarded jail, but there were no doors in our cells. The resident prisoners, who informed us we had come to Csorgo prison, introduced themselves. They also told us that this was a Jewish camp. The majority were Hungarians and the rest were from the German occupied countries. I even met two young men from Cracow. One of them, Romek Singer, was the brother of Emil, an old classmate of mine. His family was now in Budapest. They had moved from Cracow to Bochnia in 1940 when the Germans ordered the Jewish community reduced, and last year managed, for a very large sum, to hire a German truck to take them to Budapest. He was captured by the secret police when they picked up a wanted political suspect, who he had unluckily been sitting next to in a café. But he was not discouraged. His family, who were very rich, had already engaged an influential lawyer, and he expected shortly to be released. Another of the Cracow men, Richard Green, used to live a block away from the house I grew up in. In 1942 his parents were deported from the Cracow ghetto. He and his sister had escaped to the Aryan side. But their experience there had been unbearably harrowing. They had to be constantly alert for informers as well as for the Gestapo itself. Just a little less troubling were the blackmailers, so-called *Schmalzowniks,* who forced them to pay silence money, and they had to change their address every few weeks. They studied Catholic rites, which in an emergency might save his sister, though not necessarily him for he dreaded the moment when he would be ordered to take down his pants. Every time somebody looked at them for more than the usual passing moment they were terrified, and though neither of them looked Jewish, the uncertainty wore them down until they felt unable to stand it any longer. In the summer of 1943 they managed to contact somebody who helped them cross into Slovakia for a price. There they had been helped by a Jewish committee, as we had been, and like us had been betrayed on the Hungarian border. His sister, like Fela, was free in Budapest, and was taking steps to get him released. Correspondence was permitted in this camp though limited to a few short letters. Both men promised to ask their relatives to look for Fela, but I realized that without big money to hire important lawyers, my chances for release were slim.

There were about five hundred men in this prison, three-quarters of them Hungarians. There were thirty in our very clean, and fairly well-heated room. For the first time since leaving Slovakia I undressed to go to sleep but even though I was exhausted, I was frequently awakened by loud screams from the poor men who were reliving their nightmarish experiences in their dreams, and the snoring and coughing. For breakfast the next morning, served in a large downstairs hall, we were given hot coffee and plain dark bread. We were allowed to walk about inside the prison, but not to go outside. For lunch we were served the same green lentil soup I was familiar with from Tolonzhaz, but there was plenty of bread and it seemed to taste better. After lunch we were taken into the yard for exercise, walking around in circles, three abreast. Beyond the fence I spotted a vegetable and flower garden and was told it belonged to the captain. Behind the garden some big black pigs were foraging in the mud. They must have weighed at least three hundred fifty pounds each. I had never seen pigs of that color or size. They were hardly able to move in the squishy mud.

Comparing this new jail to the terribly overcrowded Tolonzhaz prison, I felt I had moved up in life. There were no criminals or murderers here, only Jews. I looked around very carefully and noted particularly that there were hills not far away. The idea of a possible escape was already taking shape in my mind. I knew that Slovakia could not be very far away, and if I could make it across the fences, I might have a chance. It was worth thinking about and when I told Mietek and Henry they were ready to join me, if a chance should come. The Hungarian in the bunk below me, Laszlo Kittay, who was about my father's age and had been there more than a year, told me that most of the Hungarian prisoners were suspected communists. The others were mainly black marketeers who had plenty of money to bribe the guards for privileges, who received excellent food parcels from their relatives, and who, in fact, did not expect to stay very long since they could afford lawyers who knew how to get around the authorities. He advised me not to talk about my escape plans because there were informers about. He also told me that no one had yet managed to make a successful escape because the jail was very well guarded. But most of the guards were friendly, and for a price brought papers, magazines, cigarettes and candies for the prisoners from nearby Satorja Ujhely. Laszlo also told me that although the Hungarian government were anti-Semites they had so far resisted German pressure to pass laws against the Jews.

One morning, when the mail was being distributed, I received a most pleasant surprise—a letter from Fela. Somehow she had found out where I was. She wrote that when she had been released from Tolonzhaz prison in Budapest with some other Jewish girls from Poland, Janek, a young Polish Jew from Kosow who lived in Budapest as an Aryan Pole, met them and found accommodations for them with Jewish families and got jobs for them in a Jewish orphanage for Polish children, many of whom had been rescued by Gisi Fleischman's Slovak group. The work was hard but Fela was happy and proud to help the miraculously rescued waifs. She was fine but was worried about me. Laszlo gave me some change to buy writing paper and envelopes and I wrote her that I was doing well, and except for the fact that I was in prison and not getting as much food as I would like, I was living in a comparative paradise. We were able to maintain a regular correspondence and in time I mentioned the lawyers who were getting prisoners released, and asked whether she might be able to enlist some Jewish organization to engage a lawyer for me.

Among a group of prisoners who had recently been brought to the jail, I met a man from Cracow named Kozma. In our conversation I learned that he was the brother-in-law of the Argentinian Jew in whose home my brothers had been captured. He knew nothing of their fate. He himself had escaped a short time ago, after they had heard that the Germans were killing off every Jew in their camps as they retreated before the advancing Russians. The SS did not want to leave any living witnesses.

When the two sergeants who actually ran the prison called for volunteers to tend the garden and the pigs, I stepped forward with a Yugoslav called Jozko. As he had "seniority" over me he got the better job in the garden, while I was assigned to the pigs. But I had succeeded in getting what I was aiming for, a job in the open air outside the wall, and although all the prisoners ruled out escape as an impossibility, I intended to try. The work in the pigsty was tough and smelly and I had to wash thoroughly before returning to my cell where I had become known as the pigman and was the butt of many jokes. I didn't mind. I was getting better food straight from the kitchen, and was excused from the afternoon exercising in the yard. Once in a while I even went outside of the compound, under guard, to dispose of loads of dirt. I got to know the guards and their schedules and the food enabled me to regain my former weight and strength. Jozko and I became firm friends and he confided that his dream was to join Tito's partisans in his home country. So the two of us shared the dream of freedom. One day Fela sent me some cakes she had baked with an apology that she had been unable to interest a lawyer in my case because she didn't have enough money. It was a disappointment but I consoled myself with the cakes which, as was the custom, I shared with my cellmates.

At rollcall one morning Jozko was found to be missing. We were immediately sent back to our cells while the staff began a search and we learned they had discovered a deep hole underneath the outside fence where Jozko had worked. Their searches continued all day but turned up nothing. The sergeants were very angry and showed it. It was the first time an escape had succeeded, and they threatened us with the feather-hatted police. We were all very nervous but nobody talked since nobody knew. Jozko was wise enough to keep his plans to himself.

My work with the pigs was now watched more closely. A few days later, as I was busy with the animals, I was dismayed to see Jozko being marched back by two feathered gendarmes. They had to support him since he was barely able to walk. He was put into solitary confinement in a cellar cell, and when he was let out a few days later, he lay limply on his bunk, his badly bruised body almost lifeless. Everybody suffered with him and brought their precious goodies to comfort him. When he recovered he told us he had almost made it to the Yugoslav border, but was caught by a patrol who tortured him until he told them where he had come from.

When I heard that one of the black marketeers who had operated the police canteen was about to be released, I asked one of the sergeants who knew me from my work with the pigs, to give me the job that was considered one of the best in the prison. In my elementary and broken Hungarian I managed to persuade him. I worked in the canteen for only four or five hours a day, and was allowed into the police kitchen where I could occasionally scrounge a good meal. I also got to taste some of the goodies I sold and even made a little money by judiciously overcharging the black marketeers who were privileged to buy things from the canteen. It would come in handy if I should ever manage to escape. I lost my old name of pigman and became Adam the Cantinosz.

A short time later Green and Singer were informed by their families that they had secured their release. I was happy for them and entreated them to contact Fela in Budapest and tell her about me. About a week later I had a letter from Fela, but she did not mention them. Those "friends" forgot me the moment they walked out free. In the next package from her there was a cake and in it documents made out in my name attesting that I was a Christian Pole who had come to Hungary in 1939, and that I had the status of a legalized refugee. Now I had enough money to travel, and papers to see me through, all I needed was to get out. From Jozko's experience I knew exactly how tough that was going to be. It became even tougher a few days later when we learned that the Germans, worried by Russian successes and no longer trusting their Hungarian allies, had invaded Hungary on March 19, 1944. This was a most devastating and tragic development for us. I knew that soon the SS and Gestapo would come too. The news profoundly upset all of us and particularly the Polish Jews who had experienced these killers first hand. I put out some cautious feelers to Henry, Mietek and Jozko, and we agreed to try to get to the Slovak border. There was no point in thinking of an uprising in the prison for most of the prisoners were naive Hungarians who had not had a taste of the Germans and were therefore not ready for such a desperate gamble. In any case we had no weapons. We made up our minds that if we were to make the attempt, it would have to be very soon. From the newspapers our guards brought in for the Hungarian prisoners, we learned that the pro-German prime minister, Sztojay had established a new cabinet comprised of many anti-Semites, whom the Germans could rely on to do their bidding. Nevertheless the SS and Gestapo took over the most important offices in the new ministries and were virtually running the country. In our prison the guards were reinforced and they became harsher. I was dismissed from my canteen post and at our daily exercises, we were put through push-ups and other strenuous drills in the muddy yard. Those unable to keep up had to do them all over again. To further humiliate us, the guards mockingly changed the name of the prison from Vidias Tabor (Attention Camp) to Zido Tabor (Jew Camp). The mail was now more carefully censored, and I no longer dared to exchange news with Fela, not even in the coded language we believed only we could understand. From some of the new return addresses on the letters that arrived for the Hungarian prisoners, we understood that the Hungarians were hastily "resettling" the Jews of Hungary, who were the last group of relatively untouched Jews in occupied Europe. God had allowed the Germans more than four years to perfect their methods of killing Jews. It seemed our fate was now to be shared by the Jews of Hungary as well.

In May 1944, our exercise walks, which had been a pleasure, became an ordeal. It hurt me to see the sadistic sergeants humiliating the older men. Yet this was child's play compared to a new experience to which we were exposed. One afternoon a freight train passing by on the railroad tracks only three hundred meters distant, drew our attention. There were human voices coming from it. We saw that the small ventilation vents had barbed wire stretched across them, and between the strands, hands were reaching out, a silent, desperate signal for help that did not come. How well I knew those death trains from my *Ostbahn* work. Now they were taking the Jews of Hungary to the extermination camps. We told the Hungarian prisoners about these trains and they began to fear that their own relatives might be on the train. The religious Jews grouped together and started reciting Psalms, the traditional way of averting evil, but I could have told them that Psalms had not stopped a single extermination train. From a friendly guard we learned that some very high-ranking German officers, accompanied by senior Hungarian officials, had visited the ghetto in Košice and had then come to Satorja Ujhely. It reminded me of the catastrophe that followed Himmler's visit to Cracow, and I knew it boded no good. Those of us who had escaped from Poland would be the first they would turn on. The SS and Gestapo never forgot Jews who dared elude the fate the Master Race had prepared for them. We were the eyewitnesses to their horrible crimes. During the night we heard several more trains with their disembodied voices passing by and each one increased our apprehension. The religious

Jews urged us to pray with them. I had seen how ineffective
prayers had been. Even the most God-fearing rabbis and their
faithful disciples had gone to a cruel death, still wearing their
prayer shawls.

At rollcall one morning there were more than the usual
number of policemen on guard. The prison commandant came
out and handed a list to one of the sergeants who looked at it
and then told us that all those whose names he would call
should wait in the yard. The rest must go back to their cells,
pick up their belongings, and come back down. When he got
through the list and my name had not been called, I realized
with a shudder that I was to be deported. So was Henry.
Mietek, Kawecki and Jozko, our close friends would stay. We
said goodbye to them and went up to our cell. I had no
illusions. this was it. The net had closed around me at last and
there was no escape this time. I worried only for Fela. When
we came down the others were ordered to return to their cells,
and from the windows they called goodbye to us. I waved
back. We were marched out, about two hundred fifty of us,
escorted by twenty armed guards on both sides of our column
and behind it. They warned us that anybody attempting to
escape would be shot at once, and I knew they meant it.

On the way I told Henry that we would try to make a getaway from the train. We both carried files which Mietek, who
was never without some tools, had given us. We might have a
chance to force our way out. It was about ten in the morning
when we reached the Satorja Ujhely railroad station. There
was not a single passenger waiting there, only a large contingent of feather-hatted gendarmes. It was a bad sign to me.
The station had been cleared. We were ordered into the large
waiting room and I noticed at once that every door and
window was guarded. Soon a long column of well-dressed
men, women and children were marched into the station,
guarded by gendarmes and accompanied by some Jews who
had special identification tags on their yellow armbands, probably *Judenrat* officials. With great surprise I saw that there
was no German official, uniformed or plainclothes, in evidence. Even more astounding was the fact that all those Jews
were completely relaxed, conversing calmly as they stood by
their luggage. The children were playing unconcernedly
around their parents, and the whole surrealistic scene looked

more like an outing of a social club than a deportation to death. Only ignorance could have kept them that calm.

The day wore into evening and we were still standing around, thirsty and hungry. The sight of the police guards already having their second meal did not stop our hunger pangs. At last some officers arrived and went into the dispatcher's office. When they came out they ordered the ghetto column to start marching back where they had come from. It was beyond my understanding. However, the religious immediately told us with deep conviction and great relief, that God had performed a miracle at last. We didn't have much time to consider this, because as soon as the column had gone, we were ordered to line up and start marching also, but into the city and not back to our camp. We thought we might be taken to the ghetto, and I hoped that would give us a fighting chance for an escape—the break we were looking for. No matter how carefully the ghetto was watched, Henry and I knew enough to make good our flight. But they did not take us to the ghetto. Instead they marched us to a small jail in the city and ordered us to wait in the yard. We sat down on our luggage and I speculated that we had been kept apart from the ghetto Jews because we were considered jailbirds, criminals needing special attention. We were given hot coffee and bread, handed out to us by convicts from the jail. After our hungry day it tasted like manna and only when I had eaten the last crumb did I look around and saw that there was no chance to escape from the walled yard, sealed in by our highly disciplined guards. It was cold and damp but I managed to get a few hours of sleep. In the morning we were given more coffee and bread and then lined up to wash. Then there was a second line for the primitive toilet facilities. Again we sat and waited. We speculated that perhaps the deportation train had had a breakdown yesterday and would come today. But the morning passed without anything at all happening, except that the religious among us were now completely convinced of a miracle and were quite cheerful. I knew better. God had already had many years to perform His miracles, but the suffering I had witnessed, and the hundreds of thousands who were dead, had not shown Him to be a willing miracle worker. We were given hot soup and bread for lunch and spent another night in the yard. Very early the next morning the guards got us up and marched us out. They kept their rifles ready for instant use, and when they led us back in the direction of the Csorgo camp, we didn't know whether to feel relieved or suspect something really bad. When we got there we were lined up in the yard for a rollcall by the commandant and sergeants. Nobody was missing, yet we were not allowed back into our cells, but were told to wait in the yard. We could see our comrades watching us from their cell windows, and when the guards left the yard, a lot of questions were shouted back and forth between us and our cellmates at the windows. It was good to be back, we thought, but wondered what would come next.

As darkness fell the commandant came out and ordered us to return to our cells. The reunion was a happy one. Perhaps this really was a miracle. We slept in our old bunks again, almost like a return home. Almost, because throughout the night we heard the trains. The deportations had not stopped, they had only been interrupted. The next day was uneventful routine, but early in the afternoon at the rollcall, the commandant brought out his list, called our names again, and ordered us to bring out our belongings. In an instant the happy jail was enveloped in a graveyard mood. Our cellmates cried as they waved goodbye once more. We just stood waiting, resigned to the point of virtual indifference.

11

Hungary, Csorgo Camp, Suicide Attempt and Escape
End of May 1944

When the captain and two sergeants arrived, I decided not to wait any longer but to carry out the plan that had been taking shape in my mind since we were brought back from Satorja Ujhely. I got out my razor blades from my suitcase, rolled up my left sleeve, and cut my wrist. The blood spurted out and the men next to me started screaming. The last thing I remembered was policemen running toward me. When I came to, I was lying in a bed with Henry in the bed next to me. Weakly I asked him where we were, and he responded equally as weak that we were still in the camp, in the sickroom. When he had seen me being carried away by the police, he had despaired too and drunk the benzine from a small bottle he had kept for an emergency. The last thing he had discerned was a general panic breaking out which the sergeant stopped by immediately marching everybody off, out of the gate toward Satorja Ujhely.

I looked at my arm and saw that it was heavily wrapped in white bandages. My fingers were swollen, and there was a lot of blood on my arm and clothes. Our commandant came in and asked why we had done such a stupid thing. We replied almost in unison that the thought of being taken back to Poland, where we had lost all our families, had driven us to despair. He made no comment but wished us a speedy recovery, then he left. Later in the evening Mietek and Laszlo sneaked in. They told us that nobody, except the sick, was allowed into the infirmary which was not guarded, and had no bars over the windows. They had taken advantage of the fact that half the guards were escorting the men to Satorja Ujhely, to come and see us.

At that moment it struck me that this was our opportunity. We could not expect such favorable circumstances again, and I told them so. They began discussing it, but I cut them short. My mind was made up. I would go that night whether they were coming or not. Henry was with me and Mietek agreed, but Laszlo declined. He was too old to run, he said, and went out, but immediately turned back and held out his gold pocket watch and chain to me, remarking that if we make it they would come in handy and easily converted into cash. I refused to accept them, so he simply walked away leaving them on the bed. But when I called "thank you" after him, he came back and embraced me for a long moment. We both cried and expressed our wish to meet again as free men, hopefully in the not-too-distant future.

Henry got up and checked the room then took all the sheets off the beds, rolled them tight and knotted them into a long rope. Together we checked the windows and found a heavy metal rod securely fastened to the outside wall and going all the way down to the ground, probably the lightning conductor. It could provide a handhold for extra safety as we climbed down. We waited for the lights-out buzzer, allowed another short time for the camp to fall asleep, and then Henry helped me to dress. I suggested we tie our shoes to our belts until we would be across the fence, to keep down the noise. Next we tied the ends of the sheets to the inside pillar and after a final check of its strength, I was ready to go. I knew the yard very well from the observations I had made in my pig-keeping days, and knew just where the fence was easiest to negotiate. We agreed that when I reached the ground I would signal by giving the rope two sharp pulls and the others would follow. Grasping the sheet-rope with my right hand, and holding onto the lightning conductor with the bandaged left, I slowly made my way down. I arrived safely, pulled twice, and crossed quickly to the fence to wait for them. Henry came down next and began to tie the barbed wire on top of the fence together to create an opening, and I helped him hold the wires. Now we waited for Mietek, but instead of his arrival we heard noises coming from the infirmary and a light was switched on.

Something had gone wrong but we realized we had no time

to find out. Henry helped me through the barbed wire and over the fence and followed me. We both started running across the open field. At that moment the whole camp was illuminated and an alarm siren started wailing. We ran as fast as our feet could carry us in the direction of the railroad tracks. The hills which had been our original target were too far away. The flashlights of the guards were already bobbing behind us. We decided to lie low, flush with the cold, wet ground, blessing our luck that it was a very dark night. We could hear the shouts of the guards looking for us with flashlights and lanterns, but they gradually faded into the distance. We started to crawl, keeping close to the ground, but stopped short of the rail tracks because we seemed to see vague figures there. We remained lying on the ground for some hours and then decided to risk a run across the road into the thick undergrowth by the tracks.

From the bushes we saw the camp lights going out and felt we had made good our escape. Soon we heard a train approaching, and when it passed us the voices marked it as another deportation train. When its whole length had gone past we got up and started following it, because now it had shown us the way west. Using the rails as our guide we walked fast, not bothering about the wet and dirt on our clothes. We were free and intended to reach Slovakia. When dawn broke we found ourselves a hiding place in the thick of the bushes because we assumed that the search for us would continue over a wide area. We looked back, but the camp was out of sight. We had gone even farther than we had estimated during the night, spurred on by fear and expectation. Now we were exhausted and took turns sleeping and watching. During the morning we saw more trains passing in both directions; some passenger and some freight trains but also the cursed deportation trains, going west with their unhappy cargo and returning empty to pick up more Jews.

Henry took the first watch while I lay down to sleep and for the first time I thought of my injured arm and it immediately started hurting. The fingers were swollen purple and I feared infection, but I fell asleep and slept well until late in the afternoon. We had no food and though we were hungry we were elated to be free, even though our happiness was marred by Mietek's failure to escape also.

When it got dark we started walking again, sticking close to the tracks which were our guide to the west. We walked all night, resting very little, and when dawn broke lay down and took stock. It was very quiet. Not far away there were some hills, and a little later some peasants appeared on them and started to work. We picked our way cautiously toward them. They were frightened by our appearance, but Henry reassured them in Hungarian until at last they grudgingly offered us some bread and milk.

12

Back in Slovakia
June 1944

When we had eaten, Henry asked them how far it was to the Slovakian border, and we were pleasantly surprised when they told us that we were already in Slovakia. My wrist was bleeding again and we asked them to show us the way to the nearest village. We proceeded with great caution because we were still in border country which could be dangerous, and stopped some distance from the village and hid, waiting for the dark. We were wary of running into patrols. When darkness fell we entered the village stealthily and walked slowly through it until we spotted an isolated house. We knocked on the door and, speaking Polish, told the man who opened that we were refugees in need of help. I showed him my arm and asked for hot water. He let us in, though both he and his wife looked frightened, but when they got used to our presence he told us to take off our jackets and shoes to dry while she heated water. Their children were asleep in the next room.

I painfully ripped off the bandages and found that my wrist was bleeding slightly, my fingers were still swollen, but the purple color had faded. I washed the wound with hot water and the woman helped me wrap my wrist with some clean white linen. While our clothes were drying by the stove she served us some hot soup and bread and they watched us fascinated as we wolfed down the food. We didn't want to risk staying too long, and they looked relieved when, early in the morning, we put on our dry clothes, thanked them, and went on our way. We headed back to the high hills. When it got dark we lay down in some bushes, and slept until early the next morning. This time we decided to continue through the hills. It seemed safer than walking along the exposed tracks, and also gave us an overview of what was going on below. We followed the sun west, heading for Poprad. Although we spotted some villages on the plain below we decided not to take unnecessary risks and moved on through the hills, putting as much distance between ourselves and the border as possible. In the afternoon we came upon some peasants at work in the hills who gave us more bread and milk. We kept going until dark and then bedded down on some soft grass and slept well with occasional disturbances from roaming animals. Early the next morning we started out again, keeping to the shelter of the trees at the edge of a forest. Henry told me that his stomach pains, caused by the benzine he had swallowed, had gone but my wound was still hurting and we agreed that in the evening we would again seek help in a village. Late in the afternoon we spotted a village below us but decided to wait until dark before going in. We were by this time soaked to the skin by heavy rains that had begun falling. When we felt it was dark enough, we made our way down the hill and entered the barn of an outlying farm. It was empty, except for a single cow, so we took off our wet outer clothing and shoes and bedded down in some dry straw. The cow, after apparently thinking over our intrusion must have decided she didn't like it, and started bellowing loudly. The noise brought the peasant and he was very angry. When we arose, two nearly nude, unshaven men, one with his arm in a bloody bandage, he was frightened. Fortunately he made no scene, but simply gave his cow some food and walked out. We watched to see that he went back into his house and continued watching for a long time to make sure he would not go to bring the police. We then took turns sleeping and watching.

In the morning my wound was hurting so badly that I told Henry I must risk asking for the peasant's help. We went to the house together. His wife gave us hot water, a fresh dressing, and some food. I was glad to see that my wound was healing, and the swelling was subsiding. It was still raining but we decided we must return to the safety of the hills. The wet ground made the going tougher, and since there was no sun to guide us we lay down to rest in the shelter of a large tree. The next morning the rain stopped and we could just make out the sun behind the clouds, enough to indicate our direction. In the afternoon we met some peasants in the hills who gave us some more food, and just before it got dark we were happy to see the lights of a city in the distance. Hoping to find some Jews there to help us, we headed for it the next morning. We found most of the stores closed, and very few people in the streets. It must have been some sort of holiday. Only in the town center did we find anything open, a bar, a restaurant, and a candy store. We went into the store and I asked the owner in Polish, whether there were any Jews in the town. He was taken aback by our dirty appearance but told us that the nearest Jews lived in Liptovský Svätý Mikuláš, and that we would have to take a train to get there.

Now the time had come to sell the gold watch and chain. I offered it to the storeowner. He suggested a sum and since I had no way of judging his price, and since we needed the money at once, I took it. He showed us the way to the station, and we were stared at all the way by passers-by whose holiday best made us look even shabbier and dirtier than we actually were. At the station we found we were in Prešov. Henry bought two tickets to Liptovský Svätý Mikuláš and as we were studying the timetable on the wall two policemen suddenly materialized out of nowhere. They asked for our papers, but since these were in the office of the commandant in Csorgo, we just looked foolish. They were both armed so we didn't try to get away. They took us to a building in the city center, the local jail, not far from the candy store. We were ordered to empty our pockets and were searched, but except for taking away our belts, they left us alone in a ground-floor cell.

We were flabbergasted by this fresh stroke of bad luck and wondered whether we had been betrayed, not that it mattered. Only the candy store man could have done it so fast. Certainly only he knew we were going to the station. We had not reached any conclusions when a policeman brought us lunch, hot soup and bread. At least they didn't intend to starve us. We were still discussing what had gone wrong and what we might do next, when we heard a determined knocking on the wall from the adjoining cell. Somebody was obviously trying to get in touch with us. We looked all over and finally at ground level found a metal pipe, probably for heating, going through the wall. By lying down close to it we were able to converse with our unknown neighbor. He told us he was a Polish Jew from a small town near the Slovak border, and after he had crossed it, he had been picked up by a border patrol just one week earlier. He had told the police the truth—that he was a Jew who had escaped from Poland. He was brought back to this jail and every day had been interrogated by the secret police, the so-called USB. The day before they had informed him that he was to be returned to Poland and he knew that it would be the end for him.

Without asking who we were, or, indeed, giving us a chance to get in a word, he urged us, if we were Jewish, not to speak Polish, not even to mention Poland, and never to admit we were Polish. Our one-sided conversation through the wall was cut short when the guards came in with blankets, hot coffee and bread. But the fair treatment was no consolation for being behind bars again.

When the guards left we got back down on the floor and asked our neighbor if there was any way we could let his family know about him, but he told us all his family had been killed in Poland. We tried at least to cheer him up, saying that perhaps he would not actually be sent back. We were very grateful to him. Condemned himself, he was nevertheless eager to save other Jews, people he did not know and could not even see. Henry and I immediately agreed to talk only Yiddish or German to each other and to justify it if interrogated, by claiming that Henry was a Hungarian and that I was born in Spiska Stara Ves and also lived in Carpatho-Ukraina, which had belonged to Czechoslovakia until 1938. The Jews there generally spoke Yiddish. In order not in any way to be associated with Poland, we would admit having escaped from Csorgo, and not try to deny being Jewish. We knew how easily they could check just by making us take down our pants. Every policeman knew it too.

The cell was clean and warm and we laid down in the bunks and got a good night's rest. The next morning after a breakfast of coffee and bread, we were taken to the first floor and placed in separate rooms. In mine there were a few men in civilian clothes sitting around a table. An older man, sitting by the wall facing me, told me in Slovak to take the vacant chair between four younger men. He started questioning me in

Slovak and I replied in German that I did not understand. Then he switched to German, which most of the others appeared to understand. I said I was born in Slovakia but that my family had moved to Munkaczewo in Hungary when I was still a boy. I told them of my suicide attempt in Csorgo, and after the older man examined my arm, no doubt to make sure I was not putting on an act, asked me why. Sensing his sympathy I told him about the deportation trains. They then questioned my political affiliations and my attitude toward Russia. I told them I had been a clerk and in my spare time engaged in sports, had never gone to a political meeting, or ever met a Russian, and had no interest in politics. As we had foreseen, they asked about Csorgo and I told them I had met Henry there, that we had escaped together, and that a third partner in our attempt had been caught. When they finished questioning me, I asked to see a doctor and was told there was no doctor in the jail but that I would get iodine and fresh bandages. When I returned to the cell Henry was already there and, speaking Yiddish, we told each other about our interrogations and what we had said. We believed we had done well. Then we tried to get in touch with our neighbor but got no answer to our knocking. We hoped that the man, whose advice had been so valuable, was not being sent back to Poland, but feared he may have been.

The warders, who were very polite, served us three reasonably good meals during the day and the next morning we were taken for more interrogations. I noticed that not all the officials were the same. The older man who I was sure was the chief was there again and nodded to me. He did not ask the questions this time, merely kept his eyes glued on my face while I answered. The questions focused on our escape and our doings until we were caught in Prešov. This was easy. I simply told them the truth. They asked me if we had met some escaped Russian POW's in the hills we had moved through. I could answer truthfully that we had met only peasants who had given us food. Before I left I was given white bandages.

We were not called during the next two days and just sat in our cell, taking care to walk around for long stretches to keep our legs in shape and prevent cramps. The window was too high for us to get a look at the street below. On the third morning I was taken upstairs alone. Again there were the five men but they told me they had no further questions. I was required only to sign the statements I had made so far. When I returned to the cell it was empty and my heart missed a beat, but in a few minutes Henry was also brought back. He too had only been asked to sign his statements. The next day we were given lunch a little earlier than usual and then told to get ready to leave. The anxiety this caused spoiled the meal. Two armed guards took us to the station and one of them came on the train with us. The guard sat by the door and paid no attention to our talk, which he could not understand. I told Henry we must escape because we did not know where we were going and it might be back to Poland. We decided to make our move at the very next stop before it was too late. As soon as the train started off we would jump. I instructed Henry as best I could how to land safely. I had had experience from my pre-war work in the chocolate factory, which was located between two stops of the streetcar, and I used to jump off of it every morning to save the walk.

The train stopped and the moment it started again we asked our guard for permission to go to the toilet. He allowed us out and watched us going through the passage. When we passed the exit I tore the doors open and jumped. Henry followed me at once, and we hit the ground together. My pants were torn but I was not hurt and neither was Henry. We got on our feet and scrambled to some nearby bushes to hide since we had to reckon with our guard pulling the emergency brake. But to our delight the train went on undisturbed. We were safe, and after waiting a little longer to make sure, went back to the tracks and followed them, not sure where they would take us. We didn't have to wonder for long, because when we rounded a bend in the tracks we walked straight into the arms of an armed patrol, two Slovakian border guards. They were as surprised as we were but before we had a chance to make a run for it, their rifles were pointing at us. They told us to start moving and walked close behind us, in the same direction the train had taken. From their uniforms we gathered they were Slovaks and asked them where they were taking us, but they ignored our questions, and only waved their rifles at us to move on. It was getting dark and as we walked we made a new escape plan. We agreed on a "go" signal—a single longish scratch of the head—and then a quick dash for the nearest bush, but only after it had become almost dark. Meanwhile we gradually walked a little faster to put a longer distance between us and the guards and when I judged we were far enough away, and I felt it was dark enough, I scratched my head and the two of us jumped into the bushes and ran like hunted rabbits. The guards started shooting and we could hear them call to each other but we were getting away from them, and after we had run for some time I threw myself on the ground. Henry and I had gotten separated in the rush but I did not risk calling to him. I felt sure he was not far away and we could meet up again at first light. I sat in the bushes, unable to sleep, and at the first crack of dawn I called for Henry and soon heard him calling back. We decided not to risk any more cities and, taking our direction from the sun again, started moving west and into the hills. We had had our fill of rail tracks. They brought us bad luck.

We saw peasants working in the fields but decided not to risk an encounter just yet, but rather to get farther away from the border. We kept to the edge of a forest and only after many hours, when we again came upon some peasants at work, did we feel safe to ask for food. They invited us to eat with them, never saying a word, not even to ask who we were, and appeared relieved to see us leave when we had finished. Nevertheless we realized they were good people, not like Poles who would have suspected we were Jewish and would have given us away. We decided the cover of the forest was our safest bet and went on through the trees. The weather turned bad. It started raining hard again and we were quickly soaking wet and cold. So we decided that rather than catch a bad cold, or even pneumonia, we would be better off to find an isolated village. Unfortunately there was none in sight. So we walked on and when we came to a road in the evening we were so exhausted that we simply lay down and fell asleep beside it. It was a very bad mistake. Though we did not know it we were in fact very near a highway and were awakened by two armed gendarmes, a foot patrol—a very unpleasant awakening. They motioned us to get up and move, not even bothering to ask us anything or demand to see our papers.

Henry and I said nothing to each other. We were both feeling sheepish about the silly mistake we had made. The gendarmes took us into a small village where they got a peasant to carry all of us on his horse drawn cart. We were still upset by our capture but noted that at least we were going west and not toward the feared east. A few hours' ride brought us into a small town in the late afternoon and we were delivered to the local jail. We gave different names from those we had used in Prešov, and since we had no papers there was no way for them to check. A warder took us into a room where we faced an elderly man, and from his bearing I guessed he must be some sort of judge or magistrate. He looked at us and without further ado sentenced us to seven days in jail for vagrancy. It was, as a matter of fact, a lucky break for us. It was a minor offense that boded no danger provided they wouldn't get the real lowdown on us.

In the cell to which we were taken we met a young peasant in his early thirties. We said hello to him and took off our soaked clothing down to our underwear, but that was soaked as well. The cell was warm but there were no bunks, only some very narrow benches. The peasant had a basketful of food and offered us some. It was the best we had eaten for a long, long time. He told us he was from a small village thirty kilometers to the west, and was in the fifth day of a seven-day sentence for failing to pay his taxes. He told us he was a poor farmer, scraping a living from a small plot of land, and couldn't spare money for the government, needing all he had to finish a roof on the house he was building. We told him we were Jewish refugees from Hungary and were looking for Slovak Jews. He said he did not know very much about Jews. He was from a remote little village, and may never even have seen a Jew. We took stock of our situation. It could have been worse. We were a long way from the border. Our cell was clean and warm, our clothes were drying, the warder brought us supper, and if they did not enquire deeper into our past, and the chances were that minor criminals were as much as they expected here, we could hope to be free in a week. So we bedded down on the narrow benches and had a good, untroubled sleep.

We found out that the date was June 7, 1944. When the early morning guard who brought our breakfast, was very excited. Waving a newspaper, he shared with us the news that the Allies had landed in Normandy the day before. All of us rejoiced even though the Slovaks were officially allies of

Germany. But Henry and I of course had the biggest stake in an early end to the war, which now seemed possible, and as we ate we wondered whether it would come early enough for us. Our cellmate was in such a good mood. He was about to be released and hopefully the war might be ending soon. He insisted we use his shaving kit, and for the first time since we fled from shaving we looked presentable again. He gave us the name of his village with an open invitation to visit if we ever came his way. Our jailers also turned demonstratively friendly and brought us candies and cigarettes. The general well-being helped our jail term pass quickly, and on the eighth day we were set free.

We decided this time to keep away from railroad stations and major roads which were always guarded, and returned to the mountains, vowing to be more careful. We had had our fill of being captured. The peasants we met in the fields gave us generously from their own food. We asked them about the village that the peasant we had met in jail had mentioned to us, and their information led us to conclude that it might be best to take up our recent invitation rather than risk more highways and unknown places. Three days of brisk walking brought us almost exactly above the village, and recalling what he had told us about his roof, we managed to spot his house which stood alone a little way from the village center. We waited for the dark and then made our way down. He was very surprised to see us, but his practical wife, whom he had probably told about us, asked us to sit down and she served an excellent hot meal. After supper he took us to his barn, made us a bed of dry straw, and invited us to stay for a few days to rest while his wife would wash and mend our clothes. We undressed to the skin and as we fell asleep on the snug, if prickly straw, I could not but compare this simple good-hearted man with the bigoted anti-Semitic Poles. We happened to have met in a jailcell by pure chance, but in his straightforward way he considered that reason enough to be our friend. He instinctively understood that we needed all the friendliness we could get. The next day he went into the nearby town to make some purchases and we asked him to make some cautious inquiries where the nearest Jews might be found. When he returned in the evening, our clothes had been laundered and mended. He brought us a big bowl of hot water for a good wash, and the information that we would find Jews in a town called Mikuláš to the west.

We immediately made up our minds to head there, and asked him to wake us early next morning. Then we went over to the house with him and thanked both of them for their great kindness. The next morning on his way to the field, he woke us with some food for the road. They gave us an old blanket for the cold nights in the mountains to the northwest, toward which we would be heading. We went straight up into the hills and then turned west toward Mikuláš. The days were longer now and we made brisk progress, avoiding all contacts with peasants for as long as our food lasted. Then we approached some peasants who were working in a field. They gave us food, and told us we had at least another four or five days of hard walking before us till we would reach Mikuláš. Two days later, in the morning, we were awakened by the noise from an itinerant gypsy tribe. They stopped to talk with us in any language we chose, and moved on. Not even an hour had passed when we spotted two armed gendarmes coming straight at us, led by one of the young gypsies. We had been betrayed this time by gypsies with their reputation for dishonesty and theft, who themselves shared our Jewish fate wherever the Nazis could lay hands on them. It was an unkind twist of fate, but we saw there was no point in resisting, and so raised our hands. After the gendarmes searched us, they chained us to each other and took us to a village where they ordered a peasant to drive us in his cart on the long, bumpy way to Kežmarok, close to the Polish border near the city of Nowy Targ where my grandmother was born, a small distance from my own birthplace, Spiska Stara Ves. It was the biggest danger we had faced since Prešov, because we were now very close to the Polish border and the menacing Gestapo. We realized now that we made a big mistake going so far north.

Late in the evening we reached the town where the gendarmes delivered us to the jail. A policeman took us to a cell, which was partly below street level. Through the open windows we could see the legs of the people walking in the street. We called for help and after our calls were ignored for what seemed an eternity, one man finally bent down to respond to us. We asked him if there were any Jews in Kežmarok and he told us he knew a few Jewish families who lived in the town. We begged him to tell them that two Jewish men were in the jail and in urgent need of help. He promised, and soon came back with an elderly woman who, happily, was from Spiska Stara Ves, the same city that my mother's family came from, and she even knew the family. She promised to enlist the Jewish community to get us free.

We were afraid that there would be Germans in the town, but when the guard opened our cell door next morning instead of the Germans we had expected, he was accompanied by a short Jewish man. The man greeted us in Yiddish, but as soon as the guard left us alone, switched to German. He introduced himself as Bergmann, a leader of the Jewish community in Kežmarok, and assured us we were in no danger and could expect to be let out, if not today, the day after. It depended on the presence of his friend, the local judge who, though of German origin, was friendly to Jews. Bergmann stayed to ask many questions about our experiences and after he left, someone from the Jewish community brought us some delicious food. Bergmann returned later and told us our case would be heard in two hours and advised us to plead guilty to all charges. The judge, he promised, would then order us to be placed in charge of the Jewish community in Mikuláš. The hearing proceeded just as he had said despite our qualms as we pleaded guilty, and we were placed in the charge of Bergmann's deputy who had come to see us through. The judge gave him the sentence in writing to serve us as makeshift papers if we should be stopped on the way. As we waited for the train in the station, Henry confided that he had always been skeptical about my stories in Csorgo about how good the Slovak Jews were, but now he was quite convinced. The three-hour journey was uneventful and in Mikuláš our escort took us to a building which had been a schoolhouse and was now a shelter for refugees from Poland. There we were given camp beds in a small room of our own. We had at last made it to Mikuláš, or to give it its full name, Liptovský Svätý Mikuláš, which had been our original objective before going through the ordeals of escape and recapture. The next morning we met some of the refugees, including entire Polish-Jewish families who had lived near the Slovak border and had managed to get across back in 1942. I could not help envying them their luck, indeed, in my mind it was a miracle to actually see Jewish families from Poland still intact.

After breakfast, served from normal dishes at a clean table, we were told that the community president, Mr. Rosenzweig, wished to see us in his private office. A tall and distinguished-looking man, he asked many questions about Hungary, especially about the situation since the Germans took over, as well as about Csorgo and all the names of Slovak Jews we could remember. When he had written everything down, he agreed to have a telegram sent to my sister in an indirect way, through our friend in Csorgo, Kawecki, who knew her address. He wrote a safe message for her, just so she would know I was all right. Later he asked his assistants to issue us documents. I registered as Adam Budkowski, but Henry used his real name. After a hot bath, with lice disinfectant, we were taken to the city and outfitted from head to toe in the Jewish stores. After lunch the committee gave us some "pocket money" for small expenses. They thought of everything for their refugees. In the days that followed we got to know many Jews in the city. We were told that many local Slovaks had gone out of their way to help their Jewish fellow citizens, foiling the anti-Jewish decrees issued by the puppet government in Bratislava, going as far as effecting fictitious takeovers of Jewish enterprises to save them from confiscation by the Hlinka guards. Unlike the church in Poland, the local Catholic Church backed the Jews to the best of its ability, and often intervened in their behalf. After D-Day when the Allies landed in Normandy, even the anti-Semitic authorities became friendlier to the Jews.

After lunch one day, as we were relaxing in the big yard of the shelter, my attention was caught by a tall figure at the other end of the yard. I rubbed my eyes, but there could be no mistake, it was Mietek! He had spotted us too, and in a flash we all ran toward each other for a tearful reunion. With his usual Jewish gallows humor he said to me with a straight face, "But Adam, I was sure that Henry and you had long since become gentlemen farmers in heaven." He was very emaciated and we got him a good meal and a camp bed in our room.

When we were all convinced that this miracle had really happened to us, Mietek told us how he had been caught during our escape from Csorgo. He had just hoisted himself out of the window when two guards who were passing through the prison yard heard some noise and spotted him. They grabbed him as he hit the ground and raised the alarm. Very soon our escape was discovered. The two sergeants took Mietek into the cellar and gave him a terrible beating, but he refused to answer their questions. He told us that hard as they hit him, it was nothing compared to the blow he suffered when one of the guards came in and informed the sergeants that they had discovered bloodstains at the fence, which made him fear we had been shot. He was kept in solitary confinement for several days without food. The sergeants became even more brutal to the prisoners and before long the feathered police arrived and started deportation selections. Mietek was picked for the first transport; Kawecki remained in Csorgo. They were put on cattle trains in Satorja Ujhely. Conditions were bad but not quite as bad as in the overcrowded wagons in Przemyśl in 1942. What made the whole thing unreal for him was how the naive Hungarian Jews still believed they were going to work camps, and indeed had put on their best clothes for the terrible journey. The first thing he did was to get himself a place near the door and talk to the men from Csorgo, but to his astonishment they declined to join his escape scheme and actually distanced themselves from him. Some of the Hungarian Jews who suspected what he was up to, attempted to dissuade him and even to physically restrain him, but they were no match for him. He was a big, strong man, steeled by his determination to survive. He was really sorry for them, urged them to stop being so blind, and warned that from his own experience he knew they were on the way to Auschwitz, a horrible extermination camp where they would be mercilessly killed, as so many hundreds of thousands of Jews had been murdered. He talked to them until it was dark and then began making good his escape. He had his usual tools with him and managed to get the door open. But before he jumped he turned around once more and asked whether anybody would come with him. Instead of clutching at this last chance to save themselves, some of the poor misguided Jews started calling for the guards, but luckily their shouting was swallowed in the noise of the speeding train, and Mietek jumped alone. It was dark, but he landed more or less unscathed and quickly moved away from the tracks. He did not know where he was, but reckoned that since they had been traveling for nearly seven hours he was most likely in Slovakia. It could no longer be Hungary. The next morning he found a village and at the first house he came to, realized he was in the southeastern part of Poland, not too far from the Tatra Mountains and the Slovak border. He kept away from the Poles, preferring to go hungry, because he remembered the stories the Polish prisoners had told about them in Csorgo. He walked mostly at night, got what food he could from peasants in the fields, and ran away as soon as they handed something to him, and so finally made it into Slovakia. He was caught by a patrol near a town but luckily was seen by some Jews as he was being marched to the jail and they had a word with the judge who sent him to Mikuláš, like us. He could not get over those naive Hungarians and talked about them again and again with both burning anger and profound pity.

Mr. Rosenzweig, who we had learned, was a well-known industrialist, became our sponsor. He admired our courage not to give in but to escape, again and again, until we had finally made it. He invited us to his office whenever he visited the shelter and brought us the war news, which was improving. The Russians had already pushed the Germans out of the Ukraine and were closing in on Poland; the western Allies were in Rome, and advancing in France; and the Germans in a final lash of their crocodile tail, were now bombarding London with a new type of destructive rocket.

One morning he told us he had been informed by a friend who was an influential Slovak official in the local police department, that a high-ranking Slovak leader was to pay an official visit to Mikuláš, and he was worried. A few nights later the shelter was surrounded by police and panic gripped the refugees. From a window I could see the police. They were armed only with revolvers, and they ordered all of us to assemble in the gym. People brought their belongings and blankets because there was a rumor that we would be sent away, though nobody knew where, and the panic made rational thinking impossible. When the lights were turned out the three of us immediately started talking and decided to escape. We were now on the ground floor. The windows were not barred, and the police with their pistols would not be very dangerous in the dark, and in any case, we estimated, were unlikely to fire on civilians, even Jews. The three of us did not undress, only took off our shoes. I fell asleep, and when Mietek woke us my shoes were gone. I thought I would not be able to make a barefoot breakout but Henry and Mietek insisted they would not leave me in the lurch and postponed our break until the next opportunity. In the morning one of the refugee women, Mrs. Schwert, brought me my shoes. She had taken them because she suspected I would try to escape with Henry and Mietek and feared we would compromise all of them, especially Mr. Rosenzweig. He himself soon arrived, terribly upset. The visiting dignitary had been Macho, the Interior Minister of the puppet government. He was a known anti-Semite. This morning he had ordered that all the Polish refugees be deported to a labor camp in southwestern Slovakia. Mr. Rosenzweig tried to reassure us all that we were not going to Poland and that many Slovak Jews had been working in the labor camps for the past two years. While conditions there were certainly tough, they were all alive and not in danger.

The policemen escorted us to the station and got on a train with us. The three of us decided not to attempt an escape so as not to compromise the Jews of Mikuláš who had been so good to us, and see what the labor camp was like. On the way Mrs. Schwert came to me and apologized for commandeering my shoes. I told her she had done the right thing. We would certainly have harmed Mr. Rosenzweig, his community, and probably the refugees as well. We were free to walk about the part of the train that had been taken over for the refugees and found there were about one hundred of us, in five compartments.

After a five-hour journey we were ordered to get off, and after a march of an hour and a half, reached the camp which was called Novaky late in the afternoon. It stood isolated, with hills on the horizon, a few long barracks surrounded by barbed-wire fences but no guards in evidence around them. We lined up for a rollcall which was taken by the commandant himself. He assigned everybody to a job, according to their skills and professions. As a candymaker I was assigned to the kitchen, Mietek the mechanic to the metal workshop, and Henry as a leather expert to the shoemaking shop.

We were put into the single men's barracks where a camp

elder gave us blankets and a pillow and assigned each of us one of the double-decker wooden bunks. I was awakened before everybody else to make breakfast for the more than two thousand prisoners and the police guards. Actually there were two adjoining but separate kitchens, one for the prisoners and one for the police. I had to clean the huge, copper pots which were the biggest I had ever seen, after every meal, and before the meals I had to carry the provisions from the warehouse to the kitchen. In the kitchen everybody was friendly and polite. There was not a loud word spoken, and there was no rushing. The chef told me I was free to help myself to any food I wanted. When we finished cleaning up we had to take out the garbage and, ever on the lookout for a way out, I observed that the small garbage gate was not guarded. Beyond the wire there were fields of high grass stretching to the picturesquelike mountains. But it was a prison camp and no one could tell how long the quiet might last. I told Henry and Mietek what I had seen and urged we begin to plan our escape before serious security would be introduced. For now it would be easy, just to walk out of the garbage gate, and we agreed to make our break the following Sunday, five days later. During that time we were told that the religious Jews were excused from work on Saturdays. There was a kindergarten and a school which kept the children busy. The camp was, in effect, run on a kind of tacit honor system. The prisoners would not attempt to escape and the commandant demanded nothing more than good work. Prisoners and guards would do everything to accommodate each other under the benign supervision of the commandant who, like all of his staff, was decent and fair. But imprisonment was not for us. We held freedom to be better than the best of camps. We still had enough money from Mikuláš to pay our train fares back and from there we would look for the Russian partisans, who we were told, were active in eastern Slovakia.

On Sunday, which was not a working day, we took our small bundles and lay down on the grass near the garbage gate, as though we were enjoying a rest in the open. We hid our bundles there, returned to the barracks and in the evening went out, saying we were going to visit friends in another barrack. Then we simply made for the gate, picked up our belongings, and walked out. Since I had studied the area previously I led the three of us to the mountains. We went some way up and then lay down on the soft grass and slept well in the warm night air. We got up very early and started moving in the direction of the rising sun. By noon we were on top of a village and went down to get information on the nearest railroad station. It was about fifteen kilometers to the north, three hours of brisk marching along the road. But we chose not to take the road, preferring instead the more difficult, but safer, route through the hills. Late in the afternoon we spotted a town and went straight to the station. This time we were able to move freely since we were well dressed and clean and aroused no attention. We took seats in different compartments, to spread the risk of capture, and relied on the only documents we had, the court order sending us to Mikuláš. We had to change trains, which entailed an hour-long wait at a junction. We finally reached Mikuláš late at night and made straight for the shelter. The man at the desk was quite upset at our sudden appearance but agreed to allow us to spend the night in our old room, but only one night. He did not want to court trouble by sheltering prisoners on the run.

We were awakened early the next morning by Mr. Rosenzweig himself. At first he was angry, but eventually promised to find a temporary place for us. He thought it would be too dangerous for us to remain in the shelter. He took us to a Slovak family who gave us a room and warned us not to go out in daylight. When we confided our intention to join the partisans we were told that the situation in Slovakia had changed, and had taken a turn for the worse for Jews. The Russians had already crossed the Romanian border in the north and Romania was trying to reach a separate peace settlement with the Allies. The Germans had begun moving from Romania into Hungary and when their position there would, as he expected, become untenable, would fall back into Slovakia, which was like a corridor to Austria and Bohemia. This possibility disturbed the community and for the first time many Jews were searching out hiding places with Christian families. He asked us to come to the school that evening for a meeting of the community. We found the hall packed. First the Hungarian situation was discussed, and several men who had come back from there recently, reported that the deportations to Auschwitz had been temporarily suspended after four hundred fifty thousand Jews had been sent there. The SS had already taken over Jewish affairs and the situation in Hungary was desperate. We now had to reckon with the possibility of Slovakia being next. We told them that from our own experience, we had learned that every sinister rumor about approaching doom for Jews proved tragically correct and urged everybody to get out while they still could, warning that the SS inevitably followed the Wehrmacht to deal with the Jews. As for the three of us, we would try to join the partisans. After the meeting many young people asked to come with us and told us there were confirmed reports of partisans operating in the Niske Tatry Mountains in central Slovakia, and also in eastern Slovakia. The Niske Tatry was nearer and we would go there, but agreed to wait for two days to give them a chance to wind up their affairs, which included entrusting their property to Slovak friends who had proved trustworthy.

A few days later we met at the railroad station and an uneventful four-hour ride took us to the junction where we were to catch our connecting train. Since there were still three hours till it was due some of us decided to look around the town and make some purchases. While we were shopping there was a sudden loud explosion not far away. German planes were bombing the station we had just left! We started running back and saw it going up in flames, and when we reached it, just after the fire engines, there were wounded and dead, and blood all over. Some of our party were dead, and others wounded, some badly burned. Chance had been on our side for a change and we had had a lucky escape. The surviving members of the party decided to stay in the town to be with their hospitalized friends, and the three of us had to continue on alone, first visiting the hospital and bidding everybody farewell. We decided not to risk any more trains or cities but head straight for the mountains on foot. We spent the night in the hills above the town and the next morning started going toward Niske Tatry.

13

Slovakia, Joining the Russian Partisans
July 1944

W e moved higher into the mountains and soon were surprised to spot a village, almost completely surrounded by forests, perched high up in the hills. We decided to go there. Suddenly the quiet was torn asunder by the sharp bark of machine-gun fire. A few moments later, from our hiding place behind the trees, we saw a sight we had long dreamed of: German soldiers on their trucks with their hands up, surrendering to civilians. The captors called for the peasants to come and receive the guns they were taking from the Germans. I did not think twice but ran up and grabbed a rifle. It was the greatest treasure I could have wished for. I had a gun and was pointing it at German soldiers. Henry, Mietek and a few peasants followed suit. The Germans were on four trucks and as I came closer I realized that most of them were in SS uniforms. The partisans who had captured them were Russians, the very partisans we were looking for. The Russian in command ordered the Germans to get off their trucks. It was a mistake, because as they jumped down some of them managed to make a run for the village. But the partisan commander was alert, curtly ordered the civilians to get out of the way and gave the order to open fire. We shot at them while those who had not run stood with their hands above their heads. The commander called for some of us to come with him and took us to where the Germans we had shot were lying. He kicked each body to make sure they were dead. I stayed close to him because I was eager to see a dead SS man. When he came across wounded men, I translated their pleas for mercy, but the commander merely signaled for me to shoot them. I held my rifle close to their heads and watched their eyes begging me before I pulled the trigger, shooting them between the eyes. If I had had an axe I would have used that. Nothing could be bad enough for SS men, and there were so few of them, but at least I had the elation of making a start at paying them back. When we finished our shooting, the commander asked whether any of us wanted to join his band. The three of us raised our hands as well as some of the Slovaks. We helped ourselves to grenades and ammunition from the German trucks. The Russians ordered the uninjured SS men to board and stood guard over them with their own guns. The commander followed the convoy in a small car, of a type I had seen the Germans driving in Rzeszów when they first went to the Russian front back in 1941. We drove along a narrow track deep into the forest, but the higher we climbed, the narrower the track became until at last it was too narrow for the trucks. The commander told us to get off and take the Germans off too and watch over them. He talked with his own men and then ordered the Germans to line up in single file against a truck and told his men and us to shoot them all. We complied with pleasure, one by one, and then made sure that every single one of those SS beasts was dead. We then poured gasoline over the trucks and set them afire. They soon exploded, incinerating the dead SS men, a wonderful sight in my eyes.

This was what I had lived for, what had kept me going through those terrible years, to avenge the Jewish blood they had spilled like water. I only regretted there were so few of them, but I was ready to go on doing the same thing, night and day, to my dying breath.

We continued deeper into the forest and when it was completely dark the commander ordered a halt. We sat on the ground in a rough circle and lit a bonfire to warm us and to roast some meat, which we ate with a lot of bread. The Russians had vodka but I did not want any.

This was the first time I had met free Russians and I took a good look at them. Most of them were older than I was. The commander was a short, strongly built man of about thirty-five. They were well armed, carrying automatic weapons across their shoulders of a type I had never seen, with circular magazines over a short barrel, pistols at their waist, and hand-grenades hanging from their chests. They were all in civilian clothes and wore caps. They spoke Russian to us, the first time I had heard the language, and I could more or less understand it if they spoke slowly. I answered in Polish which they seemed to understand quite well. I had seen Russian soldiers before in the railroad station in Rzeszów. But then they had been POW's, packed in cattle trains, many of them dead, or being marched to POW camps, hungry and beaten, condemned to die by the SS. These Russians were a different kettle of fish, proud, tough and determined fighting men, ready to face the German oppressors of their people with uncompromising guts.

Before we bedded down on the ground the commander posted guards and he included me in his choice. I held my rifle close to my body, as if it were a fragile baby needing care, and kept on thanking my lucky stars that I had lived to see this day. I looked up into the sky and wished that my parents could see me avenging them.

Early the next morning we moved on, heading west, and by noon had almost reached the crest of the mountain when the commander called a halt. With a few of his men he went into the forest and after a few minutes returned and told us that the volunteers would be allowed into their bunkers one at a time. When my turn came I was taken into a sort of deep cave hewn into the mountainside. Inside there were some men on benches and one who was sitting alone at a table and who was probably an officer, called me over and started asking questions. I gave my Adam Budkowski name, born in Poland, a Roman Catholic. I did not mention the ghettos and the camps. When he got through he stood up, embraced me, and solemnly informed me that I was now a member of the Russian partisan units operating in Slovakia, an element of the second Ukrainian front. Then Henry and Mietek were questioned and all three of us were taken before a short and husky man in his early forties who was sitting apart in a far corner. His name was Velicko and he was the commander of the unit. He shook our hands, signifying that the three of us had been accepted as their comrades-in-arms. It was a proud moment for us.

Later we learned that the man who had questioned us was the political commissar, and he had been very cautious because some deserters from the Vlasow army, who had abandoned the Germans when they sensed they were losing the war, had attempted to join up with the partisans, but they were considered incorrigible traitors and were rejected and I suppose shot. There were other turncoats: Ukrainians, Kalmucks, Tartars, Volga Germans and even some Cossacks who had joined the Germans and now realized they had backed the wrong horse after all. The partisans not only detested them for what they had done, but feared them as possible double agents, who must be rooted out. They represented themselves as escaped POW's, but might actually be serving their Germans masters as spies. The next morning we were given instructions in handling grenades and explosives and were then ordered to move on to an unknown destination, taking everything with us. It was warm, even though we were high up in the mountains, and we ate only cold food, since making a fire might give us away to the German planes that occasionally flew over. We got our drinking water from the streams we crossed. It was only when we stopped for the night that a bonfire was lit and as we sat around it our new comrades told us some of their experiences. Their hatred for the Germans matched my own. They had seen their own villages razed by the invading Germans and their families killed. Some had fought on different fronts, a few of them since the first German attack in 1941. There were even a small number who had somehow escaped from POW or forced labor camps where they had been made to watch patriots being hanged. It was hatred for the Germans that had created the partisan movement, armed at first with nothing more than axes and old rifles, until they could capture weapons from Germans they ambushed, but now they were being supplied by the Red air force. They told us that the Germans had murdered Russians numbering in the millions, and now they had no intention of taking prisoners, but only of killing every German they came across. I could not agree with them more.

The next morning we continued on, heading southwest for Banská Bystrica, following orders received by wireless from the Kiev headquarters of Marshal Malinowski, the O.C. of the Second Ukrainian front. We reached Banská Bystrica at about noon and received a big welcome from Russian partisans and Slovak soldiers. The civilian population was overjoyed to see us as well. The town, which was situated in the mountains, was small but very picturesque. We were shown to the military headquarters where our officers received instructions and then all of us marched to the outskirts of the town to a large Slovak military compound, where we were billeted in barracks. The soldiers served us a big meal in a large dining hall, and that night we slept under a roof in clean bunks again. The next morning we were given permission to spend the day in the town, but were ordered to carry our arms, to return before dark and not to get drunk or create disturbances. The latter was a vital order for the Russians, whereas we were not big drinkers.

As we were leaving, the leader who had been in charge of the attack on the Germans came over and presented me with a big German pistol, a personal gift in recognition of my having been the first to volunteer, and for my conduct in the action. The gesture touched me profoundly and I felt I had truly achieved my dream to fight the Germans, confirmed by a hardened partisan leader. More than that, with my own gun in my belt I felt like a man again, after four years of having been reduced to the status of a slave.

When we got into town we started looking for Jews, but it was still early and there were only a few people about. So we decided to have some coffee, and when the café gradually filled up we noticed some people a few tables away who looked Jewish to us. When they confirmed our guess we joined them. They were Slovak Jews and told us about the Slovak resistance that was being organized to show the world that they were not all followers of the puppet president Tiso. They were ready to rise up if the Germans would enter Slovakia en masse. The arrival of the Russian partisans, first by land from the Carpathian Mountains, and later by parachute, had given the movement momentum. That night our unit held a party and for the first time we met some women partisans, tough girls ready to do everything the men did, from fighting to carrying heavy loads through the mountains. When the drinking started I had one glass of vodka but then went to bed. I knew they could drink more vodka than I could drink water, so there was no point in starting a one-sided competition.

During the following days we happened to run into a man who worked in the editorial office of the local radio station, a

Jew who was living as an Aryan, and he gave us a full rundown of the news. In Slovakia the partisan movement was growing fast, and they were carrying out an increasing number of operations in the eastern and central parts of the country. On the eastern front, the Russians were routing the Wehrmacht in all sectors. They had already captured Lwów. A new democratic Polish government had been established in Lublin shortly after the city's liberation by the Russians, and the Red army had liberated the Majdanek extermination camp near Lublin. They had arrived so fast that the SS had no time to destroy it. But they did not find any Jews alive in it, only some Polish and Russian prisoners. They did capture most of the SS guards, however, and after a one-day public trial, at which overwhelming evidence was presented against them, they were hanged. The Russians wanted to make sure that their verdict would be accepted as just by the world and invited western reporters to Majdanek to see the evidence for themselves. At last the civilized world could see the actual mechanics of Hitler's demonic Final Solution: the gassing trucks, the gas chambers, the crematoria and the mass graves.

On the western front, the journalist told us, the news was good too. The Allies were progressing steadily through Normandy and had landed in southern France, tightening the noose around Hitler's neck. But the German retreat from the east boded greater danger for us. They were likely to pull their forces out of Hungary and fall back into Slovakia. Coming as a wounded beast they would probably be even more deadly than before, especially for the remnants of the Slovak Jews.

Meanwhile our Russian comrades were working like a well-oiled propaganda machine, constantly telling us how superior their communist political system was. However, I was convinced only that their partisans were well organized and functioning famously. Then, on August 25, there was some sensational news. Slovak partisan groups had begun hitting out at the Germans in full force. At the railroad station in Turčiansky Svätý Martin, in the center of Slovakia, a German train, carrying the senior officers of their military mission to Romania back home, had to stop because the partisans blew up the nearby tunnel, blocking the way. Before the Germans had time to react, the partisans arrived at the station in force and called on the Germans to surrender and lay down their arms. When some of them refused, the partisans shot them all, including a general, Paul Otto, and his staff. At the same time the city of Turčiansky Svätý Martin and nearby Ružomberok and Liptovský Svätý Mikuláš, as well as some other smaller towns, were taken over by partisans with the full cooperation of the Slovak garrisons and police. In Diviaky the partisans, assisted by the population, seized a large munitions dump and carried the materiel off to the mountains.

Four days later, on August 29, 1944, people streamed into the streets and started dancing when the local radio station announced that the Slovak national uprising had started. Pictures of Tiso and his so-called ministers were torn up and thrown away, and were replaced by patriotic posters calling on the population to join the armed forces of Free Slovakia. The celebrations turned into a full holiday and in the restaurants and bars the drinks were on the house. The Russian partisans were joyously mobbed. Happiness ruled and happiest of all were the Jews.

But a rude awakening was in store. The very next day the Germans invaded Slovakia from all directions, mostly Waffen SS troops supported by tanks and planes. In the Tatra Mountains, the whole area of Spiš and the city of Kežmarok were taken, whereupon the western part of Slovakia declared its loyalty to Tiso. He and his henchmen berated the uprising and its leaders, whom they denounced as Jewish Bolsheviks. It was a bitter irony—there were so few Jews left but we were still the scapegoats. However, while Tiso's ranting was predictable, the people were stunned by the Slovak general Malar's failure to make good his promise to bring his two divisions in eastern Slovakia over to the uprising. The Germans quickly exploited his hesitation. They moved into Prešov, took over his headquarters, took his men prisoners, and arrested him. Some of his men managed to join the partisans, and others took off their uniforms and went home in disgust, but most of them fell into German hands. The planned opening of the Dukla passage for the Russians by Malar's troops did not materialize. All supplies to the rebellion had to be flown in through the one available military airport, at Tri Duby, near Banská Bystrica. This gave the Germans a breathing space to deal with the Slovak partisans, who suffered heavy losses before they retreated in small bands into the mountains. There was a lot of manpower in the Free Slovakian forces, about sixty thousand men, one third of them with the partisans, but they lacked training and were no match for the battle-hardened Germans. The Russian air lift could not provide the heavy weapons to stop the German tanks we knew were on their way. The Germans were desperate to hold Slovakia and the Czechoslovakian Protectorate, their last buffer protecting the Reich, and Austria. Banská Bystrica was now teeming with refugees, many of whom were Jewish.

Our station was bombed by German planes, but went back on the air immediately with a makeshift transmitter. There was a lot of political intrigue. Some groups were supporting the democratic President Beneš in exile in London, while others, mainly leftists, and particularly the communists, were striving to take over power under their communist leader Karol Schmidke, who worked hand in glove with the Russians and commanded the major partisan forces. Different newspapers published and opposing points of view and posters sprouted on every wall advocating the different causes. The Jews tried to keep out of the rivalry. They wanted only to survive and the recent developments were not encouraging. The SS was coming closer, burning whole villages in their path, and shooting people by the dozens on charges of aiding the partisans. And, where the Jews were concerned, they acted as though they had no other concerns but to hunt and kill them.

Among the refugees, we met three Jews from Bochnia, near Cracow, who had been living as Aryans in Budapest, supported by a Polish committee. They had thought it was wise to flee when the Germans took over the Hungarian capital. They were two brothers named Finder, and a lawyer by the name of Morgenbesser, and they decided to keep their Aryan identity because we all knew that the Russians were not great friends of the Jews, either. Later our little group was joined by many more Polish-Jewish refugees, among them a man called Kargul, who had been a lieutenant in the Polish army, and a Józef Jakubowicz, who had been a sergeant. They were impressed by the shoulder patches of foreign allies some soldiers in the town were wearing and came up with the idea of forming a volunteer Free Poland unit to serve with the Free

Czechoslovak army, and asked us to join them. After thinking it over we agreed. Lieutenant Kargul approached headquarters and received their enthusiastic blessing. Our partisan commander allowed the three of us to go, but required us to leave our weapons behind, the exception being that I was permitted to keep the German pistol. We were sworn in as a Polish unit of the First Czechoslovak army, attached to the element stationed in Banská Bystrica. We were taken to a barracks and issued uniforms and arms. At first we looked strangely at each other. It was the first time we had worn military uniforms, but we quickly got used to being real soldiers, and proud of it.

One day we met among the many Slovak Jews a young mother with her small son and daughter. She was the wife of the Chief Rabbi of Slovakia, Dr. Armin Frieder, a most distinguished leader and very active in rescuing the Polish Jews. They had been separated from him by the rapid events in Slovakia. She was a pleasant woman and we were happy to offer our help and kept in touch with her and her children.

On another occasion, I happened to hear French and English being spoken in our coffee shop. I went over to the table where these men were sitting, and did my best to talk to them in my poor English. They were escaped POW's—Australians, New Zealanders and Frenchmen—who had made their way to Slovakia in the hope of getting back to their own forces. We found someone who knew English and his interpreting made conversation easier. They told us they were waiting to be flown out in the first British or American plane that would land in Tri Duby and take them to Italy or England. The leaders of the uprising expected military help from the western Allies. I asked them to take a message to my relatives in the U.S.A. and gave them the address I remembered. They would take no letter but promised to try and let the relatives know they had met me. I took the home addresses of the Frenchmen and promised to try and contact them after the war.

A more exciting surprise was in store for us. We were told by the Slovak Jews in town that a group of Jewish paratroopers from Palestine who had been dropped into Slovakia had reached Banská Bystrica and wanted to meet us. The next morning they were waiting for us. It was an unforgettable moment. They were three men and one woman in British uniforms with a Palestine shoulder patch. It was hard to contain our emotions actually meeting Jewish officers from our Holy Land. They had gone to Palestine as pioneers from Hungary and Slovakia before the war, to live in a kibbutz and had all volunteered for the mission to parachute into occupied Europe, to establish contact with whatever Jews were still alive and to try to rescue them. They were also ordered to gather witnesses and evidence of Nazi atrocities to be presented to an international war crimes tribunal the Allies intended to establish when the war was won. Their mission was sponsored by the Jewish Agency for Palestine and supported by the British. They were part of a larger group who had parachuted into Yugoslavia and then split up to make their separate ways to Italy, Hungary and Slovakia. The Hungarian detachment was headed by a woman, Channa Senesz. The Slovak unit, led by Haviva Reik comprised Chaim Chermesh, Rafael Reiss and Zvi Ben Ya'acov. All of them were members of the Kibutzim. The Yugoslav partisans had received them and assisted them on their way, and Chermesh had actually met Tito himself. They all held the rank of British officers and were devoted Zionists ready to lay down their lives in the cause of saving the remnant of Europe's Jews.

The first thing they did in Slovakia was to establish contact with sympathetic church leaders and arrange with them for the issuance of false birth and baptism certificates for Slovak Jews. It was very touching for us to learn at first hand, after so many years of silence, that we had not been totally forgotten by the civilized world, at least not by our fellow Jews. They asked us to recount our experiences under the Nazis and were visibly touched by our stories. Chaim Chermesh and I became close friends and met often. We exchanged our addresses hoping that with God's help we will have a chance to survive this war. He gave me his photo and took mine.

Soon we heard that Hitler was no longer satisfied with his commander in Slovakia, General Berger, under whom the Germans had failed to smash the uprising. He was replaced by an SS and police general, Hermann Hoefle. Our town was raided by German bombers several times, but they did no serious damage. What was serious, however, was that the lightly armed Slovak resistance fighters and partisans were no match for the Waffen SS divisions attacking Telgar and Spišská Nová Ves in the east, and breaking through in the Hron valley in the south with the intention of taking Zvolen and Banská Bystrica. Rumors were in fact already circulating that the Slovak army would withdraw into the mountains, where they had a better chance to carry out guerrilla warfare, and the way for the German advance would thus be left open.

These reports of the coming Germans created tension in the town, which had been deliriously happy only a short time ago; and among the Jews fear reached panic proportions. It was terrible to contemplate that after having survived so long under such terrible circumstances, we were now to fall into the vicious hands of the SS, just when the war was nearly over, and the liberation of Slovakia by the Russians, who had already reached the borders, was at hand. When I managed to get a break from our training to come into town I advised the Jews I met to keep close to our camp in case we would have to move into the mountains too, so that they could come with us. I also went to see Mrs. Frieder and told her to contact Chaim to get Aryan papers for her and her two children.

Meanwhile the Germans were closing in. Our forces evacuated the Tri Duby airfield, and on October 25 we heard that the Germans had taken Brezno, just twenty kilometers away, and only Zvolen and a small strip of land still separated us from them. The last order given by General Viest was that all units of the Czechoslovakian army should become part of the Russian partisan brigades.

14

Slovakia, Retreat to the Mountains
End of October 1944

Our hopes took another blow the next day when the Germans captured Zvolen and our forces were ordered to evacuate Banská Bystrica which was rendered helpless by the fall of Zvolen. We dashed into town to tell our friends we were going into the mountains but we were unable to find Chaim. Mrs. Frieder begged us to take her with us but we feared the mountains were no place for her and her young children. It would be rough and freezing up there. However, she insisted and one of our men, Morgenbesser, undertook responsibility for them and we took them to our camp. During the night more Jews joined us and told us that immediately after the military had left the city, the mob had taken over and were looting the stores, particularly the liquor stores. Early in the morning on October 27, 1944 which was the day of Czechoslovakia Independence, all fighting men and civilians began moving, on foot and in a variety of vehicles and carts, heading for the Stare Hory valley which was the only way to the Niske Tatry Mountains. There we hoped to link up with the main partisan forces. The weather was cold and misty with damp sleet, and it was still quite dark. Our unit split into two sections, and put the refugees between the two to avoid having people get lost. Our group numbered about seventy-five soldiers and refugees, mostly men, and the Frieder family. There were a large number of Slovak troops and different groups of partisans in front of us. We progressed very slowly over this narrow mountain road which was filled with all kinds of people and military vehicles. We had to make frequent halts to let the vehicles pass. At noon the fog lifted and we could see the mountains enveloping our valley like a towering pitched tent. Suddenly German planes appeared above us and began dropping bombs on the columns and straffing with their machine guns. There were heavy casualties among the terrified crowd. Everybody ran for cover away from the exposed road. Some of us found shelter under a small stone bridge over a brook, and as I hit the ground another man fell on top of me. I could hear the screams of the wounded, the explosions of the bombs and the staccato of the machine guns but when the planes left I was unable to get up. The man was lying across my legs. I called for help and some men came and pulled him out. He was dead, hit by a bullet or shrapnel. It was my closest shave yet. When I came out into the open a scene of devastation met my eyes. The dead were mingled with the wounded, blood was running everywhere, and parts of torn bodies were lying among the burning vehicles and mangled horses. The medics were unable to cope with so much work. We feared that the Germans were close on our heels and that their planes would be back to complete the massacre. Henry and Mietek were unhurt. They had taken shelter under a large tree, but many of our group were dead. As we went around covering their bodies we came on the bodies of Mrs. Frieder and her daughter. Her little boy, Gideon, was standing next to them crying forlornly, unable to understand what had happened. I could not tear him away, and only when I promised we would soon return to see his mommy, did he take my hand and came with me. There were many wounded who might have been saved if we had had doctors and medicines and a way to get them to a hospital. As it was, there was nothing we could do for them. We tried to close our ears to their pitiful cries for help and avert our looks from their pleading eyes. The only rational thing to do was to save those who were able to walk. The others were beyond help, and though it was cruel there was simply no point in waiting for a similar fate to befall the rest of us. We began looking for a path into the mountains away from the road which had proved a death trap for us. We discovered a gap in the rocks and started climbing. The ascent was steep and difficult, and we had to move in single file and help the walking wounded by pushing them on. The expectation that every step was taking us nearer to safety kept us going.

The higher we climbed the colder it got, and when it began
to rain we were quickly soaked and freezing. We took turns
carrying little Gideon who was still crying for his mother. The
whereabouts of his father, who had sent them to Banská
Bystrica for safety, was unknown.

In the evening one of the partisan commanders called a halt
and his experienced forest fighters managed to get a bonfire
going even though all the wood was wet. We let the wounded
and children sleep next to the fire while we took turns at guard
duty. When it was my turn I could see many bonfires glowing
in the valley and knew the Germans could see them too, but it
didn't matter. Their pilots would provide information to the
troops on the ground anyway. At least they would not bomb
us during the night. Very early the next morning we put out
the fire and started moving again, higher and higher up into
the mountains. It was raining hard but we didn't mind. The
rain, which turned into sleet as we went higher up, was our
best protection against sneak raids from the air. But the cold
and the slippery ground slowed our progress to a snail's pace.
Many of those ahead of us were dumping their loads, unable
to carry anything but the most essential items.

From my pre-war mountainclimbing I knew the danger of
standing still for very long in the freezing cold. The rest that
standing still affords is deceptive, and can easily result in
death by freezing, especially since we were wet and perspiring.
So I warned everybody in our group to keep their arms moving
and stamp their feet when resting, and indeed not to rest
alone, so that we could keep an eye on each other. They
realized how right I was when we passed some frozen bodies
of people who had been ahead of us, and had stopped to rest.
They sat there stiffly, as though asleep. We came upon ever
growing quantities of abandoned belongings on the way and
left them lying there. We could not carry extra loads, but
every time I came across a gun I picked it up and gave it to
one of the refugees, hoping he would be able to use it if need
be. From below we heard occasional firing. The Germans
were catching up with the rear of our escape column, and the
ominous sound gave us renewed strength to continue. When
it got dark we found a large level spot to camp on and made a
big fire to keep all of us warm. I had some bread and washed
it down with snow and then sat down to rest by the fire until

it would be my turn for guard duty. The pleasant warmth from the fire made me drowsy and I must have dozed off, because I was suddenly brought to by a shooting pain in my right foot, and I saw that my shoe was on fire. I jumped up and stamped my shoe in the snow and quickly put it out, but a large hole had burned through the sole. I despaired. It would be impossible to go on across the rough and freezing mountain with only one shoe. Mietek, and another man from my unit, Stefan Kocan, saw what had happened and called over one of the Russian partisans. The man calmly took stock of the situation, measured my foot with a piece of string, and told me to wait for him by the fire. He came back a short while later with a pair of boots which fitted me nicely. In fact they were just a shade too large, enough to let me put on another pair of socks, which was fine. Stefan spontaneously took the watch off his wrist and gave it to the Russian. He couldn't have done better. We were aware just how fond of wristwatches all Russians were. I wasn't sure where he had got the boots, and I didn't ask because I suspected he had probably taken them from a dead body. Not knowing gave me the hope that it may have been a German. I told Stefan that if we should survive, the moment the war was over I'd get him the best wristwatch in sight, no matter if I had to buy or steal it, and he consented.

The next morning we took a northeasterly direction for Prasiva on the crest of the mountain where we knew some partisan units had camped, and hoped they might still be there. In fact, they were not, but when we stopped for the night, we found a site that looked promising for building a bunker. The Russians who were experienced in these things agreed, but we needed tools for such a big job, and the only way to get them was to go back down into the valley. That was dangerous work for only strong young men to do. There was the risk of running into the Germans and the hard work of carrying heavy loads back up the mountain. Nevertheless there was no lack of volunteers and Henry, Mietek and myself were among them. Our biggest concern was not what might happen to us, but for the little Frieder boy, who was still crying for his mother. We told him we would meet her in the next village which quieted him.

We were excused from guard duty that night to rest for the next day's hard work. We started out very early in the morning, and never stopped until we were directly above the road. Nothing had changed there, except that the dead bodies had frozen. We made our way down cautiously and collected everything we could use from the wreckage, cutting parts we needed from the trucks when necessary. Mietek, the mechanic, knew exactly what to look for and where to find it, and when we had collected as much as we could carry, started the long trek back. Our heavy loads forced us to make frequent stops, but we made sure to stamp our feet and clasp our arms to keep the blood circulating. When we reached our perimeter guards at last, we asked them to send down more men to help us up the last stretch. During the day those who had stayed behind had gone through the belongings left lying along the track and picked up everything useful to bring back to the camp. The experienced Russians had cut chunks of meat from the carcasses of the horses killed in the air raid. They understood that we could not afford to waste anything edible and buried the meat in a layer of snow to keep it fresh.

The construction of the bunker was started immediately with the tools we had brought. Some men cut down trees for timber and others dug into the mountainside. It was tough work cutting through the frozen earth and the rocks. But morale was high and we all worked with a will. We decided on another trip down the next day and started well before dawn so as to get there before the Germans could come and destroy everything usable. When we were on top of the road again we sent down two men to make sure it was safe and then we descended swiftly. Without resting for even a single moment we picked up what we thought was useful and headed back. This time the loads were smaller and we could move faster. By noon the next day the bunker was ready for roofing, but first we moved in a stove to dry the muddy floor. Then we brought the tarpaulin we had cut from the trucks and stretched it tight to cover the bunker. Finally we covered it with the earth we had dug up, both to remove the traces of digging and to camouflage our bunker, and then to complete the disguise, we topped it all with snow. We had a problem with the chimney. The experienced Russians advised against placing it through a hole in the roof because that could be easily spotted by low-flying planes. We compromised on some ventilation holes in the side which meant we could use the stove only at night and only for cooking and melting snow into water. We were by now well organized, almost like an extended family, which was a good feeling, and we spent many hours recounting our experiences.

When we had settled in we decided to try to make contact with other partisan groups we were sure were hiding out in the mountains just as we were. When it was my turn for night guard I marveled at the peace and beauty of the place, so high up that it almost touched the sky. It was nature at its best. Only the cursed Germans, whose machine-gun fire occasionally echoed up the mountain to our lair, spoiled the idyll.

Since the weather was turning harsh and very cold, Henry, Mietek and I decided that we must take little Gideon Frieder to a village. This was no place for a child. Stefan asked to come along to secure our trip and we all set out together early in the morning. We carried the boy piggyback in turn, but when we got to the place above the road of death we immediately saw that human hands had been at work there. Everything had been cleared. There were a lot of rough graves, and the broken-down vehicles had been pushed to the side. We watched and waited until we felt pretty sure there was no one around and then quickly crossed the road and continued in the shelter of the tree-covered hills, keeping the road in sight, until late in the evening when we spotted lights in the distance. It was a small, remote village at the foot of the mountain. When we were directly above it, we halted for observation and when everything looked quiet, came down near the last house. Mietek and I knocked on the door while Henry and Stefan covered us, keeping the boy with them. When the door was opened we obviously gave the people inside a fright. We had not taken into account that two strange, rough men with guns and hand grenades around their waists were not welcome after-dark visitors. But I knew there was no point in long explanations and simply told them curtly that we had a boy with us who needed looking after and expected them to take him in. Without waiting for an answer I handed Gideon to the man. I told Gideon that these people were our friends and he must stay with them until we could come to take him back to his family. We gave the peasant no opportunity to say no, or for that matter, yes. Mietek and I simply told him quietly that the boy was an orphan who had lost his mother and sister in a

German raid a few days earlier and that his father was an
important Jewish leader. They would all be accountable for
the boy's safety and well-being to our partisan unit and if
anything should happen to him we would come back and burn
their house down with all of them inside. They were impressed
by our businesslike attitude and agreed without a murmur, in
fact, the woman offered us a hot meal which we accepted. I
noticed that the peasant was a shoemaker and wrote down his
name and that of the village. Little Gideon was so overwhelmed by the pace of events that he did not even cry when
we said goodbye. I think we were actually sadder than he was,
but as we made our way back up the mountain I felt we had
left him in good hands. It was certainly impossible to keep
him in the mountain during the winter. I prayed we would
soon join up with the Russian army and be able to take him
back to his father who I hoped was safe somewhere in Slovakia. Perhaps I had been too rough with the peasants, but I
had enough experience to know that their fear of reprisal
would be Gideon's life insurance.

We returned to our encampment without mishap and were
glad to see that the newly fallen snow had made our bunker
virtually invisible from even a short distance although it
occupied a commanding position that would allow us to re-
pulse any sort of attack the terrain made possible. There was
no danger of tanks coming up that far. However, our main
objective now was not to lead a pastoral life in a mountain
bunker but to fight the Germans, and to do so effectively we
must link up with other units. A group of us, headed by some
experienced Russians set out toward the northeast, moving
very slowly because of the thick snow and also to forestall
surprises. We found no footprints in the snow, which was
reassuring, and at night we looked out for fires or smoke, but
there were none. We spent the night resting around a small
fire. The next morning we spotted some men and called out to
them. They were as wary as we were, and two of them
approached us with rifles at the ready while we kept them
covered with our guns. They spoke Russian and after we
checked each other's papers, embraced, and both groups then
mingled joyously. They led us to a well-guarded bunker with
a lot of men and some women around, all speaking Russian.
They were a large, organized partisan unit, named the Stalin

Brigade, commanded by Major Jegorow who had parachuted into Slovakia in August with a few men and in a few weeks had gathered all the small partisan bands he could find around him and formed them into a fighting brigade, one of the largest in central Slovakia. They had already fought at Niske Tatry and Fatras, and had given a good account of themselves. Jegorow readily agreed to accept us into his brigade and promised to send one of his officers to take command. We stayed overnight and found that our own bunker was much cleaner than theirs. It was secured by heavy guns and a large number of fighting men and women. Jegorow received his orders directly from Kiev and the partisan groups under his command were hitting the Germans at every opportunity.

We were happy that we had looked for them instead of waiting until they should find us. That could have been dangerous, because everybody was now very suspicious of spies and traitors. It was also lucky that we had found the top brass at our first attempt. So we arrived back in high spirits and told our comrades the good news that we were now part of a partisan army.

A few days later Jegorow's representative, Captain Marcuk, arrived. He was accompanied by some armed men. He was a Polish-speaking Ukrainian and immediately took over command of our unit. He was very satisfied with our bunker and the amount of arms and ammunition we had accumulated and promised to bring us a radio transmitter, explosives and some light submachine guns. Then we got some unpleasant visitors, lice. I don't know how they reached us but they were a plague, multiplying in front of our unbelieving eyes. We suspected the Russians from Jegorow's camp had brought them. No matter what we did we could not get rid of them. Even burying my shirt in the snow didn't help, for they found their way out. The problem was complicated by our having to sleep with our clothes on, in case of a surprise attack. Marcuk nonchalantly advised us to just get used to them since they were part of the partisan's life. He warned us to be very careful because some units had already been tricked by traitors from the Vlasow army and the Hlinka guards, who had wormed their way into their camps and then killed them. The Germans also were active, air-dropping leaflets in the mountains calling on Slovaks to give themselves up in return for safe passage home.

Those who did were first tortured for information and then shot, he told us. Even generals Viest and Golian of the Free Slovak forces who had been hiding in a peasant home in Bukowce had been betrayed. There were also fairly reliable reports that the members of the American mission to the uprising had been captured, as well as other foreign and Czechoslovak officers, handed over to the Gestapo and taken to Germany. The Germans massacred Slovaks who refused to cooperate and razed the villages of Nemecka and Hronom and killed their inhabitants.

Marcuk also told us that according to reports that had reached Jegorow, President Tiso and a senior dignitary of the church had come to Banská Bystria on October 30, decorated the SS and police chief Hoefle, and celebrated a thanksgiving mass at which Hoefle himself played the organ with his blood-stained hands. If it hadn't been so sad it would have been funny, a gallery of rogues and murderers in communion to the greater glory of God and Adolf Hitler. Father Tiso pinned a lot of medals on the chests of the killers of his own people, and blessed them in the name of God and Christ.

Jegorow's camp had radio transmitters and Marcuk gave us a rundown of the news from the fronts. The only bad news was that the Warsaw uprising had failed. One hundred thousand Poles were dead, the city was destroyed, and many survivors dragged away to concentration camps. But the Russians had cut off the Baltic, linked up with Tito's partisans and reached the Adriatic. Athens was liberated. They were encircling Hungary and entering Slovakia from the north and south and in the east had already liberated some Slovak towns.

Marcuk started at once to beef up our military proficiency: organized a better guard system, issued new passwords morning and evening, made us exercise and train all day, and instructed us in the latest guerrilla tactics. He decided to set up his headquarters in our bunker and picked six men to accompany him to Jegorow's camp to get explosives and automatic weapons. Mietek and I were in the group. From a storage bunker he got us several crates of ammunition and ten automatic guns, three of them for us. Some of our comrades were disappointed when we did not bring any for them, but he promised soon to get more automatics. We also brought thousands of leaflets, in Slovak, calling on the peasants and workers to join the partisans and destroy their enemies: the Germans, the Hlinka guards, and the government of Father Tiso and its henchmen. We distributed the leaflets in the villages on our missions. Our first assignment was to comb the mountains for other groups who were isolated just as we had been until not long ago, and get them to join Jegorow's brigade. We went out scouting in the mountains every day, and found some bunkers. First we had to convince the people that we were genuine partisans, after that it was easy; they were glad to become part of a larger group. In one of the bunkers we came upon we discovered a lot of Jews, some of them from Poland. The bunker was in bad condition and they told us that a few days earlier some men in Russian uniforms had approached and asked to join them. But their guards felt there was something fishy about them and sent them away. That same night their bunker was attacked with grenades and machine guns. Some of them were killed before they were able to drive off the attackers.

We urged them to join Marcuk's unit but advised them to use non-Jewish names for safety. Only two of them, the Zeller brothers from Sanok in Poland, who had lost a third brother in the recent attack, insisted on using their Jewish names. Marcuk didn't care one way or the other. On our way back he told me that Jegorow was receiving weapons and supplies by parachute and by light planes that were able to land on small strips in the mountains.

In a couple of days two men arrived at our bunker. Marcuk spoke with them and told us they had parachuted into Slovakia only a few days earlier. They turned out to be instructors in the use of the latest explosives of the type that Jegorow had sent us to be used in the next operation he had planned. We were to carry it out the next evening. Henry, Mietek, Stefan and I were among those picked for the operation. We started out early and on the way had to pick up more men from some of the other bunkers. We took along guns and explosives for them. From each bunker Marcuk picked the men he wanted and they included some Jewish men too. When our complement was full we marched to our target, the railway tracks connecting eastern and western Slovakia. Beyond the valley, as we neared the main road, we spotted a long German army convoy, heading west, coming in our direction. We estimated they were coming from Hungary or Poland and were heading for Austria or Moravia. Marcuk decided they were too inviting a target to be missed. We spread out on both sides of the road and on a signal from Marcuk threw grenades at them. When the astonished soldiers jumped out of their trucks in confusion and began firing wildly into the forest, we picked them off with our machine guns. Killing those Germans made me happier than I had ever been. Marcuk then gave us the order to move on and we climbed higher up into the mountain, away from the road, and continued on toward our targeted railway tracks. We took up covering positions overlooking the tracks while below the two Russian explosive experts, backed by some of our men, placed the explosives. Then all of us withdrew higher up into the mountains and lay down to wait for the train. It seemed a long time coming, or perhaps we were simply impatient, but when it came and they set off the explosives, the train blew up with a big bang, its coaches falling over each other and going up in flames. As we moved on higher up, I kept looking back to savor the havoc we had wreaked on the enemy of our people. Another little account was settled and I thought of my parents and all the other helpless victims of the Germans. Now I was no longer helpless, and I looked forward to the next opportunity of repaying the Nazis.

Marcuk called a short halt and told us we would enter the nearest village to obtain food and information about the Germans. Our comrades took up covering positions while Marcuk, with one of the Slovaks and the three of us, entered an isolated house. In short order some peasants came out with empty sacks. Marcuk told us he had given them one hour to obtain the supplies we needed, and threatened to burn down the whole village if they failed to deliver. They were soon back, accompanied by more peasants who helped to carry the load. We took the provisions from them and immediately climbed back up into the mountains because it was already getting light. We didn't stop until we were high up, and after a short rest proceeded to our bunker.

Marcuk told us that the peasants had informed him about an SS unit operating in the area. He also got information of a massacre in Kremnica village. The victims were mostly Jews, including some members of the Palestinian mission. The next morning he took the three of us to Jegorow's camp to report on our operation and on the intelligence he had gathered about the SS encampments. It was not far from the scene of our mission, and their task was to protect a rail junction through which the retreating Wehrmacht was passing. Jegorow issued sixteen more submachine guns for the men in other bunkers and also sent four Russian officers with us to take over their command. The next morning we guided them to the bunkers that had been assigned to them.

When we returned to ours, our women were busy sewing white overalls from parachutes, to camouflage us when operating in the snow. Orders for another big operation had come in and we insisted on taking part in it, although Marcuk wanted to give us a rest. The objective was to blow up an important rail junction and nearby tunnel. We marched all night taking only very short breaks, remembering the danger of the so-called white death. When we reached the vicinity of the junction we split into two groups. One, headed by the four Russians, was to blow up the tunnel, and the other larger group, under Marcuk's command, to destroy the junction. When darkness fell our group moved in on the junction, camouflaged by our white overalls, and after checking the junction and its switching post, placed our explosives and wired them to a detonator. On a signal from Marcuk we drew back into the forest and set off the charge. The sight of the shooting flames piercing the dark sky were a delight, but on Marcuk's instructions we did not fire at the men who came running out of the switching building in panic, because they were most likely Slovak rail workers. We moved higher up for our link-up with the other group. We had not gone far when we heard their explosion shattering the silence of the cold night. They were soon back and together we hurriedly moved on. I personally could have flown for I was so elated to have delivered another deadly message to the German killers. At last the shoe was on the other foot.

Following these operations we rested for a few days and then received orders from Jegorow's headquarters to send small parties into the neighboring villages to gather intelligence on the disposition of German units operating in the area. Mietek and I jumped up as soon as Marcuk asked for volunteers. The only purpose for living now was to strike at the Germans.

We reached a position above the first village late in the evening, and as we moved closer we were surprised to see a lot of German soldiers going into the local inn. We could not risk entering this village with so many Germans about, and decided to lie in wait for them until they finished their drinking, and then attack as they came out. They outnumbered us by far, but we had the advantage of surprise, and we also reckoned that they would be more or less drunk. We moved in as close as was prudent and waited. When at last they started coming out, we held back until the last one had emerged and closed the door. Then we opened fire. All of them fell to the ground, but we could not be sure that they were all dead. Some may have dropped to the ground instinctively on hearing the first shot. We ran up to where they were lying and found that a few were indeed only wounded, but they raised their hands as we approached them with our automatics pointing at them. We ignored their pleas to let them go and drove them ahead of us into the mountains at the double, because the shooting may have alerted the main German force. When our prisoners complained of their wounds, or asked to rest, I told them their wounds were nothing, and the Russians would take care of them when we reached our base. They were men of a supply company and there was one sergeant among them. As I watched the scared faces of these murderers, I seemed to see them killing or mistreating Jews in Poland. I thanked my lucky stars that I had lived to see this day.

On our return we reported to Marcuk and he congratulated us for a job well done and decided to send the Germans to Jegorow the next morning for interrogation. I begged him to allow us to go with them and persuaded him that our knowledge of German would be a great help. He consented.

When we reached Jegorow's bunker Henry and I were enlisted as interpreters. The first thing the Germans said in reply to the interrogator was that they were only regular army men and had nothing to do with the SS or Gestapo. The interrogator promised he would have their wounds dressed after they would volunteer the information he wanted, about their units, where they were camped, and the movement of German units from Poland and Hungary. They made a pretense of not knowing until he called in a couple of tough-looking Russians who, he said, had ways of making them talk if they would not do so voluntarily. They got the message and started talking, slowly at first, until they had revealed everything he wanted to know and had cross-checked the information. We translated as fast as we were able, and when the interrogation was completed the Germans asked for medical attention and fair treatment. The commissar promised they would soon be taken care of. And they were. He ordered them to strip and made them run naked through the snow into the forest where they were shot. The next morning we returned, taking back a few crates and a letter for Marcuk. He read it and told us that Jegorow was happy with the way our group had carried out our mission and ordered us to go the village to try and confirm the Germans' information.

The villagers told us what they knew about the German deployment in the area and also informed us that some large SS and Tyrolean mountain troop units had attacked partisan units in Lucerna, Horna, Lehota and Bukowec killing many of them. They had discovered the partisans by following some peasants who were taking food to them and subsequently burned their villages too. Some villagers had been burned alive. In addition a Jewish partisan unit commanded by Karol Adler, whom we had met in Banská Bystrica, had also been ambushed and killed, after Hlinka guards disguised as peasants surprised and attacked them. The action took place near Ružomberok. Adler and his unit put up a brave fight killing and wounding Hlinka guards and Germans even though they were outnumbered and outgunned. Karol Adler and twenty of his brave men were taken then to a nearby village. After long hours of torture by the SS men all were hanged in front of the villagers. I was dismayed at the bad luck of Jews still being killed at this stage of the war, after they had survived so many horrors. But at least they had gone down fighting.

We returned as fast as we could to inform Marcuk. He considered the matter so serious that Jegorow must be informed at once. We volunteered to escort him and Jegorow immediately issued a general alert. Jegorow had recently been promoted to colonel by the Kiev headquarters, and expressed his satisfaction with our work. We were proud of his praise but Marcuk left the headquarters very disappointed for he had expected to be promoted to major.

The next day we were sent down to the village again to get food. On the way we decided not to go back to the same village. Toward evening we came on some footprints in the snow and followed them to a small bunker that was surprisingly unguarded. We had an even bigger surprise when we found only civilians inside, a few families with children. The three of us realized right away that they were all Jewish, and suspected that the others in our group would realize it too. We knew the Ukrainians hated Jews and made no bones about their feelings. Since Marcuk had put me in charge of the mission I had the authority to give orders to the Ukrainians. I commanded them to go ahead and wait for the three of us at a certain spot. I wanted a chance to talk to the Jews in the bunker to warn them that they were risking their lives by their carelessness. As soon as the Ukrainians had gone I first told them that the three of us were Jewish and I could see the relief the revelation caused them. Then I reproached them for failing to guard their bunker and gave them most of our grenades and a short lesson in their use as well as in the posting of sentries. We told them of the dangers they faced from the SS, the special Tyrolean mountain units, the Vlasow and the Hlinka guards, who were all known to be in the area. My warning shock them, but they had to know the truth and how to protect themselves. We told them to make sure that the peasants who brought them provisions were not being followed, always to sleep with their clothes and shoes on to be ready for any emergency, and we promised to be back. We also told them about the Frieder boy and gave them the address of the peasant we had left him with. We wanted somebody Jewish to know, in case something happened to us.

We quickly caught up with the rest of our group and continued cautiously toward the village. We made our usual check and entered the last house after posting guards around it. The peasants were shocked when we appeared out of the dark, draped in white overalls like bona fide ghosts. We made them a list of the provisions we needed and gave them an hour to get them. The peasants told us that many Slovak and foreign high ranking military and civilian leaders were betrayed to the

Hlinka guards and SS, and soon after many were shot and the rest were sent to Germany.

In every village we entered searching for provisions, we promised the peasants that if they delivered we would not trouble them again, and we kept our promise. It made them a little more sympathetic to our demands but we knew they were angry, especially because we were not the only foraging partisans.

When we returned, Marcuk was particularly pleased with the vodka we brought. He was still sulking about not having been promoted, but while he would drop an occasional hint about his displeasure to us, he never mentioned it to the Russian partisans. Indeed, I had noted that the Russians tended never to complain. All of them always praised Stalin as though he were a saint, and talked with admiration of their marshals and war heroes. Marcuk began sending out small groups composed of men from different bunkers for hit-and-run operations against the Germans. One morning he sent me to lead a small group to try and get some German prisoners for Jegorow's intelligence commissars. I remembered that not long ago the peasants had told us of a location where Germans were camped and headed there, taking a route we had not used before. When we reached the target area and started descending from the high mountain, we found footprints in the fresh snow. We followed them cautiously and they led us to a small bunker. We checked carefully but there were no guards and it looked a little too quiet. I closed in carefully and was horrified when I noticed some human limbs sticking out of a pile of earth and snow heaped in front of the entrance. I called the other men over and inside the heap discovered the bodies of men, women and children, who had been killed in cold blood. They had obviously been robbed, either before or after they were put to death, because there was not a single ring, watch or piece of jewelery on any of the bodies. We could not risk staying long enough to dig graves for them, and in fact did not have the tools for it, so we quickly covered them again with snow which would keep the bodies from rotting until we could return and bury them properly. I had no doubt that they were Jewish because inside the bunker, which had been ransacked, I found some Jewish prayer books lying on the floor. The large pools of blood indicated that the Jews had put up a fight. I strongly suspected that the massacre was perpetrated by the Ukrainian anti-Semites. We made a close check of the surroundings and found that all footprints led into the mountains, confirming that the killers had indeed been partisans. Since I had no authority to investigate, but did have Marcuk's orders for an operation, I commanded the men to carry on, though I did so with a very heavy heart. We moved down toward the village and looked for an isolated house. Since it was now safely dark I went down with Mietek and entered the house while the rest of the unit stood guard. I asked the peasants for any information they could give me on the German dispositions in the area. One young man told us that on his way home that afternoon he had seen some German trucks and armored cars being repaired. He gave me the location and I asked him to show us the place. He took us through the hills until we spotted some lighted tents. I thanked the peasant and sent him back home. We moved slowly down and surrounded the tents. There were no guards and we could hear the soldiers inside talking. We closed in very fast, threw in some grenades and then charged with blazing automatics. The wounded Germans came out with their hands up. Inside the tents we found a lot of Germans lying dead. Our aim had been good. We checked the vehicles and found crates of food which we ordered the prisoners to carry for us, and before we left we wrecked the vehicles with hand grenades. We took the slightly wounded with us.

When we returned to our camp Marcuk was not there. He had gone to see Jegorow. This was a break for me. It allowed us to take the prisoners to Jegorow's camp. There I reported our discovery of the massacre in the Jewish bunker, emphasizing that the killers had come from the mountains. The Russians who had been with us confirmed my report. But the officer I reported to never batted an eyelid and made no comment except to say that the interview was over. I was deeply disappointed and then and there decided that the Russian system was not for me. As long as it suited me to be with them killing Germans I would cooperate, but not a moment longer than necessary.

When I told Marcuk about the massacre, he appeared sincerely sorry. He congratulated us on our successful action against the Germans. I told him we were all convinced that the massacre had been perpetrated by partisans from the mountains. I did not mention Ukrainians since he was a Ukrainian himself. But he was also a fair man and he gave us permission to return to the bunker to give the victims a proper burial, which we did the next day. Stefan, who was religious, recited the appropriate prayers while I prayed for the punishment of the killers. When we returned to our bunker, I came down with a fever which grew worse during the night, and I developed diarrhea. We had no medicine, and the only available treatment, hot tea, was ineffective. My condition deteriorated rapidly, so much so that Henry, Mietek and Stefan became anxious and got Marcuk's permission to try to get medicine from the villagers. When they returned in the evening, Mietek fixed a drink for me from the dark liquid they had brought. Actually, I was so weak he had to pour it down my throat. As an additional treatment he applied cold compresses to my forehead. The next morning I felt a little better and was able to have some dry bread, my first solid food in several days. Mietek told me that the dark medicine he had made me swallow was *Borowczak* (pressed juice of blueberries), a folk medicine we had known as an effective cure for diarrhea in Poland. In a day or two I felt stronger. Mietek and Stefan had again saved my life. I already owed them for the boots they had found for me when my shoe was burned. We had in fact been like brothers since Tolonzhanz, and this brought us even closer.

I recovered gradually and Marcuk relieved me from duty to help restore my strength and told me he planned to appoint me as his liaison to Jegorow's headquarters. Meanwhile I spent many anxious days waiting for the safe return of my unit from their operations. We received reports of SS and Vlasow men searching out bunkers and killing or capturing the partisans inside them. To be captured by them was worse than being killed. It meant torture before being put to death. A week later I was firm enough on my feet to lead a small unit to Jegorow's headquarters, to bring dispatches and supplies. I was soon at home in Jegorow's camp, and when we stayed overnight had a chance to see movies and newsreels flown in from Russia. They emphasized German cruelties and sometimes the partisan audience got so worked up that they shot at the Germans on the screen. I could not blame them. I felt the same way.

One day Jegorow ordered all of his men and us to stamp on the newly fallen snow with our boots to firm up a site for a light plane to land which was bringing in a senior Russian officer. It was very exciting for me to witness a landing so high up in the mountain and when the propeller stopped, a general and his staff stepped out. We also received other new arrivals, Siberian parachutists. They were very rugged men who thought nothing of sleeping out on the snow. They told us how Leningrad had been liberated and Stalingrad saved. They also brought the latest news from the front. Cracow had been liberated along with Rzeszów. I was happy with the thought that the Lopatowskis, Zwolinskis and Magrys were safe now if, as I fervently hoped, they had survived. No less hopeful was the news of the liberation of the cities of Košice, Poprad and Prešov. They were only a few hundred kilometers away, which meant that every day was bringing the Red army and our own liberation closer. The men never mentioned the western Allies at all. Listening to them you got the impression that only the Russians were fighting the Germans.

Our operations now focused on hitting the retreating Germans as they passed through Slovakia. We were to destroy tanks and trucks, blow up railroad tracks, tunnels and bridges, and above all to kill as many of them as we could. We received special orders to catch Vlasow officers and men who were now desperately trying to worm their way into our units to save their skins. They were despised as traitors to their own people. The commissars shot every one we caught, after they had finished interrogating them.

One day, early in February 1945, we received orders for a large-scale operation. We were given rations for four days, longer than we had ever stayed away before, and were ordered to pick up more men from the other bunkers on the way. Our target was the Ružomberok area, where important rail and highway junctions were located on the German withdrawal route from Poland, Hungary and eastern Slovakia to Austria and Moravia. Our large column made its way through the mountains, avoiding the valleys, the roads, and the villages, to assure us the element of complete surprise. We wore our white overalls, and all smoking and loud talk was forbidden.

For the first time no vodka had been brought along. There were to be no errors. About noon next day our forward patrols reported sighting a large body of men, who turned out to be the contingent from Jegorow's camp coming to join us. The force was then divided into two groups, one under Marcuk to attack the highway and the other, commanded by one of Jegorow's officers, to blow up rail tracks, tunnels and bridges. As we approached our target area and descended from the mountain, Marcuk divided our group into small units which spread out over a wide area around the main road and some bridges that were our main targets.

We waited for the dark and then started to move forward, getting down on the snow to crawl the last stretch. The sappers were right behind us. We observed that the bridge was well guarded and we held our fire until the sappers reached the other side of the bridge and then opened up, firing with everything we had at the Germans on and around the bridge, and their comrades in the tents. When we were sure that they were all dead we signaled the sappers, who quickly placed their charges and we all made our way back into the hills. There the sappers set off the charges and we saw the bridge going up with a lot of noise and smoke, whereupon we immediately moved higher into the mountains to join up with the column. As each unit returned, they happily reported success. We had taken the Germans by surprise, inflicted substantial losses and damage and had suffered no casualties ourselves. When we reached the crest late in the evening, we made a large fire and enjoyed a good meal. We were all in a festive mood but since everybody was in a hurry, we didn't delay. Marcuk had to report to Jegorow, and we wanted to get back to rest. Now for the first time I felt that I was not completely recovered. My legs tended to drag, but the elation of having taken part in a small offensive against the Germans, kept me on my feet. I had a long and deep sleep and dreamed I was reporting our successful action to my parents, as though I were assuring them that I was paying off our debt for their suffering.

When I arose the next morning, Marcuk sent me to Jegorow's headquarters with dispatches. There I learned that the Red army had taken Auschwitz and had liberated many prisoners, saving them from certain death at the last moment. In

East Prussia hundreds of thousands of Germans, troops as well as civilians, were fleeing in a panic and many were killed on the way.

Russian bombers were attacking Berlin day and night. The Russian artillery was sowing destruction on the German troops, and their Katyusha rockets, the so-called "Stalin Organs," put the fear of God into them. It could not be much longer before the Russians would join up with our units.

I brought sealed orders back to Marcuk and after he studied them ordered us to prepare for another operation. We were to take possession of an electric power station in the Jesenska valley, which supplied electricity to a large area that was important to the Germans and their Tiso puppets. He picked forty men and personally led the unit. Our progress through the heavy new snow was laborious and it was late in the evening by the time we got to a small village where Marcuk obtained information on the Germans from the peasants. Then we moved through the hills until we were above the power plant and surreptitiously surrounded it, effectively camouflaged by our white overalls. We established that the entrance was guarded by two sentries with more men, presumably guards in reserve, in a small lighted building just inside the gate. We had no way of knowing whether they were Germans or Hlinka guards. At a given signal we opened fire on the guards and rushed the gate. The men inside the building came out immediately with their hands up. There were six of them and from their broken German we identified them as Vlasow soldiers. We tied their hands behind their backs and locked them up in a storage room, under guard by one of our men. Marcuk placed guards around the plant and some of our men who knew something about the machinery, stopped the generators and shut down the power. Marcuk left half of our men to hold the station and the rest of us went back with him, taking the six prisoners with us. We all knew what the commissars would do to them but felt no pity; they were the traitors who searched out partisans, and pretending to be Russians come to help them, delivered them into the hands of the Gestapo.

In Jegorow's camp there was great excitement. They were expecting the Red army to arrive very soon. When one of the commissars handed me the new orders for Marcuk he remarked that they may be the last. Soon we would be part of the regular army. He smiled and shook my hand, the longest conversation I had had with the commissars, who were always tight lipped and never said more than was necessary to make their orders clear.

The new orders were to confine our attacks to German convoys in our immediate vicinity. Every day one of our units went down, lay in wait for German vehicles to pass, fired on them and then withdrew back into the mountains. I felt wonderful every time I took part in one of these actions, especially when my bullets hit home, to pay off another installment of my debts. When we caught Germans alive we gave them the commissar treatment, forcing them to strip and run into the snow and shooting them as they ran. It pleased me to hear them begging for mercy and then to shoot them just as they had shot defenseless Jews in the ghetto.

One morning we heard the first distant artillery fire coming from the northeast. It sounded like beautiful music to us and we looked forward at last to greeting our comrades. Everybody was happy, embracing and kissing, giving vent to their long-suppressed emotions and profound relief. It had been a long time since we had allowed ourselves the luxury of showing our feelings. When we were picked for the party to go down to check on our men in the Jesenska power station, we decided to make a detour to visit the bunker in which we had met the Jewish Slovaks in hiding. We were happy to see that they had heeded our warnings and posted guards. We asked only the men to come out, as we did not want to panic the women, and I told them of the massacre in one of the refugee bunkers, and urged them to be more alert than ever as the Jew-hating Ukrainians were still around. But I also informed them that salvation was at hand for the Russian artillery was approaching, heralded by the exquisite rumbling of their cannons. They had heard them too. We left them all the grenades and ammunition we could spare and then went on to Jesenska. Our men there reported to us that a German unit had tried to storm the plant but they had successfully repulsed them. One of the buildings was damaged in the skirmish.

On our return we found that Marcuk had been urgently summoned to Jegorow's headquarters. He returned the next day and before he could say a word we read the good news on his face. Jegorow had told him to prepare to move down into the valley. Marcuk told our women to bake a large quantity of bread, suspend the rationing, and dish out more generous portions. No definite date had yet been set, but Marcuk was very happy and invited us to have a drink. For the first time we all accepted. Though the camp went on functioning normally, there was a palpable undercurrent of excited expectation. To get ready for the great day we all scrubbed our clothes in hot water and launched a general hunt for lice; we did not want to return to civilization scratching. I personally began sketching plans in my mind. First I would find Fela and then search for any trace of Szymon and Nathan.

Actually we now felt pretty safe. The Germans were in very poor shape, and in such a hurry to get back to their *Heimat,* that they were unlikely to bother us in their scramble. Moreover, the Russians were hard on their heels and did not allow them a moment's peace. They had a lot to answer for, to us as well as to the Russians. I did my best to be included in every one of our operations, to swoop down on the retreating Nazis, kill as many of them as possible, and retreat back to the safety of the mountains. In the villages we sometimes came upon them foraging for food or getting drunk, and since we no longer needed the information they could give us, we killed them before they knew what hit them.

Marcuk kept meticulous records, *sprawkas,* of each man's activities which would be important when we linked up with the regulars. They would show what we had been doing these five months in the mountains and our contribution to the fight against the enemy. They would also help us to enlist, which all of us would be required to do, and save many of us from the suspicion of having been in the Vlasow army, whose men were now deserting in the thousands. When he completed writing those *sprawkas,* he sent me to Jegorow's headquarters to have them typed and signed.

In Jegorow's camp I learned that the Russians had reached the Oder-Neisse and encircled Danzig. Hitler's excuse for invading Poland, as well as Koenigsberg. Soon after that our big day arrived. A messenger brought the order that we were to leave the mountains the next day. Marcuk briefed us on the road we were to take down from the south side of the Low Tatras in the direction of the Jesenska and Bukewska valleys, there to meet the Red army. We started packing and Marcuk warned us not to overdo it because the route was difficult and the weather was still wintry, even though we were in the second week of March. It was hard to fall asleep that night, waiting for the five o'clock H-hour.

As we assembled to go, I took another look at the mountain peaks. How I loved those mountains. They had sheltered us safely for nearly half a year and afforded us a chance to settle our score with the Germans. How majestic were the mighty Dumbier and Prasiva peaks. I looked up at them in admiration and silently expressed my thanks to them.

We started out, leaving behind everything we would no longer need. Six men made up the vanguard and then came Marcuk, with Henry, Mietek and myself behind him, followed by the rest of our camp. We stopped at every bunker along the way and were joined by our comrades. When we reached the bunker of the Jewish partisans they received us with eyes sparkling like stars on a cold, clear night. I almost cried at the sight of their happy faces which so plainly said "We made it." I immediately thought of the Frieder boy and how we might retrieve and deliver him to his father or to some Jewish organization. But our plans did not include entering any village, so I had to withgo that for the moment. Soon recollections of Cracow and Rzeszów went through my mind, the Zwolinskis and Magrys and the Lopatowskis, and then where I might find Fela, and what chances there were of finding Szymon and Nathan still alive. Henry and Stefan were hoping too. Mietek also talked about his family but he entertained no illusions. He did not expect to see any of them again. His memory of them was of the deportation train that took them to Belzec.

We still had twenty hours of marching before us and Marcuk called for a steady pace with many stops for rest and food, so that all could keep up and there would be no stragglers left behind. In the late afternoon our forward patrol reported sighting a concentration of armed men in the valley below. In fact, they were the main force of Jegorow's Stalin Brigade.

Most of our men had never seen the Brigade commander Jegorow in person, and when he greeted us we responded with a resounding hurrah which the mountains echoed back, as though to leave no doubt that they were ours now. But

Jegorow insisted on continued caution since there might still be some desperate elements of the SS or the Tyrolean mountain infantry roaming about. Late in the evening we built a huge fire and sat around it to enjoy our meal. We stayed close to the Jewish partisans for we craved the feeling of fellow Jews being free and together. The next day we passed above many of the villages I had visited during the past five and a half months, but the village where the Frieder boy was lay across the other side of the mountain. We moved without stopping now, eager to meet the Red army at last. I felt my heart pumping, not from exertion, but excitement. When I spotted a small town below us I knew we had reached the end of the road. Jegorow did not stop us from rushing forward with only a semblance of orderly marching, but when we came to the edge of the town he ordered a halt. Then he commanded us to form an orderly column, four abreast, and march into the town as soldiers and not like a bunch of wild men. When he gave the order to go I felt as though we were flying.

15

Slovakia, Joining Hands with the Red Army
March 1945

At last I spotted a few large tanks, their red stars prominent on their sides. There were some soldiers standing beside the tanks in green uniforms and odd-looking leather helmets I had never seen before. Some were carrying the same type of automatics we had. When they saw us they climbed on their tanks to get a better view. We waved to them and they waved back. It was a day to remember, March 18, 1945.

When we reached them they jumped off the tanks and embraced those who were nearest to them. Inside the town there were more tanks and a lot of Russian soldiers waiting for us. We were ordered to line up in a large circle and a Russian general stepped onto a small podium and greeted us in the name of the Red army, the Soviet people, and their Tovarich Josef Stalin. When he went on to thank us for our heroic deeds and sacrifices, a hurrah went up that set the tanks rattling. Then Jegorow got up to speak. He thanked the general and the Second Ukrainian Front, which had been in charge of our Brigade, and expressed the gratitude of all of us to the Soviet flyers who had kept the partisans supplied with arms and explosives. Finally he bade farewell to each of his units, and the responding cheer outdid the hurrah we had given the Soviet general. We realized that as we bade farewell to Jegorow, we were parting from a brave man who had given direction to our will to hit the Germans and channeled it into cohesive action. I was personally thankful to him for having given me the chance to avenge myself, my family, and millions of anonymous Jews whose blood had been so cruelly spilled by the German beasts.

A Russian officer was assigned to each of our units and instructed us where to go and what to do. First we were assigned bunks in barracks and then were given a wonderful hot meal, served on clean dishes, in a large mess hall. It was my first real Russian-style army meal. After the meal we had hot baths, and were sprayed with some chemicals and had our hair cut to get rid of the lice. Our old uniforms, which had meanwhile been disinfected, were then returned to us. Marcuk told us we would be formally discharged from the partisans and be issued our personal records before leaving the town.

After breakfast next morning we reported to Marcuk, who, together with some of Jegorow's aides, gave us our *sprawkas* and identity papers. We had to surrender all our weapons. They would not even allow me to keep the pistol I had received as a personal gift from our commander. Then we divided into groups according to nationalities, the Russians being the largest. Finally Jegorow came to thank us once more and say goodbye. He was followed by Marcuk who shook the hands of each man and woman. He spent the most time with our group, the Poles, almost all of us being Jews. He told us we were getting a month-long furlough to go back to Poland to look for our families. I felt he knew we were Jewish, but even now he did not mention it. But the fact that he had gotten the longest furlough for our group, because our desperate search for our families would be the longest, spoke for itself. Then he embraced and kissed each one of us.

While the Russians, Slovaks and Czechs were ordered to enlist and were immediately inducted into their armies, we were free for a month. We exchanged our last addresses in Poland and promised to look each other up. Mietek, Henry and I decided to stay together, and we took a tearful farewell from Stefan and the Zeller brothers. I told Stefan we would meet again when the war was finally over and I would get him the watch I had promised him in the mountains.

In the Russian headquarter offices we were given free passes for all public transport facilities, rail and highway, in the areas under Russian control, and decided first to go back to Liptovský Sväty Mikuláš, where we had made so many good friends among the Slovak Jews. I also hoped to get the Frieder boy and put him in their care, but found that the village where I had left him was still in a combat area. On the way to the railroad station we asked whether there were any Jews in the city and when we were told there were a few we decided to find them. As we walked through the town center somebody called to us, and looking around we saw a small group of men and children running toward us. They asked whether we did not recognize them. We did not. They told us they were some of the Jews we had helped in the bunker in the Niske Tatry Mountains. I looked at them very closely but could not recall their faces. Then I remembered that both times we had gone inside their bunker it was dark. It was a heartwarming reunion for all of us. What a great delight it was to meet Jews who had survived the horrors. They insisted that we come to one of their homes to meet all the people who had been in the bunker with them. They quickly got a party going with all the delicacies the women were able to make with the available food, from recipes not to be found in cookbooks.

I told them again about the Frieder boy and they solemnly pledged to look for him as soon as the fighting would pass the village, and then to do everything possible to find his father, Rabbi Frieder. They persuaded us to stay the night and the next morning took us to a store which had been Jewish before the war, and was now partly owned by a Slovak Aryan. The owner had legally registered the store in his name back in 1940 and in that way it was kept safe for the Jewish owner. Even in my elated state I could not but muse how different the Slovaks were from the Poles who, I recalled bitterly, took over Jewish property the moment they had the chance with no intention at all of returning it. In the store they fitted us out with shirts, socks and underwear. But we drew the line at suits for our uniforms would make our travels easier.

As we walked and looked about, we met some more Jews whom our host recognized and there were happy reunions right on the street. Then somebody called our host's name and the two fell into each other's arms. The man's name was Schwarz, a native of the town, who had just returned after several years in Romania. The trip back had taken him ten days.

16

Slovakia, Finding Fela
March 1945

Our host introduced us as young Jews from Poland who had also been with the partisans and had saved many Jewish lives in the mountains. As we were talking, Schwarz interrupted saying he was looking for a young Jew from Poland, and produced a little notebook containing the name of the man. Actually there were two names, both mine—Herzog, and Adam Budkowski, the Aryan name I had assumed. I froze. It took me a few moments before I was able to call out, "That's me!" I had to pinch myself to make sure I was not dreaming such a fantastic coincidence. I jumped to embrace him before he could dissolve into thin air, and inquired how he had gotten my names. I knew there was only one person who knew my two names. My dear sister!

"From a young lady called Fela," he told me. Mietek, Henry and our host stood stunned. This must be too good to be true. But Schwarz had the details to prove it. He told me Fela was married to a young man called Janek, and they were living in the building he had lived in in Bucharest. I remembered the name Janek. He was the young man who had taken care of Fela and other Jewish girls when they were released from the Tolonzhaz prison in Budapest. I was happy that Fela had married, but was concerned by Schwarz's report that her husband had been wounded in the leg and had to use crutches. He was wounded while he and Fela were going by train to Bucharest from Timişoara in northern Romania, where they had been married. The train was attacked by German planes and Janek had been seriously hurt and spent a long time in the hospital in Timişoara.

Schwarz told us the hardest part of his long journey home was through Hungary, which had suffered terribly from the battles between the Soviet and German armies, and he had to change trains frequently, and walk many miles to get past blown-up tunnels and junctions. He gave me Fela's address and I decided to set out for Bucharest early the next morning. With tears in my eyes I embraced this messenger of such wonderful news.

Mietek and Henry decided to come with me since there was nobody left for them to look for in Poland. I was touched by their gesture. We got up very early the next morning and parted from our Slovak friends, promising to return. At the station we were told there would be no trains before noon, so we went to the Russian headquarters and asked for assistance to get to Romania. The commissar wanted to know why we wanted to go there and I simply told him the truth. He was moved by my story and issued us documents requesting Russian officials to extend us all possible help. As soldiers in uniform we were given priority boarding the train and were given good seats. As soon as the train started, Slovak military police accompanied by Russian NKVD (secret police) officials went through the compartments to check documents. When we handed ours to them we noticed that they looked impressed and handed them back with best wishes for a good trip. The landscape from the train window was beautiful; the snow still covered everything like a white blanket, and in the distance I could see the magnificent Niske Tatry Mountains that had sheltered us for so many months. They made me think of the many Jews lying buried under the snow up there, murdered by anti-Semites when they had been so close to freedom. I also thought of those who had been caught by the SS, the Vlasow army and Hlinka guards, and were tortured and hanged. Then there were the remnants of the Slovak Jews I was concerned about and I worried for Chaim Chermesh and the other Palestinian paratroopers, and wondered what had become of them. The train moved very slowly because of the bad state of the rails, the bridges and tunnels which had not yet been properly repaired. Every now and then there were burned-out tanks and trucks lying by the side of the tracks.

In the afternoon the train drew in to a station and the conductor announced that it was the last stop and everybody had to get off. It would be the end of the line until the nearby tunnel, which had been totally destroyed, could be repaired. We had to walk through the snow over the tunnel, and then along the tracks for a few hours until we reached the next station. We were quite happy that we had only a few belongings to encumber us. At the station on the other side we were told there were no traffic schedules and we would know that a train was coming when it arrived. We decided this was too uncertain and went into the town to find a truck to take us east. We walked up to a military checkpoint, which was manned by Czech and Russian military police, presented our documents and asked for transport to Romania. They told us there would be nothing until the next morning and got us a room in a little hotel for the night. Early in the morning we went back and watched them stop all vehicles and carefully examine the papers of every soldier and civilian on them. From one truck they ordered some men to come down and had them taken away by NKVD. They told us that the men were suspected Vlasow or Hlinka members for whom they had been watching. We had to wait for some time until they found us places on an empty Russian truck which was heading for Kosice. It was a lucky break. The area we drove through had been densely built up but now it was devastated. Homes were destroyed and tunnels and bridges blown up, the latter rather inadequately replaced by pontoon bridges that Russian army engineers had built. In the evening we reached Kosice and began looking for a restaurant and Jews. We made some enquiries but nobody knew of any Jews. However, when we found a large restaurant we felt certain that the young people at a nearby table were Jewish. We went over and put the question directly to them, explaining that we were ourselves Polish Jews who had fought with the partisans in Slovakia. This reassured them and they acknowledged they were Jewish too. They had been in Hungary, and some of them had also fought with the partisans in eastern Slovakia and had returned with the Red army. They were now employed by the provisional Czechoslovak government which had been set up in Kosice. From their conversation, I understood that it was now communist controlled. Benesz was never mentioned.

They told us about the tragic fate of the Jews in Slovakia after the 1944 uprising and how the Germans who came in to help Tiso's puppet government quell the uprising, made the Jews their first victims. Himmler himself had visited Bratislava, and had sent in one of his top killers, Alois Brunner, who had had a hand in the extermination of the Jews in all the occupied countries. Tiso had blamed the Jews for the uprising and threatened their annihilation. The threat was carried out starting with the roundup of the Jews of Bratislava on November 20. Jews were hunted all over Slovakia and deported. Among those sent away were the Jewish leaders which included Gisi Fleischman, the woman who had saved so many Polish children. Having survived for five years, the Slovak Jews were caught in the Nazi death machine just four months before the end of the war, and paid the price for the uprising. It was estimated that ten thousand Jews were killed in Slovakia, and another fourteen thousand were deported during those tragic months.

At the railroad station next morning we were again advised to try road transport because the trains were still very unreliable. At a checkpoint we were offered a lift on an empty army truck that was going to Uzhgorod, a large city in the Carpatho Ukraine area. Although it would take us northeast we got on. The driver told us we would have no trouble getting a ride to Bucharest, via Budapest, from there. There was still snow on the bumpy roads, and after we had traveled a short time I realized we were crossing the border into Hungary. I could not help recalling how Fela and I had crossed this border in 1943, and how we were betrayed by the border guide. Now I was coming back as a free man.

The signs of war were still fresh everywhere. The roads were lined with burned-out German and Russian tanks and vehicles. There were many makeshift graves topped by German steel helmets. To me they made the landscape beautiful, except there were not enough of them.

We passed through many villages and towns which were completely or partially destroyed, and when we stopped to get something to eat, we noticed how the Hungarians jumped to serve the Russians, anxious not to get into trouble with them. They took our uniforms to be Russian too, so we got prompt service. They did not even ask us to pay, they were so relieved to see us leave. We reached Uzhgorod in the afternoon and the driver put us off in the town center. We saw some Jewish stores but they were closed, and the passers-by we asked knew of no Jews. The town was in that part of Czechoslovakia that Hitler had handed over to Hungary after he took over the country in 1939. Now it was called Carpatho-Ukraine and a part of the Soviet Union, annexed when the Red army entered it. Finally we found a Jewish shop that was open and we talked to the owner in Yiddish. He was still bewildered, having returned from hiding only a short time before. He had lost almost all of his family. He told us that we might soon find some Jews assembling for the evening service in the nearby synagogue. It was a small building and there were already some men inside, some of them Russian soldiers. Elderly men always make up the majority in synagogues but here there was not a single elderly man in the congregation. They had not survived. After the service, in the Jewish tradition of hospitality to strangers who had come to pray, we were invited for supper and to stay overnight in the home of one of them. After the meal we sat around the table recounting our experiences. Our hosts had suffered much from the anti-Semitic Hungarians, Ukrainians and Germans. A few were helped by sympathetic neighbors. One family was actually hidden in a cemetery by gentiles who brought them food at night or under the pretext of coming to place flowers on the graves of relatives. Their worst times came when the Germans took over in 1944 and when the mass deportations began. I nodded for I remembered the despairing cries and pleading hands from the deportation trains going past our prison in Csorgo the year before. We talked late into the night. Each Jew was a book, an incredibly sad autobiography.

Entry to the station was strictly controlled by Russian soldiers and NKVD officials. Only people with special travel passes were allowed in at all and they had to apply weeks in advance for them. A year ago those local Urkrainians and Hungarians had been happy to see the Jews dragged away by the Germans, and now they were themselves trapped by the Russians. How quickly the tables had turned on them! Our passes were good and when the train arrived at last, we were given seats next to some Russian soldiers. The train made very slow progress and there were frequent checks made by

NKVD officials, but our documents gave us no trouble at all. The journey which was scheduled to take six hours lasted ten, and when the conductor ordered everybody off, we had not yet reached Budapest and had to go the last few kilometers on foot to reach a small town. A military officer assigned us to a small hotel for the night and there we found that all three of us had lice again. We hunted down as many as we could and washed our clothes, which gave us the impression that we had gotten rid of them, though we feared we had not.

The next morning we reached Budapest where we got on a crowded streetcar headed for the Jewish section. Almost every building we passed was damaged, some completely leveled, witnesses to the tremendous battles that had been fought there. It was sad to see the city, so beautiful the last time I had seen it, in its devastation. But I could not feel sorry for the Hungarians who had been so brutal. In the Jewish section it was depressing to walk through the streets where the houses still had yellow stars painted on them and the stores bearing Jewish names were closed. The few Jewish-looking people we met were like ghosts, shabbily dressed, hungry-looking and hurrying on their way with downcast eyes, afraid to look at men in uniform. Henry, who spoke a little Hungarian, asked one of them the way to a Jewish restaurant and we were guided to one on Kiraly utca. We asked the cashier whether there were any Polish or Slovak Jews about and he showed us to a table occupied by some young people. I recognized a young man, Kranz, who was from Cracow and had been a member of the Maccabi sports club. He recognized me too. He was sitting next to a young Catholic woman and told me that she had hidden him in her apartment and after the liberation they were married. The group invited us to have tea and pastries with them. As we talked I sensed a terrible sadness. All of them had lost their families and were the sole survivors. The hunt for Jews had continued until the last moment when the Russians entered the Peszt part of the city. But the killings continued on the other side of the Danube until the Russians forded the river four weeks later on February 13. One of the worst oppressors had been a monk, Father Andreas Kuhn, who searched for Jews with a gun hanging from his religious habit, killing both Jews and the Aryans who had sheltered them. He was one of the leaders of the bloody Nyilasz party.

In the evening we got seats on a train bound for Bucharest. Its slow pace made me drowsy and I finally fell asleep, but was awakened occasionally by military police making their inspection rounds. Before dawn the train reached a place called Debrecen, not far from the Romanian border, and everybody was ordered off again. We sat huddled on a bench in the cold, badly damaged station, waiting for the Bucharest train to arrive. Late in the morning we were informed there would be no train and we should try to go by road. In the city we met an old Jew who invited us to his home. The faces of his family told the Jewish tragedy more graphically than volumes. They were one of the few families who had survived, saved by a noble Hungarian family. On our way to the checkpoint to look for a ride, we saw that this city also had been devastated by recent battles. The many burned-out tanks standing about indicated that a tank battle had been fought there. We found places on a Russian truck which took us to a town called Oradea Mare and there, after the NKVD officials had checked our passes, we were assigned places on a train to Bucharest. Some Russian soldiers who were on their way home greeted us merrily and generously shared their food and drinks with us.

When we reached the station in Bucharest it was difficult to find anyone who could understand us. So we looked for Jewish people who could speak Yiddish. But for the first time I found that my uncanny instinct for Jewish faces failed me. It was hard to recognize Jews among the Romanians. Everyone was short and dark. We did eventually find a Jew who spoke German. I showed him the address I had been given to find Fela and he told us it would be impossible for strangers to locate it, so he took us there on the streetcar. Before we reached the building in Mosilur Street, we passed a large building which, our escort explained, was now the main shelter for Jewish refugees. Mietek and Henry decided to wait there for me, so that I might have a private reunion with my sister.

17

Romania, Reunion
April 1945

Every step that took me nearer to her home accelerated my heartbeat. Her apartment was on the third floor, and I ran up the stairs three at a time. When I reached the landing I rested for a moment to get my breath. Then I knocked on the door and waited. At last it was opened and I faced a tall young man on crutches looking at me curiously. I knew from the description I had received that he must be Janek, Fela's husband. He asked me in Romanian whom I was looking for and I answered in Polish that I was Adam, and was looking for my sister. He smiled and let me in. We embraced warmly and he told me that Fela was out shopping, but should be back soon. We talked about each others' experiences for a while. I apologized that I had been unable to let them know I was coming, but actually my ears were listening for Fela's footsteps. At last I heard her coming up the stairs and turning the key in the door.

We stood up facing the door. Fela came in, her arms full of packages, but when she spotted me she dropped them and shouted my name. We fell into each other's arms repeating one another's name, and cried for joy. Janek stood there crying too. When finally we separated Fela stepped back to look at me closely and remarked how skinny I was. I told her how happy I was that she had chosen Janek for a husband. He was a fine figure of a man, his injury notwithstanding. She told me he had taken care of her from the moment she had met him and had gotten her out of Hungary to Romania, and they had been married in a town called Timişoara.

We sat down, unable to take our eyes off each other, and said nothing for a few minutes. We did not mention our parents or brothers, finding it wiser not to open the wounds that would never heal, at our first reunion. Janek was the only member of his large family who survived this horrible war. His father died of a broken heart at the age of forty-three. Janek and his cousin Lipinski buried him at night at the Jewish cemetery. His mother, age forty-two and his younger sister and four brothers were deported and gassed in the death camp on September 7th, 1942. At that time he was only seventeen years old.

I told Fela that the lice were bothering me and while I took a hot bath she washed my clothes. Janek, who was about my size, gave me some of his to wear. Dressed in them, I took Fela to meet Mietek and Henry. Janek, who was not too steady on his legs, waited for us at home. In a large hall at the shelter, I found them with a small group of refugees, all talking at the same time. I introduced them to Fela but they refused to come to her apartment because of the lice. She promised to take the three of us for disinfection the next day.

Back at Fela's apartment I met their neighbor, Duda, who came from Stryj in Polish eastern Galicia. Janek had met him in Budapest as he was being set upon by some hoodlums and rescued him. They had met again in Bucharest when Duda spotted Janek walking on crutches through the snow, and Duda had spontaneously given him his own room.

They told us of their experiences in Budapest from the time the nightmare began. The refugees knew that the Germans would look for them first through their agents, the Hungarian Keogh (secret police). The Polish Jews made their way to Romania, while the Slovak refugees tried to return to Slovakia. Janek met Maciek Fiedler and together they helped the Jews by providing forged documents and even getting doctors to surgically disguise circumcisions to allow them to assume Aryan identities. But one of their "clients" was caught and under torture revealed Janek's name which led to his arrest and incarceration in the Schwabhed SS prison in a cell with some leading Jewish and Hungarian personalities. Executions by firing squad were a matter of course there. Janek took the initiative and managed to break through the heavy bars on the window and jump out into the yard, followed by several other prisoners. Despite the heavy guard they all managed to get away. He and Fela hid together, changing addresses frequently, until they made their run for Romania. On the train they were approached by a German policeman but managed to get away when Fela hit him with her shoe. They crossed the border on foot and reached Timişoara where some Jews took them in. A short time later the rabbi of the community married them. When on August 23, 1944, the king surrendered Romania to the Red army they, along with many other local Jews, decided to move away from the border area and headed for Bucharest. Their train was attacked by German bombers on the way. Fela, Janek and some other refugees managed to take shelter in a field. However, when Janek heard the crying of a child, he went back to the train, and as he was carrying him into the field a bomb exploded nearby and he was badly injured. The boy escaped unhurt but Janek spent many weeks in the hospital. The local Jews called him a hero. When he was released from the hospital, he and Fela continued on to Bucharest. In consideration for his crutches, some Russian officers made room for them in their compartment on the train. During the trip they fell asleep, and when they awoke the Russian officers were gone as well as all their belongings.

I found Bucharest to be a beautiful city and life was almost normal there. Food was rationed, but everything was available for a price. The stores had lots of goods to sell and many customers. When I asked Fela if she had heard from our relatives in America, she told me that she had sent them several letters but had received no reply. I checked and found that she had the wrong address, so I immediately sent a telegram to our uncles.

At the shelter sponsored by the American Joint Distribution Committee where Mietek and Henry were staying, I met some emaciated-looking Jews wearing pajama-type attire with wide stripes. They were survivors of death camps in Germany and Austria waiting to go to Palestine. I considered every one of them a living miracle. We knew what a hell-on-earth the death camps were. We had also heard that when the Germans withdrew from Poland they completely leveled the death camps and murdered every last prisoner in order to leave no trace of their crime. Yet these people had survived. They told us that after their liberation they had returned to Poland to search for their families and found much to their consternation, that the Poles were extremely hostile to them. So they left Poland again and made their way to Romania.

Mietek and Henry liked Bucharest and decided to stay there. But I was determined to go back to Poland to seek information about my brothers and to visit the Lopatowskis, the Zwolinskis and Mr. Magrys. After the three of us were disinfected, and appeared to have gotten rid of the lice, I took them to visit Fela and Janek. Mietek had them spellbound with the hairraising stories of our escapes and subsequent activities as partisans. (I had not spoken about them.) Fela served us a meal, my first taste of her cooking, and when I complimented her she explained she had learned to cook from Mrs. Zwolinski.

The next morning a messenger from the HIAS (Jewish refugee assistance) organization summoned us to their office where they gave us one hundred dollars our uncle had telegraphed through their New York office. In Romanian terms it was a small fortune, but with the windfall came a request for detailed news about the family. We were at a loss how to inform our grandmother that our parents, her daughter Antonia and son-in-law Emil were dead, murdered in an extermination camp, and that we did not know what had happened to our dear brothers. So we took the easy way out, cabled our thanks for the money and promised that a letter about the family would follow.

Fela felt very rich with all that money and immediately started planning how to spend it. First she bought some expensive delicacies to prepare a festive meal for all of us, and invited Duda too. He told me that in Romania a thriving black market had developed between the various parts of the country and that our uniforms and Russian passes made it possible for us to make a lot of money. Certainly we all needed money and decided to think it over. After dinner Fela and Duda took me into town to show me the city at night. The city center was vibrant, with the many cafés, restaurants, dance halls and night clubs all crowded, and long lines outside the cinemas. The people wanted to forget the war and so for the duration of the evening, I abandoned myself to the same great feeling.

The next morning Duda and I went to see Mietek and Henry

at the shelter and Duda told them about his black market scheme. They were agreeable, and while Duda and Mietek went shopping for the goods we thought we could profitably sell, Henry and I went to the Russian command post and got travel passes to Poland through Hungary and Slovakia. In fact our own documents impressed the NKVD official and he wished us a good trip.

The four of us set out from Fela's apartment the next morning loaded with suitcases, but we had not gone as far as the streetcar stop when a Russian patrol stopped us, and despite our documents took us to the police station. We worried that they would search our luggage, but they were satisfied by our papers. We explained Duda's presence by telling them he was helping us carry our suitcases to the railroad. A ten-hour train ride took us to Arad, close to the Hungarian border, where we sold our wares, fabrics and clothing. We got very good prices for them and on Duda's advice bought cooking oil, for which there was a great demand in Bucharest. We got back safely and the next morning sold the oil at a good profit. We took a two-day rest and then, with our capital, bought more goods and luggage to carry them in, and came back even richer. To celebrate we took Fela and Janek out to a Jewish restaurant.

But we did not forget that the war was not yet over. The Germans were still putting up resistance to the Allied armies that were closing in on them from east and west. For the first time we met Jews with numbers tattooed on their arms like branded cattle. They were survivors of Auschwitz. One morning the news came that President Roosevelt had died. I noticed that the refugees did not mourn him. Nor did we. We all felt that he could have done much more to save the Jews from the Nazis. The other allied leaders as well as the Pope were not without blame. I left the judgment on them to history. I personally would never forgive them for abandoning us to the most vicious mass murderers history had ever known. The refugees told me that when the Russians liberated their extermination camps, they did not bother with trials. They simply shot all the SS men and women they could lay their hands on. It was my kind of justice.

I bade farewell to Fela and the three of us started off for Poland, accompanied by Duda. We decided to leave the black market alone this time and only took along a few pieces of luggage which we filled with cigarettes to sell so as to pay our way through Hungary, Slovakia and Poland. I felt more hopeful about the chances of finding Szymon and Nathan alive, now that I had met quite a few survivors. We rode in a compartment with some Russian officers. Duda, who had lived under the Russians and spoke their language, had lively discussions with them. But he also knew their reputation for stealing luggage and as a precaution slept on his suitcase. But when he woke up the Russians were gone and so were his cigarettes. They had cut open the side of his suitcase and stolen them. Duda was so discouraged that he decided to go back to Bucharest and got off at the next stop. We continued on without him.

During our long train journey we saw a lot of freight trains going east loaded with machinery. They were German factories the Russians had dismantled and were taking back to Russia as reparation for the destruction the Germans had wreaked on their country. They were not waiting for the niceties of peace treaties. Going through Hungary we were in a compartment with civilians for a while and they were obviously afraid of us, until Henry explained that our uniforms were Polish. Then they opened up with complaints against the Russians who had robbed and raped, but since they were the law, they could not be taken to court for redress. Finally we arrived in Kežmarok, close to the border with Slovakia, and were told there were no trains going to Poland. We went into the city and found a Jewish family. Henry and I were dismayed to learn from them that the leader of the community, Bergmann, who had been so helpful to us, had been deported and had not returned, and that almost all the other Jews of the town were gone too. But there was some good news. The Germans were on their knees. Mussolini, the Italian dictator, and his mistress had been caught by partisans and shot, and their bodies strung up by the heels on public display. One of the Axis dictators was gone, and the end was approaching fast. Buoyed by the news we made the rest of our way to the Polish border on foot.

18

Return to Poland
1945

The Czechoslovak border guards checked our papers and let us through and we had no trouble on the Polish side either. My feelings on returning to Poland were mixed; I was hopeful of finding Szymon and Nathan, but at the same time I also recalled how I had crossed this border with Fela, in November 1943. We got a lift to Cracow on an empty Russian army truck. Occasionally the driver stopped and took on Polish hitchhikers, a mixed lot of refugees and black marketeers, loaded down with bundles. But they all knew there was a price, a bottle of vodka, and paid it before being allowed on. After a few more kilometers there was a backfire from the exhaust and the truck stopped. The driver's escort came down from the cabin and ordered all the Poles off and asked them to help push to get the truck going again. They pushed with a will, but when the engine sprang to life the two crooks drove off at full speed taking all their belongings with them, leaving them standing openmouthed. Some tried to give chase but it was hopeless, the truck was going too fast. The breakdown had evidently been staged. We were not involved, being in uniform. Soon our truck reached a small town where we were told that a train for Cracow was expected soon. Our papers again got us good seats. We noticed that every passenger was loaded with baggage, all obviously trading on the black market.

After an uneventful journey of two hours the train made a stop at the Cracow-Podgorze station, which I knew so well, and then continued to the main station, Cracow Central. The station looked exactly as I remembered it. We asked for the Russian headquarters and were directed to the city center. On the way I noticed that the town had suffered very little visible damage. We found the headquarters in an imposing building that had once been the palace of a prince. An officer checked our papers and sent us to the nearby Francuski Hotel, one of the best in town, where we were given a large room, free of charge.

The next morning we asked for the local black market and were matter-of-factly directed to a nearby square where Polish peasant women used to sell flowers before the war. We sold our cigarettes to the highest bidder and got a lot of zlotys for them. We looked around hoping to spot a Jewish face in the crowd, and finding none we walked toward the Jewish quarter of Kazimierz. We noticed that most of the shops had Polish names painted over those of their original Jewish owners. Although I knew it was to be expected, it nevertheless hurt to see it. These were the familiar stores we used to patronize and I had imagined I might find the old names back. The new Polish merchants looked well, and not as frightened as the Hungarians. There were more Russians in the streets of Cracow than in Slovakia, and more patrols, on foot and in open military cars. The Russians in the patrol cars were NKVD units. The Polish soldiers wore uniforms that looked very much like those of the Russians. Actually these Poles were members of Colonel Berlings Kościuszko army, established in Russia, which had fought along the Russian army. I pointed out some sights to my friends, including the place on Grodzka Street where the Germans carried out the first mass arrests and killings in September of 1939, and the site, adjoining Wavel castle, where Jewish-owned buildings had been demolished to make room for Governor Frank. But our search for Jewish faces was fruitless until we reached Krakowska Street where I spotted a small group of Jewish-looking people outside a store. I asked them, in Yiddish, where the owner was, and they directed us inside. I did not recognize the man, but he told me the store used to belong to his late father and I remembered the family name. He himself had survived in hiding, and when he returned the Pole who had taken over the store refused to return it. He went to court and won, but the Polish neighbors now pointedly boycotted his store and insulted him and his Jewish clerks. His case had not been unique. The few Jews who survived the war and returned to retrieve their property, generally had to resort to the courts, and if they won, to enlist the militia to enforce the judgment. In the small towns, the Jews who dared ask for the return of their property met with violence, and if they were lucky enough not to be killed, had to run for their lives. The Poles had not changed.

There was only one synagogue still open, in nearby Miodowa Street, which we used to attend on Friday nights before the war to hear the inspiring sermons of Rabbi Dr. Osias Thon, who had been a Zionist and a member of parliament. In the temple we were told that there was a Jewish committee on Dluga Street which registered returning Jews and there, if anywhere, I might get information about my brothers. We took a streetcar and I noted that nothing seemed to have changed in Cracow, except that the Jews were gone. We found the committee offices at the back of a large building and there were a lot of people waiting outside. We were told to register, and I put down both my real name and the Aryan one I had assumed, as well as Fela's address in Bucharest, just in case somebody would want to contact me. When my turn came, the clerk looked through her register and told me she could not find either of my brothers' names. Her "no" stabbed at my heart. It was the grim confirmation I had feared but repressed, because I wanted to hope. She sensed my distress, let me look through her register for other familiar names, and when I found none she told me not to despair, more Jews were returning every day and registering wherever they happened to land. The committee's central office was in Łódź, where the largest number of Jews now lived. It collated the names collected by all Jewish committees in Poland. She pointed out that every survivor was a miracle, as I well knew, and urged me not to give up hope for two more miracles, the reappearance of my brothers. She also advised me not to go to Rzeszów as yet because there had been some ugly anti-Jewish incidents there, and it would be foolhardy to take unnecessary risks.

At our request we were received by the new Jewish leaders: Community President Dr. Isydor Horowitz, and his deputies Michael Borwicz, Maria Marianska and Dr. Henry Reichman.

I could recall only Borwicz who, before the war, as Maksymilian Boruchowicz, had been a well-known writer and PPS activist. They asked us about our war experiences and where we were living now. Later they asked us whether we would be willing to take some Jews back to Romania with us—Hungarian and Romanian Jews who wanted to go home, and others who hoped to find a ship to Palestine in Constanca harbor on the Black Sea. We agreed and explained what documents they would need to get through all the controls and patrols.

Back in the hotel I wrote a detailed letter to the Zwolinskis in Rzeszów, and promised that as soon as we could Fela and I would come to visit them. I took it to the main post office to mail. As I entered, a feeling of sadness overwhelmed me as I recalled how often I had come here with Mother to mail letters to the U.S.A. From there I set out to Kollataja Street to meet the Lopatowskis. The corner building in which we used to live came into sight. But now there was nobody at the window on the third floor to wave to me. I had to remind myself that our family was gone. As I entered the building I recalled the evening when we had left to go to Rzeszów, when I had still dared hope that we might all return one day. I resolved not to go up to the third floor, where our apartment was, because the apartment without my loved ones was more than I could face. The Lopatowskis lived on the ground floor, and when Mrs. Lopatowski answered my knock she did not recognize me and just stood there staring at my uniform, puzzled. I said, "I'm Henry," she repeated my name and then came forward to embrace me. We kissed affectionately and her son, attracted by her call, came out too, accompanied by a young woman, and he also embraced me. But when they invited me to come in, I noticed that Mr. Lopatowski was not there. Without thinking I asked for him. Mrs. Lopatowski's face clouded and she asked me to sit down. After I was seated she sadly told me that her husband, my dear, dear friend, and a wonderful human being, Władysław Lopatowski, was dead. He had been arrested by the Gestapo ten months earlier, and on June 24, 1944, was hanged in public, together with forty-nine other Polish patriots. Her words made my eyes water and the tears almost blinded me. She told me he had been betrayed by a Jewish woman for whom he had obtained forged identity papers, who was caught by the Gestapo and under torture revealed his name to them, and was then shot herself.

When Mrs. Lopatowski got over the emotion of her account she proudly revealed that her husband had been one of the leaders of the "Zegota" organization which had helped Jews in the camps, and had also been active in the "Rada Pomocy Zydom" another organization which specialized in helping Jews escape. She assured me that when my brothers were caught they had never feared, convinced that whatever tortures the Gestapo might subject them to, they would not betray their benefactor. She also told me that Mr. Gelb had been taken away in 1943 and never returned. She knew nothing of the fate of his German wife who moved out later.

Her son had married, the young woman whom I had met was his wife, and he was now working in the Zieleniewski metal plant, where his father had been a foreman and leader of the PPS branch.

They told me that when the Red army was approaching Cracow the Germans calmly packed up and prepared to demolish the city, but the final Russian push was so swift that they had no time to carry out their plan but left helter-skelter, destroying only some ammunition dumps and the bridges over the Vistula. The city was spared when the Russians arrived on January 19, all the inhabitants were saved. But there was no love lost between the Poles and the Russians, who were hated almost as much as the Germans themselves; for centuries both had been Poland's traditional foes. The Poles had been particularly upset by the Red army's failure to come to the aid of the Warsaw uprising in the fall of 1944. They had sat tight on the other side of the Vistula while the Germans massacred the Polish rebels. It had been an obvious political maneuver. Moreover, since the liberation the NKVD* and their Polish servants, the UB**, had systematically deported the leaders, as well as many rank and file members of the Polish rightist underground and even the socialist PPS. They had not been seen since. The pictures of Hitler that the Germans had displayed about the city were replaced, by equally big ones, of Stalin. The Poles were now as bitter about the western

*National Commission of Internal Affairs
**Polish secret service

leaders, who had abandoned them to the Soviets and acqui-
esced in their slicing off part of the country, as we Jews had
been about them for abandoning us to the Nazi killers.

It was a sad day for me. My brothers' deaths were confirmed
almost certainly, and I had learned of the terrible end of the
noble Mr. Lopatowski and Mr. Gelb. We kept our appoint-
ment with Mr. Borwicz in a restaurant full of boisterous
Russian soldiers. The few Poles there stared at our unfamiliar
uniforms. Borwicz noticed my somber mood and I told him
about Mr. Lopatowski and how much he and the PPS underground had done for our family. Borwicz then told me that he
himself had been saved by the PPS underground who had
rescued him from the Janowska camp near Lwów in November 1943, at almost the same time we had been rescued from
Rzeszów. It had been his second salvation. He had actually
been strung up by the Germans, but the rope broke and the
hangmen, who apparently were superstitious, let him live.
After his escape, the PPS sent him to the Miechów area,
where he became the commander of a PPS partisan unit and
got the nickname Zygmunt. Actually, when the Germans
invaded Poland in 1939, he had been in Switzerland, but
decided to return. He went to live in Lwów, which the
Russians had occupied as part of their deal with Hitler but
lost again to the Germans in 1941. He had witnessed many
German atrocities and was busy recording his personal experiences. The books he was writing about them were to be
published soon.

He told us that although he was still an active socialist, as a
Jew he must inform us that the situation with the Jews in
Poland was again very bad and especially dangerous in Cracow, now that Warsaw was destroyed, had become the center
of anti-Soviet and anti-Jewish agitation. It was also a hotbed
of opposition to the new government, in stark contrast to the
general passive acquiescence to the German occupation by
the population in 1939. All over Poland, underground journals
put out by students and rightists with the full support of the
Church, were hostile both to the Jews and the Russians, who
had lost six hundred thousand men liberating Poland from the
Germans. In Cracow Jews and Russians were avoided so-
cially, and in the public places and restaurants they fre-
quented, nasty remarks were made about them. However,

officially the new government recognized Jews as citizens of equal standing, and there were two Jews appointed to senior posts in the cabinet, Hilary Minc the minister of industry, and Jacob Berman, the deputy foreign minister. The government was going out of its way to help the surviving Jews to rebuild their lives and institutions in the new Poland. The Jewish institutions were themselves busy returning to the fold the many Jewish children who had been hidden with Christian families by their parents, most of whom had perished.

The Polish government-in-exile and rightist Polish circles in London were disseminating poisonous anti-Semitic propaganda. Jews had been attacked all over Poland culminating in the killing of five Jews in Polaniec, near Kielce on April 10. It was quickly followed by other, similar outbreaks.

He told me that the Bund leader, Samuel Zygielbojm, who had been one of the two Jewish members of the Polish government-in-exile in London, committed suicide in his hotel room on the night of May 11–12, 1943, when the report of the deaths of his comrades in the Warsaw ghetto uprising reached London. He left a letter to the president of Poland and the leaders of the western Allies explaining he had found it impossible to remain passive while the Jews of Poland, whom he represented, were being slaughtered and the Allies failed to intervene to save them. By the sacrifice of his own life he wished to record his protest against the world's indifference to the extermination of the Jews in Europe. Borwicz's researches had established the facts and figures of the extermination and clearly demonstrated that the Allies had, in fact, been informed about the German extermination operation as early as the beginning of 1943, often at the risk of the couriers' own lives. The pretext that they did not know did not hold water. I told him I would like to go to the camp in Belzec to which my parents had been deported in September of 1942, but he advised against it. There was nothing left to see there. The Germans had leveled the camp in 1943 and covered all traces of their crimes. They had even reopened the mass graves, exhumed the corpses of the murdered and cremated them, dispersing the ashes. It would be foolhardy to risk the trip since Jews were still unsafe in Poland. One of the two Jews who had survived the Belzec camp, a certain Rudolf Reder, was writing a book about the camp that was soon to be published in Cracow. It would provide me all the information I sought. A few days later he introduced me to Mr. Reder. He was an elderly man, almost blind. I was told that the Auschwitz-Birkenau camp on the other hand, had not been completely destroyed, because the Russians had advanced so fast, and I might wish to go there.

I accepted his advice and for a start went to the Montelupich prison in Cracow where, I believed, my brothers had been taken after they were caught by the Gestapo. It was a three-story building, a military jail before the war, which the Gestapo had made notorious. My papers got me in and a guard showed me the cellar in which the Gestapo tortured their prisoners. The metal hanging hooks and other torture instruments were still there and, horrific though they were, revived my pride in my brothers. Despite everything, they had not given away the Lopatowskis and the Zwolinskis.

The guard showed me only one cell, because the prison was again in use but this time for Polish political prisoners. The cell was so narrow that prisoners could only stand in it, with no room to lie down, or even sit. The Gestapo kept solitary prisoners in it for days at a time.

I was told there were no records left from the Gestapo period. They had destroyed them before they left. Now only a plaque on a wall recorded that the Gestapo had run the prison, from September 29, 1939, until January 16, 1945. I was glad to get out of the place, and despite the evidence I had just viewed, still dared hope that my brothers might yet be alive somewhere. Shocked and upset though I was I went on to the Plaszow camp in the suburb by that name, where some of the prisoners from the jail, particularly Jews caught with Aryan identity papers, were taken. A streetcar took me there. All of the camp buildings had been destroyed. An elderly Pole working there pointed out the hills across the camp where many thousands had been executed. I felt I did not have the mental reserves to enter the camp. My visit to the prison had opened a deep wound, and to go inside the camp would have been like turning the knife in it. Instead, I walked through Podgorze Street, the old Jewish quarter, part of which had been the Cracow ghetto, now destroyed.

When I returned to the hotel I told Henry and Mietek I wanted to go to Auschwitz, and they agreed to come with me.

An hour's drive on a truck got us to the city of Oświęcim within walking distance of the camp. It was still enveloped by barbed wire and high watchtowers, and the Russians were using it as a prison camp for Germans. The Russian sentries carefully guarded it. A black arch over the entrance was obscenely inscribed *Arbeit Macht Frei* (Work Liberates). It was, it struck me, a perversion of language by the people who had made an ideology of the slaughter of humans. Our documents got us through, and when we told the Russian officer in charge that we had come all the way from Slovakia to see the camp, he detailed a soldier to show us around. Later we went to Birkenau where the almost incredibly large size of the place astounded us. As far as the eye could see there were hundreds of wooden barracks as well as some larger brick buildings. Our escort told us that millions of people had perished in Auschwitz which was already known as the world's largest cemetery. We walked along the rails on which the cattle trains had brought the victims, and saw the area where the gas chambers and crematoria had done their grisly work. The guard told us that the Germans electrified the barbed wire around the camp and many prisoners had deliberately thrown themselves on it, choosing to die a quick death rather than endure the torment of life in Auschwitz. The SS had blown up the crematoria before they fled the advancing Russians, but they did not have time to dispose of the mountains of Jewish clothing, shoes, eye glasses, and even the women's hair they had shorn from their victims' heads before they gassed them. There they were, silent but devastating witness to a crime so immense, so appalling, and so incredible as to overwhelm human imagination.

We were told that the Soviets liberated Auschwitz on January 22, 1945, and had saved about six thousand prisoners, including a few hundred children, and eight thousand sick, who were still alive. Most of them were Poles with only a few Jews among them. As soon as the SS fled, the Poles who lived near the camp had gone in, not to save or help the survivors, but to search for treasure the victims might have buried. I was shattered by the size and diabolic planning of this death factory. It was estimated that about four million men, women and children who were mostly Jews put to death in its gas chambers, twenty-four thousand in one single day, June 28,

1944, and their bodies cremated. There was no punishment on earth bad enough for the German beasts and I was happy that at least I had lived to be able to kill a few of them.

By the time we returned to Cracow we decided we had had enough of Poland. The next morning, April 29, we went to the offices of the Jewish committee and told them we were leaving the next day. We would wait for the refugees we had agreed to take to Romania from the Podgorze railroad station. We were still talking to the officials when someone came running in and shocked us with the news that the bodies of Hitler and his mistress, Eva Braun, as well as his propaganda minister, Joseph Goebbels, his wife and their five children, had all been found in the Fuehrer's bunker in Berlin by Russian soldiers. They had committed suicide. The Goebbels couple had poisoned their children before taking their own lives. After the first thrill I considered it bad news. It had been my prayer that Hitler and his close henchmen would be caught alive, like Mussolini. The Russians, and only the Russians, could fittingly repay them for their crimes. A quick and painless death by suicide was too easy a way out for them. I had not cried at the news of the death of Roosevelt and did not rejoice about Hitler's now, but it did mean that Berlin was in Russian hands, and it could not be much longer before the war would be over.

In the afternoon I went to say goodbye to Mrs. Lopatowski. She wanted to give back the belongings we had given her for safekeeping in 1941, but I declined and told her I did not intend to remake my life in Poland and would try to join my relatives in the U.S.A. The three of us then walked to the station in the Podgorze section, and on the way I pointed out to Mietek and Henry the chocolate factory where Father and I had worked. In the station we met the large group of men and women we were to take to Romania. They were accompanied by Polish-Jewish soldiers. The combination of uniforms and the papers the Jewish committee had obtained for the refugees helped us get them all on the train. The soldiers got the conductor to find compartments for us and then left.

On the long journey we discussed our war experiences in Yiddish. Every one of the refugees had gone through hell, and just talking about it, or hearing others do so, reopened the wounds which had not healed, and never would. But it was also a relief to get it off our chests, and to know that others had gone through similar horrors and survived with their sanity intact.

Many of them were from Łódź, where two hundred thousand Jews had lived, and had run a well-known textile industry before the war. They told us that their ghetto, Bałuty, had been kept open by the Germans almost until the end of the war, and as late as August of 1944 there were still seventy-five thousand Jews in it, allowed to live in order to keep the Łódź textile factories, which were vital for the Germans, in production. The ghetto leader had been a man called Chaim Rumkowski, who had been given almost unlimited power over them by the Germans who appointed him. He maintained fairly good relations with the Germans, but to his own people he behaved like a pocket dictator, or self-crowned princeling. Special banknotes were printed for use in the ghetto with his picture on them, and his portrait looked down from the sides of the ghetto streetcars.

Only when the Russian advance threatened Łódź did the Germans start to liquidate the Bałuty ghetto. They ran into a logistics problem. The nearest extermination camp, Chełmno, which, from 1942 had been employed for the mass extermination of the Jews of Łódź and western Poland, had been closed and leveled in 1943. So the Germans had to transport the surviving Jews of Łódź to Auschwitz. Chaim Rumkowski was among them. His service to the Germans did not save him. They left some eight hundred fifty men to clean up and collect all usable materials for shipment to Germany. Just before the Russians arrived they intended to shoot them, and had already dug graves for them, but many were saved by going into hiding before the Germans could carry out their plan. When the Soviets liberated Łódź, on January 18, they found only eight hundred seventy-seven Jews alive.

The train came to a full stop at Nowy Targ, and from there we had to make our way to the Slovak border on foot, a walk of several hours. The border guards did not trouble us. We told them we were escorting concentration camp survivors, and since some were still wearing their striped camp uniforms, they asked no questions. In the afternoon we reached Kežmarok and made straight for the station. Our wards were exhausted for their dire experiences had weakened their physiques. Our papers impressed the Slovak military police and they secured two compartments in the train for us. We had to change trains again at Koszye and reached Budapest the next morning. There we caught the train to Bucharest. On the way I again noticed freight trains taking German machinery to the east. They gave me a feeling of satisfaction. I was sure the Russians were doing the right thing. In Bucharest we delivered our refugees to the Jewish committee and took leave of them. We had made a long and strenuous trip together, but for such veterans of hardships, it was child's play.

Fela was glad to see me back, and when I told her about the execution of Mr. Lopatowski she cried for a long time. The next morning, when we were discussing our future, a neighbor came in and told us that the war was over. Germany had just surrendered unconditionally. It was May 8, 1945. The street below broke into spontaneous celebration. Total strangers embraced, dancing got under way and every Russian soldier was covered in kisses. But at the refugee shelter there were no celebrations. They had been through too much and lost too many of their relatives to be in a mood for rejoicing. The news obviously provided us profound satisfaction that we had lived to see this moment. But it was also a time for somber reflection and remembrance, and the gnawing agony that the free world had chosen to stand by and allow the Germans a free hand to carry out their "Final Solution." I wondered whether the victorious Allies would now mete out their just deserts to the murderers. I felt confident that the Russians would. I had seen them in action in the mountains. We had already heard that many high-ranking Nazis had fled to the west to surrender to the Americans and British, precisely in order to escape Russian retribution.

Fela, Janek and I agreed that we should not attempt to rebuild our lives in Romania, where we were strangers. We had had enough of being refugees. Nor would we return to Poland. That unfriendly land was soaked with Jewish blood and its hostile people had the blood of many dead Jews on their hands. I suggested Slovakia. Fela and Janek wanted to go to Palestine, but this was very difficult. We hoped that perhaps our family in America might help us get to the U.S.A. But we felt we were jumping the gun for the war in Europe had ended only a few hours ago, and in the Pacific the

Americans were still fighting, so we must be patient. In any case we wanted to stay until Janek would recover and be able to walk without his crutches. What I desired most, regardless of where we would eventually go, was to be with them so as not to be alone. Fela took Janek to a Black Sea resort to recuperate, and when they returned I made my way back to Cracow with Mietek and Henry. We took Hungarian cigarettes and other popular goods with us and did a good trade selling them.

From the Jewish committee in Cracow we learned that the Polish government had issued a decree ordering Poles to register all former Jewish property that had come into their possession during the war, in whatever way, on pain of heavy fines and jail terms for failure to register. The government coupled the decree with an undertaking to assist Jewish survivors to recover their property, and to permit all Jews who had fled Poland to return. The decree met with open hostility from the population, and when the first refugees returned from Russia many outbreaks of anti-Semitic violence occurred. In many places Jews were beaten and robbed, a few even killed, and Jewish property and synagogues that had survived the Germans were vandalized. The old blood libel from the Middle Ages, of the ritual murder of Christian children by Jews, was dusted off and recycled, and the leaders of the Catholic Church did nothing to stop them. I heard that in Rzeszów an anti-Jewish riot had occurred and one Jew, Siudek Meryl, was killed. I had known him personally. He had been a sergeant in the Jewish police in our ghetto and had not been well liked.

I visited with the Lopatowskis again and they told me about the new Poland, which, in fact, was under total Russian domination. Though they had been staunch socialists, they did not like it and complained bitterly. I was sorry for the Lopatowskis, but I had little sympathy for the rest. They had not minded when the Germans were murdering the Jews, now I could not feel sorrow for them.

On the way home a newsboy raced past me with a special edition of the evening paper with a giant headline proclaiming that the American air force had dropped the world's first so-called "atom bomb" on Hiroshima. From the report it was not clear just how the bomb worked, but it had devastated the whole city. I could only regret that the Allies had not dropped such bombs, many of them, on the Germans. Three days later another atom bomb was dropped on Nagasaki.

On the following Saturday we slept late and when we went out were met by the wailing of sirens on speeding militia and police trucks going in the direction of the Jewish section. We jumped on a streetcar, but it was stopped by the police when we reached the section. However, our uniforms got us through the police cordon and we came upon a scene of great commotion outside the main synagogue, the Miodowa temple. Some of the worshipers told us that in the middle of the service a mob of hooligans had forced their way in and had broken up the prayers with screaming allegations that the worshiping Jews had tried to kill a Polish boy for use in their ritual. The old blood libel brought to life. The mob began beating up the worshipers and smashing the beautiful stained-glass windows. But when some uniformed Jewish soldiers in the congregation confronted them with guns they made off, running through the streets assaulting passing Jews and smashing Jewish property. Before the police were able to put a stop to their rioting, they had killed two Jews, a fifty-five-year-old woman, Roza Berger, and a sixty-two-year-old man, Anshel Zucker, and badly wounded several more who had to be taken to the hospital.

Outside the temple a Jewish officer showed us a leaflet the ruffians had distributed. It denounced the Jews as Poland's ancient enemy and charged that they carried out ritual murders of Polish children in the Miodowa temple. It also asserted there was no room in Poland for the Jews and their Bolshevik protectors. The officer, who had fought with the Red army, told us that during the war he had heard of the killing of Jews by the Germans, but had never imagined the scale and intensity of the genocide, and now he was distressed to see the Poles carrying on where the Germans had left off.

He was serving as a liaison officer between the Polish authorities and the Jewish committee, and had already been instrumental in recovering many Jewish children who were being brought up as Catholics by Polish families to whom their parents had entrusted them. Many of the Poles were reluctant to return the children. Some had also been found in convents and were taken to special shelters in western Silesia. The new mayor of Cracow, Dr. Bolesław Drobner, a well-known socialist who was himself Jewish, was very helpful in finding Jewish children and returning them to their own people.

The next day we went to the Jewish committee and offered to escort another group of Jews out of Poland. We were introduced to one of the committee heads, Mr. Wulf, who also was a writer, and he showed us the newspaper in which the pogrom of the day before was widely condemned officially by some Polish leaders. But behind the backs of the officials, he told us, many Poles openly advocated forcing the Jews to leave Poland, with the exception of those who had fought with the Anders army. In my mind it was tragic that Poles could still hate the few surviving Jews, after everything the Germans had done to us. No wonder the Germans had chosen Poland as the site for their extermination camps. Their instincts had not been wrong.

On Tuesday morning we met a large group of Jews at the Podgorze railroad station, and a two-day-long journey got us to Bucharest where we took them to a refugee shelter. It was August 15, and the news of Japan's surrender came, the final end of the long war which had started almost exactly six years earlier. We stayed in Bucharest for four months and since Janek was much better and now needed only a cane to get about, we left for Budapest, and Duda came with us. We found a nice apartment in a good section of the city.

One day, when Mietek and I were out walking, we recognized one of the sergeants from the Csorgo camp. He was now in civilian clothes but his face was the same. We followed him at a distance, and when a Russian mobile patrol passed, we stopped them. They took us and the sergeant to the headquarters of the Hungarian secret police. It was the same building to which Hannah Senesch, one of the Palestinian Jewish parachutists we had met in Banská Bystrica, had been brought in 1944. We told the duty officer of the sergeant's past and he was put under arrest. Some time later we were summoned to testify against him along with four other guards from the Csorgo camp, in a so-called citizens' court. We gave a matter-of-fact account of their cruelties but stressed that their despicable behavior was not demanded of them because the commandant was a fair man. They were all sentenced to fifteen years at hard labor.

Some time later Henry got married to a young Hungarian

woman called Bezi who had survived Auschwitz. She became part of our extended family. The atmosphere in Budapest was bad for Jews. Just as in Poland, we were castigated as Bolsheviks and collaborators with the Russians, mainly by the Catholic Church. Jewish leaders appealed to Cardinal Mindszenty to condemn the defamation, but he declined.

Mietek and I decided to make another trip to Poland and on the way to explore the possibility of all of us going to live in Slovakia. In Cracow I went to see an old Jewish book dealer whom I had met earlier, to see if he had gotten any new written material on the fate of the Jews. He had collected a lot of books, and an album of photographs of Jews being mistreated by Germans. He and the Jewish institutes came across the pictures in Polish photo shops which had developed films for German soldiers and SS men and had kept copies. Other photos of atrocities being perpetrated by the Germans had been obtained from Russians who found them on German soldiers they had captured or killed. All those books and few albums were published by the Jewish Historical Institute in Cracow and Lodz. I spent many hours reading them.

In the office of the Jewish committee I met some more Jews from Rzeszów who had arrived since our last visit. None of them knew anything about my brothers. Then, on one of my walks in the city, I spotted Maciek Fiedler and his twin brother, Ludwik. Maciek spotted me too. We embraced warmly. His first question was for news about my brothers and I told him the tragic story of their capture. It made him cry. Ludwik had survived as an Aryan on the estate of a Polish nobleman. He joined the Armja Krajowa underground and had taken part in their operations. Now he held a senior post in the Cracow district government, as a department head.

I went to see the Lopatowskis and told them of my plan to settle in Bratislava. They were unable to understand why I would not stay in Cracow and I did not want to hurt their feelings by telling them the truth. I knew they were great patriots and told them that as a veteran of the Czechoslovak army and the Slovak partisans I would enjoy privileges I could not hope for in Poland. They were themselves bitter about how the Russians were taking over the country and turning it into a satellite of the Soviet Union, and in the process wiping out all traces of democracy. The NKVD and their Polish collaborators were everywhere, and people were starting to fear their own relatives, indeed, their own shadows. But on the surface little had changed in Cracow, except that the Jews were gone. Once there had been sixty-five thousand of us. Now, as we looked everywhere for Jewish faces there were only a few.

A few days later I took a trip to Warsaw. In this ruined city I hired a taxi to take me to see the ghetto, or rather what the Germans had left of it, which was only rubble. Walking about with bowed head I found some everyday things, a rusty spoon here, some broken pieces of mirror there, which with a few other small things I saw lying around, were all that was left of a once flourishing and proud Jewish community of over six hundred thousands. I felt sick and quickly returned to Cracow.

Mietek and I decided to stay over Passover because we wanted to spend it in company with the few Jewish survivors. The Jewish committee was happy to invite us to their Passover seder in the Przemyska Street shelter. The day before the seder, Mietek took me to the black market in the main square where we bartered for German goods from Russian soldiers who were on their way home. We sold them wristwatches for which all Russian soldiers, were eager to own. We noticed that there were many women soldiers among them.

It was the first Jewish holiday I had celebrated since September 1939. The hall in the shelter was full, but instead of the usual festive atmosphere of the seder, which traditionally is a family affair par excellence, there was sadness. The sadness of remembrance of all who were gone, and the fact that there were so few whole families left. How tragically different this Passover was, only the recital of the Exodus story by Rabbi Steinberg from Brody, was the same as it had been for thousands of years. As the story unfolded I reflected that we too had survived a Pharaoh and a Haman, a modern and more vicious one. His name was Adolf Hitler. But how few of us there were. What a price we had paid for survival.

We decided to stay for the whole eight days of the holiday, so that on the last day we might attend the service at which the Yizkor memorial prayer for the departed is recited in the synagogue. I also wanted to recite the Kaddish mourning prayer which close relatives of the departed recite in the

synagogue on the anniversary of the death. I had consulted
the chief rabbi and he had told me that since I did not know
the exact dates of the death of my parents and brothers, I
should select one day of the year.

During the week we visited the Jewish committee several
times and met some of the young men of the Bricha (Escape)
organization, set up by the Jewish community in Palestine to
rescue the survivors of the Holocaust from war-torn Europe
and smuggle them through the British blockade into Palestine.
Most were young Slovaks, dedicated Zionists who allowed
nothing to stand in the way of what they considered to be their
holy work. With our Slovak partisan background we became
their trusted friends.

But even in this festive week tragedy struck. Four Jewish
men and a woman, on their way back from Cracow to their
hometown Nowy Targ, were ambushed and murdered. The
papers played it down, devoting only a few lines to the
incident, and blamed it on "bandits." At the offices of the
Jewish committee, we got more details and the names of the
victims, all of whom were survivors of camps and had looked
forward to returning to their homes in hope of finding their
loved ones. Their car was stopped at a fake military checkpoint on the highway to Nowy Targ on Easter Sunday at three
in the afternoon, by a group of armed men in uniform. While
other travelers were allowed through, the five young Jews
were ordered out of their car at gunpoint and taken to a nearby
woods where they were forced to undress and then shot. Their
naked corpses were left lying there by the perpetrators who
made off into the Tatra Mountains. The names of the victims
included a Lindberg, whose father had been a customer of my
father before the war, and we used to call on the family
every time we visited in Nowy Targ. Everyone in the Jewish
committee was deeply disturbed. It was clear that no Jew was
safe in Poland.

The authorities denounced the killings and blamed them on
reactionaries acting on orders of General Anders in London.
They arranged a state funeral for the victims, to be held in
Cracow on April 23, but Rabbi Steinberg convinced them to
postpone it until the next day because April 23 was the last
day of Passover, a holiday which no Jewish funeral could
be held.

It is one of several holidays in the year when the Yizkor memorial prayer is recited during the festive morning service. It was the first time in my life that I had attended it, because as long as one's parents are alive it is customary to go out into the foyer when the prayer is said. I particularly wanted to attend my first Yizkor prayer in the city in which we had lived, indeed, that is what kept me in Cracow. The last time I had attended a holiday service both my parents were alive. Now I prayed for their souls. I could not bring myself to pray for the souls of Szymon and Nathan, because against all odds I still hoped that they were alive somewhere. The poignancy of the Yizkor prayer, this first festival after the war, was brought home to all of us when not a single person left the temple. Everyone had lost close relatives for whom to say the Yizkor prayer.

Rabbi Steinberg gave a moving sermon, mourning those murdered by the Poles and denouncing the senseless killing of the five unfortunate young people who had survived the Holocaust as well mourning all Polish and European Jews murdered by the cursed Nazis. There was not a dry eye in the temple. After the service we told some worshipers that there was life for Jews outside Poland, another world, where Jews did not have to live in fear.

We stayed for the public funeral of the five latest victims of the hatred for Jews. We all cried as their coffins were lowered into the earth that had already swallowed so many Jews, but the Polish officials stood in silence, their faces sealed. A few hours after the funeral we started on our way back to Budapest. This time there was no need for us to take refugees with us; the Bricha men were now doing that job.

Mietek met a young Jewish woman from Przemyśl he had known during the war. They moved into an apartment together, although they did not marry. Mietek did not as he put it, want to clip his own wings just yet. I too did not think that the time had yet come for me to settle down. I wanted first to make sure that I would be able to go to America with Fela and Janek. Meanwhile I was planning one more trip to Cracow on business, and Mietek agreed to come with me. Fela tried to stop us, fearing for our safety, particularly since in one of the popular cafés we met a Jew who had just come from Poland and told us that another five Jewish women and two men had been murdered by the killers from the mountains, just one week after the previous victims were buried.

We gave in to Fela's pleadings and postponed our trip for a week. This time we stopped for the night in Czesky Cieszyn, which is located just short of the Polish border. In the evening we went to the synagogue to meet the local Jews. When we introduced ourselves my name struck a chord to a Mr. Katz. He came over and asked me about myself and then told me that he had lived in Cracow, under the protection of an Argentine passport. But in November 1943, at the time my brothers were caught, he was arrested and taken to the Montelupich prison. In the prison he had seen my brothers for a few moments. He knew that they were tortured for many days and were then transported to Plaszow together with some Jews who had been captured on the Aryan side. I kept questioning him but that was all he knew about them. (I already knew from Mr. Borwicz that many Polish and all Jewish prisoners taken from the Montelupich prison, had been shot in Plaszow camp and were buried in mass graves.)

When he finished his account I broke down. Now I knew what I had feared since that day I had left them lying hand-cuffed in an unknown apartment in Plaszow. The days of my hoping were over. From now on I would have to include them in the Yizkor prayer. How terrible was this accidental meeting with the harbinger of the tragic news, but it had laid to rest once and for all the ghost of nagging doubt, and I had to come to terms with a world in which I would never see them again. I lost my appetite for going on to Cracow, but Mietek pointed out that we had invested all our money in the goods we intended to sell there. So we continued our journey but I could not face the market and Mietek went alone. However, he returned later with all the goods intact. He had not been able to get a good price and decided to try again the next day. On our way to the shelter we ran into a man I had known before the war, Olek Ameisen, who used to have a soda water factory in Cracow. He had survived the war in Russia and had returned a few weeks earlier with his Russian wife and their child. He spoke fluent Russian which was now a great advantage. He had won his court fight to get his factory back but was still busy with the formalities and was happy to do business with us since he had as yet no income. We gave him all the goods we had brought, with the exception of a few cartons of cigarettes which I kept for the Lopatowskis. He promised to get the best possible price for us. In the offices of the Jewish committee we heard more bad news. A group of eleven Jews who had tried to cross the border into Slovakia had been murdered near Kroscienko. Twenty-three Jews had been murdered in a single month in the surrounding area. They too had been given a state funeral. But Poles had openly made anti-Semitic remarks as the procession made its way through the streets.

Our next trip was to Bratislava. We arrived late in the afternoon and in the evening went to the synagogue where we hoped to find some Jews. The first person we met was old Mr. Schwerd. It was a happy reunion for all of us. He told us that when the Slovak national uprising failed, he and his family were hidden by a Slovak family and they all came through safely. I was particularly happy to hear that Rabbi Armin Frieder had survived the war, though he was in poor health. He had remarried and was back in Bratislava, in the position of Chief Rabbi of Slovakia. His son Gideon, the little boy we had saved when his mother and sister were killed in the German air raid at Stare Hory and had then entrusted to the care of a peasant, had been restored to him.

Schwerd told us that as army veterans and partisans who had fought against the Nazis, we would be eligible for significant benefits if we settled in Slovakia. These included apartments and even small businesses and he urged us to give it serious consideration. We spent the night in the Schwerds' apartment and I joked with Mrs. Schwerd that I would hide my shoes from her. We thought over Schwerd's suggestion and a few weeks later Fela, Janek, Mietek and I moved to Bratislava for good. Henry and Bezi stayed behind.

At the Bratislava veterans' office Mietek and I received Czech identification papers. I was actually a little sad to take off my uniform and become a civilian. We were given nice apartments. After we bought some new clothes, we obtained travel papers to enable us to travel to Hungary and Poland to trade. In Czesky Cieszyn we contacted Mr. Katz and he put us in touch with a professional smuggler who undertook to take any merchandise we wished across the border, in both directions. It was technically smuggling, but it was the way trade was done at the time. We gave him our goods and the next morning he delivered them to us at a pre-arranged address on the other side of the border. With the goods we went on to Cracow. Since we knew what was in demand, we had no trouble selling them quickly and profitably. Later I went to visit the old chocolate factory which was in operation again, but I could not spot any familiar faces. However, in the owner's private office I was happy to find Mrs. Wang, whose husband, Arthur, used to be in charge of the factory finances. She looked at me puzzled for a moment and then recognized me with a happy shout of, "My Henryczek." She kissed me and held me tight, but when I asked about her family she started to cry. Only her son was still with her. Her husband and brother-in-law were murdered by the Nazis in Cracow in 1942. The surviving family members had moved to Russia and there she was separated from her sister, Sabina, who was sent far into the east with her small daughter. Because her factory had more than fifty workers it had been nationalized and she was now the general manager, employed by the state. Of the Jewish workers, only Mr. Feiner, who used to be in charge of sales, survived in Russia, and was now helping her with the management. Soon he would be leaving for a senior post he had been offered in a small wine import firm, and she was sorry to lose her only remaining Jewish employee, and dear friend. I walked around the production hall and was warmly greeted by the workers. Mrs. Wang asked me to come back to Cracow and become an executive in the factory. I told her I would not live in Poland any more, and she then confided that she too was eager to leave, and was already in contact with friends in Belgium about moving there.

In the evening I went to visit Maciek who was living with his aunt. She had married a Christian Pole before the war and survived as a Christian since no one had known she was Jewish. Although she had two children of her own she loved Maciek and Ludwik as though they were her sons too. Ludwik, who came in later, told me that hundreds of Jews who had survived the war as Aryans, decided not to return to Judaism. Many married Christians and now denied their origins, even moving to other cities to avoid being recognized as former Jews. Many of them held high positions in the government and army. As I looked at Ludwik while he was telling the story, I realized that he himself was completely assimilated and no longer had anything in common with Jews. Maciek was different, perhaps because he had suffered as a Jew in the ghettos and camps. It struck me how great our tragedy was, to lose more Jews by choice after the war in which millions of our people were murdered by the Nazis. But I felt I had no right to judge others. God alone knew why they had chosen as they did; at least they were still alive.

From the Jewish committee we learned the tragic news about Chaim Hirschman, who was one of the only two Jews who made good their escape from the Belzec death camp, in which about six hundred thousands Jews were gassed. My dear parents perished in Belzec. Hirschman made a big mistake staying in Poland. When a special commission appointed to investigate the Belzec atrocities opened its hearings in Lublin, he had been summoned and gave eye-witness testimony on March 19, 1946. He was asked to come back the next day. On his return home, he was stopped on the road and murdered by Polish anti-Semites. It seemed incredible to me that he had survived a notorious German death camp where about six hundred thousand Jews were gassed only to fall victim to Polish beasts.

In a similar account, another Jewish man, Czesław Mordowicz from eastern Poland, survived Auschwitz twice. He was first sent to that terrible extermination camp in 1943. The next year he and a Slovak prisoner were able to make a successful getaway with the aid of the Polish underground. They reached Slovakia and joined the partisans. Mordowicz was captured and sent to Auschwitz again. On the deportation train he told the Slovakian Jews exactly where they were being taken and what awaited them in Auschwitz. He urged them to join him in an escape attempt. But they refused to believe him. Fearing that his escape might in fact result in retribution to themselves they stopped him physically. When he tried nevertheless to get to the door they beat him unconscious. When they arrived in Auschwitz some of the Polish auxiliary staff, who were members of the Polish underground, noticed the Auschwitz number tattooed on his arm before the Germans did. They realized that it would give him away as an escaped prisoner which would lead to torture and certain death for him and all those Poles who were risking their lives to save his. They spirited him to the sickroom before the SS

men noticed him. In the sickroom they disguised the Auschwitz number by tattooing a large fish over it. He managed to
survive. After the war he did not want to go back to Poland.
We met him for the first time in Bratislava where he settled
with his wife and we became close friends. He told us that he
and his family planned to settle in Palestine.

I also discovered a book about the Belzec camp written by
a Rudolf Reder whom I met in Cracow. He was the other
survivor from this tragedy. As I read the book the faces of my
parents appeared before me and I could see them being taken
out of the cattle train that brought them to Belzec, separated
from each other, and rushed into the gas chambers where they
suffered agonies for as long as half an hour before death
released them from the ordeal. All my old fury against the
German beasts welled up again as I read of the sadistic killing
of small children in front of their mothers, or their being
thrown alive into burning pits, and of the selection of young
Jewish girls for the SS orgies, culminating in their being driven
into the gas chambers after the night of rape.

I began gathering detailed information about the Belzec
death camp. It was located in the Zamość district of eastern
Poland, close to the Russian border, on the main Lublin-
Tomaszów railroad line. Its official German name was "SS
Sonderkommando Belzec. Dienststelle Belzec der Waffen
SS." It was conceived as an extermination camp, not a labor
camp, the first death camp in the general government. It
therefore did not have a lot of barracks to house a large
number of inmates and in fact only four barracks were built in
it. Its only purpose was to kill as many people as possible as
quickly as possible. Its total area was about two and a half
square kilometers, surrounded by triple barbed-wire fences
which were electrified to make it escapeproof. Trees were
planted around the fences to camouflage the camp.

The Germans built it at a small railroad station, which they
enlarged to an eight-track depot by the time they started
operating the camp on November 1, 1941. The staff consisted
of thirty SS men, and two hundred to three hundred Estonian
and Ukrainian SS guards. From one thousand to fifteen hundred Jewish workers were employed for various tasks. They
were used for only a short time and then gassed, and replaced
by young new arrivals.

The victims were brought to Belzec in cattle trains from southeastern Poland, eastern Galicia, Austria, Belgium, Czechoslovakia, Germany, Holland, Norway and Romania. The trains, usually comprising forty to sixty cars, each crammed with one hundred to one hundred forty people, stopped at the Belzec station. There the Polish engineers and SS guards were replaced by guards from the camp. The trains then continued into the camp, a journey of five to ten minutes. The moment a train stopped, the doors were opened by the Estonian and Ukrainian guards who screamed at the exhausted, starving and frightened Jews to jump from the cattle cars onto a ramp. To speed the process, the guards had vicious dogs and freely used their whips and rifle butts on the unfortunate Jews. While this was going on a small orchestra played relaxing music nearby.

Many of the arrivals were injured in the frenzy. These together with the invalids, the sick, the old and the infants, were carried into an isolated part of the camp on stretchers by the Jewish workers. There they were thrown into long, deep pits that had been dug in advance, and were shot dead by the SS men.

Meanwhile at the ramp the arrivals were surrounded by the SS guards. A German SS officer assured them, in German, that they had been brought to Belzec to work. First they would be taken for a bath and disinfection and then be assigned to different jobs. His reassuring speech calmed the frightened and bewildered Jews. But immediately after it the selections started. Men were separated from the women and children and all were ordered to undress and put their clothing, jewelry and valuables into neat heaps. They were promised that they would return to retrieve them after their bath. A bunch of SS men walked through the throng and picked out the stronger men and young women and also asked for artisans, whom they ordered to step aside. Those selected were permitted to pick up their belongings and were taken to the barracks.

The naked men were ordered to march toward the barracks which were marked by German signs reading "Bath and disinfection facilities." When they reached the doors the SS guards, freely wielding their whips and bayonets, pushed them into a forty-five-square-meter room. Many were already badly bleeding. When the SS had squeezed seven hundred fifty men into the room, which actually was a gas chamber, they closed and locked the door, and the gas was pumped in. The victims suffered for twenty to twenty-five minutes until all were dead. The SS men and their Jewish slaves, the so-called Sonderkommando, waited for another fifteen minutes before opening the doors. Then the Jews had to drag out the twisted bodies. Outside, another group of Jewish slaves, "dentists," extracted gold teeth from the mouths of the corpses.

The women and children were taken to another barracks and made to sit on long wooden benches to have their hair shaved off by a large group of barbers, under the watchful eyes of the SS guards. When all the hair had been cut they were brutally pushed into the gas chamber by the merciless SS men. When the full number had been squeezed in, the doors were locked and the gassing started. When it was over the corpses were picked over for gold teeth and hidden valuables and then taken on small rail wagons to the burial area where they were dumped into the pits and covered with earth. All this work was done by the Jewish Sonderkommando.

Another group of Jewish workers picked up the clothes and belongings at the ramp and took them to a barracks for sorting by Jewish men and women. Some small children were also employed in the barracks. Their job was to tie up the shoes in pairs. All currency, coins, gold and jewelry were taken by the SS. The hair and the better items were prepared for shipment to Germany while the cheaper stuff was sent to Lublin and sold to the Poles.

Altogether six hundred thousand Jews were murdered in Belzec, as well as about twelve hundred Poles accused of taking part in the resistance or giving shelter to Jews. In late 1943, when the Germans feared the arrival of the advancing Red army, they began to cover up the crimes they had committed in Belzec. The Jewish Sonderkommandos were ordered to reopen all the mass graves, spray the corpses with gasoline and burn them. The bones were crushed by special machinery and the ashes of the corpses, and the powdered bones, were spread over the nearby fields. After the Jews finished the grisly task of getting rid of the bodies they were ordered to help the SS level the camp. When they finished, in November of 1943, no sign of the camp was left. The last group of the

Sonderkommando, about five hundred Jews, were then taken by train to the Sobibor camp, under heavy SS guard, and shot.

The SS intended to leave no living witness to Belzec. But by a miracle two survived to tell the world, Reder and Hirschman.

After the camp was leveled, the Polish population of the neighborhood, who had not been allowed near it while it was active, infested the site and searched every inch for buried treasures. The ultimate scavengers.

In a Cracow newspaper I read that Rudolf Hess, the commandant of Auschwitz, was caught by the British forces in Germany and sent to Poland to stand trial. I was confident that the Polish National Tribunal, established by special decree on January 22, 1946, to try the war criminals, would punish him severely, but I also knew that there was no punishment, however severe, that could compensate for his crime. But at least he was going to be tried and punished, whereas so many thousands who had been part of the Nazi murder machine would get away scot-free in West Germany, Austria and other countries which took them in.

One morning I went to Warsaw to see the new exhibition in the National Museum, which the old book seller had advised me not to miss. There was a long line outside, but with my foreign documents I was given tourist priority and shown in without waiting. The whole exhibition was devoted to the crimes the Germans had committed in Poland during the occupation. I was impressed by the tremendous amount of material the curators had managed to assemble so quickly. I spent the longest time in the section illustrating the extermination of the Jews. The documentation was extremely interesting and the photographs shocking. A whole department was devoted to the Auschwitz and Majdanek extermination camps, in which so many Jews, as well as many Poles, were put to death. There was a tremendous quantity of documents, photos, maps, paintings, articles of clothing, eye glasses, and many other items testifying, both by impersonal documentation and poignantly heart-rending articles of children's clothing, to the greatest crime man ever committed.

In another section, devoted to the martyrdom of the Polish people, overwhelming evidence was displayed of the Nazis' attempt to totally destroy Polish culture with the eventual objective of stamping out the Slavic race, including the "pacification" of hundreds of villages, in fact, the destruction of them. The exhibits had been collected by the "Central Commission for the Investigation of German Crimes in Poland from 1939 to 1945" and the Jewish Historical Institute, with the assistance of several associations of Polish prisoners of the Nazis. The president of Poland, Bolesław Bierut, was the patron of the exhibition.

When I was ready to leave I was astounded that I had spent a total of six hours in the museum. I immediately took the train back to Cracow, and the next day, together with Mietek went to see Olek. We also made one more visit to the offices of the Jewish committee to see the latest lists of returning survivors, but after I checked and rechecked them, I realized again there was no hope left that I might find my brothers alive.

The next morning we returned to Bratislava where I heard that our partisan commander, Captain Marcuk, was living in the city. It surprised me because I knew the Soviets did not allow their citizens to leave. I went to visit him and he explained that before the war he had been a Polish citizen, something he had never told us, indeed, he had always evaded talking about his past. He must have come from the Polish Ukraine which had a long history of anti-Semitism, and I decided not to see him again.

I also met some other old partisan comrades from the mountains who were now high government officials. They assured me that the hunt for traitors and collaborators was being vigorously prosecuted, and that already an extradition demand had been presented to Austria where Father Tiso, and many other traitors were known to be living. But I could get no news about Chaim Chermesh and his brave parachutists, except the fact that they had been part of a group of thirty-two Jewish volunteers from Palestine who had been dropped into Romania, Yugoslavia, Hungary, Italy, Slovakia and Bulgaria in the summer of 1944. By now it was known that eight of them including Hannah Senesch had been caught, tortured and hanged. When we learned that Mother's first cousin, Milek Birn, who had survived the war in Russia, had come back to Prague, I went to see him. Next I went to visit the Jewish Museum, which the Germans had not only left untouched, but actually augmented with Judaica from all the countries in Europe they occupied. Their intention had been, after they would win the war, to turn the museum into a display of an extinct race of subhumans.

Meanwhile, at home Janek had got a new shipment of goods, and Mietek and I took them to Czesky Cieszyn where our trusted contact man took us across the border to Poland. In Cracow I went to see Maciek and the first thing he told me was that tragedy had struck him. His twin brother Ludwik had been arrested and was in jail. During the war Ludwik had been involved with the rightist underground. But after the war he obtained a senior post in the district government and was given access to secret files which included the names of all Jews who had chosen to retain the Aryan identity they had assumed in the war to save themselves from the Germans. Many of them were now working for the new government under their Aryan identity. Ludwik passed their names, the Jewish and Aryan ones, to the rightist Poles in London. They broadcast the names back to Poland with the intention of creating embarrassment both to the Jews involved and the authorities. The security police spent a long time investigating the affair until they reached the source, Ludwik. Maciek had desperately looked for a first-class lawyer to defend him, but the few remaining Jewish lawyers refused to take his case, and I could not blame them. They considered him a traitor. Finally a Polish lawyer who had experience in defending prisoners of the underground, undertook his defense. The prosecutor was Jewish, a man called Rumpler whose family I knew well. His younger brother Romek had been my classmate in the commercial academy. The trial lasted a single day. The evidence was overwhelming, and Ludwik was sentenced to fifteen years of hard labor. The affair disgraced Maciek and he wanted to leave with us, but I advised against this, pointing out that Ludwik had made a mistake, and might even have been blackmailed, and he should get a better lawyer to lodge an appeal against the sentence. But we found that for such crimes no appeal was allowed. All Maciek could do for Ludwik was to send him small food parcels once a month. It was one more Jewish tragedy, twin brothers who had survived the Holocaust, had found each other again, and were about to be parted once more, for fifteen years.

The next day, July 4, 1946, after we completed our transactions with Olek, we heard on the radio that there had been some "disturbances" in Kielce. A pogrom had been perpetrated in which forty-two Jews were killed and another fifty wounded. The report blamed "antigovernment" forces and pledged that those responsible would be sternly punished, and that many arrests had already been made. We were stunned; this was not a local outbreak on a highway or in a remote village, but a pogrom in a large city. We went to the offices of the Jewish committee where we found many other Jews as eager as we were to hear exactly what had happened. Mr. Wulf related the full story. On the evening of July 3rd, a Pole named Blaszczyk came to the offices of the militia in Kielce with his wife and their nine-year-old son Henry. He claimed that the boy had just returned home after having been missing for two days. The boy told him that a Jew had lured him, with a gift package and twenty zlotys in cash, and taken him to the Jewish Community Center where he locked the boy in the cellar. There Henry had seen the bodies of Polish children, victims of Jewish ritual murder.

After making his accusation, Blaszczyk shouted to the passers-by in the street that his son had been kidnapped by Jews and escaped with his life only by a miracle. A mob followed him to the Jewish Community building at 7 Planty Street, joined on the way by dozens of others armed with sticks, metal pipes, axes, knives and stones. The women incited the mob with hysterical screams about the Jews killing Polish children. When they reached the building, the community chairman, Dr. Seweryn Kahane, alarmed the district governor's office and pleaded for protection. But before any help arrived the mob broke into the building and set upon the Jews they found inside, ignoring the pleas for mercy from women and children, and did not desist until they had killed many of them including Dr. Kahane, tore the clothes off the bodies and ripped off rings and other jewelry. One pregnant woman gave birth to a child before she died. Some of the corpses were found outside the building, apparently those who had tried to escape the wrath of the mob. Many of the murdered were survivors of the German camps, and some had only just returned from the Soviet Union. The pogrom was witnessed by a Polish woman employed in the center. While the mob was running wild in the center others went to Jewish homes wreaking damage and injury. In one case, four armed militiamen entered the apartment of the Fisz family where they found Mrs. Fisz, her three-week-old baby and a neighbor, a Mr. Moszkowic, who was visiting them. They drove them out of town in a truck, took their money, and shot Mrs. Fisz and her baby. Moskowicz managed to escape into a nearby forest where he spent the night, too frightened to come out. Before dawn the next day he walked back to the city and went to the militia headquarters to report the killing, and there recognized the four murderers who were placed under arrest. The authorities made no real attempt to stop the rampage which lasted for seven hours. The Church leaders, the local security forces, and the army units stationed in the city, all failed to act and, worse, some soldiers and militiamen actually took part in the beatings, robberies and killings. This was not an isolated attack by bandits striking from the mountains but an outbreak of hatred in which hundreds of ordinary townspeople had taken part.

The pogrom terrified the few remaining Jews and made them realize they had been tragically misled by the Bundist propaganda which had persuaded Jews to remain in the "new" Poland, as free and respected fellow citizens. It was a disaster for the community which numbered a total of only two hundred of the eighteen thousand Jews who had lived in Kielce before the war. Their mood changed, the Bundist propaganda was discredited, and many realized that it was the Zionists who had been right all along, that there was no place for Jews in Poland, and looked to the Bricha to get them out of Poland and into Palestine. Meanwhile reports were coming into the office of seven more Jews murdered on a train near Kielce while Russian and Polish security forces were ambushed in various places and murdered.

Mietek and I decided to attend the funeral of the victims and went to Kielce the next day in the company of a large group of Jews. A large delegation also came from Silesia and Łódź. The funeral became one of the largest and saddest demonstrations of Jewish mourning and anger I had seen. Forty-one army trucks bore the forty-two caskets. The first one was that of Rabbi Kahane, draped in the blue and white colors of the Jewish national flag, which later became the flag of the State of Israel. One truck bore the bodies of a mother and her child. Some bodies could not be identified at all.

The procession route was lined with soldiers and security personnel. Representatives of the government and Jewish leaders attended the funeral. The government spokesmen condemned the "reactionaries" who, they charged, had ordered the pogrom, and promised swift and stern action against the suspects already arrested, and the officials who took their time in sending help or had stood by and failed to stop the killings. They also pledged that the government would take all necessary steps to root out the rightist underground and anti-Semitism. Jacob Berman, who as a member of the government had become the highest-ranking Jew in the country, was one of the speakers.

The chief Jewish chaplain of the Polish armed forces, David Kahane, made a moving speech and recited the Kaddish mourning prayer, and he was followed by the famed American cantor Moshe Kousewitzky, who chanted the traditional El Male Rahamim (God Full of Mercy) prayer for the dead.

When the caskets were lowered into the ground there was not a dry eye in the cemetery and there were heartbreaking scenes when relatives of the dead stood over the graves to say their last goodbyes.

And then there was the long walk back, hundreds of Jews who had miraculously outlived the Nazis had now buried forty-two of their brethren, murdered by their own countrymen only one year after the war had ended. The way to the graveyard had been tragic, the way back pathetic.

The next morning I bought all the papers, curious to read what they had to say about the Kielce murders and the funeral, and what steps were being taken to bring the guilty to trial. The papers representing the labor unions were very sympathetic to the Jewish community and demanded swift and stern punishment. But the mouthpieces of the rightist Mikołajczyk and the Church only published short reports of the funeral without comment or word of condemnation.

There were articles both by Polish writers who denounced the killers, and Polish anti-Semites in London who supported them. They called for the dismissal and punishment of the commanders of the Kielce militia and security forces who had allowed the pogrom to proceed. They also called on the leaders of the Church to speak up and explain why they were silent while Catholic Poles were violating God's commandment "Thou shalt not kill." It was the same question, I mused, that we had asked during the long night of our suffering under the Nazis, but there had never been a reply, neither from the pope nor from his clergy in Poland.

In the afternoon we returned to Bratislava. We found that the Czech press had given extensive publicity to the killings. Fela made me promise to limit my trips to Poland to the bare minimum. But she herself wanted to visit once more the Lopatowskis and Zwolinskis before our visas for the United States would come through. Janek could not expect to visit his hometown as it was now part of the Soviet Union. But he did want to see Warsaw again for he had lived there for some years.

One of the few happy moments I experienced, after all these sorrows, happened when I went to the Jewish section with Janek. Quite unexpectedly we ran into the Zeller brothers who were with Stefan Kocan, Stefan's brother, and some young women. We embraced warmly and the Zellers introduced the girls as their sisters who had survived the war in Budapest. I was particularly happy to see Stefan. Now at last I would be able to pay off the debt of honor I incurred in the snowbound mountains, when he had taken off his wristwatch and given it to the Russian partisan who found a pair of boots for me when I burned my shoe. He recalled the incident only when I reminded him of it, and I told him he was entitled to choose the best watch in Bratislava. I took him to the dealer I traded with who had a large selection, and when he picked out a watch he liked, I bought it for him. At last we were even and I was gratified that I was able to repay the debt.

In the evening all of us had a joyous meeting, with everybody talking at once, there was so much to tell. Fela and Janek were extremely happy to meet Stefan and the Zeller family. The next day was a happy one too. We received a letter from our family in the U.S.A. I was amused to see it was addressed to me, in care of Adam Budkowsky. They had evidently been unable to figure out what my relationship to Adam Budkowsky was. It struck me that this was a sure sign I should straighten things out and the very next day I went to the local registry office and officially got my real name back.

I would need it for my U.S. visa. Later I went to Prague to inquire at the U.S. embassy about the possibility of our early emigration to the States, and while I was there I went to see Mother's cousin Milek Birn and his wife Rozia. We had never met and the meeting was very emotional. He used to live in Brno, Czechoslovakia, but his family had lived in Tarnów near Cracow. Milek told me that before the war he had held a high position in the Czech banking industry and as a hobby did amateur photography at which he became so proficient that he was soon one of the best-known photographers in Europe, and won many prizes. When the Germans took over, he escaped through Poland to Russia and there got a job with the ministry of propaganda, taking photos for them all over Russia. When the war ended he was one of the few Czechs the Soviet government sent home in a military plane. Now he worked for the Czech tourism ministry and was again traveling extensively taking photographs. It was good to meet relatives who had survived the war.

Accompanied by Mietek I took Fela to Poland. Janek's leg was bothering him again and we thought it better that he not make the trip which would be a strain for him. On the train I very gently told Fela for the first time what I had heard from Mr. Katz, the efforts I had made to find the names of our brothers in the registers of the survivors, and that I had regretfully reached the conclusion that there was no real hope left in finding them alive. She burst out crying and cried for a long time. But eventually she confided that in her heart she had long suspected they had not survived their capture by the Gestapo.

In Cracow, I first took her to the section where we used to live, and to the school she had attended. It was a sentimental visit for her, but also a very painful one, to see the scenes of her childhood which had been so cruelly obliterated. She had another emotional experience meeting with the Lopatowskis. She was eager to make a short trip to Rzeszów to visit the Zwolinskis. I told her I preferred not to go with her because some Poles might recognize me, and it had by now become an embarrassment, even dangerous for Poles to admit they had sheltered Jews during the war. It was tragic that noble humans had to conceal their good deeds, but I knew of several cases where Poles, who had risked their lives to save Jewish fellow citizens from the Germans, were being boycotted by their neighbors for it. Fela on the other hand could keep up the pretense of being their niece who had come to visit them. She still had the identity papers in their name. But since I was nevertheless anxious for her, and since the intercity phones hardly ever worked, I made her promise not to stay more than two days.

After I put her on the train I walked to Szpitalna Street where my old bookdealer had his store. He gave me all the newspapers with the reports of the Kielce pogrom trial, which had been heard by a military tribunal. The first witness was the boy Blaszczyk, the "victim" of the alleged Jewish lust for the blood of Christian children. This time he told the truth, that he had been picked up on the street by a friend of his father's whom he knew well, and had been taken to his home in a village a few miles outside Kielce. There he was coached to say he was kidnapped by Jews.

The accused admitted their guilt but refused to express remorse, and nine were sentenced to death and quickly executed. Now at last the Church intervened, but to condemn the verdict, not the crime the accused had perpetrated of killing innocent Jewish men, women and children. The commanders of the local militia and security forces, who were charged with failing to stop the killings, pleaded innocence on the grounds that they had refrained from ordering their men to open fire for fear that they might hit bystanders. All of them were dismissed. The boy's parents and their friends were given short sentences.

The papers' reaction to the verdicts varied with their politics; the socialist and communist press, for instance, put the blame on the members of the former government-in-exile in London and on General Anders, accusing them of inciting their followers. The government was evidently embarrassed by the affair, mainly because the world reacted very strongly, and publicly condemned both the perpetrators and the authorities who failed to restrain them. The outcome was that the government issued a decree making violence against people of a different nationality or religion a grave crime punishable by long jail terms and even the death sentence, and also decreed severe punishments for spreading anti-Semitic rumors or propaganda. It was the only good thing resulting from the pogrom, and was coupled with a pledge from the government to aid Jews wishing to emigrate to Palestine.

I went to see Olek and did some business with him. He told me that on June 30, the last repatriation train bringing home surviving Jews, had arrived from the Soviet Union. The Jewish leadership estimated that a total of two hundred thousand had returned from Russia. All ethnic Germans who had lived in Poland before the war, and all the German settlers who had come on the heels of the Wehrmacht, had been driven out immediately after the war ended. The Ukrainians were taken back to the Soviet Union by the Russians who did not forgive them their collaboration with the Germans, and the Bialorussians were repatriated as well.

So the only "foreigners" left now in Poland were the Jews, the "Moszeks" and "Iceks" as they had always belittled us, now adding that we were communists and Christ haters.

The next day I went to the Jewish committee where I learned that many German killers were being brought back to Poland to stand trial for their crimes, among them General Stroop, the annihilator of the Warsaw ghetto. I was surprised also to hear the name Kurt Schupke, and checked whether he was the Schupke I had known in the Rzeszów ghetto. I found that his name was linked with Rzeszów, Zaslaw and Plaszow, where he had been commandant, so there could be no doubt it was he.

When Fela returned she could not get over her meeting with the Zwolinskis. They had hardly slept a wink, recalling her stay with them during those dark days. They treated her like a daughter and gave her all our family photos and the letters we had written to her from the ghetto. But I could not bring myself to read them. She had also visited the Magrys family in Rzeszów.

I refrained from taking Fela to the Jewish quarter. I thought it would be too emotional for her, and instead took her to the Jewish committee and introduced her to its leaders. There I ran into Janek Rosenman who, like me, had been among the last one hundred Jews in the Rzeszów ghetto. He was a mechanic and had looked after Schupke's car and also did other repair jobs for him. He told me what had happened after my brothers and I had escaped from the ghetto. Schupke and Garelik, the commander of the Jewish police, had been very angry but soon more young men fled, and when an informer told the Gestapo, they ordered Schupke to impose retributive punishment on those still left. At the rollcall next morning Schupke ordered fourteen men to lie down on the ground in front of his house and shot them one by one. A few hours later he also shot his personal servant Berkowicz and his son. In the evening he ordered the arrest of more young men but word of the coming doom got out and they fled. A few days later the Gestapo arrived and searched Garelik's apartment. They found two Argentinian passports made out in his and his wife's name and subsequently tortured and shot them both. There were rumors that Garelik, who had been very close to Schupke, had promised to protect him from the Russians. Schupke, after the ghetto was finally liquidated, took the remnants of the Jews to Plaszow. Among them was Rosenman. Schupke became the commandant after Amon Goeth was arrested by the Gestapo for stealing confiscated Jewish treasures that belonged to the SS. Rosenman went through several other camps till finally he was liberated. After Rzeszów was liberated, mass graves of thousands of Jews were discovered in the Glogow forests outside the neighboring village of Rudna Mala. When Rosenman returned to Rzeszów after the liberation, he and the other returning Jews met with open hostility from the population who boycotted them, and their plans to resettle in Rzeszów were quickly nipped in the bud by anti-Jewish riots. When the NSZ movement shot Siudek Meryl, who had been a sergeant in the ghetto police, and allegedly had informed on Poles who had helped Jews, all but a handful of the Jews got out. Rosenman moved to Silesia where he felt safer because most of the Polish residents were themselves newcomers to what used to be a German province, he settled in Wrocław, formerly Breslau, the main city. He had information about the few people from our ghetto who had survived. Oszerowicz the undertaker, and his two daughters, were now in Berlin; Mrs. Kleinmuntz, the good lady from the community kitchen and her son had returned; and Dr. Heller, that good Samaritan, was on his way to Palestine. Lotka Goldberg, the young woman who had been the only one to make a successful escape from the Szebnia death camp in 1943, was also on her way to Palestine. Dr. Beno Kahane the hated head of the *Judenrat,* was either in Germany, or on the way to the U.S.A. Rosenman himself was still uncertain about his future, and I told him how I saw the situation and advised him to ask those from the Bricha movement to take him to Palestine.

Another man I ran into was Karol Hauptman, who had been my classmate and fellow soccer player on the Maccabi team in Cracow, where his family had lived near us. Karol survived the war in Russia. He worked for a Russian widow on her small farm. He had come back a few months earlier. He confided that he wanted to leave Poland and knew that the Bricha was his best bet, but was afraid to travel with a large group because he was now playing soccer for the Cracow's militia team and might be recognized by the militia at the border. I promised to obtain Czech travel papers for him and take him with me. But I swore him to secrecy and warned him not to tell anyone, not even his brother, Poldek, who had returned as a lieutenant with the Polish forces and had fought with the Russians. There were too many informers about, eager to earn rewards. Karol told me about other men I knew who now held senior positions in the local and district militia forces, which accepted Jews. A fit, young man like me who had been with the Czechoslovakian army and the Russian partisans could get a high position with them. I told him I had no intention of ever living in Poland again, and was in fact waiting for my papers to go to the U.S.A. to join my family.

Fela, Mietek and I left for Bratislava the next morning. Fela told me she was happy to get out of Poland and had no intention of ever coming back again. Though conditions had been difficult for her in Romania, Hungary and Slovakia. There at least Jews were not exposed to open anti-Semitism, discrimination, and worse, the wanton killings that had taken place in Poland so recently. She told me that the Zwolinskis were now pensioners but their government pension was not enough to make ends meet, so we decided then and there that as soon as we could earn money in the U.S.A., we would help them. The Magrys family, on the other hand, were doing well with a paint shop they owned. The Lopatowskis also managed, more or less, on the three salaries they earned.

Janek was glad when we returned and now I had an ally in Fela to persuade him to drop his plans to visit Poland. But he insisted and got travel documents in his Polish name and I went with him. We took along a shipment of watches and got them across the border in the usual way, and I sent a telegram to the Lopatowskis to pick them up at a certain address. I preferred to travel clean because I did not want to invite trouble while Janek was with me. In Cracow we picked up the watches from the Lopatowskis and delivered them to Olek.

It was the first time Janek had been in Poland since 1942. When we reached Warsaw he was very quiet for the town held so many memories for him. He had spent many years in Warsaw, before the war working together with his older cousin Ignacy Lipinski. Lipinski, his son and Janek escaped together from Poland to Hungary. Janek was always close with them.

We took a taxi and went to see the site of the totally destroyed ghetto, and then to Praga, where Janek had an old Jewish hometown friend who was a very high official in the government. I bought some more books about the Jews of Poland and then we went to shop for cameras. Janek was the expert, and knew which were most in demand in Bratislava. I noticed that he was becoming very tired both mentally and physically. We had been doing more walking than was good for his leg, although he did not complain even when the pain must have been excruciating. While he rested, I bought some more books for my collection and the next day we returned by train to Cracow and took a bus to Katowice and then on to Cieszyn where we crossed the bridge back into Slovakia. Janek confided that he had seen enough of Poland and, as Fela had told me, this was his last visit. Though he looked like a typical Pole he had sensed the hatred for Jews in the air. When we got back home Janek joined Fela in urging me to give up my travels to Poland. I did not agree entirely, but I did promise that I would restrict my trips to the barest minimum.

But a few days later I got a telegram from Olek, written in our private code, asking for more wristwatches. Janek got them for me and I went alone to Cracow. Olek took the whole shipment and then I went to see Maciek who told me that he had recently visited his brother in the prison in northern Poland. He was heartbroken to see how bad he looked. Ludwik, who had been used to the good life of fine food, old wines and young women, was kept in an isolation cell, subsisting on the barest foods. But Maciek had some good news too; he had fallen in love with a Jewish woman and they intended to marry. He introduced her to me in the evening and I liked her very much. She was very intelligent and had a good sense of humor. I told them I intended to make a trip to Zakopane, a popular resort in the Tatra Mountains not far from Nowy Targ, and invited them to be my guests. I hired a taxi to take us to this area which had been dangerous not so long ago, but now the security forces had cleared it of the threat of bandits from the forests.

It was the best time I had spent since before the war. I climbed the highest peaks and visited all the tourist sites but also the notorious "Palace," the Gestapo headquarters, where many Polish patriots and Jews who were caught while trying to escape from Poland to Slovakia were brought and tortured.

When we returned to Cracow I went to see Mrs. Wang who told me that she had received her visa for Belgium and had applied for a passport. I bought some more books, old Jewish ones, in the Tandetta market and in some bookshops for a pittance. They had, after all, been left behind by the Jews free of charge.

I also met Karol Hauptman. The first thing he told me was he had met Ignac Haber, our close friend and former teammate in the Maccabi soccer club. Immediately we hurried to the Przemyska Jewish Center where all the returnees were staying. It was a very emotional encounter. The last time I had seen Haber was in August 1939. Our families used to live in the same building in the Jewish section. This young, strong sportsman was now bent and thin and bitterly complaining about his eyesight. When I asked him about his family, he answered that only he and his older brother had survived. He told me that he had recently returned from the Sudeten part of Czechoslovakia from the Brinlitz camp. About twelve hundred Jewish men and women had been working there since October 1944 after they had been transferred there from the Plaszow camp. Haber had been one of the first workers for the Emalia factory before the Ghetto. On March 13, 1943, when the Cracow ghetto was liquidated, Haber and all the other Emalia factory workers, were marched into the newly formed Plaszow camp. From this camp all of them were escorted back and forth to work in the factory under guard. The owner of the factory was Oscar Schindler and he was a Sudeten German. During their stay in the Plaszow camp,

Haber and his coworkers witnessed the most cruel and sadistic crimes committed by Amon Goeth, the commandant of the Plaszow camp. Schindler managed to obtain special permits from the Gestapo chief and from Amon Goeth to transfer his machinery and his twelve hundred workers to Brinlitz. He protected his workers from the bloodthirsty SS until the Brinlitz camp was liberated by the Soviet army in May 1945.

I also learned that the trial of Rudolf Hoess, the commandant of Auschwitz was about to begin in Warsaw. The rest of his henchmen would be tried in Cracow. In most East European countries and especially in Russia, all of those who had collaborated with the Germans were tried, and hanged soon after. There were no long trials such as in Nuremberg before the International Tribunal. I hoped that more of those who had committed crimes against innocent civilians would be brought to the East European countries.

People in the Bricha movement said that the borders between Poland and Czechoslovakia were being closely watched. Polish rightists who were running from the Polish secret police were trying to escape by using fake Jewish documents. This was a strange twist, killers of Jews pretending to be Jewish. I hoped that the Jews who returned to Poland from the camps, and those who were coming back from Russia and those who had survived the war in Poland would leave this hostile country.

We had already decided that we would not live there again. The only ties with Poland were the Lopatowskis, the Zwolinskis and Mr. Magrys. We would never forget what they had done for us and what they had risked to save us.

When I traveled to Cracow, I went to the militia headquarters where I met Karol Hauptman. He had prepared a special pass for me to witness the upcoming trial of Amon Goeth, who had been brought to Poland from Germany by an American military plane. My pass was for the first day. Goeth was to stand before Poland's highest tribunal on August 27, 1946. He sat facing the Jewish witnesses dressed in his gray prisoner garb. That day was the third time I had seen this killer. But this time he was not dressed in his black SS officer's uniform, or wearing his black cap with the shining silver death skull or his high boots. He was not carrying his long, black leather whip and his revolver. Amon Goeth was accused of violating all human rights by beating, torturing and killing eight thousand Jews in Plaszow camp. Together with Haase, the chief of the Gestapo in the Jewish section in Cracow, he was responsible for the liquidation of the ghetto in Cracow on March 13 and 14, 1943 where more than two thousand Jewish men, women and children were murdered. He was also accused of the bloody deportation and later the liquidation of the Tarnów ghetto where another two thousand were murdered in 1943, and another eight thousand were marched to the death trains. Goeth also was in charge of the liquidation of the Szebnia camp where fifteen hundred Jews were shot in the nearby forest. The trial ended on September 3, 1946. The verdict was announced on September 5. Amon Goeth was found guilty on all counts. The sentence was death by hanging. The plea for mercy was denied by the president of Poland and on September 13, 1946, Amon Goeth was hanged in Cracow by the militia hangman. The same day Dr. Leon Gross, a Jew, was also hanged. Gross was the basest collaborator in the Plaszow camp.

From the beginning of the war when we lived in Cracow and later in Rzeszów, we were aware of many dangerous Jewish informers working for the Gestapo and other German authorities. Most of them were eliminated by those whom they served. But we also knew about many Jewish heroes. I read about them in the books I had collected. I was proud to read about the brave Jewish underground fighters, including my good friend Szymon Draenger and his wife Justina. She wrote her record on toilet paper in prison, and in this way it was preserved for the world to know. It listed many unknown heroes who fought the mighty German army with little hope of success but out of the need to survive, and who carried out acts of sabotage and hit-and-run killings. The stories revived my faith in my fellow Jews and did miracles for my morale.

One evening in Bratislava when we were standing in line for a movie, I recognized Moszkac Selinger. Before the war he had been a well-known player for the Maccabi soccer team in Cracow, but I knew that under the German occupation he and his wife who was a German Jewish refugee became the most dangerous and hated informers for the Gestapo in Cracow. Both were hunted after the war by Jews and Poles. My anger rose when I spotted him, and without thinking I ran toward him. He was alert and made off into a side street. I followed but quickly lost him in the dark and was extremely angry with myself for having allowed him to get away. If I had not lost my head I could have waited for a policeman or soldier to help me arrest him. I hoped I would run across him again. He had the blood of many Jews on his hands. Anyway, I lost interest in the movie and we all went home.

The next day Mietek and I decided to travel to Budapest on business and at the same time to visit Bezi and Henry. We were happy to see how well they looked. Henry told us that lately he was traveling to Vienna on business and was doing very well. He told us that it was not as risky as going to Poland. Mietek was enthused and told me that we should do the same. I told him that I had made myself a promise never to enter Germany or Austria for any reason. A Jew who had survived the war and suffered from the hands of those killers should never be among them. The Austrians, in my opinion, were more cruel than the Germans.

In Bratislava I began to study the trial of Father Tiso, the puppet head of Slovakia under the Germans. He, as well as many of his henchmen, managed to escape to Austria with the retreating Wehrmacht on April 5, 1945, and were caught there in November and handed over to the Czechoslovak government. On May 15, 1946, the Slovak National People's Courts, to try German war criminals who had committed crimes in Slovakia, along with Slovak traitors, collaborators and the notorious Fascist Hlinka guard.

The intention to put Father Tiso on trial was not easy sailing for the government. On the one hand the communists, supported by former partisans, soldiers, and many workers, demanded his trial and conviction. The Democratic Party, on the other hand, headed by Jozef Letrich who had swept the polls with a majority of 70 percent in the election, and was supported by the Catholic Church, opposed it. But the trial began in December of 1946, and caused much friction between the communists and Letrich and the Church. I considered it beneath my dignity to go to the court to see Tiso, the erstwhile small town cleric from Banovce. In my opinion the man had the deaths of thousands of Jews and Slovaks on his conscience but I refrained from discussing his case with Slovaks since I did not want to get involved in religious arguments. Simultaneously with the Tiso trial, many local people were being tried all over Czechoslovakia for collaborating with the Germans or the Slovak Fascists. The press was complaining bitterly about the leniency of the western Allies who were letting thousands of killers go free without even attempting to check that their hands were clean. At the same time, in the new German government and army, Nazi war criminals were being appointed to important positions. As I saw it only the Soviets and eastern European countries were meting out justice commensurate with the crimes.

I picked up the travel document I had obtained for Karol Hauptman and took it to him on my next trip. We came back to Bratislava together, without any of the border troubles he had feared, and we put him up in our home until I could arrange the trip to Germany for him through my friends of the Bricha. While in Poland I was happy to learn that Maciek and Basia had gotten married, and that as a result of a general amnesty the government declared his brother Ludwik's sentence would be reduced by six years, and he had been moved to a more lenient prison where he enjoyed more visitation rights.

Because travel to Poland was becoming constantly more dangerous I restricted my business to Slovakia with only occasional trips to Budapest. Each time I found Hungary more red and the communist party, which did poorly in the elections, receiving only a minority of the votes, was in fact becoming more powerful by the day. Many of my friends there left for Czechoslovakia. Henry and Bezi managed to wind up their affairs and leave while the gates were still open. I was happy to see them safely out of there and in Slovakia. They stayed with us until they could get an apartment of their own.

The American embassy informed me that my visa had come through and I could go to the U.S.A. But, because Fela and Janek were of Polish birth, they were on the Polish quota which entailed a very long wait. I decided to wait until we all could go together.

On one of my now rare trips to Cracow I met Kuba Kranz who had been in the Rzeszów ghetto and various camps with me. He was the sole surviving member of his family. He invited me to his engagement to a Jewish girl he had met. I also visited Mrs. Wang, who was about to leave for Belgium, but she still hoped first to be able to recover her property and sell it. She told me that many former Polish Jews now living in the U.S.A. were coming to try to sell their properties to Poles. But her claim was more difficult because the factory was nationalized and legally belonged to the government.

On April 15, 1947, the trial of Father Tiso in Bratislava ended, and he was sentenced to death. The reaction was unexpectedly passionate. The Democrats, led by Letrich, were protesting vigorously inside the country, to the West and to the Vatican. The communists on the other hand sponsored demonstrations demanding the immediate carrying out of the death sentence. The Pope did not intervene on the grounds that the Vatican had frequently warned Tiso not to govern Slovakia under the Germans. Fortunately, a majority of government ministers staunchly supported the execution, and after President Beneš rejected the pleas for clemency, Tiso was hanged in Bratislava on April 18, 1947. The execution sent shock waves through the nation. The Catholic Slovaks refused to acquiesce in the execution of a Catholic priest, notwithstanding his having cooperated with Hitler for six years. He had personally blessed and decorated SS troops in Banská Bystrica in October 1944, shortly after we had fled from the city. He conferred his blessings on the murderers before and after they killed Jews and Slovak partisans, and again after the national uprising failed.

My book dealer got some more books for me about the German occupation. One, *Pharmacy in the Cracow Ghetto*, by a Polish pharmacist, Tadeusz Pankiewicz, was a very comprehensive description of the events in the Podgorze ghetto, from the day it was established in early March 1941 until its liquidation on March 13 and 14, 1943. He had been a personal witness to many murders and tragedies inside the ghetto, and recorded the names of the criminals and the dates of the crimes and the deportations in the summer of 1942. As I read it and relived our times in Cracow, I found it hard to believe that the Gestapo had allowed a Pole to carry on his business among the confined, and indeed doomed, Jews and to witness their crimes. The only explanation was that they had not considered the lone pharmacist a threat and had in any case been too confident to care. I managed to meet this wonderful human being who had helped many Jews, and expressed my admiration of him.

On March 11, 1947, the butcher of Auschwitz, Rudolf Ferdinand Hoess, the commandant of the extermination camp which became the symbol of the calamity of the Holocaust, was put on trial in Warsaw. I closely followed the Czech and Polish newspaper reports of the eighteen-day-long trial which ended with a death sentence. Among the many witnesses was the Prime Minister of Poland Jozef Cyrankiewicz, who himself had been a prisoner in Auschwitz, and lived to testify against its commandant. Cyrankiewicz was one of the prominent figures in the PPS underground movement to which Mr. Zwolinski and Mr. Lopatowski belonged. The evidence revealed that the Germans had prepared special units of professional killers and had run schools, and even universities, for their cadres, in addition to the training camps for the rank and file killers. What amazed me particularly was Hoess's background, the scion of a very religious Catholic family, who nevertheless became one of the most vicious killers in human history. He personally used to visit the Belzec and Treblinka camps to study their methods and give advice on how to perfect the killing, and it was he who proposed the use of Zyklon for gassing Jews by the thousands. Auschwitz, though the most notorious, was only one of hundreds of camps where Jews were put to death. Now the terrible truth was coming out, as it were, from behind the triple strands of electrified barbed wire, and I fervently hoped that the other mass murderers would be brought to justice too.

On April 16, Hoess was hanged, fittingly in the very camp he had commanded and made so infamous. Justice was done, at least as far as humans can do justice to so incredible a mass murderer. I knew that already many SS officers and guards of Auschwitz had been brought back to Poland to be judged and forty of them were put on trial in Cracow.

My book dealer informed me that he had received reliable information that our family friend, the engineer Hochwald, had been murdered by Goeth in the Plaszow camp on November 11, 1943. The news that he too had perished was a personal tragedy for me. I had hoped to meet him once more and thank him for everything he had done for us. In one of my visits to the Jewish committee I met Rosenman again and he was bursting with some exciting news. Kurt Schupke was shortly to be put on trial. Schupke's court-appointed lawyer had approached those of the few survivors of the Rzeszów ghetto whom he could find, including Rosenman himself, and he wanted to see me, too. I agreed to meet him and he told me that several Jews would appear as defense witnesses and asked me to testify on Schupke's behalf. I told him that regardless of what the others wished to say, for me he was an SS man who had killed Jews in the Zaslow camp and personally shot fourteen young men, as well as the man who had been his servant, and his son, in the Rzeszów ghetto itself. For me he was therefore a German with Jewish blood on his hands, and I would say nothing in his favor. I asked the lawyer not to put my name on his list of witnesses for the defense. He begged me to reconsider, but I made no promises and went to talk to Maciek about it. Maciek agreed that I had done the right thing and said that if he would be approached he would refuse too. Like me, he thought Schupke had been fair to us, but he was also a proven killer and had to face the consequences of his deeds.

Maciek also told me that he was trying to get visas to France for himself and Basia who had a sister there, but the outlook was bleak and he was ready to consider going to Palestine instead.

On my return to Bratislava I was delighted to hear that Fela and Janek had good news about their U.S. visas, and Mietek, too, had found his relatives in the U.S. and contacted them with a view to joining them. Bezi and Henry also had a good chance to get U.S. visas, thanks to a brother Bezi had in the States.

It seemed that almost every Jew in Poland, and in the more hospitable Slovakia as well, was ready and eager to leave, to tear up our roots that in many cases went back for many generations because there were too many tragic memories from the immediate past for us here.

In the veterans' office I was told that as a volunteer in the army and a member of the partisans I could get a Czechoslovak passport, which would help me in my travels. On their advice I went to Prague to the Ministry of Defense and the Interior Ministry about it. Soon after, by special decree from President Beneš, I became a Czechoslovak citizen.

While traveling on a streetcar in Bratislava I spotted Moszkac Selinger again walking on the street. I jumped off, but

decided to be more careful this time and keep an eye on him
until I could find a policeman to arrest him. I followed him to
a café, watched him go in and take a seat, and waited outside
until a policeman came by. I stopped him, told him who I was,
and pointed to Selinger who, I said, was a war criminal wanted
in Poland, and asked him to arrest him. He agreed and we
went in together and I could see Selinger freezing the moment
he realized we were coming toward him. But as there was no
chance for him to run, he tried to deny his identity and claimed
his name was Novak, and that he had the papers to prove it.
The constable told him he would be able to do that in the
station and took him along in a streetcar. I accompanied them.
Selinger was booked for questioning and I was asked to return
the next day to sort the matter out. I was proud at last to have
caught a Jew who had blindly served our mortal enemies at
the expense of his own brethren. I asked the police to arrest
his German wife too and they promised to go to his apartment
and search it.

The news of the event spread fast throughout the small
Jewish community and many people came over to congratulate
me. Everybody knew about the Jewish informers and Kapos
who had served the Germans in the ghettos and camps, and
many had personally suffered at the hands of these despicable
men and women who had acted as they did to save their
own necks.

The next morning I hurried back to the police station and a
constable showed me to the room of the officer who had been
put in charge of the case. He was studying some papers on his
desk when I came in. The moment he looked up a shudder
went through my body. I recognized him as the man in charge
of the interrogation when Henry and I were caught in Prešov
in 1944. After I told him why I had come, and he had studied
all my papers, but gave no sign of recognition, I told him that
I remembered him as the man in charge of the policemen who
had interrogated Henry and me in Prešov. This former senior
officer of the *Ustrednia Statnej Bezpecnosti* (USB) secret
police of the Tiso government, which had fully cooperated
with the Germans, went pale at the realization that the tables
had been turned and now his life was in my hands, and that
both of us knew it. I wondered how a man with a record like
his had got a high position in the new democratic government.

I knew that functionaries of the USB had been hunted down and punished. Perhaps he had changed his identity. I recalled how he had examined my open wounds and ordered them to be dressed, and that when our lives had been in his hands he had sent us to the Hungarian border, and not back to Poland which would have been a death sentence for us.

In fact I owed my life to him in a way, and I told him exactly who I was and that in my heart I knew that he had with a stroke of his pen saved my life and Henry's. Now I wished to repay him in the same coin. The color returned to his ashen face and he jumped to his feet, grabbed both my hands, and thanked me again and again. I told him I would keep his secret and he had nothing to fear from me. Actually I was happy that I was able to repay a life-saving good turn. It felt as good as it had done to kill Germans when I was a partisan.

When we had both regained our calm again he brought out Selinger's file which showed that he was living alone with a Slovak family. His wife, he had claimed, was killed by the Germans in 1944. In his room the police found a lot of expensive watches, gold jewelry and even gold teeth, as well as some foreign currency. They had informed the Polish embassy in Prague, and the Ministry of Justice in Warsaw, of Selinger's arrest, and were holding him pending an extradition request. I worried that they might release him on bail, which Selinger would obviously jump, but he assured me they would not. When I stood up to go he came over to me, clasped me by the arms and thanked me again. He had tears in his eyes when I again reassured him that he had nothing to fear from me, and gave him my address if he would ever need me. I left with the feeling that I had repaid a debt.

A few days later I was notified that Selinger had been expelled to Poland and was being held in the Montelupich prison in Cracow. I decided to go to Cracow at the earliest opportunity to find out for myself what had happened to him. As usual, I combined the trip with business through my established channels. On arrival in Cracow I immediately went to the Jewish committee to inquire about Selinger and told Borwicz that it was I who had caught this traitor. He and the other officials congratulated me and he took me to see the committee's legal adviser, a Mr. Salpeter, whom I had heard of before the war when he was one of the young leaders of the

Zionist movement in Cracow. He was preparing the list of local Jewish witnesses for the prosecution to testify about Selinger's activities in the ghetto and of several Poles to give evidence about his activities outside the ghetto. He told me that in Warsaw a very well-known Jewish champion boxer, Rotholz, had also been caught and brought to court on charges of cooperating with the Germans, was found guilty on all counts and sentenced to a long jail term. I recalled that two other Jewish collaborators had also been executed: Dr. Gross, who had worked with Amon Goeth, and a certain Hochberg, who had been an official in the organization of Slovak Jews and had at the same time collaborated with the Hlinka guards and the Germans. There had been more Jewish collaborators but most of them had been killed by the very Germans they had served. However, many of those traitors would get away because there were no living witnesses to discover them and testify against them. Salpeter told me he could get me a pass to the Schupke trial which had opened in Cracow on June 12, but I had no stomach to see the SS man I had known. I only wanted them all dead. On June 18, he was, in fact, sentenced to death and was hanged almost immediately. Justice was done—the way I understood it and wanted it. Before I left I went to see Salpeter again and he told me that Selinger would probably get only a life term because those he had betrayed were no longer alive to testify against him.

I was bemused by a report of another trial, held in Cracow in August 1947, of some of the former leaders of the rightist, Armia Krajowa. They were charged with betraying socialist activists to the Germans and killing Jews. One of them, a certain Strzalkowski, who had been the leader of the movement in Rzeszów, testified in his defense that they had known that a certain Jewish girl, named Fela, was being sheltered by a Pole named Tytus Zwolinski. They suspected that she had even traveled to Cracow as a courier for raising money to help Jews and had blacklisted her. Yet, in his mercy, he had never done anything to harm her, he claimed.

When I returned to Bratislava, I was dismayed to hear that Dr. Armin Frieder, the Chief Rabbi of Slovakia, had succumbed to the illness he had contracted during his flight from the SS and Hlinka killers.

Now his son was an orphan and his second wife a widow,

and I mourned for the devoted and wonderful man. Soon after both emigrated to Palestine and his brother Emanuel took over the leadership of the Slovak Jews. I knew the Frieder family had documents on the history of the Slovak Jews in their possession, including correspondence of their leaders with the leaders of the Jews in Hungary, as well as with the International Red Cross and the Catholic Church, and no doubt one day he would put them to use for a historic record.

We were still waiting until Fela, Janek and I would be able to go to the U.S.A. together, and meanwhile we were kept busy saying goodbye to many of our new friends who were emigrating, mostly to Palestine. I made another trip to Poland and, in Cracow, Salpeter told me that Selinger had indeed been sentenced to life imprisonment for collaboration with the enemy. The trial of the forty SS officers and guards from Auschwitz was then being heard by the National Tribunal, in a hall of the National Museum on Aleje Maja and I agonized whether or not to go there. Finally I decided to attend a single session.

The accused, which included five women, sat on long benches and one of the women, Maria Mandel, had been in charge of the Birkenau women's camp, which functioned exclusively as an extermination camp for its victims who were mostly Jewish. They were either put to death in the gas chambers or used as human guinea pigs for medical experiments. Mandel had been known as a particularly cruel beast. Another of the accused was Artur Liebenhenschel who replaced Hoess in November 1943. I observed them sitting there fearful of their fate, deprived of their whips and guns, and now it was their lives that were at stake. I hoped they would suffer at least a fraction of the tortures they had inflicted on the thousand of innocents who were their victims. They knew they could expect no pity from this court of Poles whose country had suffered so terribly under the heels of the Germans, unlike the misplaced compassion British and American judges were showing to the criminals being tried in occupied Germany. The trial ended on December 14, and twenty-three of the killers were sentenced to death and were executed on December 22. Six received life terms, and one was acquitted.

All over Poland, as well as in Czechoslovakia, Hungary and Romania, swift justice was being meted out to the German oppressors and their collaborators. It was exhilarating for me to be alive to see this retribution. Soon we heard that the American and British military tribunals in Germany were being dissolved and that the Nazi criminals they had captured, but not yet tried, were being handed over to the German courts. We were dismayed by the news. It had been pathetic enough when the British and American judges, who could not begin to imagine the cruelty of the Holocaust, were judging them. But this was a farce. It recalled to my mind the old Polish folk saying "One dog won't bite another dog." In fact, Western Germany had become a haven for the criminals who had done everything possible to evade justice. Now they would be safe there. We knew it, but there was nothing we could do about it.

One morning the mailman brought an invitation to the American embassy in Prague. Fela and Janek got their visas on the spot, but I had to wait another month. We telegraphed our family in the U.S.A. and asked them to arrange transportation for us. A few weeks later tickets, for January, arrived for Fela and Janek. It was a happy moment for all of us.

I decided that before I would leave, to make one last big business trip to Poland, to try to break the bank. I invested everything I had in the purchase of a large quantity of the best available watches, and transferred them through my channels. The young Lopatowski picked them up as usual, but when Olek came to get them, Mrs. Lopatowski informed him that the shipment had been intercepted and confiscated by the Commercial Commission. I almost fainted when I got the news. All the hard-earned money I had made since the end of the war was sunk in those watches. When I arrived, Mrs. Lopatowski told me that her son had been arrested and she had no idea where he was being held. She advised me not to stay and not to come back. She feared the commission agents would watch her apartment because she knew that her son had told them everything about my business network and operations. I had a sneaking suspicion that the young Lopatowski had got wind of my imminent departure to the U.S.A., from something Olek had let slip, and decided to seize the opportunity to get rich by getting away with my valuables, and that he had made up the story about being caught.

I did not want to voice my suspicions to Mrs. Lopatowski.

The loss of her husband had been enough of a blow for her, and I also considered it judicious not to stay until I could find out the truth. So the only thing to do was to return immediately to Bratislava financially ruined though I was. I would also have to tell Fela and Janek that we had lost everything. I didn't look forward to it, but it had to be done. I was afraid to go to Olek, just in case the story was true and his house was being watched. Instead I went to see Maciek. He brought Olek over and they were very angry and upset, convinced that the young Lopatowski had made up the story to get away with my fortune. But they agreed that it would nevertheless be best for me to cut my losses and leave. Olek provided a car and I drove to the border. There I waited until it was dark and crossed the river separating Poland and Slovakia, preferring not to go through the official border post, just in case they were looking for me. When I returned home and told Fela and Janek what had happened they were upset but their relief that at least I had got away free made up for the loss.

The time came for them to leave, but this time we were confident that we would soon be reunited for good in the United States.

19

Leaving Europe for the U.S.A.
February 1948

W hen notice of my visa arrived I said goodbye to all our friends, hoping that we would soon meet again across the ocean. Then I went to Prague to pick up the visa and took the international train which took me through that cursed Germany. I made a point not to set foot on any German station, and in Belgium I caught the ferry to England. I visited London and got on the ocean liner in Southampton. As the ship sailed across the Atlantic the news came through that the government of Czechoslovakia had been overthrown by the Communists. It was a shock for me but I was glad I was no longer there, and immediately started worrying for my friends, and all the other Jews who were still waiting to emigrate. I was especially concerned for Milek and Rozia. He was elderly and she was sick. I knew very well that the Russians, who were surely involved in the communist takeover, would already have closed all the borders tightly. We had a very rough trip through heavy storms and arrived twenty-four hours behind schedule. As we approached the shores of America I became thoughtfully sad, thinking of my parents and brothers who had not lived to come to America with me. I vividly recalled the day, early in 1938, when our family in New York had sent the papers for all of us to join them. The U.S. embassy in Warsaw had approved our applications and assured us we would get our visas sometime in 1939. But before they came through, Hitler invaded Poland on September 1 and put an end to our dreams and hopes. Only Fela and I survived to see America. They, or more probably their cremated ashes, were buried somewhere in Poland, together with six million other Jews. At that reflective moment, as the Statue of Liberty came into view and my heart was filled with thoughts of my murdered family, I pledged to myself that I would put my experiences in writing and let all who wished to hear know what I had witnessed and learned during those dark years of tragedy known as the Holocaust.

Fela, Janek and my two uncles were at the pier as the boat tied up in New York on February 24, 1948. It was a tearful meeting for all of us, a mixture of joy and sad reflections. The streets of New York were deep in snow and we drove slowly to the Bronx where my beloved grandmother lived. But as we reached the building, my uncles told me that Grandmother no longer lived there. A year ago they had taken her to a nursing home in Westchester, after she had lost her memory, could no longer recognize anyone and was unable to take care of herself. Her illness was diagnosed as Alzheimer's disease. It was a great blow for me. I had looked forward so longingly to seeing her. Mother had always talked about her, and we had had a big photo of her on the wall of our sitting room. In the old days, before the war, not a month passed without a letter from her and she had often sent us packages. The uncles saw that I was heartbroken and promised to take me to visit her on the weekend. In her apartment I met our youngest aunt, Lola, who was living there with her husband Arnold, and their two young sons, Elliot and Leonard. Soon all the other members of the family arrived to meet me, four uncles with their wives and children, and four aunts with their husbands and children, a full house. Though this was our first meeting I did not feel they were strangers. Mother had told us so much about them that it was as if we had known them all our lives. We talked a lot but, as though by tacit consent, did not raise the subject of our missing dear ones. When they left I had a chance to talk to Fela about her impressions of our family and of New York and the U.S.A. in general, and found that she and Janek were very happy. The first Sunday our youngest uncle picked us up and drove us to Grandmother's nursing home. On the way he told me that early in 1945 he had received some letters from Australia, and later also from France, with regards from me, and I knew at once that they were from those escaped allied POW's I had met in the Tatra

Mountains in October 1944, who promised to inform my family. The nursing home was very big. Grandmother was in bed and did not react to our coming. I bent to hold her hands in mine and kissed them, and then kissed her head too. But she did not react at all, not a sound. I started to cry as I had not cried since I lost my brothers. On the way back to New York, I reproached my uncle for confining that wonderful old woman to a home, all alone, in the care of strange nurses and doctors.

A few days later I started to work for my uncle Sam, in his large factory making ladies' dress buttons. Janek had started to work there the month before and it was a good job. In the evenings, Fela, Janek and I went to night school to learn English. Most of the class were refugees like us and they told us that Jewish newcomers met regularly every Sunday near the HIAS building in the Lower East Side. The next Sunday the three of us went there by subway to see whether we might meet, or find out about, people we knew. There were hundreds milling around and we started scrutinizing the crowd. My heart leaped when I spotted my good friend Leon Horn, and after an affectionate greeting he introduced me to his wife, Maria. She was Jewish. They had met in a displaced persons camp in Germany and married there. He told me that his only brother, Hersch, had survived, too, and was living in Sweden.

From the HIAS building meeting place, we went to Brooklyn to meet Chaim Mojshe Halbersztam, whom Fela had never met, and his wife. The wife was American and, like him, very religious, and they had no children. Of his very extensive family only his sister-in-law and her son had survived. But he had given up the rabbinate and was doing very well in business, running a small textile firm he opened. The next Sunday at the HIAS building Janek spotted Duda. We embraced and as we stood talking, noticed that many such meetings were occurring all over. It was the accepted way for old friends from Europe to meet again in our new country. The truth was that we had not expected to meet many friends again. Each Jew who survived the Nazis was a miracle. Later in the week we went to see Duda who lived with his mother, his older sister and her husband, in the Jewish section on the Lower East Side. We made friends with them and met frequently, and Janek and I often had lunch with Duda who worked near our factory.

When we were out walking in the midtown section of Manhattan one Sunday, we came across one of the Schwerd boys who told us that all of them had opened a jewelry factory with their father on 48th Street. We had a happy reunion with them and they told us about the events in Bratislava after we left. Many Jews, especially those known as Zionists, had been arrested and many anti-Semitic incidents occurred there as well as all over Slovakia.

Our circle of friends from Europe grew, and all of us were thrilled when the United Nations voted to accept the State of Israel into the community of nations as an equal member. How very proud and happy we were. At last the Jews had their own country. But as though the curse of the Holocaust would pursue us forever, our mood was tempered by our solemn thoughts for the six million who had not lived to see this day. We were also very worried by the onslaught of the combined Arab armies on the small and poorly armed new state. It was as though our old curse, that nothing could turn out entirely good for Jews, which had haunted us for so many terrible years in Europe, was now turning up in the Middle East. Happily the war turned in Israel's favor, though at a terrible cost of more Jewish lives, many of them survivors of the Holocaust who had taken up arms for their new country the moment they had stepped ashore in our Holy Land. But at least they had died honorably, nay gloriously, fighting for a great cause, rifle in hand. How proud of them the six million victims would have been, had they but been spared to see the day.

In one of our Sunday HIAS visits we met Jankiel Breitowicz, his wife Jadzia, and their young son Herbert. Jankiel looked sick and explained that he suffered from latent tuberculosis. I also noticed that he had a deep scar in his face, near his left eye. He told me he had gone through many concentration camps in Germany and had contracted tuberculosis in them. When the war was ending he had been in a camp in Flossenburg. When the American army approached, the SS took all the remaining Jewish prisoners to a nearby forest and shot them and threw the bodies into a pit. Jankiel happened to be one of the last to be shot and was thrown on top of the heap of corpses. The bullet entered his head near his left eye, went through his head and out again, but did not kill him. Next to him another man was still alive too, and when the killers had left, they started calling for help. A German farmer heard their cries and extracted them and kept them in his barn until the Americans arrived. The soldiers took them to a nearby German hospital where they were nursed back to health and when they were discharged they went back to Poland to look for their families. Jankiel found his wife, Jadzia, and his son, Herbert, in Katowice. Both survived the war in Germany. As a Polish Christian she volunteered for work in Germany in 1941. From Katowice Jankiel and his family went back to Germany and stayed in a DP camp until they were able to come to the U.S.A. They had no income and were supported by HIAS.

I often visited Leon Horn and one day he told me that his brother Hersch had returned from Sweden and he had bought a luncheonette in Spanish Harlem for him. He immediately offered me a partnership, and since Uncle Sam's factory was in trouble, and our jobs were in jeopardy, I accepted. A little later Leon bought another nearby business and Hersch became my partner. Janek rented the space outside our window and sold costume jewelry, and all of us did very well. When Janek and Fela rented an apartment near Lola's house I moved in with them. Then my sister Fela had a child, a boy, and they named him Robert after Janek's father and Emil after our father.

We never forgot the Zwolinskis and wrote to them every month, always including money in our letters. Once in a while we also wrote to Mr. Magrys, but we never wrote to the Lopatowskis. I was too angry about the son's betrayal. We asked our uncles to bring Milek, who was their first cousin, and his wife Rozia to the U.S.A. and meanwhile we regularly sent him small sums of money. Sadly, Rozia died of heart trouble before their papers came through and he remarried soon after, to a non-Jewish woman. It upset me but after all it was his life and we maintained our close relationship. On a trip to Italy, Fela and Janek met Milek in Milano, where his older brother Romek lived with his family. I was also very happy to hear that my dear friend Chaim Chermesh was back in Israel in his kibbutz.

Fela gave birth to her second child, a girl, and she was named Toni, for our mother. After some time they decided to move to Dallas, Texas, where Janek started a large and successful manufacturing and wholesale business. Soon they had another daughter and named her Marcie, for one of Janek's relatives.

All through the Holocaust I had not given much thought to women in a romantic way, but at last my turn came and on June 14, 1964, I got married to the finest woman in the world. Soon after our wedding we went to Israel where her family lived. For me it was a very touching moment when I stepped off the plane onto the ground of our own country, and I was very proud and happy to see how much the Israeli Jews had accomplished in such a short time. I met many people I had known in Cracow before the war, as well as a few survivors from Rzeszów. We surprised Chaim Chermesh when one day we unexpectedly turned up in his kibbutz, Kfar Glickson. He was sincerely happy to meet us, but we were unfortunately not able to meet his two sons. They were both out of the country on an assignment for the government.

Now I had a chance to hear what happened when we had all fled from Banská Bystrica. Chaim and some of his comrades had taken a large group of armed Slovak Jews with them. The German raid, which had hit us too, dispersed and separated them. They then had the same idea we had, to climb high up into the mountains for safety. There they met up with another group of Jews and together built a bunker. But they were too trusting and one morning, when they spotted some civilians approaching, they gave them a friendly greeting instead of suspecting their purpose as they should have. That night, after they had fallen asleep, their bunker was attacked by armed men with grenades and gunfire and most of them were killed or wounded before they knew what hit them. Only a few, including Chaim and one of his comrades, managed to get away into the woods. The attackers took the wounded away with them and turned them over to the Gestapo who first tortured and then hanged them all. Chaim and his comrade found a cave whose entrance was covered with snow and burrowed their way in and hid. They could hear the attackers for some time looking for survivors, and stayed in the cave without food, for almost a week before venturing to dig their way out and then ascended higher up into the mountains. Luckily, they came across another bunker and after they had been interrogated and cleared by its inmates, who included a few Polish and Slovak Jews were allowed to join them. They stayed with them and operated as partisans until they could join the Russians, as we had done. When they at last came down from the mountains they had a tough time convincing the suspicious Russians in the valley who they were, but finally were given permits to travel through Poland to the Soviet Union. After a long and difficult trip they reached the Black Sea port of Odessa where they got passage on a ship to Turkey, and from there made their way back to Palestine.

After he finished his story, Chaim found a photo of me that he had snapped in Banská Bystrica, and also showed us a book he had written about his experiences in Europe and in the Slovak national uprising. In it he mentioned the group of Polish Jews he had met in Slovakia and named me (as Adam) and Henry Lubelski. The book was published in Hebrew by the Israeli Defense Ministry's education department and I bought a copy when we went to Tel Aviv, and my wife read it to me. I told Chaim that I still had a photograph of him, along with his address which he had given me back in the Slovak mountains.

Shortly after our return home we received a letter from Mrs. Zwolinski saying that her wonderful husband, the friend we owed so much to, had passed away. Not very long after that we received another letter from their niece that Mrs. Zwolinski had died also. We had not yet gotten over their deaths when Milek's wife wrote us that Milek had died in a hospital in Prague.

On our next visit to Israel I bought some books about the Holocaust, one of them about the Slovak Jews. In it I found the name of Emanuel Frieder who, I knew, was the brother of Rabbi Armin Frieder, the father of Gideon, the boy we had rescued and placed with a shoemaker in a remote Slovak village. My wife got on the phone and after a lot of inquiries got Frieder's number in Nethanya, and after I explained to him who I was he was very excited and insisted we come to see him at once. We took a taxi there, and the first thing I asked was for news of Gideon. He told me that he lived in Ann Arbor and was a professor of computer sciences at the

University of Michigan, and gave us Gideon's address and phone number.

Mr. Frieder himself was the principal of a Nethanya high school and the head of the Slovak Jews in Israel. After the first excitement of our meeting had worn off, he took us to his study and showed us six boxes of documents about the Jews of Slovakia he had smuggled out of the country with him. These were the documents I had heard about back in Bratislava, a historical treasure trove which included the correspondence between Rabbi Frieder and Jewish organizations in Switzerland and Turkey, and with senior officials of the Vatican from 1939 to 1945. There were also copies of thousands of appeals for help and the responses to them. They made it clear that the world had done nothing to try to save the sixty-two thousand Slovak Jews who were deported to eastern Poland and Auschwitz in 1942 and never came back.

After we returned to the U.S.A., we called Gideon. His wife answered the phone, and when I explained who I was and asked to speak to Gideon she said he could not talk about his past anymore. I was so upset that I hung up and did not call again. But on our next visit to Israel, I told Emanuel Frieder about it and asked him to put me in touch with Gideon. He told me he would see to it that Gideon would call us when we returned to New York. He did and soon after came to visit us. The little boy from the mountains was now a grown man with two grown daughters and a son of his own. Since then we have become like one big family and often go to see each other.

From Montreal we received bad news. My dear friend Maciek Fiedler had died as a result of minor surgery, and his wife Basia did not long survive him. In both cases I was notified too late to attend the funerals.

In 1978 we went to Israel again for the Passover holiday and in Tel Aviv I met an old friend who was also a friend of Mietek. He told me that Mietek was visiting in Israel, too, but he did not know the hotel where he was staying. We got on the phone and began calling all the large hotels until one of them informed us that Mietek had been registered there but had already returned to Frankfurt. I called him there and told him I had been looking for him in Tel Aviv and he entreated us to make a stopover in Frankfurt on our way home. Before I gave an answer I remembered that I had sworn never to set foot on German or Austrian soil. But Mietek was one of my best friends who had gone through so much with me, and when my wife nodded, I agreed.

We arrived in Frankfurt in the evening and Mietek was waiting for us at the airport to take us to his house in the suburbs. There we met his wife and their three grown sons. Over coffee we two close friends started reminiscing about the old days, our first meeting in the Tolonzhaz jail in Budapest, our escape, our adventures in Slovakia, and our fighting the Germans in the mountains. But when I started talking about our suffering in Poland he abruptly switched to Polish, and curtly told me to stop talking about the German cruelties. He had never told his wife and sons that all his family had been gassed in Belzec and that he alone had got away with his life. He said they were happy in Germany and he had become a rich man doing business with the Germans. My wife, who did not understand Polish, was surprised when I suddenly got up and told her we were going to our room and would be leaving first thing next morning. Mietek showed us to our room and on the stairs tried to explain his behavior. But I cut him short and told him our friendship had come to an end. In our room I explained to my wife what had taken place downstairs and she justified my stand. But although I felt I had done the right thing I could not sleep. I was troubled through the night thinking about how my friend had sold his soul to the devil. I deeply regretted that I had broken my own vow and come to Frankfurt at all. I never could understand how Jews, especially Polish ones, could live among Germans and Austrians, when every man or woman they sat next to in a bus or café might have the blood of Jews on his hands, which all their courtesy and smiles could never wash clean. Whenever I met anybody from Cracow or Rzeszów who told me they lived in Austria or Germany, I told them straight to their face that in my book they were betraying every one of the six million Jews their neighbors had murdered, and walked off without shaking hands.

Late in 1983, I ran into Mietek again in midtown New York. He spontaneously came over and embraced me, and the first thing he said was that he would never be able to forgive himself for his despicable behavior in Frankfurt. He implored me to let him come to our home in the evening, and as he was so genuinely sorry, I did not have it in me to refuse him. We spent many hours talking and it was like old times again. The next morning he flew back home and not long afterward I heard that he had died of a heart attack in a Frankfurt café. It was a great blow. I was very upset that his wife, Julia, had not even bothered to inform me. I called Henry to tell him of the death of our old friend and comrade, and he was as upset as I was.

I sat down and wrote a long letter to Mietek's wife and sons to express my sympathy and described in detail to his sons everything I knew about their father, starting with our first meeting in the Tolonzhaz prison. I told them his Jewish name, and the names of his parents and brothers, where they had lived in Poland and where they had perished at the hands of the Germans. I wrote that I had truly loved their father and would forever carry his memory in my heart. I never received an acknowledgment and I believe that perhaps their mother, who was an Austrian and not Jewish, did not want the sons to know how very Jewish Mietek had been. They were raised by a father named Sam Donner of Frankfurt, and she apparently wanted him to remain Sam Donner even after his death. It was a sad irony. In the war the Germans did not want him to live because he was a Jew, and now his Austrian wife did not want him to be a Jew even in death.

20

Visit with My Wife
Poland, September 1984

I n September 1984, I took my wife to Poland, to show her Cracow and the house we used to live in there, as well as Warsaw and Auschwitz. We arrived in Warsaw, from Amsterdam, on a cold and rainy fall day. First we visited the old Jewish section. Our Polish guide, whom I had told we were Jewish, told us that the Poles living there now had built their semidetached, two-family houses, on the ruins of the Warsaw ghetto. Apparently they had not bothered to remove the remains of the thousands of Jews who had been buried under the ruins and give them a decent burial. The Germans had blown up all the buildings when they squashed the heroic uprising in the spring of 1943. At the Jewish Historical Institute, which was also a Jewish museum, we met some Jews who were still living in Poland. But most of the people working there were not Jewish, and it was, in fact, a sorry museum that did not do justice to what had been the largest Jewish community in all of Europe. When I expressed my distress to one of the Jewish directors he responded that the government was not supporting the institute. They still did not like the Jews.

As we walked through the miserable streets of the capital I kept looking out for Jewish faces. I had always been able to spot a fellow Jew, but was unable to find a single one in a city where almost six hundred thousand Jews had lived a mere forty-five years ago. We left for Cracow and immediately after we checked into our hotel, took a taxi to the Jewish section and the street where we used to live. We entered the building where Fela and our brothers were born and checked the names in the lobby. There was not a single Jewish one among them. We walked on and I showed my wife the place where the Maccabi stadium once stood and the site of the public school we had attended. It too was gone. We went on to Kollatja Street, to the house from which we had fled to Rzeszów in March 1941. It was a poignant moment for me. I knocked on the door of the Lopatowskis' old apartment from which the devoted Mr. Lopatowski had taken Fela and me to the Slovak border in November 1943. A middle-aged man, who must have been his son, opened the door, and when I asked to speak to Mrs. Lopatowski, he said his wife was not at home. I asked for his mother and he told me she was living in the old section ever since she had remarried many years ago. He had not recognized me and when he asked who I was, I gave him the first name that came into my head. I had no wish to talk to this scoundrel who had denounced me to the authorities in 1947. We turned away at once and went up to the third floor where our apartment had been. But when we reached the door I hesitated and could not ring the bell. I feared that seeing the familiar rooms would be too much for me and, should I recognize any of our old furniture, might not be able to endure the pain. So we went down again and on the way I pointed out the apartment where the dear Gelb family had lived. I could never find out what had happened to him and his German wife.

The next day we visited the old section, the city center, behind the famous Mariacki church. When we came to the building where Mrs. Lopatowski lived, my wife asked me to go in alone. This was my meeting, she said. An old lady opened the door and asked me in. She did not recognize me, just as her son had failed to recognize me the day before, so many years had passed since our last meeting. She looked very poorly, hardly able to walk or talk, and did not react when I tried to explain who I was. Her memory was gone. So I just asked her for a photo of her first husband, and on looking through some albums I had spotted on a shelf, we found a small one and with a nod she indicated that I might have it. Before I left I asked her whether she was in need of money or anything else, but she did not answer. I was terribly sorry to leave her in such a state, this once resolute woman, who with her husband had saved the lives of Fela and mine at the risk of their own for no other reason than that they were decent human beings who considered it right to stand by friends in the hour of their need. I left some money anyway, and went out with bowed head. I did not have to give an account to my wife. My face told the story.

We walked to the Kazimierz section, where the Jews had lived, and I told my wife that almost all the stores we passed had belonged to Jews, and had been handed over to their new owners by the German murderers. It was incredible to me how rundown this once beautiful city looked now, a picture of dilapidation well on the way to ruin. Many historic buildings were propped up by heavy beams, and when we passed the Wavel castle, I noticed that the Jewish street names had not been changed, but there were no Jews left in them. There were no more Jewish stores or workshops and the Jewish market was now being run by Poles. How they had looked down on the Jewish peddlers selling their vegetables, live poultry and fish, and now they were doing it. Through a back door we entered the Miodowa Street synagogue and found that this once rich temple of worship was also little more than a ruin. It was Friday, and I asked the old caretaker when the Sabbath Eve service would begin. They had none, but the next morning at nine they would have a Sabbath service. He looked poor and ragged and I gave him a large tip which he gratefully accepted. We walked on through the area the Jews had lived in. I remembered it as being old but very clean. Now it was so filthy and in so bad a condition that it was hard to believe that people could live there at all. Once these Poles used to call us "dirty" Jews. The old synagogue we used to belong to was closed, and in very poor condition, and some other synagogues were now warehouses. Except for the Miodowa temple, only the Remuh synagogue was still in use, serving the few religious Jews who still lived in Cracow. The Old Synagogue, six hundred years old, was now a museum. We went in. A young Polish woman sold us tickets and gave us a brochure about the history of the Jews of Cracow. But the interior was a disappointment to me. A few bad copies of Jewish paintings hung on the dirty walls, and in the center of the hall, where the "bimah" altar had stood, there was a pathetic display of some small local relics, and the music that was playing in the background was repulsive to me. It was a very disturbing experience. The Jewish museum of a city in which almost seventy thousand Jews had lived had little to show. There were only about six hundred Jews still living in Cracow; some three hundred of them were married to Poles and did not practice their religion, and the rest were elderly.

We took a taxi to Auschwitz. The road ran parallel to the railroad tracks that led to the site of the extermination camp. We could see the tracks all the way, and I mused about the hundreds of thousands of Jews who had made their last journey on them in tightly packed cattle trains, to a terrible death waiting on the inside. Our driver told us that the road had been used by the Germans to transport Polish and Jewish prisoners from the Cracow jails in 1941.

It was my second visit to Auschwitz. When we reached the gate with its infamous inscription *Arbeit Macht Frei,* we had to get out and enter through a small side door. No vehicles were allowed. It was a solemn moment for both of us. I could see that my wife was visibly shaken. A group of elderly Poles had just arrived for a visit and we followed them. First we reached the ramp where the deportation trains had stopped and the Jews had to jump out and face the waiting German killers with their dogs. They had concealed their true purpose by having Jewish prisoners calm the distraught newcomers by saying that if they would obey the orders they would get work and food. Then the SS officers started their selections, deciding who was to remain alive for the time being to be worked to starving exhaustion, and who must go to the gas chambers. Now it looked like any old railway ramp, but it held a story of such baseness and cruelty of man to man as to defy the most morbid imagination. In Birkenau we turned away with a shudder but did not spare ourselves the sight of the barracks, where the poor, completely exhausted and starved Jewish women were sent after their eighteen-hour day of slave labor to sleep in narrow wooden bunks, three high, covered against the bitter cold of the Polish winter by bug- and lice-infested ragged blankets. We saw the cold cement floors, the inadequately closed roofs, and the broken windows that were no barriers for either the winter frost or the summer heat. I think nothing had been changed since the last victim had died there, or had been taken away in January 1945. We saw the outhouses and the miserable washing facilities the prisoners had been forced to use for just five seconds each. Then we walked along the road where so many had passed to the gas chambers. The gas chambers and crematoria were gone, blown up by the SS before the advancing Russians.

We went to see the monuments dedicated to the four million men, women and children who had died in Auschwitz and Birkenau. I was glad to see their memory was honored in many languages including Hebrew. Remembered after their death but forgotten by the civilized world when they might yet have been saved.

We also went into the most horrible barracks of them all: Barracks 11, where the prisoners, Poles and Jews, who had attempted to organize resistance or had been caught in any other illegal activity, were brought. The cells were so low that the tortured prisoners had to crawl into them and there was not enough room inside to stand or even sit up. We saw the interrogation rooms, actually torture chambers, and outside the barracks the wall at which the half-dead prisoners were finally shot. There were no survivors from Barracks 11. On this same spot, Commandant Rudolf Hoess was hanged after the war. It was the right place for his execution. We went on to see the stream where the ashes of the victims were dumped after they had been cremated.

We never said a word to each other all the time. Both of us were devastated, and I saw that my wife was deathly pale. I did not know what I could say to reassure her. I was myself occupied with very somber thoughts of the past.

Before we left, my wife recited some prayers from her Hebrew prayer book. It was a terrible visit but one I felt I owed to my murdered brethren, and despite everything, I did not regret we had come. When we returned to our hotel we were unable to think of eating and retired to our silent beds. The next morning we took a taxi to attend the Sabbath service in the Miodowa temple. Only the back door was open and inside we found a few poorly dressed men, some of them invalids. I asked my neighbor on the bench beside me whether the man who was conducting the service was the community rabbi and he told me there was no rabbi or cantor in Cracow. After the service we walked to the Remuh synagogue, but the service there had been concluded and the famous cemetery adjoining the house of worship was closed because of the

Sabbath. The only man still there was Czesław Jakubowicz, the head of the city's Jewish community. He was a native Cracowian and he told me that only about ten percent of the community were born in Cracow, the others had come after the war.

We took a taxi and asked the driver to take us to the former ghetto in the Podgorze section. As in the Kazimierz section, there were no Jews or Jewish stores left in this once exclusively Jewish quarter. It too was rundown and miserable; its streets filthy and its buildings badly neglected. We traveled on the main road and reached Plaszow, the industrial suburb of Cracow. At that moment the most tragic memories came back to me.

We were now very close to the house where about 41 years ago I saw my brothers alive for the last time. In a few minutes we reached the former concentration camp in Plaszow. Through the gates we saw a large monument honoring the eighty thousand Jews and Poles who perished there. We felt it would be too much for me to enter and view this horrible place, where many of my family's friends and local Jews we knew were murdered and their bodies burned. Instead we crossed the road and climbed the small hills overlooking the camp.

I knew that these were the hills where my brothers were executed. As we were climbing, I realized that maybe my tortured brothers, Szymon and Nathan, together with other condemned fellow prisoners passed on this very path on the way to be machine gunned and than thrown into a mass grave.

As we continued up the hill, it started to rain. We noticed two small monuments and moved toward them. The smaller one was topped by a metal cross surrounded by barbed wire. I went closer and read the Polish inscription: "This cross was placed here in memory of the Poles who were executed in these hills by the German occupiers. May they rest in peace forever."

We walked over to the larger monument and the first thing I noticed was a Menorah, the candelabrum symbol of Solomon's Temple, which was topped by a Hebrew inscription my wife read for me. "Revenge our spilled blood."

Underneath the Menorah there was a long inscription in Polish: "On this site tens of thousands of Jews, rounded up in

Poland and Hungary, were tortured and murdered in the years 1943–1945. We do not know the names of the murdered and substitute one word for them: Jews.

"Here one of the most horrid crimes was committed. Human words can not describe the abomination of these crimes, the incredible bestiality, the ruthlessness and cruelty of the perpetrators. We substitute one word for them: Hitlerism.

"In memory of the murdered, whose final cry of anguish is the silence of the Plaszow cemetery, the Jews who survived the Fascist pogroms offer their homage."

When I translated the inscription to my wife she handed me the prayer book she was carrying and suggested I recite the prayer for the dead, the Kaddish, for my two brothers and for all the other Jewish martyrs. I tried, but no words would come, and all I could do was to whisper, "Sh'ma Yisrael, Hear O Israel," the words I had so often exclaimed when I had been in mortal danger. We both broke down and slowly descended from those hills. I looked around thinking that my brothers might be buried somewhere near and silently bade them and their fellow martyrs goodbye.

We returned to our hotel and the next morning flew back home. I thank God that He let me survive and gave me the strength to commit my experiences to paper. We Jews have survived many killers of whom Hitler was the biggest and the worst. It is this thought that gives me the courage to trust that we shall outlive all our enemies.